T0358356

MICROFINANCE IN ASIA

MICROFINANCE IN ASIA

Christopher Gan
Lincoln University, New Zealand

Gilbert V Nartea
University of Waikato, New Zealand

World Scientific

NEW JERSEY · LONDON · SINGAPORE · BEIJING · SHANGHAI · HONG KONG · TAIPEI · CHENNAI · TOKYO

Published by

World Scientific Publishing Co. Pte. Ltd.
5 Toh Tuck Link, Singapore 596224
USA office: 27 Warren Street, Suite 401-402, Hackensack, NJ 07601
UK office: 57 Shelton Street, Covent Garden, London WC2H 9HE

Library of Congress Cataloging-in-Publication Data
Names: Gan, Christopher, author. | Nartea, Gilbert V., author.
Title: Microfinance in Asia / Christopher Gan (Lincoln University, New Zealand),
    Gilbert V. Nartea (University of Waikato, New Zealand).
Description: New Jersey : World Scientific, [2016]
Identifiers: LCCN 2016035726 | ISBN 9789813147942 (hc : alk. paper)
Subjects: LCSH: Microfinance--Asia.
Classification: LCC HG178.33.A78 G36 2016 | DDC 332--dc23
LC record available at https://lccn.loc.gov/2016035726

British Library Cataloguing-in-Publication Data
A catalogue record for this book is available from the British Library.

Desk Editors: Chandrima Maitra/Alisha Nguyen

Typeset by Stallion Press
Email: enquiries@stallionpress.com

Printed in Singapore

Contents

Preface   vii

Acknowledgements   xi

About the Contributors   xiii

Chapter 1   An Overview of Microfinance   1
             Christopher Gan, Gilbert V. Nartea and Judy Li Xia

Chapter 2   Rural Credit Market and Microfinance in Vietnam   23
             Phan Dinh Khoi and Christopher Gan

Chapter 3   Microfinance Institutions in Malaysia   47
             Mohamad D. Revindo and Christopher Gan

Chapter 4   Credit Market and Microcredit Services
             in Rural China   93
             Mohamad D. Revindo and Christopher Gan

Chapter 5   Microfinance System in Thailand   147
             Satit Aditto

Chapter 6   Rural Financial Markets and Credit Delivery
             System in the Philippines   177
             *Salvador P. Catelo, Maria Angeles O. Catelo
             and Ceptryl S. Mina*

v

Chapter 7   Islamic Microfinance in Indonesia   227
Bayu Arie Fianto and Christopher Gan

Chapter 8   Microfinance Market in Bangladesh   271
Mohammad Monirul Hasan and Mohammad Abdul Malek

Chapter 9   Conclusions   307
Christopher Gan, Gilbert V. Nartea and Judy Li Xia

Chapter 10   Accessibility and Impact of Rural Credit Cooperatives Microcredit Programmes to Rural Households: A Case Study from Hubei Province, China   319
Mohamad D. Revindo and Christopher Gan

Chapter 11   Rural Microfinance Banking Viability and Outreach: A Case of Bank Rakyat Indonesia   337
Mohamad D. Revindo and Christopher Gan

Index   357

Preface

The development and role of microfinance has grown rapidly in recent decades. Microfinance plays an important role in poverty reduction and in providing financial access to households in rural areas. Providing financial services and helping people who have difficulty in meeting loan contract requirements (e.g., the legality of business and collateral) are predominant features of microfinance institutions compared with other financial institutions such as commercial banks. Based on this principle, the objective of this book is to provide an overview of microfinance programme development and the determinants influencing the accessibility of microcredit by rural households in Asia. A special feature of this book is a chapter devoted to Islamic microfinance in Indonesia. The principles of Islamic microfinance are derived from Islamic law and people's religious beliefs. Unlike chapters in a traditional textbook, each chapter in this book is self-contained with specific rural credit characteristics and examples.

Chapter 1 provides an Overview of Microfinance and Microcredit. The chapter discusses who are microfinance providers, who do they serve and how do they help the poor. The chapter also provides a summary of empirical evidence on the impact of microfinance.

Chapter 2 presents the Rural Credit Market in Vietnam. This chapter describes the Vietnamese rural credit market, including credit supply, credit demand and credit accessibility by rural households, credit policies and the Vietnam Bank for the Social Policies (VBSP) microcredit programme.

Chapter 3 deals with the Microcredit System in Malaysia. The chapter discusses the experience of the main microfinance providers in Malaysia such as the Amanah Ikhtiar Malaysia, the Economic Fund for National Entrepreneurs Group and Yayasan Usaha Maju institutions.

Chapter 4 discusses China's Rural Credit Market. The chapter provides an overview of rural credit markets in China, including microfinance, credit demand and credit accessibility by rural households, and the performance of government rural credit programmes.

Chapter 5 presents the Rural Financial System in Thailand. The chapter discusses the efforts of microfinance institutions to reach the poor with financial services in Thailand concluding that this goal can only be met on a sustainable basis through permanent, viable institutions. The chapter also addresses how an MFI can exclusively target the poorest of the poor.

Chapter 6 discusses the Rural Financial Markets and Credit Delivery System in the Philippines. The chapter discusses the role of microfinance in rural development in the Philippines. It particularly identifies the effects of microcredit on input use, productivity and income in the context of Philippine agriculture.

Chapter 7 introduces Islamic Microfinance in Indonesia. The chapter begins with a historical overview and landscape of Islamic microfinance in Indonesia followed by shari'ah compliance and the principles of Islamic values in Islamic microfinance and the factors that influence the performance of Islamic Microfinance Institutions (MFIs).

Chapter 8 provides an overview of the Microfinance market in Bangladesh, often known as the hub of MFIs in the globe. The chapter explores the evolution and presents the status of the microfinance market in Bangladesh, supply and demand factors, opportunities for further research and innovations and provides policy recommendations.

Chapter 9 — Conclusions

Chapter 10 — Case study 1 draws the case of Rural Credit Cooperatives (RCCs) microcredit in Hubei Province and looks at whether the implementation of RCCs' microcredit is an effective instrument to improve the rural households' welfare and whether it actually reaches the poorest population in rural areas. The case highlights that poor rural households are still constrained to access microcredit due to some household-related factors as well as obstacles at RCCs' institutional level.

Chapter 11 — Case Study 2 gives a historical overview of Bank Rakyat Indonesia and its successful transformation from being government-reliant towards becoming a commercial and capital self-sufficient microfinance bank without overlooking its main mission of catering to rural poor population. The chapter shows how a well-managed microfinance banking system can weather economic crises and help the rural poor cope with economic shocks.

Acknowledgements

The motivation to write this textbook came primarily from the encouragement of our postgraduate students. Several of our students' thesis on microfinance helped shape the outline and structure of this book.

We would like to acknowledge with thanks the financial support from both the Faculty of Agribusiness and Commerce, Lincoln University and the Waikato Management School, University of Waikato for research on which some of the chapters in this book are based.

Special thanks are accorded to the Department of International Economics, Senshu University, Kawasaki-shi, Kanagawa, Japan for providing Professor Gan with an office and computing support to work on the book while he was on study leave last April 2016.

Microfinance is a fascinating subject to us. We are happy to undertake a book writing project such as this from the ground up with the hope that readers will provide us with critical comments.

About the Contributors

Salvador P. Catelo is a Professor in the Department of Agricultural and Applied Economics (DAAE), College of Economics and Management (CEM), University of the Philippines Los Baños (UPLB). He has taught economic analysis and planning of agricultural projects, agriculture and economic development, agricultural policy, farm management, both at the undergraduate and graduate levels. Dr. Catelo has served as Dean of CEM and Chair of the DAAE. He was also a Visiting Professor at the Tokyo University of Agriculture and Nagoya University and has worked with local and internationally-funded development projects. His fields of specialisation and research interests include policy and development, global food systems and value chain analysis, production economics and farm management, and impact analysis of agricultural projects.

Maria Angeles O. Catelo is an Associate Professor in the Department of Economics (DE), College of Economics and Management (CEM), University of the Philippines Los Baños (UPLB). She served as Chair of the DE and has handled courses in introductory economics, microeconomics, money and banking, public finance, and cost–benefit analysis. Her research interests include the economics of green growth with focus on smallholder livestock producers and their inclusion in markets, health and environmental impacts of air and water pollution, and economic instruments for environmental management. These research interests were borne out of her collaborative undertakings with various institutions such as the Economy and Environment Program for Southeast Asia (EEPSEA), the Food and Agriculture Organisation (FAO) of the UN, and the International Food Policy Research Institute (IFPRI).

Ceptryl S. Mina is a Research Assistant at the College of Economics and Management (CEM), University of the Philippines Los Baños (UPLB). She is currently involved in the project "Production Economics of Selected Natural Food Colorants and Flavors in the Philippines", where she assists in the analysis of the economics of producing and processing selected natural food colourants and flavours in the Philippines; identification of various market channels; assessment of the competitiveness of these locally produced natural food colourants and flavours. She is currently pursuing a Master of Science in Agricultural Economics degree from the same university.

Satit Aditto obtained his PhD in Agricultural Economics at Lincoln University, New Zealand in 2011. He is currently an Assistant Professor in Department of Agricultural Economics, Faculty of Agriculture, Khon Kaen University, Thailand. His current research emphasises risk analysis of smallholder farmers in Northeast of Thailand, microfinance in rural Thailand, agricultural supply chain management and factors affecting business success of small and medium agribusiness enterprises in Thailand.

Bayu Arie Fianto is a PhD candidate in Finance at Lincoln University, New Zealand. His PhD research focuses on investigating the impact of Islamic microfinance institutions on Indonesian rural households. Fianto received his Bachelor's degree in Management from Brawijaya University, Indonesia (2007) and an MBA in Islamic Banking and Finance from International Islamic University Malaysia (2009). In 2010, he joined the Islamic Economics Department, Faculty of Economic and Business, Airlangga University, Indonesia as a Lecturer. Prior to joining Airlangga,

Fianto worked as Account Officer at Bank Muamalat Indonesia, the first Islamic bank in Indonesia. His current research interests include Islamic microfinance, Islamic bank, and equity financing in Islamic finance.

Christopher Gan is the Professor of Accounting and Finance at Lincoln University, New Zealand. He earned his PhD in Agricultural Economics (with a specialisation in rural finance) from Louisiana State University, his Master of Economics and Trade from Indiana State University, and his Bachelor of Arts in Economic Development from Warren Wilson College, the United States. He has published more than 100 refereed journal articles and has more than 50 professional presentations. He is the Chief Review Editor of *Applied Economics* and the Associate Editor of the *International Economic Finance Journal*. He is also on the editorial board of several refereed journals. He has won Best Paper Awards at international conferences in 2014, 2013, 2012 and 2010. His research interests include microfinance, banking, the Asian economy, development economics and financial economics.

Mohammad Monirul Hasan is a PhD Researcher at Center for Development Research (ZEF), University of Bonn, Germany. He was Senior Research Associate at Institute for Inclusive Finance and Development (InM) from 2008 to 2015. Over the last 8 years, Monirul has worked broadly on microfinance and poverty, agricultural efficiency, food and nutrition security and health. He is currently investigating the impacts of Food Hygiene Education, a randomised controlled trial experiment, within agriculture–water–sanitation and hygiene nexus for the rural households in Bangladesh. Monirul holds three Master's degrees in Agriculture and Food Economics (University of Bonn, Germany), Rural Development and Agri-business (Corvinus University of Budapest, Hungary) and Economics (University of Dhaka, Bangladesh).

Mohammad Abdul Malek has been leading the Agricultural Economics Research Unit at BRAC Research and Evaluation Division (RED), Dhaka since its inception in 2012 and has been associated with Center for International Research on Japanese Economy (CIRJE), Faculty of Economics under University of Tokyo, Japan and ZEF, Germany. During his 15 years research and evaluation career with the Government, INGO and University/think tanks, Dr Malek gained extensive experiences on mobilising resources and implementing research projects from 3ie, Bill and Melinda Gates Foundation, Australian DFAT and International Growth Center (IGC), among others. He publishes scientific outputs and presents research results in academic and public forums including television media. His recent research interest tests the acceptability and adoptability of different technological and institutional innovations which generates significant public policy interests.

Gilbert V. Nartea is Associate Professor of Finance at The University of Waikato, New Zealand. He has a PhD in Agricultural Economics (specialisation in finance) from the University of Illinois at Urbana-Champaign, Master in Economics from the University of New England, Australia, and BS Agribusiness Management (*cum laude*) from the University of the Philippines. He has published in the *American Journal of Agricultural Economics, Journal of the Asia Pacific Economy, Journal of Asian Economics, Pacific Basin Finance Journal, Journal of International Financial Markets, Institutions & Money, Accounting and Finance, International Review of Economics* and Finance among others. His research interests are in microfinance, empirical asset pricing, decision analysis, risk management and investments.

Mohamad D. Revindo is currently a PhD candidate in International Business at Lincoln University, New Zealand. He is a recipient of New Zealand-ASEAN Scholar Awards (2013–2017). Revindo earned his BA in Economics and Development Studies from University of Indonesia (2000), MSc in Economics from KU Leuven, Belgium (2007) and MA in European Studies from KU Leuven (2008). Revindo has worked as a Research Associate with the Institute for Economic and Social Research, University of Indonesia (LPEM-UI) since 2009. His research interests include small and medium-sized enterprise, microfinance, local economic development and international business. He previously worked for 5 years as a surveyor and survey coordinator at PT. Surveyor Indonesia, a state-owned enterprise specialised in survey, inspection and certification services. He has also taught at the Graduate School, University of Indonesia and Prasetiya Mulya Business School, Jakarta.

Phan Dinh Khoi is currently a Lecturer at Can Tho University. In 2009, he joined the doctoral research program at Lincoln University on the Vietnamese Government Scholarship. After completing his PhD program, Phan Dinh Khoi returned Vietnam and was appointed as Head of Department of Finance and Banking at Can Tho University in 2012. He currently teaches microeconomics and development finance courses for both undergraduate and graduate levels. He also works on a number of development projects focussing on rural development and poverty reduction in Vietnam. His recent research papers has been published in the *Journal of Asian Economics* and *Journal of the Asia Pacific Economy*.

Judy Li Xia is a finance Lecturer at New Zealand College of Business. She completed her PhD degree in Finance from Lincoln University, New Zealand in 2011. She holds a Master's degree in Financial Management, Central Queensland University, Australia in 2004. Her research interests are rural finance, microfinance and credit constraints. She has published in *Journal of Asian Economics*, *Journal of Socio-Economics* and *Journal of Chinese Economic and Business Studies*. She was a bank manager in Wuhan, China before starting her doctoral study.

Chapter 1

An Overview of Microfinance

Christopher Gan*,§, Gilbert V. Nartea†,¶ and Judy Li Xia‡,||

*Professor in Accounting and Finance,
Faculty of Agribusiness and Commerce,
Department of Financial and Business System,
PO Box 85084, Lincoln University, Christchurch, New Zealand

†Associate Professor, Chairperson, Department of Finance,
Waikato Management School, University of Waikato,
Private Bag 3105, Hamilton 3240, New Zealand

‡Lecturer, New Zealand College of Business,
15A Bishopdale Court,
Bishopdale 8053, Christchurch

§Christopher.Gan@lincoln.ac.nz
¶narteag@waikato.ac.nz
||Judy.Li@lincolnuni.ac.nz

Abstract

Microfinance has been recognised and considered as the common mechanism to provide credit for the poor and low-income people, especially people in rural areas. Since its initiation in Bangladesh in the seventies, it has been gradually embedded in national strategies of many developing countries as well as universal goal to combat with hunger and poverty in the new millennium. The chapter provides an overview of microfinance and microcredit. The chapter discusses who are the microfinance providers, who do they serve and how do they help the poor. The chapter also provides a summary of empirical evidence on the impact of microfinance.

Keywords: Capital, credit accessibility, microfinance, poverty, rural household.

1.1 Introduction

Lack of ability to obtain credit from the formal financial sector has long been viewed as the biggest obstacle to improving households' livelihood (McCarty, 2001; Pham & Lensink, 2007). To fulfil credit demand, rural households have to seek informal sources of credit at higher a interest rate to support their production and consumption. This informal debt is believed to marginalise household income and likely leads the borrower into a cycle of debt and poverty. This market failure is eminent in many developing countries where the rural financial market is not functioning well (Musinguzi & Smith, 2000). Therefore, credit inaccessibility in rural areas impedes the development of the rural sector, which potentially decelerates the development of the rural economy. To increase credit access for rural households, many governments have implemented microfinance programmes targeting agricultural and rural areas nationwide particularly in developing countries. The policies aim to assist rural poor households' access to microfinance products through banks at a preferable interest rate. In addition, the governments have recognised microfinance products as a strategic tool to provide cheap credit to rural households.

Microfinance refers to the provision of financial services to the poor and low-income households (ADB, 2000). These services can include credit, savings, insurance, money transfers and equity investments. The feature that most distinguishes these services from those given by traditional financial institutions (FIs) is the small size of the transactions. Hence, microfinance institutions (MFIs) provide mainly microcredit, microsavings and microinsurance. New innovations in microfinance include microtransfers and microequity.

Microcredit involves lending capital in small amounts to poor people who are traditionally considered unbankable to enable them to invest in self-employment (Kasim & Jayasooria, 2001). The World Bank (2006, p. 12) describes microcredit as "a process in which poor families borrow large amounts (or lump sums) of money at one time and repay the amount in a stream of small, manageable payments over a realistic time period using social collateral in the short run and institutional credit history in the long run". Different forms of microcredit are available such as individual lending, group lending and village banking. Particularly, microcredit programmes have been developed to provide rural households with greater credit accessibility.

Microsavings are small amounts of money saved by poor people with FIs, mostly MFIs. Some schemes involve a daily collection system and service delivery at the doorstep of clients. As these small savings accumulate they provide a source of lump sum cash for future emergencies, investments and consumption needs of the poor (Mersland & Eggen, 2007).

In some cases, microcredit programmes would involve saving services, but the services are limited to the collection of compulsory deposit amounts from the borrowers to collateralise the loans issued. Borrowers cannot access these compulsory deposits and cannot have voluntary saving accounts in microcredit programmes (World Bank, 2006; Cornford, 2000).

Though microcredit has taken a more prominent role in microfinance, it appears that the poorest of the poor find the provision of savings opportunities more important than the provision of credit facilities (Collins *et al.*, 2010). There is empirical evidence suggesting that in some regions of the world the poor use savings products more than credit. For example, Maes & Reed (2012) report that The Opportunity International Bank of Malawi has 45,000 borrowers and 250,000 savers, the Equity Bank in Kenya has 715,000 borrowers and 4 million depositors and the Grameen Bank (GB) has over US$1.4 billion in deposits, which is 145% of its outstanding loan portfolio of US$965 million. Khan & Ashta (2012) also report that 28 Bangladeshi MFI's collectively have 27.8 million depositors compared with about 20.6 million borrowers with 26 out of the 28 MFIs reporting more depositors than borrowers.

Microinsurance is a programme which provides insurance services to the poor and low-income populations and small businesses. It operates similarly to regular insurance except for the fact that regular premium payments and therefore the payouts are also smaller. Just like regular insurance common types of risks covered are life, health, disability and property including agricultural production. Microinsurance could be directly provided by traditional insurance companies but could also be delivered by MFIs. Some MFIs also provide loans to cover the payment of microinsurance premiums like CARD in the Philippines (Reinsch & Metcalf, 2010).

Microtransfers are a new innovation wherein small amounts of money or remittances sent by migrants and overseas workers back to their home countries. Another new innovation is microequity, which refers to the provision of equity instead of credit to finance projects of the poor. It is so far only in its early stages of development and is being done mainly in developed countries.

1.2   Who Does Microfinance Serve?

Microfinance caters to the financial needs of underprivileged groups including female heads of households, pensioners, displaced persons, retrenched workers, small farmers and microentrepreneurs (CGAP,[1] 2003). In addition, microfinance borrowers are typically self-employed, household-based entrepreneurs who have relatively unstable income sources and can be divided into two groups: rural and urban. In rural areas, the borrowers are usually small farmers and others who are engaged in small income-generating activities such as food processing and petty trade; while in urban areas, microfinance activities are more diverse and borrowers include shopkeepers, service providers, artisans, street vendors and small–medium enterprises (Sapovadia, 2006). However, the client-focus of microfinance varies in different regions. For example, in Latin America, microfinance has been developed into a business rather than an anti-poverty programme, which is a branch of commercial banking and focuses more on urban small–medium enterprises than the rural poor

---

[1]CGAP refers to the Consultative Group to Assist the Poor, which is a consortium of 33 public and private development agencies working together to expand access to financial services for the poor in developing countries.

(Poyo & Young, 1999). By contrast, in Asia where the poor population is more numerous, especially in rural areas, microfinance would inevitably be directed to serve the rural poor as an anti-poverty instrument (World Bank, 2006).

The most common financial service provided by MFIs is microcredit, hence microfinance and microcredit are commonly used interchangeably, but microfinance is obviously much broader than just microcredit. In the next section, we will describe the basic characteristics of microcredit.

1.3 Characteristics of Microcredit

Compared to traditional lending, microcredit has its own vivid characteristics. Loans from the microcredit programmes are usually in small amounts and have relatively shorter repayment recycles. Du (2004) argues that a major difference between microcredit and conventional lending is that the former targets borrowers from the poor and low-income groups. In addition, microcredit emphasises lending to the poor women who are disproportionately represented among the world's poorest people. Another outstanding difference between microcredit and traditional lending is that microcredit is usually offered without the requirement of collateral compared to compulsory collateral requirement in traditional lending (Yunus, 2003). However, in place of collateral, microcredit disciplines borrowers through a special strategy such as group lending, which represents another characteristic of microcredit: mutual accountability. Borrowers form into groups to monitor each other. The potential pressure on the groups helps to keep individual repayment records transparent and the collective responsibility works as 'social collateral' on the loans (Hussain, Maskooki & Gunasekaran, 2001). We discuss these differences more fully below.

1.3.1 *Targeting the poor*

A major difference between microcredit and conventional lending is that the former often targets borrowers from the poor and low-income groups. Microcredit programmes are poverty-focused, which aim to facilitate the access to financial services such as credit for the poor globally who are usually regarded as disadvantaged groups in accessing conventional financial services from formal FIs. In addition, microcredit emphasises lending to poor women who are disproportionately represented among the world's poorest people. According to Cheston & Kuhn (2002), about 74% of microcredit borrowers in the world are women. The rationale behind lending to women is that most women borrowers have been proven to be more credit-worthy than men, in addition to the better ability of controlling the use of loans by women (Garikipati, 2006; Ang, 2004).

1.3.2 *Collateral free*

Collateral is always a compulsory requirement in traditional lending as a way of minimising default risk anticipated by lenders. Such collateral requirement becomes more rigid if borrowers are economically poor. However, the poor usually do not own valuable assets which can be used as appropriate collateral when applying for loans from traditional FIs, and as a result, poor people are historically considered unbankable and precluded from the traditional credit markets. Microcredit is an innovative idea that challenges the traditional lending wisdom of 'no collateral means no credit'. It deems the poor as creditworthy as the rich and provides collateral free loans to the poor to develop entrepreneurial activities.

1.3.3 *Group-lending scheme*

In place of collateral, however, microcredit disciplines borrowers through a special scheme such as group lending. Loans are made to an individual borrower who is a member of a borrowing group. However, each individual borrower assumes responsibility for the loan repayment of his or her group members, which means all group members are jointly liable. If only one member from a group defaults, the rest in the group will be denied future access to loans from the microcredit programme. As a result, the principle of joint liability creates an incentive mechanism by which individual borrowers are stimulated to select credible members to group with, to monitor the other members' activities once the loan is received and to enforce repayment in case a group member fails to fulfil his or her obligation. In other words, the group-lending scheme creates a special kind of collateral called 'social collateral' on the loans, which reduces the costs of screening and monitoring borrowers, and ensures timely repayments for lenders (Anderson & Nina, 2000; Besley & Coate, 1995).

1.4 Who are the Microcredit Providers?

A variety of organisations have been involved in the delivery of microcredit services during the last two decades. The World Bank (2006) categorises these organisations into seven types which include commercial banks, wholesale development banks/funds, retail development banks/companies, apex organisations funded by multilateral or bilateral donors and/or governments, MFIs and non-profit non-governmental organisations (NGOs), cooperatives and community-based organisations. Institutions such as wholesale development banks/funds and apex organisations provide lending only to institutions such as MFIs and cooperatives, instead of individuals; by contrast, cooperatives and community-based organisations only lend to individuals.

Different countries have fostered their own local organisations to provide microcredit and such local organisations can be generally classified as NGOs and formal FIs. For example, the Bangladesh Rural Advancement Committee (BRAC) and the Association for Social Advancement (ASA) are two major NGOs, while the GB is the biggest FI providing microcredit in Bangladesh. These three major microcredit providers serve around 11 million borrowers throughout Bangladesh (ADB, 2000). Similarly, Amanah Ikhtiar Malaysia (AIM) is the largest NGO in Malaysia providing microcredit to about 50,000 borrowers for a total loan amount of RM200 million (Kasim & Jayasooria, 2001). In addition, the Unit Desa of Bank Rakyat Indonesia (BRI-UD) in Indonesia is a successful rural FI which has attracted more than 2.5 million borrowers with total outstanding loan of US$781 million (World Bank, 2006; Timberg, 1999).

Among the most successful microcredit programmes is the GB microcredit, introduced by Muhammad Yunus in the late 1970s. As a pioneer in microcredit, the GB promotes innovative ideas in poverty reduction through its lending programmes. Yunus (2003) advocates that credit should be promoted as a human right and should be based on 'trust' rather than collaterals or legally enforceable contracts. Furthermore,

Yunus stresses that in order to eliminate poverty, appropriate changes must be made in the institutions and policies surrounding the poor, rather than just providing charity to the poor. Based on this belief, the GB created an accessible mechanism for the poor to access credit on reasonable terms to improve their welfare (Yunus, 2003; Latifee, 2003). The Grameen model has been implemented in more than 50 countries in Asia, USA, Australia and Europe (Hussain *et al.*, 2001). Today, the GB has a network of nearly 1,300 branch offices that serve 3.8 million borrowers of which 96% are women, and has disbursed loans worth US$4.5 billion (Chowdhury, 2004). More significantly, 5% of GB's borrowers graduate from poverty each year and sustain their living standard (Hussain *et al.*, 2001).

1.5 How Does Microfinance Help the Poor?

It is often argued that financial services such as credit, savings and insurance can positively affect the livelihood of the poor thereby improving income distribution (Latifee, 2003; Claessens, 2006). According to Latiffe (2003, p. 2), "credit is a powerful instrument to fight poverty" because "it creates opportunities for self-employment rather than waiting for employment to be created". Credit gives poor people a means of investing and breaking out of the "vicious circle" of poverty because credit has the potential of improving credit users' income and savings, and consequently, enhancing investment and reinforcing high incomes (Mohamed, 2003).

Despite the importance of financial services such as credit in helping the poor to improve their living conditions, poor people are excluded from the formal financial system and such exclusion ranges from partial exclusion in developed countries to full or nearly full exclusion in less developed countries (LDCs) (Brau & Woller, 2004). Traditional FIs are reluctant to serve the poor mainly because poor people fail to meet the selection criteria such as the requirement of physical collateral set by FIs. The perceived high risks and costs arising from processing and servicing unsecured small loans make FIs shy away from financing the poor, mainly due to the concern of financial viability. Lacking access to formal credit, most poor and low-income people continue to rely on meagre self-finance or informal credit, which limit their ability to actively participate in and benefit from the development process.

The primary goal of a microcredit programme is to provide credit to the poor by extending small collateral free loans that purposely enable the borrowers to actively generate a range of improvements in economic conditions (World Bank, 2010). Islam (2007) hypothesised that microcredit can create a circle of growth for poor borrowers that 'low income households need credit for investment to create more income and more credit and more income'. In other words, microcredit enhances income growth, which increases a household's consumption level, hence, contributes to an immediate welfare improvement. For example, an enhanced income from borrowing encourages the poor to increase investment in working capital as well as physical assets. Capital and physical asset accumulation attributed to microcredit reinforces the income generating capabilities of borrowers (Aghion & Morduch, 2005; Hossain & Diaz, 1997).

Hulme (2000) argues further that conventional microcredit programmes lead to changes in household income, which leads to changes in economic security, educational and working skill levels. Ultimately, these changes lead to modification in household welfare and social political relations and structures. Morduch & Haley (2001) opine that microfinance helps reduce the impact of economic shocks on the poor and increase their assets and income.

Proponents of microfinance also argue that improved access to credit at reasonable cost could enable the poor to smooth consumption (food and non-food), better cope with crises, develop self-employed businesses, enhance income earning capacity and build up assets gradually. Moreover, Swain (2004) stresses that since microfinance programmes have generally targeted women as clients, access to financial services such as credit can empower women to become more confident, more assertive, more likely to participate in family and community decision making and better able to confront systemic gender inequities. Therefore, microfinance is a mechanism which gives the poor, especially women to better their livelihoods (Mourji, 2000).

Littlefield & Rosenberg (2004) argue that though microfinance is not a panacea for poverty, the poor value it highly because it can enable them to create employment opportunities that might induce improvements in a range of welfare measures, including income stability and growth, school attendance, nutrition and health.

Latifee (2003) noted that microcredit improves the poor's economic conditions by enabling them to start self-employed businesses, increasing their income, stabilising their consumption and building up their capital assets. The poor can use the generated income to pay for the instalment of loans while leaving their original capital intact. Consequently, their capital base usually increases in large amounts as they borrow continuously, which gives them opportunities to make medium and long-term investments. Therefore, microcredit borrowers are likely to sustain long-term development by participating in entrepreneurial activities and as a result, shake off poverty with economic growth.

In the case of agriculture, credit is an important element in the agricultural production process, which allows producers to satisfy the capital needs of the production cycle.

The provision of microinsurance facilities to MFI clients allows clients better capacity to withstand the consequence of many shocks and paves the way for better risk management. Since the poor are less able to cope with shocks they are less likely to take up higher yielding, albeit more risky, enterprises which might reduce poverty (Churchill, 2007). But if a farmer has crop insurance for example, he might be more inclined to take up more capital intensive cropping systems that could produce higher incomes. In addition, microinsurance also allows the poor to make full use of their loans for productive enterprises rather than having to use them to pay for unforeseen medical or funeral expenses, or having to set aside a portion of their loan as a cushion for unforeseen shocks.

Microtransfer services of overseas remittances also have important benefits to people of developing countries. Overseas remittances are undeniably a major source of external development finance (Hasan, 2006). The World Bank (2006) reports that out of a total of US$232 billion in remittances worldwide, developing countries received US$167 billion which was more than double the total development aid from all sources. De Bruyn & Kuddus (2005) report that up to 60–70% of recipient poor households' total income come from remittances. Remittances facilitate investment in both productive and consumption goods in recipient countries (Yang, 2006). Rivera & Reyes (2011) also note that while much of the remittances are used for consumption, the residual are converted into savings that could be used for investment purposes.

1.5.1 *Empirical evidence*

The empirical evidence on the impact of microfinance is at best mixed. While microfinance, particularly microcredit significantly contributes to alleviating poverty, it is not a panacea for poverty reduction. In a review of empirical studies investigating the effectiveness of microcredit in poverty reduction, Weiss & Montgomery (2004) conclude that the evidence is far from conclusive. More recently, Duvendack *et al.* (2011) reached the same conclusion.

First, we will review empirical studies suggesting a positive impact of microfinance on the poor, especially women and low-income households followed by a review of studies pointing to the contrary.

1.5.1.1 *Poverty alleviation*

There is rich evidence showing that microcredit has a significant impact on poverty reduction around the world. Pitt & Khandker (1998) report that microcredit increases consumption expenditure, reduces poverty, and increases non-land assets. Zaman (1999), focusing on the BRAC, one of the largest microcredit providers in Bangladesh, also reports that microcredit can help the poor smooth consumption and build assets. More recently, studies show that 48% of the poorest households in Bangladesh have risen above the poverty line with access to microcredit; similarly, BRI in Indonesia has witnessed an increase in its microcredit borrowers' income by 12.9% compared to only 3% increase in non-borrowers' income (World Bank, 2006; CGAP, 2003). Similarly, Kasim (2000) conducted a study on AIM's microcredit programmes in Malaysia and found that the changes in income, expenditure, savings and assets are positive and higher for the microcredit borrowers compared to non-borrowers. In 2002, China Rural Credit Cooperatives (RCCs) launched the microcredit programmes on a national scale becoming the main force in popularising and formalising China's microcredit programmes with their extensive network penetrating the grassroots level (Du, 2004, 2005; Sun, 2003). The amount of microcredit loans issued to rural households by RCCs nationwide totalled 96.7 billion yuan in 2002 and around 60 million rural households had received microcredit loans provided by RCCs. The scale of RCCs' microcredit programme has far surpassed the scales of both the NGO and government programmes (Gao & Hu, 2005; Du, 2004; Druschel, 2002).

Islam's study (2007) shows microcredit contributes greatly to borrowers' productivity, which is a crucial determinant of the economic condition of the rural poor. For example, financial support from microcredit allows the poor to invest in high-yielding varieties and advanced technology, which significantly stimulates productivity and promotes production. According to Islam, increased productivity is important for a 'concomitant' and 'secular' rise in income, which is crucial for rural poverty reduction. Furthermore, microcredit also creates employment opportunities for a vast under-utilised labour resource by undertaking economic activities on a self-employed basis. As the self-businesses expand over time, more labour is demanded.

1.5.1.2 *Coping with risk and shocks*

Latifee (2003) observed that microcredit borrowers are in better position to cope with different crises. For example, during the 1998 flood in Bangladesh, the microcredit borrowers could borrow more and repay the loans within an extended period of time so that they could maintain their daily expenses and productive investment during the crisis. Therefore, microcredit can minimise the severity of such crisis and help borrowers to recover from their losses (Latifee, 2003; Zaman, 1999).

In addition to maintaining consumption of basic necessities, access to credit can increase poor farmers' risk-bearing ability and help them alter their risk-coping strategies so that farmers may be willing to adopt new and riskier strategies with higher potential return in their production instead of risk-reducing but inefficient strategies (Diagne, Zeller & Sharma, 2000). Hence, credit is a powerful instrument to help poor people invest and break out of a 'vicious cycle' of poverty because it has the potential to improve the users' incomes and savings, and consequently, enhance investment and reinforce high incomes (Mohamed, 2003).

1.5.1.3 *Social status promotion/gender equality/women empowerment*

By joining the microcredit programmes, the poor are organised into groups where they can share diverse information to learn more about the outside world. As a result, the poor, women in particular, become more mobile and active in participating in social network and commercialisation process, and become more conscious about their life quality and their family welfare. Latifee (2003) concludes that the poor can benefit from microcredit through economic condition improvement and social status promotion.

MacIsaac (1997) acknowledges that microcredit is a powerful tool in fighting poverty and promoting gender equality. The author argues that microcredit can promote gender equality by creating employment opportunities for poor women to generate stable income. Such economic empowerment provides women with new skills, information and organisational capacity, which indirectly results in social and political empowerment. Similarly, Manimekalai (2004) asserts that microcredit plays a major role in many countries' gender and development strategies because of its direct relationship to women empowerment. This view is shared by Cheston & Kuhn (2002), who note that the impact of microcredit on women empowerment can be manifested by increased participation in decision making, more equitable status of women in the family and community, increased political power and rights, and increased self-esteem. More specifically, Manimekalai (2004) studied women borrowers from Self-Help Groups[2] (SHGs) in India and finds that SHGs microcredit programme in India has greatly helped women borrowers improve their economic conditions and promote their social status.

Since microcredit programmes have generally targeted poor women as clients, access to microcredit can empower poor women by increasing their contribution to household income and asset building, which is a significant contributor toward their increased self-worth and improved family status. As a consequence of participating in microcredit programmes, women borrowers become more financially independent, more likely to participate in social networks and commercialisation processes, and able to better confront systemic gender inequities. A regional study by World Bank (2006) reveals that 90% of women borrowers from SHGs in India

---

[2]SHG is the dominant microfinance scheme in India. The operations of SHGs composed of 15–20 members are based on the principle of revolving the members' own savings. The volume of individual borrowing is determined by the volume of member's savings or the savings of the group (World Bank, 2006).

can freely visit local markets and make small and large purchases independently, while 68% of women borrowers in Nepal can make independent decisions on property, children's education and marriage.

Other recent studies also attest to the impact of microfinance on women empowerment (see for example, Pitt, Khandker & Cartwright, 2006; Ashraf Karlan & Yin, 2010) due in large part to increased female income derived from microenterprises. This empowerment is also seen to result in changed family consumption pattern since women are more inclined to spend on children and family goods (Duflo & Udry, 2003).

1.5.2 Counter findings/criticisms against microfinance

1.5.2.1 Poverty alleviation

According to MacIsaac (1997), microcredit may be less effective, or even counter-productive, in helping the poorest of the poor to raise their living standards because the worse-off borrowers use the loans only for consumption or invest in less riskier (and generally less remunerative) activities compared to the better-off borrowers who tend to invest in riskier and more productive ventures including technological improvements, which provides opportunities of generating greater income to improve their living standards. In the same vein Bateman & Chang (2009) more recently, argue that microfinance works against technology adoption by creating an environment that helps perpetuate primitive technology. MacIsaac (1997) suggests that microcredit can be more effective when combined with other financial interventions such as savings and insurance. Chowdhury (2004) echoes this more recently, arguing that microcredit should not be viewed as a sole instrument for poverty reduction; instead, it should be included as a part of broader poverty eradication strategy combined with other intervention programmes such as social protection programmes. As an answer to this criticism, MFIs have innovated new services such as microsavings, microinsurance, microtransfers and microequity. However, Quibria (2012) notes that unless two fundamental constraints are addressed, it would be difficult for poor households to graduate from poverty. The first is the problem of the predominance of primitive or low technologies in rural microenterprises and the second is the challenge of weak domestic demand for their products.

Early studies suggesting positive impact of microcredit on poverty reduction such as that by Pitt & Khandker (1998) are now being challenged. In a follow-up to his earlier study Khandker (2005) finds a much weaker impact of microcredit on poverty. Khandker finds that though microcredit raises consumption and non-land assets of the very poor, it has little effect on aggregate poverty. In addition, Banerjee *et al.* (2009), using randomised control trials which overcome the technical econometric problems of earlier studies, also do not find any robust evidence of a positive impact of microcredit on poverty in the slums in urban Hyderabad, India. Likewise Karlan & Zinman (2010) did not find a positive relation between microcredit and poverty for microentrepreneurs in Manila, Philippines.

1.5.2.2 *Women empowerment*

Though some authors opine that microcredit leads to women empowerment, Quibria (2012) argues that this is not automatic, since female empowerment is contingent on the effect of microcredit on female income. Quibria argues further that if female income from credit falls short of male income, the female might still be marginalised in household decision making. Indeed a number of studies argue that microcredit has had little or no effect on female empowerment (see for example, Goetz & Gupta, 1996; Hunt & Kasynathan, 2001; Banerjee *et al.*, 2009). Furthermore, though Belwal, Tamiru & Singh (2012) find that microcredit can increase income and savings of female entrepreneurs, this did not have any salutary impact on their lives after accounting for loan repayment and interest.

1.5.2.3 *Mission drift*

Another criticism levelled against microfinance is mission drift (Mersland & Strom, 2010). Ashta *et al.* (2014) points out that the mission drift critiques usually centre on (a) diversion of microcredit into consumer credit, (b) larger loan sizes and (c) high interest rates. Firstly, critics of microcredit suggest that these funds are increasingly being used by borrowers for consumption rather than for entrepreneurial activities.

The second critique on larger loan sizes means that the loans are being targeted for the wealthier of the poor rather than the poorest of the poor (Ashta, Couchoro & Musa, 2014). Copestake, Bhalotra & Johnson (2001) found this to be true for PULSE in Zambia. Roth (1997) also pointed out earlier that microcredit has not reached "the poorest of the poor" but "the wealthier of the poor", and it is limited by poor political institutional framework in some countries. For example, Reeve (2006) suggests that incoherent legal framework and poorly trained management contribute to the inefficient implementation of microcredit in Indonesia. Finally, some critics also point out that a number of MFIs are so focused on profit motivation leading them to charge high interest rates which in turn leads the poor borrowers feeling deceived (Eversole, 2003). Examples include the case of MFI Compartamos which reportedly was charging interest rates as high as 99% per year (Ashta & Bush, 2009; Ashta & Hudon, 2012; Lewis, 2008; Smith & Epstein, 2007), and the case of SKS in India with allegations that its microcredit programmes led to too much borrower stress and even suicides (Ashta, Khan & Otto, 2011). Cheston & Kuhn (2002) also argue that women who borrow from MFIs suffer ill health and exhaustion because of overwork, caused by compulsory participation in the time-consuming meetings, engaging in income-generating activities to pay off the loans, and simultaneously, taking traditional responsibilities of the family, such as looking after children. In addition, microcredit remains inaccessible to the poorest of the poor because microcredit institutions intend to protect their self-sustainability to achieve larger scale of poverty reduction at moderate level (Druschel, 2002).

Despite these criticisms the World Bank (2006) argues that the overall impact of microfinance is positive but the degree of impact varies in different countries.

References

Aghion, B. A. & Morduch, J. (2005). *The Economics of Microfinance*. Cambridge, MA: MIT Press.

Anderson, L. E. & Nina, O. (2000). Micro-credit and group lending: The collateral effect. Economics Working Papers, School of Economics and Management, University of Aarhus. Retrieved from http://econpapers.repec.org/RePEc:aah:aarhec:1998-18. Accessed on April 21, 2015.

Ang, M. H. (2004). Empowering the poor through microcredit. *Entrepreneurship and Innovation Management*, 4(5), 485–494.

Ashraf, N., Karlan, D. & Yin, W. (2010). Female empowerment: Further evidence from a commitment savings product in the Philippines. *World Development*, 38(3), 333–344.

Ashta, A. & Bush, M. (2009). Ethical issues of NGO principals in sustainability outreach and impact of microfinance: Lessons in governance from the Banco Compartamos' IPO. *Management Online Review*, 1–18.

Ashta, A., Couchoro, M. & Musa, A. (2014). Dialectic evolution through the social innovation process: From microcredit to microfinance. *Journal of Innovation and Entrepreneurship*, 3(4), 1–23. Retrieved from http://www.Innovation-entrepreneurship.com/content/3/1/4. Accessed on April 21, 2015.

Ashta, A. & Hudon, M. (2012). The Compartamos microfinance IPO: Mission conflicts in hybrid institutions with diverse shareholding. *Strategic Change*, 21(7–8), 331–341.

Ashta, A., Khan, S. & Otto, P. E. (2011). Does microfinance cause or reduce suicides? Policy Recommendations for Reducing Borrower Stress. Retrieved from SSRN: http://ssrn.com/abstract=1715442. Accessed on April 23, 2015.

Asian Development Bank (ADB) (2000). Finance for the poor: Microfinance Development Strategy. Manila, Philippines: ADB. Retrieved from www.adb. org/Documents/Policies/Microfinance/financepolicy.pdf. Accessed on August 1, 2007.

Banerjee, A., Duflow, E., Glenerster, R. & Kinman, C. (2009). The miracle of microfinance? Evidence from a randomized evaluation. Department of Economics, Massachusetts Institute of Technology working paper, May.

Bateman, M. & Chang H.-J. (2009). The Microfinance Illusion. Mimeo. Retrieved from: http://www.econ.cam.ac.uk/faculty/chang/pubs/Microfinance.pdf. Accessed on April 23, 2015.

Belwal, R., Tamiru, M. & Singh, G. (2012). Microfinance and sustained economic improvement: Women small-scale entrepreneurs in Ethiopia. *Journal of International Development*, 24, S84–S99, doi:10.1002/jid.1782. Accessed on April 23, 2015.

Besley, T. & Coate, S. (1995). Group lending, repayment incentives and social collateral. *Journal of Development Economics*, 46(1), 1–18.

Brau, J. C. & Woller, G. M. (2004). Microfinance: A comprehensive review of the existing literature. *Journal of Entrepreneurial Finance and Business Ventures*, 9, 1–26.

Cheston, S. & Kuhn, L. (2002). Empowering women through microfinance. Retrieved from http://www.microcreditsummit.org/papers/empowerintro.htm. Accessed on August 4, 2007.

Chowdhury, A. K. (2004). Implementation of the first United Nations Decade for the Eradication of Poverty (1997–2006). Statement in the Second Committee of the 59th Session of the United Nations General Assembly. Retrieved from http://www. un.org/special-rep/ohrlls/ohrlls/UNGA59/HR's%20statement%2015%20Nov%20 04-item89a-Eradication%20of%20Poverty.pdf. Accessed on April 3, 2015.

Churchill, C (2007). Insuring the low-income market: Challenges and solutions for commercial insurers. *Geneva Papers on Risk & Insurance — Issues & Practice*, 32(3), 401–412.

Claessens, S. (2006). Competitive Implications of Cross-Border Banking. World Bank Policy Research Working Paper No. 3854.

Collins, D., Morduch, J., Rutherford, S. & Ruthven, O. (2010). *Portfolios of the Poor: How the World's Poor Live on $2 a Day*. Ranikhet: Permanent Black.

Consultative Group to Assist the Poor (CGAP). (2003). About microfinance. Retrieved from http://www.cgap.org/portal/site/CGAP/menuitem.9a218408ac 5bc61fae6c6210591010a0/. Accessed on August 7, 2007.

Copestake, J., Bhalotra, S. & Johnson, S. (2001). Assessing the impact of micro-credit: A Zambian case study. *Journal of Development Studies*, 37(4), 81.

Cornford, R. (2000). 'Microcredit,' 'Microfinance' or Simply 'Access to Financial Services' What do Pacific People Need? Retrieved from http://www.devnet. org.nz/conf/conference2000.html. Accessed on July 5, 2007.

De Bruyn, T. & Kuddus, U. (2005). *Dynamics of Remittance Utilization in Bangladesh*, IOM Migration Series, Vol. 18. Geneva: International Organisation for Migration.

Diagne, A., Zeller, M. & Sharma, M. (2000). Empirical measurements of households' access to credit and credit constraints in developing countries: Methodological issues and evidence. Discussion Paper No. 90, Food Consumption and Nutrition Division International Food Policy Research Institute, Washington, D.C.

Druschel, K. (2002). Microfinance in China: Building sustainable institutions and a strong industry. Master's thesis, School of International Service, American University, 2002. Retrieved from www.american.edu/sis/idp/ resources/Druschel%20SRP.pdf. Accessed on August 16, 2007.

Du, X. S. (2004). Attempts to implement micro-finance in rural China. In *Organisation for Economic Co-operation and Development (OECD), Centre for Co-operation with Non-members, Rural Finance and Credit Infrastructure in China*. Paris: OECD Publications, pp. 271–284.

Du, X. S. (2005). The Regulatory Environment for Microfinance in China. Essays on Regulation and Supervision, No. 11. Retrieved from www. microfinancegateway.org/redirect.php?mode=link&id=25978. Accessed on August 3, 2007.

Duflo, E. & Udry, C. (2003). Intrahousehold Resource Allocation in Côte d'Ivoire: Social Norms, Separate Accounts and Consumption Choices. Yale University, Economic Growth Center Discussion Paper No. 857.

Duvendack, M., Palmer-Jones, R. R., Copestake, J. G., Hooper, L., Loke, Y. & Rao, N. (2011). *What is the Evidence of the Impact of Microfinance on the Well-Being of Poor People?* London: EPPI-Centre, Social Science Research Unit, Institute of Education, University of London.

Eversole, R. (2003). Help, risk and deceit: Microentrepreneurs talk about microfinance. *Journal of International Development*, 15, 179–188. doi:10.1002/jid.972.

Gao, L. Z. & Hu, X. C. (2005). An overview of microcredit-mode in poverty reduction in China. *Journal of Jinan University*, 15(6), 61–67 (in Chinese).

Garikipati, S. (2006). The Impact of Lending to Women on Household Vulnerability and Women's Empowerment: Evidence from India, Research Paper Series No. 2006/25. Liverpool, Great Britain: University of Liverpool, Management School.

Goetz, A. M. & Gupta, R. S. (1996). Who takes the credit? Gender, power, and control over loan use in rural credit programmes in Bangladesh. *World Development*, 24(4), 45–63.

Hasan, R. A. (2006). Harnessing Remittances for Economic Development of Bangladesh. INAFI: Working Paper Series. Dhaka.

Hossain, M. & Diaz, C. P. (1997). Reaching the poor with effective microcredit: Evaluation of a Grameen bank replication in the Philippines. *Journal of Philippine Development*, XXIV(2), 275–308.

Hulme, D. (2000). Impact assessment methodologies for microfinance: Theory, experience and better practice. *World Development*, 28(1), 79–98.

Hunt, J. & Kasynathan, N. (2001). Pathways to empowerment? Reflections on microfinance and transformation in gender relations in South Asia. *Gender and Development*, 9(1), 42–52.

Hussain, M., Maskooki, K. & Gunasekaran, A. (2001). Implications of Grameen banking system in Europe: Prospects and prosperity. *European Business Review*, 13(1), 26–42.

Islam, T. (2007). *Microcredit and Poverty Alleviation*. Aldershot, England; Burlington, U.S.A.: Ashgate Publishing.

Karlan, D. & Zinman, J. (2010). Expanding credit access: Using randomized supply decisions to estimate the impacts. *Review of Financial Studies*, 23(1), 433–464.

Kasim, S. (2000). *Impact of Banking on Rural Poor in Peninsular Malaysia: Final Report for External Impact Evaluation Study on AIM Active Borrowers, Non-Borrowing Members, Dropouts and Non-Participating Poor*. Penang: Centre for Policy Research, Universiti Sains Malaysia.

Kasim, M. Y. & Jayasooria, D. (2001). Informal economy, micro-finance and non-governmental organisations in Malaysia. *Humanomics*, 17(1/2), 134–140.

Khan, S. & Ashta, A. (2012). Cost control in microfinance: Lessons from the ASA case. *Cost Management*, 26(1), 5–22.

Khandker, S. R. (2005). Microfinance and poverty: Evidence using panel data from Bangladesh. *The World Bank Economic Review*, 19(2), 263–286.

Latifee, H. I. (2003). Micro-credit and Poverty Reduction. Paper presented at the International Conference on Poverty Reduction through Micro-credit, June 9–10, Taksim-Istanbul, Turkey.

Lewis, J. C. (2008). Microloan sharks. *Stanford Social Innovation Review*, 6(3), 54–59.

Littlefield, E. & Rosenberg, R. (2004). Microfinance and the Poor. *Finance and Development*, 41(2), 38–40.

Maclsaac, N. (1997). The Role of Microcredit in Poverty Reduction and Promoting Gender Equity. Discussion Paper, Canadian International Development Agency, Quebec, Canada.

Maes, J. P. & Reed, L. R. (2012). State of the Microcredit Summit Campaign Report 2012. Washington, DC: Microcredit Summit Campaign.

Manimekalai, N. (2004). Impact of Various Form of Microfinancing on Women,' Report submitted to Department of Women and Child Development, Ministry of Human Resource Development, Government of India.

McCarty, A. (2001). *Microfinance in Vietnam: A Survey of Schemes and Issues.* Hanoi, Vietnam: Department for International Development (DFID) and the State Bank of Vietnam (SBVN).

Mersland, R. & Eggen, Ø. (2007). You cannot save alone — financial and social mobilization in savings and credit groups. Retrieved from SSRN eLibrary, http://papers.ssrn.com/sol3/papers.cfm?abstract_id=1032247. Accessed on May 10, 2014.

Mersland, R. & Strom, O. (2010). Microfinance mission drift? *World Development*, 38(1), 28–36.

Mohamed, K. (2003). Access to Formal and Quasi-Formal Credit by Smallholder Farmers and Artisanal Fishermen: A Case of Zanzibar, Research Report No. 03.6. Dar es Salaam, Tanzania: Research on Poverty Alleviation (REPOA).

Morduch, J. & Haley, B. (2001). Analysis of the Effects of Microfinance on Poverty Reduction. NYU Wagner Working Paper No. 1014. Retrieved from http://www.nyu.edu/wagner/workingpapers.html. Accessed on September 2, 2010.

Mourji, F. (2000). Impact study of the Zakoura microcredit program. Microfinance Gateway. Retrieved from http://www.microfinancegateway.org/p/site/m//template.rc/1.9.25435. Accessed on April 25, 2014.

Musinguzi, P. & Smith, P. (2000). Saving and borrowing in rural Uganda. Southampton, UK, University of Southampton, Discussion Papers in Economics and Econometrics, 0016, 20 pp.

Pham, T. T. T. & Lensink, R. (2007). Lending policies of informal, formal and semiformal lenders. *Economics of Transition*, 15(2), 181–209.

Pitt, M. M. & Khandker, S. R. (1998). The impact of group-based credit programmes on poor households in Bangladesh: Does the gender of participants matter? *The Journal of Political Economy*, 106(5), 958–996.

Pitt, M. M., Khandker, S. R. & Cartwright, J. (2006). Empowering women with microfinance: Evidence from Bangladesh. *Economic Development and Cultural Change*, 54(4), 791–831.

Poyo, J. & Young, R. (1999). *Commercialization of Microfinance: A Framework for Latin America. United States Agency for International Development Microenterprise Best Practices Project*. Washington, DC: Development Alternatives, Inc.

Quibria, M. G. (2012). *Microcredit and Poverty Alleviation: Can Microcredit Close the Deal?* Helsinki: UNU-WIDER.

Reeve, D. (2006). Indonesia: Microcredit in Indonesia. AFG Venture Group, Sydney, NSW 2000, Australia. Retrieved from http://www.afgventuregroup. com/asian_analysis/Indonesia-%20Microcredit%20in%20Indonesia.php.

Reinsch, M. & Metcalf, M. (2010). Costs and Benefits of Health Microinsurance Premium Loans and Linkages with Health Providers, CARD's Experience in the Philippines. Freedom from Hunger Research Paper No. 10B.

Rivera, J. P. R. & Reyes, P. O. (2011). Remittances as avenue for encouraging household entrepreneurial activities. *Journal of International Business Research*, 10, 85–113.

Roth, J. (1997). *The Limits of Micro Credit as a Rural Development Intervention: Prepared for the Institute for Development Policy and Management — Manchester University*, pp. 1–32.

Sapovadia, V. K. (2006). Microfinance: The pillars of a tool to socio-economic development. *Development Gateway*. Retrieved from http://ssrn.com/abstract= 955062. Accessed on June 11, 2014.

Smith, G. & Epstein, K. (2007). The ugly side of microlending. *Business Week*. http://www.businessweek.com/stories/2007-12-12/the-ugly-side-of-micro-lending. Accessed on April 25, 2014.

Sun, R. M. (2003). The development of microfinance in China. Retrieved from http://topics.developmentgateway.org/rc/filedownload.do?itemId=323395. Accessed on May 1, 2007.

Swain, R. B. (2004). *Is Microfinance a Good Poverty Alleviation Strategy? Evidence from Impact Assessment*. Stockholm, Sweden: Sida (Swedish International Development Cooperation Agency).

Timberg, T. A. (1999). Small and Micro-Enterprise Finance in Indonesia: What Do We Know? Retrieved from unpan1.un.org/intradoc/groups/public/documents/APCITY/UNPAN015693.pdf. Accessed on August 8, 2007.

Weiss, J. & Montgomery, H. (2004). Great expectations: Microfinance and poverty reduction in Asia and Latin America. *Oxford Development Studies*, 33(3–4), 391–416.

World Bank (2006). *Microfinance in South Asia: Toward Financial Inclusion for the Poor*. Washington D.C., U.S.: Pangraphics.

World Bank (2010). Access to Finance for the Poor. CGAP Annual Report 2010.

Yang, M. J. (2006). The issues in rural microcredit in Western China: A discussion. *Xi'an Finance*, 11, 7–9 (in Chinese).

Yunus, M. (2003). What is microcredit? Retrieved from http://www.grameen-info.org/mcredit/index.html. Accessed on April 15, 2007.

Zaman, H. (1999). Assessing the Poverty and Vulnerability Impact of Micro-Credit in Bangladesh: A Case Study of BRAC, World Bank Policy Research Working Paper, No. 2145. Washington, D.C.: The World Bank.

Chapter 2

Rural Credit Market
and Microfinance in Vietnam

Phan Dinh Khoi*,‡ and Christopher Gan†,§

*Head of Department, Department of Finance and Banking,
College of Economics, Can Tho University, Vietnam

†Professor in Accounting and Finance,
Faculty of Agribusiness and Commerce,
Department of Financial and Business System,
PO Box 85084, Lincoln University, Christchurch, New Zealand

‡pdkhoi@ctu.edu.vn
§Christopher.Gan@lincoln.ac.nz

Abstract

The rural credit market in Vietnam is characterised as a segmented and emerging market where the growing demand for credit by the poor and low-income households is unmet. This chapter examines the main characteristics of three pillars in Vietnam rural credit market including demand, supply and government policies. While the demand for rural credit is unmet, the supply of credit simultaneously comes from formal, informal and semi-formal providers. To improve credit accessibility, government policies targeting the poor have overcome the obstacle of collateral loan for the poor; however, asymmetric information inherently prevents the poor from having access to credit not only from the borrower's side but

23

also from the credit institutions. Therefore, improving credit accessibility to the poor and rural households continues a challenging task for policy makers in order to achieve long term development goal in Vietnam.

Keywords: Rural credit market, microfinance, microcredit, government policies, Vietnam.

2.1 Introduction

This chapter describes Vietnam's rural credit market, such as credit supply, credit demand and credit accessibility by rural households, credit policies and the Vietnam Bank for Social Policies (VBSP) microcredit programmes. The chapter is organised as follows: Section 2.2 provides an overview of Vietnam's rural financial system including formal, semiformal and informal sectors. Section 2.3 discusses credit supply and demand in the rural credit market. Section 2.4 discusses the policies and events that influence the development of the rural credit market. Section 2.5 discusses the government microcredit programme targeting poverty reduction in Vietnam. Section 2.6 summarises the chapter. Section 2.7 provides some relevant policy implications.

2.2 An Overview of Vietnam's Rural Financial System

The development of the Vietnam rural credit market is historically marked by the 'Reform' in 1986. Before 1986, under the central planning regime, the rural credit market played a minimal role in supplying capital to the agricultural sector. As the State did not recognise private investment, it ignored the need for capital investment. Official credit was delivered by the State Bank to communes, cooperatives and state farms (Fallavier, 1998). In the late 1980s, Vietnam rural credit market was established to supply capital to the agricultural sector. The establishment of the Vietnam Bank for Agriculture (VBA) in 1988 was the first step in lending to private investment in agriculture. After its official establishment, the formal credit market has been developed to serve rural clients. Meanwhile, nongovernment organisations (NGOs) and donors have joined to increase the credit supply through microcredit schemes in the rural credit market. This form of credit has been documented as the semi-formal credit channel

(Le, 2011). Further, Vietnam rural credit market is regarded as segmented and dual structured where the formal and informal credit sectors prevalently exist (McCarty, 2001; Pham & Lensink, 2007). Informal credit sector exists along the formal and semi-formal credit sectors and its existence contributes to the complexity of credit provision in the rural credit market.

For years, the formal credit sector, led by the VBA, mainly provided credit for agricultural production with a collateral requirement. The poor were mostly excluded from VBA credit. Since 1995, the establishment of the Vietnam Bank for the Poor (VBP) has directed the credit supply to cover the unreached segment, for example, the poor and landless households. McCarty (2001) documented a steady formal credit expansion where the share of formal credit increased from 28% in 1993 to 46% in 1998 and to 70% in 2001. However, a proportion of households who were not served by the formal sector seeks alternative credit from the informal sector such as friends, relatives and moneylenders at excessively high interest rates. The average interest rate charged for informal loans in 1993 was 80% per annum, which was more than double the rate of formal loans. Khoi *et al.* (2014) documented that the average interest rate is 150% per annum for an informal loan in the Mekong River Delta.

Vietnam rural financial system consists of three sectors: the formal, semi-formal and informal credit sector. Figure 2.1 shows the types of lenders in each credit sector in Vietnam's rural financial system.

2.2.1 *The formal credit market*

The formal credit sector includes bank and non-bank institutions. The bank institutions are characterised by the dominance of two state-owned commercial financial institutions, namely the Vietnam Bank for Agriculture and Rural Development (VBARD), and the VBSP. In addition, a number of commercial banks and the PCFs also play a major role in the formal credit market. According to the World Bank (2002) report, the formal credit sector accounted for as much as 73.5% of the total lending to the economy. Heavily regulated by the State Bank of Vietnam, the formal credit sector was designed to serve the rural credit market but its operations fall short of achieving the defined objectives. Recently, the rural

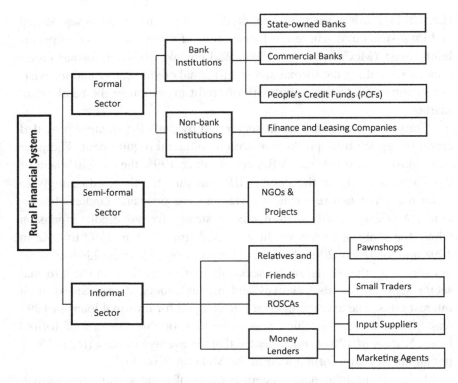

Figure 2.1:   Vietnam Rural Financial System

Source: Adapted from Le (2011).

credit market has shown an increasing trend of credit supply through a number of commercial banks and the PCFs.

The VBARD formerly known as the VBA was separated from the State Bank of Vietnam in 1988. The VBARD is the largest supplier of credit to rural households, providing credit for all types of agricultural activity in the rural areas (BWTP, 2008). The share of rural households access to credit under VBARD management increased rapidly from 9% in 1992 to about 30% in 1994 (Wolz, 1999). Although the VBARD is by far the most important financial institution in the rural areas, its lending coverage is still underdeveloped to serve the entire rural credit market, particularly the rural poor.

Microcredit lending is dominated by larger loans in the VBARD total outstanding loans. Of the total loans in 1998, small loans below VND 5 million[1] represented about 50% compared to 16% in microcredit (at an average of VND 1 million) (World Bank, 2007). A collateral requirement is another constraint in VBARD's lending practices providing rural credit. VBARD requires collateral such as residential property, movable assets, goods and land rights, when granting loans. Thus, only about 30% of the households with a "red certificate" on land use rights have access to credit. Most rural households are unable to meet the lending requirements and are excluded from the supply of rural credit.

Bias in risk assessment and complicated procedures in the lending process have also contributed to the underdevelopment of VBARD's operation. The VBARD branches prefer to provide credit to state-owned enterprises (SOEs) due to the low risk of default. SOEs are often considered zero risk clients because the government is expected to bail them out in the case of default. Lending to SOEs also incurs relatively low transaction costs for significantly large amount of credits compared with many small microcredits to a large number of rural households (Putzeys, 2002). Dealing with small loans and microloans is considered costly in terms of time and money because of the complexity in processing the loan applications. Often, VBARD credit can be used only for specific agricultural investments but not for those activities that are the priority needs of the borrowers.

The state-owned VBP, the second largest rural bank, was established in 1995 under the framework of the Hunger Eradication and Poverty Reduction Strategy. It officially started operation in 1996, providing credit at low interest rate to the rural poor who did not qualify for individual loans because of limited collateral. The VBP utilises the VBARD's branch network at the district level and, to a limited extent, at the commune level, where loan officers visit the communes on a weekly basis. This coverage and lending practice further reach the segment currently not served by the VBARD in the rural credit market. The existing network is believed to have limited outreach to the poor in the most remote and rural communes. In 1999, only 2.3 million poor households obtained loans. Due to strong demand for microcredit, 8.3 million rural households were recorded to have obtained a loan from VBARD and VBP in 2001. In terms of total

---

[1]Exchange rate: 1US$ = 16,000VND.

loans outstanding, VBARD accounted for 60% of the total loans and provided an average loan size of VND 6.45 million and 40% were from VBP with an average loan size of VND 2 million (World Bank, 2003).

In 2003, the VBP was renamed the VBSP. Its operations have been modified to target the poor. The VBSP closely cooperates with local organisations in lending procedures in which the local People's Committees help VBSP to identify the poor and socially disadvantaged groups. Meanwhile, other social mass organisations in villages such as the Women's Union and the Farmers' Associations help the bank to monitor the loans. Collateral is not required for borrowing but the social mass organisations provide a Guarantee Fund to the bank. If the borrowers default, the bank will take a portion of the Guarantee Fund. To ensure repayment, the social mass organisations organise the borrowers in credit groups. Joint-liability groups were also formed in the initial stage of microcredit lending but this lending practice has been changed to the more flexible group lending practice (Bhole & Ogden, 2010) in which the individual is liable only for her or his loan but not for those of other group members. According to the VBSP (2009) report, the total outstanding loans reached VND 72,660 billion, providing loans to 7.5 million active borrowers. The 2009 outstanding loans increased 38.4% (equivalent to 20,149 billion VND) compared with 2008 where loans to poor households accounted for VND 32,542 billion for over 3.7 million clients.

After the collapse of the rural credit cooperatives, VBP was entrusted with reorganising the rural credit cooperative system. This resulted in a network of PCFs whereby PCFs' branches have been created in nearly all provinces of Vietnam. To restore public confidence in the formal rural finance system, the term 'cooperative' has been deliberately excluded from the name of the newly established finance institution (Putzeys, 2002). The PCFs' system has been set up as a member-owned organisation that aims to mobilise savings from its members. The system is managed according to the economic principle of cost covering, i.e., no easy money is available.

The PCFs' network has been established predominantly in those areas that are economically better off and have a better developed infrastructure. Therefore, the PCFs' system plays a limited role with respect to reducing rural poverty. Its major role is to provide a viable rural finance system to farm and small entrepreneurial households to stimulate economic development, which indirectly contributes to poverty eradication (Putzeys, 2002).

The Vietnam banking sector is large by international comparison, whether measured by deposits or credit. According to the World Bank (2014) report, the banking sector dominates the financial system, with total assets amounting to about 200% of Vietnam's GDP (including the two policy banks) and 92% of the financial institutions total assets. While the banking sector is relatively large for a low middle-income country, non-bank financial institutions account for only 17% of GDP and 8% of the financial institutions' total assets. Finance companies provide project and consumer finance and represent the largest class of non-bank financial institution, accounting for 6% of GDP and 3% of the financial institution total assets (World Bank, 2014).

2.2.2 *The informal credit market*

Knowledge of the informal credit sector in Vietnam is primarily based on anecdotal evidence but its important role as the informal credit provider in rural credit market has recently been well documented (for details, see Barslund & Tarp, 2008; Pham & Izumida, 2002; Pham & Lensink, 2007). Typically, rural households can borrow money from different types of informal loan sources such as relatives, friends and neighbours, Rotating Savings Credit Associations (ROSCAs), or private money lenders, with greater flexibility than the formal credit providers.

Relatives, friends and neighbours are the first alternative sources of credit; loan size and interest rate are determined by individual relationships and reputations. Taking advantage of personal relationships, relatives and friends, in general, provide loans without collateral or loan contract with any form of written loan contract. Recorded interest rates are low for loans from the neighbours and, in many cases, loans from relatives and friends are interest free. The loan amount varies according to the loan purpose such as emergency, consumption for illness, funerals, weddings, etc. Although, these loans are rarely sufficient to finance agricultural production, they partially reflect the prevalence of informal loans in the rural credit market in Vietnam (Pham & Izumida, 2002).

ROSCAs have been traditionally known as an informal credit channel for rural households in Vietnam. Although they have existed for many generations, these financial arrangements have never been recognised as business contracts under the Law of Credit. These groups are referred to as *Hui* in the South and *Ho* in the North (Pham & Lensink, 2007). ROSCAs promote periodic savings which, in turn, are rotated as funds among a limited group of members who trust each other. Members of ROSCAs come mainly from the same hamlet or are organised on the spot among colleagues and friends at work. In general, membership averages 12 or more persons.[2] Decisions on interest rate, number of members and loan amounts are made either jointly by all members, by a bidding process or solely by the organiser. The life cycle of a ROSCA ends when every participant has obtained the total funds collected at least once. Most ROSCAs are set up to bridge short-term needs but they can also be set up to finance long-term investments. However, ROSCAs are not regulated by the Law on credit institutions, defaults are commonly associated with either ROSCA members or organisers due to the weak screening process among members and weak social sanctions.

Private moneylenders are widespread and seem to be an important source of loans for most rural households. Putzeys (2002) revealed that, in 1997–1998, 51% of credit to farm households was provided by informal channels such as private moneylenders and individuals. Private money lenders are usually rich households in rural areas with surplus money and goods. The informal interest rate is normally higher than the formal rate; in some extreme cases, the interest rates are as high as 10–30% per month. Despite the high interest rates, there are many reasons why people borrow from moneylenders. Flexibility, both in getting the loan and repayment, as well as simple lending practices for borrowers are documented as being far more important than the interest rates (Pham & Izumida, 2002). Generally, moneylenders do not ask for collateral and have no complicated screening steps to determine the loan.

Some moneylenders are traders who give cash in advance on the basis of the promise to receive or buy the products at harvest time. Others can

---

[2]Twelve people is an ideal matching number to the 12 months of the year.

be suppliers who provide credit as input for agricultural production at the beginning of the season then receive the principal payment plus interest at the end (Khoi *et al.*, 2014). This type of lenders has emerged during the last few years as Vietnam's agricultural products market became more developed. Therefore, it is widely accepted and assumed that it will become an important source of informal credit in Vietnam's rural credit market.

Similar to other rural financial markets in developing countries, the informal credit sector remains controversial in Vietnam's rural credit market reconstruction. There are opponents who traditionally regard informal credit as a violation of financial discipline despite its contribution to meeting farmers' financial needs. This is because the Vietnamese government does not recognise the legal existence of the informal sector and the development of informal credit is out of the government's supervision. Therefore, informal credit should be excluded from the rural credit market by improving the lending operations of formal financial institutions to expand outreach in favour of rural households, which is crucial in establishing a sound rural credit market and maintaining the sustainable development of the rural economy. However, according to the development finance's view, supported by the persistence of informal credit, suggests a better regulation for both formal and informal credit sectors would tap more financial resources from informal sector which would work towards improving more credit access to the rural credit market. The existence of informal credit reflects the imperfections of Vietnam's formal rural credit system, which is characterised as fragmented and unable to meet the diverse credit demands of the rural households. In terms of rural credit development, the existence of informal credit should be re-addressed both in rational views in order to facilitate credit accessibility to household in the rural credit market.

2.2.3 The semiformal credit market

The semiformal credit sector was established through microfinance programmes in late 1990s, managed by international programmes and NGOs in partnership with local organisations at the provincial level. This sector consists of various structures of decentralised financing that offer microfinance services that attempt to reach that part of the population excluded from formal credit channels. Initially, the semiformal credit sector was mainly funded by international and national donors who saw this channel of funding as a means to provide more efficient aid to poor families in rural areas and thus alleviating poverty.

Like other Asian countries, the semiformal credit sector has a significant role in the provision of microcredit to the poor but at a smaller scale in Vietnam (see McCarty, 2001). The key actors in the semiformal credit sector are mass organisations such as the Women's Union, Farmers Associations, Youth Union and War Veterans, who play a crucial role in the implementation of donor-supported microfinance schemes. These organisations are usually represented at four administrative levels: national, provincial, district and commune. This structure enables the mass organisations to have direct contact with the authority at the local level and to establish a connection at the national level. The legal framework covering microfinance services in Vietnam was established in 2010; hence, the semiformal credit sector was left outside the Law on Credit Institutions in the past decades.

Currently, the semiformal credit sector includes more than 300 small-scale microfinance programmes, of which 40 are relatively big and focus on microfinance. These are NGO-typed, with clients ranging between 1,000 and 10,000 members and the majority of the loan portfolio is below US$1 million. These programs strongly focus on the poor with typical loan size between US$150 and US$300 and their major clients are women. Among them, Capital aid fund for unemployment of the poor[3] (CEP) and Tinh Thuong Microfinance Institution (MFI)[4] (TYM) and four other MFIs account for more than 50% of market share of semiformal credit sector (Le, 2011).

---

[3]CEP is a non-profit Vietnamese MFI that operates in the provinces of Southeastern Vietnam and the Mekong Delta.

[4]Tinh Thuong is a Limited Liability MFI and the first official MFI in Vietnam. It was established by the Vietnam Women's Union with a mission to improve the quality life of low-income women and their families, especially poor disadvantaged women by providing financial and non-financial services, creating favourable conditions for their participation in economic activities and enhancing their role in society.

2.3 Credit Supply and Demand in the Rural Credit Market

Table 2.1 provides a summary of the empirical studies providing information about the sources of credit supply and the purposes of credit demand in Vietnam. Like the rural credit markets in other Asian countries, the formal credit sector fails to provide credit for production and consumption of rural households, hence, the informal sector exists in the rural credit market. Rural households are likely to borrow from different credit sources for different purposes. For example, McCarty (2001) and Pham & Izumida (2002) showed that the predominant purpose of formal loans reported by the surveyed households was for financing current production such as cultivation, livestock and handicrafts but most informal loans were obtained primarily for personal consumption and expenditure, such as house repairs, weddings and funerals. Recently, Pham & Lensink (2007) showed a mixed contribution of the formal and informal credit sectors to households' credit demands in Vietnam. Rural households borrow from either

Table 2.1: Main Sources of Supply and Demand for Rural Credit

	Production					Consumption				
Studies	Fertiliser	Other inputs for crop production	Livestock	Fixed capital	Self-employment Non-farm activities	Daily expenses	Weddings and funerals	Schooling	Health care	Housing
McCarty (2001)	D	D	D	D	D	D	D	D	D	D
	F/IF	F/IF	F/IF	F/IF	F/IF	IF	IF	IF	IF	IF
Pham & Izumida (2002)	D	D	D	D	D	D	D	D	D	D
	F/IF	F/IF	F/IF	F/IF	F/IF	IF	IF	IF	IF	IF
Ho (2004)	D	D	D	D	D	D	D	D	D	
	F	F	F	F	F	IF	IF	IF	IF	
Pham & Lensink (2007)	D	D	D	D	D	D	D	D	D	D
	F/IF	F/IF	F/IF	F/IF	F/IF	F/IF	F/IF	F/IF	F/IF	F/IF

Note: D: Demand for, F: Supplied by formal credit sector, IF: Supplied by informal credit sector.

the formal credit sector, largely to support their agricultural production, such as purchasing chemical fertilisers and raising livestock, or they borrow from friends or relatives to supplement their consumption including house building, medical treatment and children's education. Evidence of the association between formal and informal credit for production and consumption loans in the rural credit market in Vietnam has been documented but partially explained.

As the [Vietnam] agricultural input and product markets have developed, the demand for rural credit, particularly the demand for microcredit, has also changed (World Bank, 2007). Rural households have increasingly demanded more sophisticated loans. For example, a crop producer and a small trader have very different demands for loans. A crop producer might prefer a loan at the beginning of each crop planting and the loan repayment after harvest whereas a small trader requires a loan any time for cheap stocks with a flexible repayment period. In addition, the loan size also differs between the very poor and less poor households based on their income-generating activities. Though a small loan can certainly make a significant impact in raising the income-generating capacity of a crop producer, a medium-scale trader would demand a large loan for her or his business. Thus, under a supply-driven and subsidised-credit policy, the provision of credit to poor households needs to be re-addressed in order to identify the changes in demand for credit from clients as well as improve the formal lending practices.

2.4 Policies and Events in the Development of the Rural Credit Market

After the country's Reunification in 1975, the Vietnam economy was strictly regulated by the central planning model, which decelerated growth and created fewer incentives for economic agents to be involved in economic activities (Fan, Huong & Long, 2004; McCarty, 2001). Before the 1980s, the economy was characterised by: (i) state or collective ownership; (ii) the centralisation of physical input and output supplies; (iii) the absence of factor markets and highly regulated markets of goods and services; (iv) a concentration on heavy industries and (v) a passive one-tier banking system in which the state bank performed as a commercial as well as a Central Bank in order to allocate the capital to designated projects rather than to mobilise domestic savings (Fan *et al.*, 2004). Consequently, the average national income growth rate per annum during the period 1976–1980 was estimated at 1.4%, far below the targeted rate of 13–14%. Severe food shortages, trade deficits, aid cuts and budget deficits, high inflation and a declining per capita income imposed high pressure on policy makers in the early 1980s (Pham, 2009; Vo, 1987).

Faced with severe inflation and a budget deficit in 1986, the Vietnamese government reformed a number of macropolicies, starting with decentralisation of SOEs, to control fiscal and monetary policies. The economic reform had a significant impact on the economy, particularly controlling inflation in the late 1980s. Within 10 years, the near hyperinflation in 1986 was reduced to a single-digit level, facilitating economic growth (Pham, 2009). In 1990, financial reform started with separating the State Bank monopoly into the two-tier banking system with the State Bank functioning as a typical Central Bank and the commercial banks specialising in providing banking services. The newly established banking system opened the door for lending to the private sector. Currently, the commercial banking system consists of the state-owned banks and joint-stock banks, credit funds, joint venture banks and foreign banks. Interest liberalisation, flexible management of the exchange rate and the application of indirect monetary measures in market management have also been implemented. As a continuing effort of the government followed by the implementation of a number of innovative monetary policies that are expected to contribute significantly to macroeconomic stabilisation, inflation control and an increasing supply of credit to all sectors of the economy, its impact is not promising. Due to strong government intervention in the banking sector and high degree of cross-ownership between banks, the performance of the banking sector has deteriorated and probably weaker than reported (World Bank, 2014). Table 2.2 summarises major key policies and events that specifically influenced Vietnam's rural credit market.

In an attempt to foster credit through microfinance institutions, the Vietnamese government issued the Decree No. 28-ND-CP/2005 to direct the operations of MFIs in 2005. To continue to provide favourable credit to the rural area, the Resolution 26-NQ/TW/2008 was passed to

Table 2.2:   Key Policies and Events Influencing Vietnam's Rural Finance

Year	Policy/Event	Solution
1988	Development of Vietnam Bank for Agriculture	To provide financial services to agriculture and rural sectors
1993	PCFs were re-established	To mobilised savings from rural households
1995	Vietnam Bank for the Poor was established	To provide credit to poor households at favourable interest rate
2001	Decree No. 48/ND-CP/2001 of the Government to PCFs	To improve PCFs' organisation and operations
2002	VBSP was established	To provide cheap credit to the poor and rural households
2005	Decree No. 28/ND-CP/2005 of the Government	To direct the organisation and operations of microfinance institutions (MFIs)
2008	Resolution 26-NQ/TW/2008 on "Tam nong" of the Party Congress	To continue to provide favourable credit to the rural sector, and encourage the MFIs to lend to the rural sector
2009	National Microfinance Steering Committee was formed	To develop a market-based microfinance sector
2009	Decision No. 497/QD-TTg/2009 of the Prime Minister	To provide the interest support for farmers within the demand stimulus package
4/2010	Decree 41/ND-CP/2010 on Credit Policy for developing agriculture and rural sector	To increase non-collateral loans for farming households, non-farm households, farming cooperatives, farming enterprises
6/2010	The New Law on Credit Institutions (CIL) was amended to replace the CIL in 1997	To incorporate non-bank MFIs into the formal financial system and to liberalise the banking operations including rural finance

Source: Adapted from Le (2011).

encourage the MFIs to expand lending to the rural sector. In 2009, the National Microfinance Steering Committee was formed in order to develop a market-based microfinance sector. Following this, MFIs' operations were incorporated into the formal financial system under the CIL in 2010. The continuing efforts of the government in improving credit access to rural area resulted in the passage of the new CIL and the ongoing efforts to formulate the Microfinance Strategy and Roadmap are major steps in the right direction. However, according to Le (2011) the government also has to ensure that the pursuit of other social objectives will not undermine the objectives for the microfinance sector. However, the government with its "social policy lending" to the target groups could cause the exclusion of the vast majority of the poor and low-income households from accessing permanent, responsive and a range of financial services, not just microcredit.

Despite a number of limitations, the rural credit market has significantly contributed to the rural development of Vietnam in terms of the expansion of outreach and increasing credit access to the rural households (Le, 2011; McCarty, 2001). The establishment of VBARD in 1988 and the PCF in 1993 played a major role in supplying rural credits. Both institutions built a countrywide network for specialised rural credit providers to expand their services. In 1995, the VBP was established under the control of VBARD with the purpose of providing poor households with favourable credit, i.e., the poor could borrow collateral free low interest loans. The establishment of VBSP in 2003 further expanded social policy lending to the target group to ensure the inclusion of the poor as well as further establishing the microfinance sector in the rural credit market.

Government policies have deliberately encouraged the development of the microfinance sector. Several policy initiatives are implemented to ensure microfinance institutions operate in the rural financial market as well as to include the microfinance sector in the rural development process. Particularly, Decree No. 28/ND-CP/2005 provided the primary legal framework to open up the MFIs' operations to service clients. Resolution 26/NQ-TW/2008 re-emphasised rural development based on three main sectors — agriculture, farmers and the rural sector. The policy indicated a further need to continue providing favourable credit to the rural sector by encouraging financial institutions to lend to the rural sector. In 2009, the National Microfinance Steering Committee was formed to develop a market-based microfinance sector. Subsequently, two rural credit policies have been implemented. Decision No. 497/QD-TTg/2009 of the Prime Minister aims to provide interest support for farmers within a demand stimulus package and Decree 41/ND-CP/2010 on Credit Policy for agriculture and rural sector development increases non-collateral loans for farm households, non-farm households, farm cooperatives and farm enterprises. In particular, non-collateral loans increased up to VND 50 million for farm households, VND 200 million for non-farm households and VND 200 million for agricultural cooperatives and farm enterprises.

Although the MFIs have been formally directed by Decree No. 28, the Law on Credit Institutions amended in 2010 has legislatively integrated the MFIs as a subset of the formal financial system. As the landmark legislation for MFIs to operate in the rural financial market has been established, ongoing efforts to formulate the Microfinance Strategy are major tasks. Le (2011) indicated the paradox of defining the Microfinance Strategy that ensures the MFIs performance meets the social objectives while pursuing market-oriented rural finance. On one hand, the maximising profit behaviour of the banks could drive the vast majority of poor and low-income households away from accessing a wider range of financial services, not just microcredit. In addition, the dominance of the subsidy from VBSP burdens the government budget and discourages the development of market-oriented rural MFIs.

2.5 Microcredit Programmes Targeting Poverty Reduction in Rural Vietnam

Despite a number of key policies established over the past two decades in the rural credit market to support poverty reduction, Vietnam is still home to over 12 million people (14.2% of the population) living in poverty[5] (World Bank, 2008). Currently, the majority of poor households in rural areas live in poor conditions, such as temporary houses, lack of fixed assets, low and unstable income. Access to credit has remained one of the critical issues of the country's poverty reduction and rural development strategy.

The VBSP microcredit programme has been designed to target the poor who face disadvantage in living conditions and have limited access to finance sources. Since its official establishment in 2003, the VBSP

---

[5]In 2006, the national poverty line was set at VND 260,000 (US$16) per month per person in urban areas and VND 200,000 (US$12) per month per person in rural areas.

provides the poor with preferential microcredit through a '*group-based lending scheme*'. To borrow credit from VBSP, a household should join a credit group in its locality. A credit group consists of 5–50 members residing in the same village. If in a village the number of members is lower than five, they should join a credit group in another village. Each credit group sets up a management board, which is responsible for the borrowing and credit use of its members (Quach, 2005). According to the VBSP's lending policies, to become a member of a credit group a household should meet the following criteria: (i) a long-term residence permit at the locality in which the credit group is located; (ii) a household member in a work force able to work; (iii) has a poor certificate, has a demand for credit for production or for consumption necessary for subsistence, a total loan requirement of not more than VND 30 million (VBSP lending policies in 2012) or total outstanding loans may not exceed VND 30 million (VBSP, 2013).

The VBSP's policy microcredit programmes currently include the followings: poor households programme, marginal poor households programme, disadvantaged students programme, job-creation programme, programme for migrant workers abroad for a limited term, programme for business and production households living in extremely disadvantaged areas and communes, programme for extremely disadvantaged ethnic minority households in the Mekong River Delta, safe water and rural sanitation programme, small and medium enterprise programme, forest sector development programme, extremely disadvantaged ethnic households programme, business and production units, enterprises with drug-detoxified employees programme, housing support programme for the poor, credit programme for disadvantaged ethnic households in the Mekong River Delta, credit programme for traders doing business in disadvantaged areas, programme for poor households to build houses against storm and flood in the middle region, programme for migrant workers in Korea with security deposit, and other credit programme entrusted by international organisations and local authorities (VBSP, 2013).

Standard lending procedures for a member of a credit group applying for VBSP loans are as follows. First, applicants send a formal letter to their credit group. In the letter, the applicants specify the amount and purpose of the loan that they intend to borrow. Upon receiving the applications, the credit group leader arranges a meeting of all members to consider the relevance of the loans. During the meeting, the credit group, based on the consensus of members, determines which households are able to borrow and the amount and terms of each loan. A list of the successful applicants is prepared by the credit group leader sent to the People's Committee in that commune. Once the list is ratified by the People's Committee, it is sent to a VBSP branch for final approval. It often takes from 1 to 4 weeks to obtain credit (Nguyen, 2008; Quach, 2005).

'Group-based lending' has been popular in making loans to rural poor households since the start of the VBSP microcredit programmes. However, it is worth noticing that this lending practice does not strictly follow the joint-liability principle. The borrowers are required to form a group, including a number of certified poor members and a group leader, but no joint liability is specified (Quach, 2005). In terms of the lending procedures, the group leader's tasks include: (i) to provide information of group members to credit officers; (ii) to collect loan applications from group members and disperse the loans and (iii) to convince members to repay their loans. In the case of a default, the responsibility for dealing with default borrowers is the credit officer; the group leader helps persuade the defaulters to repay. According to Quach (2005), a 'lending through a group' mechanism adopts a 'group-based lending' to reduce transaction costs rather than to reduce default risk. However, lending through a group is more effective in dealing with asymmetric information than in individual lending. At the commune and microcredit institution levels, the process of lending and monitoring VBSP credit is rather stringent (Nguyen, 2008).

To ensure high repayment rates in the system, the VBSP monitors outstanding and overdue outstanding loans from its local branches. To allocate fund for next fiscal year for its branches, the VBSP headquarter compares the overdue outstanding loans of VBSP' branches at the provincial level with their allocated fund in the current year. As a result, less funding might be allocated to VBSP branches with large overdue loans. In addition to the credit groups the People's Committee is also administratively responsible for the repayment of credit group members in their commune. Often, when the applicants list is ratified, the People's Committee tends to exclude very poor households who might not be able to repay loans but non-poor or better-off households can get loans (Dufhues *et al.*, 2001). Therefore, the poverty targeting of the VBSP programme remains questionable.

Nguyen (2008) investigates how well the microcredit programme reaches the households by using the World Bank–GSO poverty line instead of the poverty line defined by the Ministry of Labour and Invalid Social Affairs (MOLISA). The results revealed that, in 2004, only 12% of the poor households with a favourable credit record obtained loans from the microcredit programmes provided by VBSP. The evidence strikingly indicates that the lending rate of microcredit programmes was significantly low. In addition, the poor usually receive smaller amounts of credit than the non-poor. The loan size per poor borrowing household was VND 3.174 million, which was lower than VND 3.715 million that a non-poor household borrowed on average.

Two main reasons explain why microcredit programmes did not reach the targeted poor households. First, the poverty targeting issue has difficulty in identifying the real poor. In Vietnam, the poverty definition is not consistent between the GSO–World Bank approach[6] and local authorities (Nguyen, 2008). At the commune level, a household is classified as poor if the household exhibits some difficulties such as lack of food or living in a damaged house while the income lies below the income poverty line constructed by MOLISA. The criteria are set up by each commune and they can differ from one commune to another. Because of the inconsistent definition of poverty, the only way to differentiate the poor from the non-poor is principally the instinctive judgement of local officers who often have an obscure and varied understanding of the poverty line set by the government. Thus, it is difficult to monitor the delivery of the subsidised loans to ensure that the loans actually reach the poor.

In addition, the non-targeting issue, in which much of the benefit from the subsidised microcredit program is enjoyed by the non-poor rather than the poor, has also contributed to the failure of these programmes. Nguyen (2008) showed that the VBSP program's coverage rate for middle and high income groups was 7.3% and 2.3%, respectively. The

---

[6]GSO–World Bank approach follows the international poverty line, which sets a minimum income of US$1.25 a day per person.

non-targeting issue in Vietnam was similar to that of China's subsidised-loan programmes in the early 1990s. Rozelle, Zhang & Huang (2003) revealed that over 90% of loans in China in the early 1990s were invested in industrial production instead of agricultural production. Likewise, bias in loan allocation and profit concerns are the main reasons that prevented banks from delivering subsidised loans to the poor from microcredit programmes (Li, Gan & Hu, 2011).

The second reason related to asymmetric information in selecting the borrowers in a poverty targeted microcredit programme reported in Dufhues *et al.* (2001) study. The authors reported that due to high costs related to lending and monitoring process, credit groups and commune heads are reluctant to include poor households in the list of credit applicants. Since commune heads are involved in the screening process and they receive incentives based on the credit volume and repayment rate in the commune, the commune heads also involve in the reinforcement of the repayment of overdue loans. This is an unpleasant duty which the commune heads try to avoid. Therefore, they are more likely to select households that may not be poor according to the national criteria but have a credit demand with potential repayment. The poor are excluded because they are assumed to have a low repayment capacity. Meanwhile, non-poor households find it easier to obtain credit because they are expected to be more reliable in using credit effectively and repaying the credit. In addition, the poor often have low levels of education, limited production skills and market information. They also tend to apply for smaller credit amounts than the non-poor, which makes the loan processing costly.

2.6 Chapter Summary

The rural credit market in Vietnam is characterised as a segmented and emerging market wherein the growing demand for credit by poor and low-income households is unmet. Three forms of credit providers, namely formal, informal and semi-formal, coexist. The formal credit sector was driven by a series of institutional changes and credit policies designed to cover the credit demand of rural households, particularly the rural poor. More credit access has been documented, however, a large portion of the poor are unable to borrow from the formal credit sector hence seek an alternative source of credit. The informal credit sector, traditionally known as an alternative source of formal credit, is prevalent as the alternative for many rural households; it exists with the formal credit sector. The semiformal credit sector, dominated by NGOs and donor support funds, participated in the market in late 1990s, and has an increasingly important role in providing microcredit and microfinance services to the poor but on a small scale.

In the development of the rural credit market, government policies targeting the poor have overcome the obstacle of collateral loan for the poor. Many credit policies in favour of the poor have been implemented; however, the asymmetric information inherently prevents the poor from having access to credit. Persistently, the subsidised microcredit policies appear to be a paradox for the Vietnam government to perform its social objectives in a market-oriented rural finance market. The dominating subsidised microcredit programme ensures a wider outreach of microcredit to the rural household, particularly the poor; however, it burdens the government budget and hampers the development of the market-oriented rural finance. On the other hand, to maintain the market-oriented rural banks with profit maximising behaviour, implementing a subsidised, credit policy could drive the majority of poor and low-income households from accessing credit.

2.7 Policy Implications

As the informal, semiformal and formal credit sectors coexist in the Vietnam rural credit market, an appropriate credit policy to direct these sectors to work better towards the rural development goal is necessary. A better linkage among these credit sectors would enable one sector to overcome its weaknesses by gaining from others' strengths. Particularly, lending through group without joint liability helps improve the participation rate of poor households. Expanding this lending to some informal lenders in the group would reduce the transaction costs of screening but likely increase the repayment rate because the borrowers can roll over their loans using the available alternative credit. For example, Vietnamese government and VBSP should reinforce the lending policy on individual contracts to reduce the leakage rate, while keeping the programme more cost-effective.

Given the persistence of asymmetric information, direct intervention of government into the provision of financial services to a wide range of borrowers is not an 'optimal' solution because the government faces the same problems of asymmetric information as the financial institutions. Therefore, to enable the rural credit market to function effectively, government and financial institutions should focus on the solutions to reduce the problem of asymmetric information and transaction costs associated with small-sized lending contracts (see Adams & Vogel, 1986; Bardhan & Udry, 1999). For the government, it is important to enhance the development of financial infrastructure and informational intermediation, while improving physical infrastructure and providing a consistent microcredit policy to ensure the bottom poor have adequate access to rural credit (see Navajas *et al.*, 1998; Seibel, 1997). For the financial institutions, it is essential to develop and employ the innovations in financial technologies such as tailored lending contracts (e.g., group lending) or partnership based lending for some actors in an agricultural value change (e.g., with credit rating, credit scoring agencies).

The downgrading strategy that separated larger scale loans from VBA to small-scale loans from VBSP shows the effectiveness gained from adapting innovation in lending practice to expand credit to the rural area (see also Le, 2011; Nguyen, 2008; Pham & Izumida, 2002). Rural and poor households have had greater access to preferential microcredit in the past decade and the positive impact of microcredit programmes has been well documented. However, as the rural credit market evolves, including the development of credit demand and credit supply, and other microfinance services, the question of whether the VBSP is sustainably operating in a changing environment remains debatable. The development strategy of VBSP operation should, however, reflect its predecessor's failure. Divesting VBA microfinance operations by setting up a heavily subsidised VBSP to disburse preferential loans targeting the poor contravenes the principles of sound banking practice and sustainable poverty alleviation. Moreover, highly regulated banking operations lack the dynamics of adequately responding to the growing demands of vast numbers of the poor for a full range of financial services (Dufhues,

Heidhues & Buchenrieder, 2004; Seibel, 1997). This issue should be seriously re-addressed in the long-term strategy of agricultural and rural development, and poverty reduction.

References

Barslund, M. & Tarp, F. (2008). Formal and informal rural credit in four provinces of Vietnam. *The Journal of Development Studies*, 44(4), 485–503.

Bhole, B. & Ogden, S. (2010). Group lending and individual lending with strategic default. *Journal of Development Economics*, 91(2), 348–363.

BWTP (2008). Vietnam Industry Assessment: A Report on the Vietnamese Microfinance Sector.

Dufhues, T., Pham, T. M. D., Ha, T. H. & Buchenrieder, G. (2001). *Fuzzy Information Policy of the Vietnam Bank for the Poor in Lending to and Targeting of the Poor in Northern Vietnam*. Stuttgart: Grauer.

Fallavier, P. (1998). *Developing Microfinance Institutions in Vietnam*. Vancouver: The University of British Columbia.

Fan, S., Huong, P. L. & Long, T. Q. (2004). Government Spending and Poverty Reduction in Vietnam. Project report prepared for the World Bank funded project "Pro-poor spending in Vietnam", by International Food Policy Research Institute, Washington DC, and Central Institute for Economic Management, Hanoi.

Khoi, P. D., Gan, C., Nartea, G. V. & Cohen, D. (2014). Impact of microcredit in the Mekong River Delta. *The Journal of Asia Pacific Economy*, 17(4), 558–578.

Le, T. T. (2011). Vietnam rural financial market — Fact diagnostics and the policy implications for rural development of Vietnam. *Journal of Economics and Development*, 41, 57–73.

Li, X., Gan, C. & Hu, B. (2011). Accessibility to microcredit by Chinese rural households. *Journal of Asian Economics*, 22(3), 235–246.

McCarty, A. (2001). Microfinance in Vietnam: A survey of schemes and issues. Hanoi, Vietnam: Department for International Development (DFID) and the State Bank of Vietnam (SBVN).

Navajas, S., Schreiner, M., Meyer, R. L., Gonzalez-Vega, C. & Rodriguez-Meza, J. (2000). Microcredit and the poorest of the poor: Theory and evidence from Bolivia. *World Development*, 28(2), 333–346.

Nguyen, V. C. (2008). Is a governmental microcredit program for the poor really pro-poor? Evidence from Vietnam. *The Developing Economies*, 46(2), 151–187.

Quach, M. H. (2005). *Access to Finance and Poverty Reduction: An Application to Rural Vietnam*. Birmingham: University of Birmingham.

Pham, L. T. (2009). *Determinants of Child Health and Contraceptive Use in Vietnam: A Microeconometric Analysis.* The Netherlands, Groningen: University of Groningen.

Pham, B. D. & Izumida, Y. (2002). Rural development finance in Vietnam: A microeconometric analysis of household surveys. *World Development*, 30(2), 319–335.

Pham, T. T. T. & Lensink, R. (2007). Lending policies of informal, formal and semiformal lenders. *Economics of Transition*, 15(2), 181–209.

Putzeys, R. (2002). *Microfinance in Vietnam: Three Case Studies.* Preparation MSc thesis of Development Cooperation, University of Gent, Belgium, The Belgian Technical Cooperation of Hanoi, Vietnam.

Rozelle, S., Zhang, L. & Huang, J. (2003). China's War on Poverty. *How Far Across the River.* Stanford: Stanford University Press, p. 235.

Seibel, H. D. (1997). *Upgrading, Downgrading, Linking, Innovating: Microfinance Development Strategies-A Systems Perspective.* Working Paper, University of Cologne, Development Research Center.

VBSP (2009). VBSP Annual Report 2009. Retrieved from http://www.vbsp.org.vn/ B202655C-B30C-48F0-B607-F133765722F2/FinalDownload/DownloadId-00A3DEA454DDBD205814FBAEC6591ED9/B202655C-B30C-48F0-B607-F133765722F2/Image_BCTN/2009.pdf.

VBSP (2013). VBSP Annual Report 2009. Retrieved from http://vbsp.org.vn/wp-content/uploads/2015/03/BCTN-NHCSXH-Dang-Website.pdf.

Vo, N. T. (1987). *Socialist Vietnam's Economy 1975–1985: An Assessment.* Tokyo: Institute of Development Economics.

Wolz, A. (1999). *Achievements and Problems of People's Credit Funds in Vietnam.* Heidelberg: FIA.

World Bank (2002). Vietnam Delivering on Its Promise. Report No. 25050-VN.

World Bank (2003). Vietnam Development Report 2004, Report No. 27130-VN, Poverty, Poverty Reduction and Economic Management Unit, East Asia and Pacific Region, November 17, 2003, pp. 1–194.

World Bank (2007). Vietnam: Developing a Comprehensive Strategy to Expand Access for the Poor to Microfinance Services. Volume I: The Microfinance Landscape in Vietnam.

World Bank (2008). Vietnam Development Report.

World Bank (2014). Financial Sector Assessment. Annual Report 2014.

Chapter 3
Microfinance Institutions in Malaysia

Mohamad D. Revindo*,‡ and Christopher Gan†,§

*PhD Candidate, Faculty of Agribusiness and Commerce,
Department of Financial and Business System,
PO Box 85084, Lincoln University, Canterbury, New Zealand

†Professor in Accounting and Finance,
Faculty of Agribusiness and Commerce,
Department of Financial and Business System,
PO Box 85084, Lincoln University, Christchurch, New Zealand

‡Mohamad.Revindo@lincolnuni.ac.nz
§Christopher.Gan@lincoln.ac.nz

Abstract

Microfinance was introduced in Malaysia in 1987 to provide financial access to the poorest member of the society and to reduce the persisting income inequality. Poverty and inequality in Malaysia are characterised by the income disparity between urban–rural populations, gender, as well as among ethnic groups and states. This chapter gives an overview of three main Microfinance Institutions (MFIs) in Malaysia, namely Amanah Ikhtiar Malaysia (AIM), Yayasan Usaha Maju (YUM) and Tabung Ekonomi Kumpulan Usaha Niaga (TEKUN). The three MFIs receive financial support from the Malaysian government but differ in the year of establishment, organisation type, lending schemes, service area coverage and target borrowers. MFIs differ in the performance of their loans' repayment rate where the high Non-Performing Loans (NPL) can be associated with the loans' lending terms as well as borrowers' certain individual and household characteristics. MFIs' microcredit loans positively affect borrowers' individual, household and microenterprise economic performances but the magnitudes of the impact vary among MFIs and across economic performance measures. The implications of the presented findings and analysis are discussed, both for the MFIs and the policy makers.

Keywords: Microfinance, institutions, AIM, YUM, TEKUN, performance, impact, Malaysia.

3.1 Introduction

Malaysia is one of the most advanced and developed economies in Southeast Asia region. Since its independence in 1957, Malaysia has developed from low-income to upper–middle-income economy with GDP per capita of US$11,307.1 in 2014, ranked 60th in the world overall (World Bank, 2015). Malaysia has also transformed its economic structure from agriculture and mining-based economy into manufacturing industry and service-based economy. On top of economic development, the improvement on education and healthcare services in Malaysia have also been rapid as indicated by high human development, ranked 62nd in 2014 UNDP's Human Development Index (HDI) (UNDP, 2015).

Economic growth, structural transformation and human development alone, however, does not bring about poverty eradication and income equality by themselves. Poverty and inequality persist in Malaysia and have been characterised by the disparity between urban–rural areas, sexes, as well as among ethnic groups and states (Hashim, 1998). Hence, the Malaysian government has always firmly asserted the need of particular economic programmes and tools to alleviate poverty and to create equality in the population.

Inspired by the success of the *Grameen Bank* in Bangladesh, Malaysia introduced microfinance in 1987 aiming to provide access to finance to the population in the poverty pockets. This chapter gives an overview of microfinance development in Malaysia, depicted through the development of the three major microfinance institutions/providers (MFIs). The first section of the chapter discusses the characteristics of poverty and income inequality in Malaysia. The next three sections give overview of different MFIs in Malaysia: the *Amanah Ikhtiar Malaysia* (AIM) in Section 3.3, followed by the *Yayasan Usaha Maju* (YUM) and the *Tabung Ekonomi Kumpulan Usaha Niaga* (TEKUN) in Sections 3.4 and 3.5, respectively. Section 3.6 discusses how the microcredit services of the three MFIs affect the welfare of their clients.

3.2 Economic Development and the Introduction of Microfinance in Malaysia

3.2.1 *Economic development and poverty in Malaysia*

Malaysia is a multi-ethnic country with three distinct ethnic groups; *Bumiputera*,[1] Chinese and Indian. The country gained independence from British rule in 1957 and a colonial inheritance of a well-developed infrastructure and efficient public administration (Menon, 2009). Prior to the 1970s, the Malaysian economy was predominantly based on mining and agriculture. However, the government promoted foreign and domestic investment, especially in the manufacturing sector, whereby the role of investment in GDP rose from about 13% in 1955 to over 20% in 1970 (Esfahani, 1994). Not only did the investment flows allow the rapid economic growth of the newly independent state but it also led to a transition towards the development of industrial and service sectors in the 1980s (Esfahani, 1994). Malaysia has since developed from low-income economy to upper–medium-income economy whose per capita income, levels of education and healthcare are well ahead of most neighbouring countries in Southeast Asia (Menon, 2009).

Figure 3.1 depicts Malaysia's GDP from 1960 to 2014. The upper panel of Figure 3.1 shows that the nominal GDP rose from US\$1.92 billion in 1960 to US\$338.1 billion in 2014. During the period, the real GDP grew annually 6.37% on average, despite interrupted with low growth in

---

[1]*Bumiputera or Bumiputra* is a Malay word that refers to the Malays and Indigenous people in Malaysia (Siddique & Suryadinata, 1981).

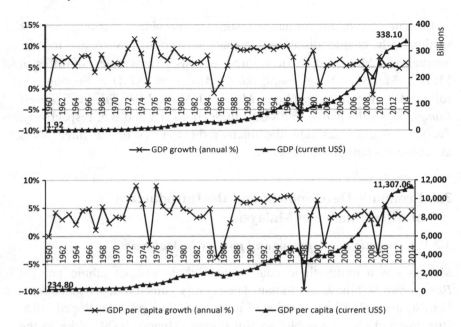

Figure 3.1: Malaysia GDP and GDP Per Capita (1960–2014)
Source: World Development Indicators (World Bank, 2015).

1975 and 2001 and even negative growth during the 1985 recession, the 1997 Asian financial crisis and 2008 global financial crisis.

The economic growth allows the Malaysian population to enjoy rapid increase in per capita income. The lower panel of Figure 3.1 shows that in the span of 54 years (1960–2014) the nominal per capita income has multiplied by more than 48 times from US$234.8 to US$11,307.06. During the period, the real per capita income has multiplied by 7.5 times and grew annually 3.83% on average despite several occasions of negative growth (World Bank, 2015).

Apart from economic growth, the development of healthcare and education services in Malaysia have also been rapid. Table 3.1 shows that the life expectancy (as a measure of health) has increased from 68.1 year in 1980 to 74.7 year in 2014. During the same period the mean years of schooling of adult population increased from 4.4 year to 10.0 year and the expected years of schooling at birth increased from 9 year to 12.7 year,

Table 3.1: Malaysia Human Development Indicators (1980–2014)

Indicators	1980	1990	2000	2010	2011	2012	2013	2014
HDI value	0.569	0.641	0.723	0.769	0.772	0.774	0.777	0.779
HDI rank	58	64	54	62	62	62	62	62
Life expectancy at birth (years)	68.1	70.7	72.8	74.1	74.3	74.4	74.6	74.7
Mean years of schooling (of adults) (years)	4.4	6.5	8.6	10.0	10.0	10.0	10.0	10.0
Expected years of schooling (of children) (years)	9	9.7	11.9	12.7	12.7	12.7	12.7	12.7
GNI per capita in PPP terms (constant 2011 PPP $)	7,315	9,772	14,500	19,725	20,576	21,074	21,812	22,762

Source: Human Development Report (UNDP, 2015).

indicating improvements in education level.[2] As a result, Malaysia's HDI value improved from 0.569 in 1980 to 0.779 in 2014 (UNDP, 2015). Nevertheless, Malaysia's HDI ranked 62nd in 2014, slightly lower than 58th in 1980. This indicates that despite the Malaysia's achievements in the development of income, education and healthcare services level, at least one of the three indicators has developed at relatively slower pace compared to other countries on average.

Malaysia has also performed well in employment provision and general poverty reduction (see Table 3.2). Unemployment rate in Malaysia has always been low and with only little fluctuation. The average unemployment rate was 3.26% with the highest rate of unemployment recorded in 1993 (4.1%) and the lowest in 2014 (2.0%) (World Bank, 2015).

The poverty level in Malaysia tends to decrease over time (see Table 3.2). Using Malaysia's national poverty line as a measure, the

[2] Since 2010, UNDP has replaced literacy rate and gross enrolment ratio with mean years of schooling and expected years of schooling respectively as indicators for education in its Human Development Report (UNDP, 2010).

Table 3.2:   Poverty, Income Inequality and Unemployment in Malaysia (1984–2014)

Indicators	1984	1992	2002	2004	2007	2009	2012	2014
Incidence of poverty (at $1.90 a day, 2011 PPP) (% of population)[a]	2.88	1.26	n/a	4.35	0.0	0.28	n/a	n/a
Incidence of poverty (at $3.10 a day, 2011 PPP) (% of population)[a]	12.01	10.92	n/a	15.38	2.71	2.71	n/a	n/a
Incidence of poverty (at Malaysia national poverty lines) (% of population)[b]	20.7	12.4	6.0	5.7	3.6	3.8	1.7	0.6
Incidence of hardcore poverty (at Malaysia national poverty lines) (% of population)[b]	6.9	2.9	1.0	1.2	0.7	0.7	0.2	n/a
Poverty gap at $1.90 a day (2011 PPP) (%)[a]	0.58	0.1	n/a	1.03	n/a	0.04	n/a	n/a
Poverty gap at $3.10 a day (2011 PPP) (%)[a]	3.13	2.34	n/a	4.38	0.19	0.49	n/a	n/a
Poverty gap at national poverty lines (%)[a]	n/a	n/a	n/a	1.4	0.8	0.8	n/a	n/a
Unemployment, total (% of total labour force)[a]	n/a	3.7	3.5	3.5	3.2	3.7	3.0	2.0
GINI index[b]		0.483	0.459	0.461	00.462	00.441	00.441	00.431	00.401

Source: [a]World Development Indicators, World Databank (World Bank, 2015).
[b]Socio-Economic Statistics (Economic Planning Unit, 2013b, 2015d).

population that live under the poverty line shrank from 20.7% in 1984 to just 0.6% in 2014 (Economic Planning Unit, 2015b).[3] The incidence of hardcore poverty (population that live in less than half of Malaysia's national poverty line) decreased from 6.9% in 1984 to 0.2% in 2012 (Economic Planning Unit, 2013a). Using the World Bank's poverty line, the incidence of poverty series in Table 3.2 shows that the population that live with less than $3.1 a day decreased from 12.01% in 1984 to 2.71% in 2009.[4] Likewise, using the World Bank's extreme poverty line, the population that live with less than $1.90 a day diminished from 2.88% in 1984 to 0.28% in 2009. Further, the depth of poverty (measured by poverty gap) series shows that in 2009 the poor population's income on average were only 0.49% shortfall of $3.1 a day, 0.04% shortfall of $1.90 a day, and 0.8% shortfall of the national poverty line (World Bank, 2015).

Despite all the achievements in per capita income, education level and healthcare standard as well as achievements in poverty reduction and jobs provision, to date Malaysia still has income inequality problem. The last row in Table 3.2 shows the GINI index has improved in a very slow pace and tend to fluctuate. As of 2014, the GINI index was still at 0.401, which indicates an alarming income inequality problem.[5]

---

[3] The 2014 Malaysia's National Poverty Line Income (PLI) by region (in RM, where 1RM = 0.25US$):

Region	Poverty		Hardcore poverty	
	Gross PLI	Per capita PLI	Gross PLI	Per capita PLI
Peninsular Malaysia	930	230	580	140
Sabah (East Malaysia)	1,170	250	710	150
Sarawak (East Malaysia)	990	240	660	160

Source: Brief Household Income & Poverty Statistics Newsletter, 2012, 2014 (Economic Planning Unit, 2015a).

[4] The World Bank previously used $2 and $1.25 as international poverty and extreme poverty lines, respectively. However, as of October 2015 the World Bank has updated the poverty line to $3.1 and extreme poverty line to $1.9 (World Bank Group, 2016).

[5] A country with Gini index value above 0.4 is regarded as a country with high inequality or at least medium–high inequality (Bourguignon, 2004; Vieira, 2012).

3.2.2 *Poverty, inequality and microcredit programmes in Malaysia*

The indication of income inequality in previous section brings to further discussion on the characteristics of inequality and poverty in Malaysia which in turn leads to the introduction of microfinance in Malaysia. Inequality and poverty in Malaysia exhibits at least four features; disparity in household income and poverty rate (1) between rural and urban areas, (2) among ethnic groups, (3) across states and (4) inequality in employment opportunity between male and female workforces.

Between 1970 and 1990, the Malaysian government introduced the New Economic Policy (NEP) that undertook social and economic development in the country, with the main objective to eradicate poverty and restructure the societies of the country (Jomo, 2004). It was hoped that the NEP would eliminate the identification of race with economic function; for example, Chinese in the business sector, Malays in agriculture and Indians in rubber plantations (Jomo, 2004). During the NEP period, in 1987, AIM was founded. AIM is a non-governmental organisation (NGO) that introduced the first microcredit programme to the country with the main objective to reduce poverty among *Bumiputeras* by granting small loans to borrowers involved in income-generating activities. The NEP successfully reduced the country's poverty level from 52.4% in 1970 to 17.7% in 1990 (Economic Planning Unit, 1991; Roslan, 2006). The economic status of the *Bumiputeras,* however, did not improve. Although the average income of Malaysian population increased rapidly, large income disparities between the Malays and Chinese ethnic groups that had inherited from the colonial period still existed (Jomo, 2004).

In 1991, the NEP was replaced by the National Development Policy (NDP) framework, a medium-term plan that brings forward the economic and social development of the country until 2000. The NDP continued the policies to reduce racial imbalances in the economic sector (Menon, 2009). The Vision 2020 was also introduced in 1991 as a long-term plan to guide Malaysia into fully developed nation by 2020. Overall, the NEP, NDP and the first 20 years of Vision 2020 development planning successfully reduced poverty and unemployment in the country (see Table 3.2), achieved positive growth in GDP (see Figure 3.1), and increased the income of the *Bumiputeras* (see Figure 3.2).

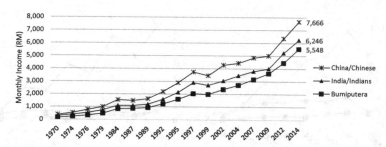

Figure 3.2: Households Monthly Income in Malaysia, by Ethnic Groups (1970–2014) (in RM)

Note: 1RM = 0.25US$.
Source: Mean Monthly Gross Household Income by Ethnicity, Strata and State, Malaysia, 1970–2014 (Economic Planning Unit, 2015c).

Nevertheless, the *Bumiputeras* still represents the ethnic group with the lowest income and largest ethnic group among those living in poverty. Figure 3.2 shows that despite the increase in households' income enjoyed by all ethnic groups, in 2014 the Chinese households were the highest income earner with an average monthly income of RM7,666. In contrast, Indian families earn an average monthly income of RM6,246 while *Bumiputera* families earns RM5,548.

Accordingly, the poverty rate also differs among ethnic groups, with the highest rate found in *Bumiputeras*. Figure 3.3(a) shows that poverty incidence steadily falls through time for all ethnic groups, however, incidence of poverty is highest among *Bumiputeras*, followed by Indian and Chinese, respectively. In 2014, incidence of poverty was 0.8% in *Bumiputeras* and 0.6% in Indian, in contrast to 0.1% in Chinese ethnic group. The same is true for hardcore poverty incidence. Figure 3.3(b) shows that in 2012 the incidence of hardcore poverty is 0.3% in *Bumiputeras* and 0.2% in Indian, in contrast to 0% in Chinese ethnic group.

The second feature of poverty and inequality in Malaysia is the income disparity between the urban and rural population. Figure 3.4 shows that despite the steady increase in household income, in 2014 the rural households on average earned RM3,831 monthly compared to RM6,833 earned by the urban households.

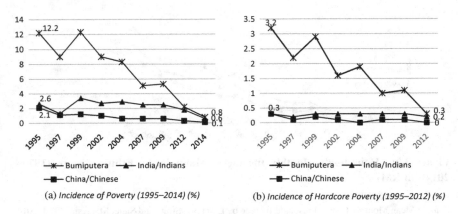

(a) *Incidence of Poverty (1995–2014) (%)* (b) *Incidence of Hardcore Poverty (1995–2012) (%)*

Figure 3.3: Poverty in Malaysia, by Ethnic Groups (%)

Source: Economic Planning Unit (2013a, 2015b).

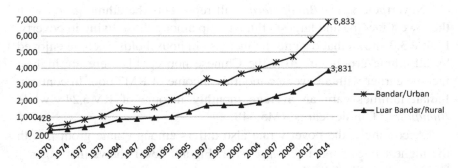

Figure 3.4: Household Income in Malaysia, by Geographical Areas (1970–2014) (in RM)

Note: 1RM = 0.25US$.

Source: Mean Monthly Gross Household Income by Ethnicity, Strata and State, Malaysia, 1970–2014 (Economic Planning Unit, 2015c).

The poverty level in rural area is also generally higher than in urban area. Figure 3.5(a) shows that despite the continuous reduction of poverty incidence since 1970, as of 2014 the incidence of poverty in the rural area (using national poverty line) was 1.6% of the rural population, in contrast to only 0.3% of the urban population. Further, Figure 3.5(b) shows that in 2012 the incidence of hardcore poverty — those who live in less than half

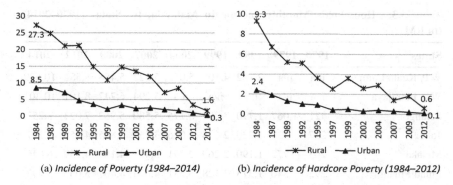

(a) *Incidence of Poverty (1984–2014)*   (b) *Incidence of Hardcore Poverty (1984–2012)*

Figure 3.5   Poverty in Malaysia, by Geographical Areas (1970–2012) (%)
Source: Economic Planning Unit (2013a, 2015b).

of national poverty line — was 0.6% of the rural population, in contrast to only 0.1% of the urban population.

The third characteristic of inequality in Malaysia is the welfare difference across states. Table 3.3 shows the persistent household income disparity across states during 1970–2014 (44 years) despite the trend of increasing income over time in all states. In 1989, the average households' income in Kuala Lumpur was 2.9 times higher than those in Kelantan and the ratio stayed approximately the same in 2014, despite both states exhibit increasing income during 1989–2014.

Unsurprisingly, the poverty rate also differs across states. Table 3.4 shows that although the poverty rate tends to decrease over time in all states, there were evidence of disparity across states. In 2014 the highest poverty incidence was in Sabah & W.P. Labuan (3.9%), much higher than Kelantan as the second highest (0.9%) and immensely differs from 0.0% in Johor and Putrajaya as the lowest. Further, the incidence of hardcore poverty tends to decrease over time in all states, but the difference across states were also sharp. In 2012 the highest hardcore poverty rate was in Sabah & W.P. Labuan (1.6%), in contrast to 0.5% in Perlis as the second highest and 0% in Selangor and Pulau Pinang as the lowest.

The fourth characteristic of inequality in Malaysia is the difference in employment opportunity for male and female workforces. Figure 3.6 shows that unemployment rate is generally higher in female labor force

Table 3.3:   Households Monthly Income in Malaysia, by States (1970–2014) (in RM)

States	1970	1979	1989	1999	2004	2007	2009	2012	2014
W.P. Kuala Lumpur	n/a	n/a	2,102	4,105	5,011	5,322	5,488	8,586	10,629
W.P. Putrajaya	n/a	n/a	n/a	n/a	n/a	5,294	6,747	8,101	10,401
Selangor	421	1,067	1,790	3,702	5,175	5,580	5,962	7,023	8,252
Johor	237	731	1,220	2,646	3,076	3,457	3,835	4,658	6,207
Melaka	265	772	1,190	2,260	2,791	3,421	4,184	4,759	6,046
Pulau Pinang	292	840	1,375	3,128	3,531	4,004	4,407	5,055	5,993
Negeri Sembilan	286	629	1,162	2,335	2,886	3,336	3,540	4,576	5,271
Sabah & W.P. Labuan	n/a	767	1,358	1,905	2,487	2,866	3,144	4,089	4,985
Sarawak	n/a	582	1,199	2,276	2,725	3,349	3,581	4,293	4,934
Terengganu	173	360	905	1,600	1,984	2,463	3,017	3,967	4,816
Kedah	189	382	860	1,612	2,126	2,408	2,667	3,425	4,478
Perlis	140	316	852	1,431	2,046	2,541	2,617	3,538	4,445
Pahang	286	702	1,092	1,482	2,410	2,995	3,279	3,745	4,343
Perak	254	559	1,067	1,743	2,207	2,545	2,809	3,548	4,268
Kelantan	151	341	726	1,314	1,829	2,143	2,536	3,168	3,715

Note: 1RM = 0.25US$.

Source: Mean Monthly Gross Household Income by Ethnicity, Strata and State, Malaysia, 1970–2014 (Economic Planning Unit, 2015c).

compared to male labour force. Despite the fluctuation in unemployment rate in both male and female labour force over time, the difference tend to be constant through time — approximately 0.3% — except in 1999 where the unemployment in male workforce was higher than female's.

3.2.3 *Overview of MFIs in Malaysia*

The characteristic of poverty and inequality in Malaysia discussed above gives more relevance to the discussion of MFIs in Malaysia. Microfinance services, particularly microcredit loans might be targeting specific group in the society (the poorest or the most vulnerable), specific gender (female), specific region (rural areas and backward states), as well as

Table 3.4: Poverty in Malaysia, by States (1984–2014) (%)

States	Incidence of poverty					Incidence of hardcore poverty			
	1984	1992	2002	2012	2014	1984	1992	2002	2012
Sabah & W.P. Labuan	33.1	27.8	16	7.8	3.9	9.7	6.8	4	1.6
Kelantan	39.2	29.5	17.8	2.7	0.9	15.5	8.7	3.4	0.3
Sarawak	31.9	19.2	11.3	2.4	0.9	10	3	1.8	0.3
Perak	20.3	10.2	6.2	1.5	0.7	6.7	1.9	1	0.2
Pahang	15.7	6.9	9.4	1.3	0.7	5.4	1.1	1.1	0.2
Terengganu	28.9	25.6	14.9	1.7	0.6	11.6	9.2	2.2	0.2
Negeri Sembilan	13	8.1	2.6	0.5	0.4	3.7	1.8	0.2	0.1
Kedah	36.6	21.2	9.7	1.7	0.3	13.5	5.4	2	0.1
Pulau Pinang	13.4	4	1.2	0.6	0.3	4.1	1.1	0.1	0
Perlis	33.7	19.8	8.9	1.9	0.2	11.7	4.1	0.9	0.5
Selangor	8.6	4.3	1.1	0.4	0.2	2.5	0.6	0.2	0
W.P. Kuala Lumpur	4.9	1.7	0.5	0.8	0.1	1.4	0.3	n.a	0.1
Melaka	15.8	8.5	1.8	0.1	0.1	5.5	1.8	0	n.a
Johor	12.2	5.6	2.5	0.9	0.0	3.1	1.1	0.1	0.1
W.P. Putrajaya	n.a	n.a	n.a	0.0	0.0	n.a	n.a	n.a	n.a

Sources: Incidence of poverty (Economic Planning Unit, 2015b) and Incidence of hardcore poverty (Economic Planning Unit, 2013a).

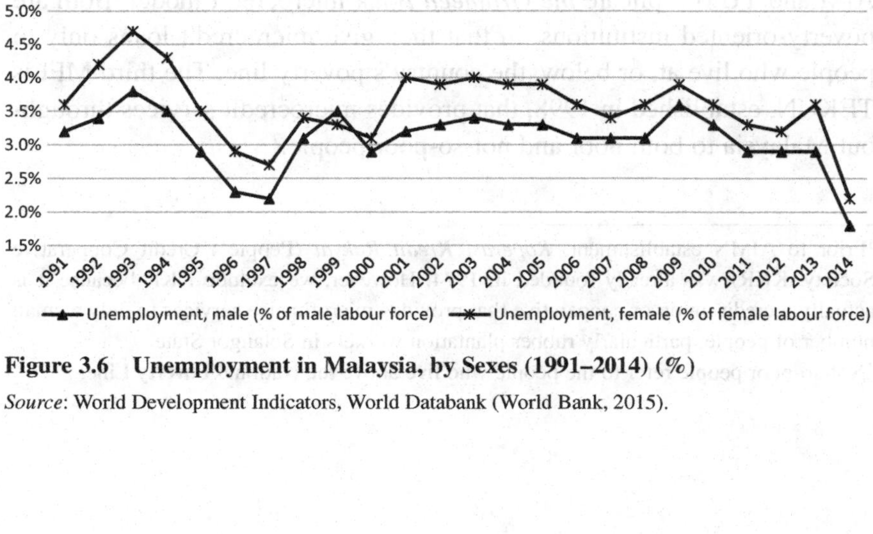

Figure 3.6 Unemployment in Malaysia, by Sexes (1991–2014) (%)

Source: World Development Indicators, World Databank (World Bank, 2015).

Table 3.5:   MFIs in Malaysia

Characteristics	AIM	YUM	TEKUN
Established	1987	1988	1998
Services area	Throughout Malaysia	The state of Sabah	Throughout Malaysia
Target borrower	Poor people	Poor people	Poor and not so poor people
Lending scheme	Group	Individual	Individual
Organisation type	NGO	Government organisation	Government organisation
Government support	Subsidised	Subsidised	Subsidised

Source: Mokhtar, Nartea & Gan (2012b).

specific ethnic group. The establishment and operations of MFIs in Malaysia were in fact part of the effort to eradicate poverty in certain ethnic group and/or specific areas.

   This section provides an overview of three major MFIs in Malaysia, namely AIM, YUM and TEKUN. The characteristics of each MFI are summarised in Table 3.5. AIM was established in 1987 and became the first MFI operating in Malaysia.[6] AIM provides microcredit services throughout Malaysia (Peninsular, Sabah & Sarawak). Not long after, in 1988 the state of Sabah established its own MFIs called YUM, with a focus on providing microcredit loans to the poor people of Sabah. Both AIM and YUM replicate *the Grameen Bank* microcredit model. Both are poverty-oriented institutions, in that they give microcredit loans only to people who live at, or below, the country's poverty line. The third MFI is TEKUN, established in 1998, that provides microcredit services throughout Malaysia to both poor and not-so-poor people.[7]

---

[6]Prior to AIM's establishment, *Koperasi Kredit Rakyat* (People's Credit Cooperative Society, KKR) was already founded in 1974. However, we exclude KKR because it is actually a credit union or cooperative that provides microfinance services to only a small number of people, particularly rubber plantation workers in Selangor State.

[7]Not-so-poor people refer to the people who live above the National Poverty Line.

AIM applies a group lending scheme, whereas YUM and TEKUN apply individual lending schemes. AIM is a NGO whereas YUM and TEKUN are under the directive of the Ministry of Agriculture and Agro-based Industry of Malaysia. All MFIs are subsidised for which they receive full financial support from the government in terms of grants and soft loans (Roslan, 2006). The charges for microcredit loans are very low and, as a result, the three MFIs have not achieved financial sustainability since their establishment (Roslan, 2006).

3.3 AIM

3.3.1 *Background*

AIM was the first MFI in Malaysia which was inspired by the success of *the Grameen Bank* in Bangladesh (McGuire, Conroy & Thapa, 1998). In 1986 two social scientists, Profs. David Gibbons and Sukor Kasim from the Universiti Sains Malaysia began a pilot project of *the Grameen Bank* concept, known as *Projek Ikhtiar* in Selangor, in Peninsular Malaysia. *Projek Ikhtiar* provided microcredit for poor people in rural area in Selangor to set up income-generating activities (AIM, 2013b).

The *Projek Ikhtiar* was considered successful as most of the borrowers managed to set up and run various microbusinesses and the repayment rate among female borrowers was more than 90% (AIM, 2013b). It was concluded that a group lending system similar to *the Grameen Bank* model can be applied in Malaysia. Following the success of *Projek Ikhtiar*, AIM was established in 1987 under the Trustee Incorporation Act 258 (revised 1981) (Chamhuri & Quinones, 2000). Since then, AIM's microlending services have been widely offered throughout Malaysia.

AIM is a poverty-oriented MFI that provides loans only to the poor. However, AIM has had a convoluted development over the years, experiencing a mission breakdown from 1992 to 1999 when the original objective of AIM to assist the poor was distorted by political motives (Kasim, 2000). This breakdown began in 1992 when the existing members in top management were replaced with new members who wanted AIM to be a mechanism to attract political supporters. The breakdown included leakage from loans to not-so-poor people with the introduction of two new loan schemes: *Skim Pinjaman Nelayan* (SPIN) loans for fishermen; and *Skim Khas Ibu Tunggal* (SKIT) loans to single urban mothers. The SPIN and SKIT participants were given very large amounts for their first loans (RM10,000) and this led to uncollectible loans since the borrowers could not afford to repay them (Kasim, 2000).

In addition, the loans were not cost-effective and were more like charity-loans (Conroy, 2002). The loss of direction resulted in managerial disarray and AIM recorded the highest non-loan repayments in the institution's history. In order to cover the cost of uncollectible loans, the management increased administration fees that was initially zero to 19%. The increased loan administrative fees contributed to higher drop-out rates among the borrowers who were significantly poor (Conroy, 2002). Following this, major reforms took place in 2003 in which AIM underwent a change of a new management with a task to re-establish AIM as a viable institution.

From 2004, the new management team began to restore AIM to its original objective —serving the poor. In addition, efforts have been made to improve the efficiency of the operation, loan repayment collection and to attract more borrowers. As a result, AIM had 59,971 new members in 2004 alone, with an average of 4,998 new members every month (Chan, 2010). Since then, AIM has also introduced additional microcredit loan schemes for economic, social and even recovery purposes and maintained the policy of charging a low management fee. Today, AIM is the leading MFI in Malaysia.

3.3.2 *AIM's loan schemes*

The loan schemes offered by AIM can be classified into two categories. The first category is economic/general loan including three loan schemes — *i-Mesra, i-Srikandi, i-Wibawa* — that differ in the eligibility of the loan amounts as well as in the type and duration of instalments (see Table 3.6). The second category is loans for social and recovery purposes, under which four loan schemes are provided: The *i-Sejahtera* is a multipurpose loan that can be used for properties acquisition, capital goods purchase including personal spending such as Hajj Pilgrimage; the *i-Bestari* loan scheme is developed to cover the fees for education or training programme; the *i-Penyayang* scheme is designated to assist the borrowers to recover or to

Table 3.6: AIM Loan Schemes (as of 2015)

Loan schemes		Details	Amount in RM	Instalment
Economic (General loan)	1. *i*-Mesra	Finance economic projects that are believed to provide good returns to the members	1,000–10,000	12–150 weeks
	2. *i*-Srikandi	Finance for those who have potential viable and successful projects	12,000–20,000	12–150 weeks
	3. *i*-Wibawa	Provide additional capital to carry out seasonal projects or opportunities that come in short periods of time	5,000 (max)	6 months paid either on a weekly basis, monthly basis or full settlement
Other loans	4. *i*-Sejahtera	Housing/multipurpose financing	1,000–10,000	12–100 weeks
	5. *i*-Bestari	Education financing	1,000–5,000	12–100 weeks
	6. *i*-Penyayang	Finance for members who face problems in repayment caused by project failure, health problems or natural disaster	1,000–5,000	12–100 weeks
	7. *i*-Emas	Finance scheme for people who are 75 years old and above	2,000 (max)	12–50 weeks

Management fees: 10% per annum for loans exceeding 6 months and 5% for loans that are 6 months or less
Group Savings: RM1–RM15 per week
Grace Period: 1 week after received the loan

Sources: Skim Pembiayaan Ikhtiar (AIM, 2015a), AIF (2015).

re-start discontinued project; while *i-emas* targets elder/senior citizen borrowers (AIM, 2015a; AIM Sabah Barat, 2012).

As part of making loans to its members, AIM is concerned about members who face difficulties in their lives, including death, accidents, chronic disease, destruction of their house or project due to fire and natural disasters. In recognition of these hardships, AIM established the Welfare and Well-Being Fund for AIM members. The funds are collected from the members and for the use of members and their families (see Table 3.7).

3.3.3 *AIM's achievements and loan repayment*

AIM offers loans to borrowers involved in various types of business activities. The AIM borrowers' major business activities include small businesses, agriculture, manufacturing, animal husbandry, fishing and services. AIM's lending activities have experienced rapid growth in the last several years. From 2009 to 2014, the number of borrowers grew by 56%, the institution branches increased by 60% and the amount of disbursed loan multiplied 2.4 times (see Table 3.8).

AIM recorded 98.98% repayment rate in 2009 and always higher than 99% since 2010 (see Table 3.9). AIM's repayment rate is higher than YUM and TEKUN's repayment rates, which reflects AIM's good achievement as a subsidised MFI in general (Mokhtar, Nartea & Gan, 2012a). AIM's high repayment rate may be attributed to the facts that AIM applies a group lending scheme, weekly instalment, gradual disbursements as well as training and education to borrowers (Amri, 2012). AIM's non-performing loan (NPL) level is very low (less than 1% of the total loans disbursed) and mostly among the borrowers that used the loan for non-income-generating activities, had low number of gainfully employed members in the household, and low number of sources of income in the household (Al-Mamun, Wahab & Malarvizhi, 2011; Wahab, Malarvizhi & Mariapun, 2011).

3.4 YUM

3.4.1 *Background*

The second MFI in Malaysia is the YUM, based in Sabah State in east of Malaysia and Northern-most part of Borneo Island. Sabah is the second largest state in Malaysia, inhabited by 33 officially recognised indigenous groups, with Kadazan–Dusun as the largest group. Sabah's economy relied

Table 3.7:   Welfare and Well-Being Fund for AIM Member (as of 2015)

Schemes/Type of benefit	Rate of contribution/ Benefit	
Death		
i. Member	RM500	
ii. Husband	RM500	
iii. Children under care aged below 18 years (except children who are still studying or disabled)	RM250	
Ward admission		
Due to accidents or chronic diseases, excluding pregnancy or birth-giving (member or husband only, 2–20 days in 1 year).	RM50 per day	
Contribution for costs of chronic disease treatment only		
Member and husband only — with approval from qualified doctors.	Maximum RM500 in a life time	
Destruction of own house caused by fire (unintentional) or natural disaster (flood, storm and others)	**House on land**	**water/squatter/long house**
i. Total destruction (100%)	RM10,000	RM4,000
ii. Partly destroyed	Ranges from RM0 (damage less than RM300) to RM5,000 (damage more than RM15,000)	Ranges from RM0 (damage less than RM300) to RM3,000 (damage more than RM15,000)
Destruction of rented/lodging house	Maximum 2,000	
Cases of natural disaster and fires in a particular zone affecting more than 5 houses	Ranges from RM0 (for damage less than RM500) to RM2,000 (for complete damage)	
Large-scale disaster		
Destruction of house or other properties caused by natural disasters in a particular area/location affecting more than 5 people (including members and non-members)	RM200 (once a year)	

(Continued)

Table 3.7:   (*Continued*)

Schemes/Type of benefit	Rate of contribution/ Benefit
Destruction of the project (affecting less than 5 members in a particular area/location)	20% of current loan or outstanding loan (whichever is lower), RM200–RM4,000
Contribution for Hajj Pilgrimage	RM300 (once in a lifetime)
Contribution for children's tertiary education fees	RM100

Source: Tabung Kebajikan & Kesejahteraan Sahabat (AIM, 2015b).

Table 3.8:   AIM's Developments (2009–2014)

	31 July 2009[a]	31 January 2013[b]	30 September 2014[c]
Total borrowers (persons)	222,559	332,355	347,907
Total branches	86	123	138
Total disbursed loans	RM3,328,694,213	RM8,338,484,403	RM11,348,728,593

Sources: [a]AIM (2010); [b]AIM (2013a); [c]AIM (2014).

Table 3.9:   AIM Repayment Rate (2009–2013)

Year	2009[a]	2010[b]	2011[c]	2012[d]	2013[e]
Repayment Rate	98.98%	99.20%	99.49%	99.60%	99.14%

Sources: [a]AIM (2010); [b]MicroCapital (2011); [c]Kosmo (2012); [d]Jamil (2012); [e]AIM (2013a).

heavily on the export of its primary and minimally processed commodities mostly petroleum, palm oil and cocoa as well as lumber milling and tourism (Sabah, 2015). Despite the continuous economic development in the state, Sabah's incidence of poverty (3.9% in 2014) and hardcore poverty (1.6% in 2012) were the highest in Malaysia — 6.5 times and 8 times higher than national average incidence of poverty and hardcore poverty levels, respectively (Economic Planning Unit, 2013a, 2015b).

YUM began as a "*Projek Usahamaju*" (PU) initiated by the *Institut Kajian Pembangunan Sabah* (Institute for Development Studies Sabah, IDS) and *Korporasi Pembangunan Desa* (Rural Development Corporation, RDC) in 1988 (Chamhuri & Quinones, 2000). The project was mainly motivated by the IDS' studies on poverty in Sabah. After a visit to *the Grameen Bank* in Bangladesh, IDS and RDC decided to launch PU, a *Grameen Bank*-modeled project in Marudu City. Marudu City was chosen for its highest incidence of poverty in the whole Sabah (YUM Sabah, 2014d). The project began by giving microcredit loan to 100 borrowers and was considered a success after the borrowers were able to use the fund for productive activities and repaid the loan as scheduled. On the 30th June 1995, the state government of Sabah decided to institutionalise PU and form YUM. YUM is registered as a foundation under the Trustee (Incorporation) ordinance 1951 chapter 148 of Sabah (YUM Sabah, 2013).

The core role of YUM is to provide loans to housewife, single mother, small-scale traders, smallholder farmers and fishermen in need of capital for their income-generating activities. YUM is a replication of *the Grameen Bank* with a few adjustments in its implementation to adapt to the socio-economic condition in Malaysia, and Sabah in particular. YUM's loans target the poor female group of the society; requires no guarantor and collateral; and relies on collective responsibility (YUM Sabah, 2013, 2014d). However, in some areas YUM also uses an individual lending system because the borrowers may live far apart within the same village. In such situation, peer/group monitoring will not work effectively because the geographical conditions prevent them to meet each other often (Mokhtar, 2011).

3.4.2 *YUM's loan schemes*

YUM provides two categories of loan scheme, namely *Business Loan* and *Life Quality Improvement Loan* (see Table 3.10). The *Business Loan* targets YUM members who need fund to start-up new microbusinesses or who plan to increase their microbusinesses' working capital. Within *Business Loan* category there are two types of loan offered; the *General Loan* Scheme and the *Usahawan* Scheme. The *General Loan* is offered for members with monthly income of RM3,000 or less, with an eligible loan amount of RM500–5,000 for the first-time loan and up to RM20,000 for the subsequent loan. The *Usahawan* scheme is offered for members with monthly income of more than RM3,000, with an eligible loan

Table 3.10:   YUM's Loan Schemes

Loan schemes		Details	Amount in RM	Instalment
Business loan	1. General loan	For members with monthly income < RM3,000	500–20,000 (max. 5,000 for first-time loan)	50–250 weeks
	2. *Usahawan*	For members with monthly income > RM3,000	21,000–100,000	50–250 weeks
Life quality improvement loan	3. House renovation	For members who have received loan ≥ 3 times	2,000–10,000	50–250 weeks
	Management fees: 7% every year			
	Compulsory savings: 2% from total loan			
	Grace period: 2 weeks after receipt of the loan			

Sources: YUM Sabah (2014c), (2014e).

amount of RM21,000–100,000. Within the *Life Quality Improvement* loan category, the only loan scheme offered is the *House Renovation* scheme. Only YUM members who have borrowed fund at least three times are eligible for this loan, with an eligible loan amount of RM2,000–10,000.

For all loan schemes, YUM members can choose the instalment period that suit them best, ranging between 50 and 250 weeks with a grace period of 2 weeks after receiving the loan. For its loan service, YUM charges a management fee of 10% for every 50 weeks instalment period.

YUM's borrowers are required to contribute 2% of the total loan amount as compulsory savings that serve as collective emergency fund. The emergency fund provides benefits for the members in various cases of hardship (see Table 3.11). The emergency fund gives benefits in the case of death, permanent disability and illness of borrower or husband. YUM also uses the fund to contribute to funeral fee in the case of death of a borrower, husband or dependants. In addition, members will also receive benefit in the case of fire on their houses or business premises.

3.4.3 *Loan achievement and repayment*

YUM's scale of operation is growing through time as shown in Table 3.12. As of 31 December 2008, YUM had just 8,252 borrowers

Table 3.11: YUM's Emergency Savings

Types of benefit	Beneficiaries	Scope
Death	Borrower and husband	Death of borrower/husband
Permanent disability	Borrower and husband	Permanent disability of borrower/husband
Fire	Borrower	Borrower's house and premises
Contribution for funeral	Borrower, husband and dependants	Death of borrower, husband and dependants
Ward admission	Borrower and Husband	Illness/disease of borrower/husband

Source: YUM Sabah (2014f).

Table 3.12: YUM's Achievements (2008–2014)

Achievements	2008[a]	2014
Number of borrowers	8,252	55,490[b]
Number of branches	20	24[c]
Number of staffs	165	n/a
Loans disbursed	RM46,070,700	RM248,840,700[b]
Repayment rate	90.72%	96.7%[d]

Sources: [a]Mokhtar (2011); [b]YUM Sabah (2014b); [c]YUM Sabah (2014a); [d]MacPee (2014).

with a total of RM46 million loans disbursed from its 20 branches. In 2014 YUM already had 55,490 borrowers with a total almost of RM249 million loans disbursed in 24 branches. These facts indicates that on the one hand YUM successfully broadens its service to reach more poor people but on the other hand also shows increasing Sabah people's interest in YUM's microloans.

The YUM's loan repayment rate had also improved from 90.72% in 2008 to 96.7% in 2014, indicating an improvement in YUM's loan management. The NPLs are mostly found in borrowers involved in agricultural business activities such as farming, animal husbandry and fisheries, borrowers who had a loan period of less than 1 year, the young borrowers (aged 18–25) and borrowers with high weekly repayment amount (more than RM201) (Mokhtar *et al.*, 2012a).

3.5 TEKUN Nasional

3.5.1 *Background*

The third MFI in Malaysia is *TEKUN Nasional* (hereinafter referred to as TEKUN), established on 9 November 1998. TEKUN was initiated following the resolution of Penang *Bumiputera* Economic Convention in 1994, which suggested an establishment of a financial institution that can channel capital to small businesses easily, quickly and with no impediment in its implementation. Such a financial institution was required to overcome business financing access problems for small *Bumiputera* entrepreneurs (TEKUN Nasional, 2013c).

The resolution was followed up by The University Sains Malaysia with the implementation of a microcredit pilot project known as TEKUN (The Economic Fund for National Entrepreneurs Group) in Penang in 1995, which was subsequently extended to Kelantan in 1996 and Terengganu in 1997. The pilot project was considered a success and as a result the Malaysian Government decided to expand TEKUN project throughout the country to benefit more small *Bumiputera* entrepreneurs (TEKUN Nasional, 2013a). To support this initiative, *TEKUN Nasional Foundation* was established under the purview of the Ministry of Entrepreneur and Cooperative Development (MECD) in November 1998 and officially commenced its operations on 1 February 1999.

In 2008, TEKUN expanded its role as a finance provider agency by also providing support services for entrepreneurial development (TEKUN Nasional, 2013a). TEKUN would provide business opportunities and business skills training to their borrowers, and to develop networking among innovative and progressive entrepreneurs from all over Malaysia. In this way, TEKUN is different from AIM and YUM in that it does not focus solely on the poor but also provides services to not-so-poor people (Mokhtar, 2011). Along with this repositioning action, *TEKUN Nasional Foundation* was rebranded to *TEKUN Nasional* and was placed under the purview of the Ministry of Agriculture and Agro-Based Industry since April 2009.

3.5.2 *TEKUN's loan schemes*

TEKUN offers seven types of assistance to the microentrepreneurs aimed to startup new business, expand existing business or to finance short-term

Table 3.13:   TEKUN's Support Services

Type of assistance/Form of financing	Details
TEKUN *Tunas* (TEKUN startup)	Startup capital for potential and new entrepreneur to operate fixed or mobile stall or business premise to undertake services, transportation and manufacturing activities
TEKUN *Niaga* (TEKUN business)	Additional working capital for fixed and mobile stall or business premise to undertake services, transportation and manufacturing activities
TEKUN *Rakan Niaga* (TEKUN business venture)	Funding for joint venture business package with TEKUN i.e., beauty products, frozen food, tuition centre and others as specified by TEKUN
TEKUN *Jangka Pendek* (TEKUN short-term financing package)	Working capital finance ranging from RM500 to RM2,000 with weekly repayment period between 1 and 3 months to operate business stall for day or night market, Ramadhan Bazaar, Exposition and Sales Promotional activities
TEKUN *Tani* (TEKUN agriculture)	Provide financing to start or expand business or project in agriculture such as planting banana, corn, sugar cane and vegetables or ornamental plant such as orchid, cactus and bonsai tree/plant
TEKUN *Pelancongan* (TEKUN tourism)	Provide financing to start or expand business or project in tourism sector for activities such as Homestay programme, chalet, recreational equipment, agro-tourism and others as specified by TEKUN
TEKUN *Ternak* (TEKUN animal husbandry)	Provide financing to start or expand business or project in animal husbandry such as cattle and goat rearing, breeding bird (Quail), fresh water fish and prawns

Sources: Perkhidmatan Pembayaran Agensi Kepada Komuniti/Syarikat (Malaysian Government, 2015); Tekun Financing Scheme (SMEinfo, 2015).

business opportunities (see Table 3.13). The TEKUN financial assistances target the microenterprises in various fields of business including retail & business, services, agriculture, animal husbandry & aquaculture, manufacturing, education, transportation, tourism/recreation, wholesale and construction (TEKUN Nasional, 2013b).

In terms of eligible loan amount, TEKUN offers four classes of loan scheme including two classes of microloan schemes, and one for each

Table 3.14:   TEKUN Loan Schemes

Loan schemes	Eligible amount	Instalment
Skim Pinjaman Mikro (Microloan scheme)	RM1,000–5,000	Up to 3 years
Skim Pinjaman Mikro (Microloan scheme)	>RM5,000–10,000	Up to 5 years
Skim Pinjaman Kecil (Small loan scheme)	>RM10,000–50,000	Up to 5 years
Skim Pinjaman Sederhana (Medium loan scheme)	>RM50,000–100,000	Up to 10 years

Source: Maklumat & Syarat Pinjaman (TEKUN Nasional, 2013d).

small and medium loan scheme (see Table 3.14). The value of the loans ranges from RM1,000 to RM100,000 for which the borrowers have flexibility to choose the repayment period between 6 months up to 10 years and modes of loan payments of either weekly, monthly or semi-annually depending on the types of business involved and TEKUN management's decisions (Mokhtar, 2011; TEKUN Nasional, 2013e).

TEKUN provides loans to both male and female population, small–medium-scale entrepreneurs from the *Bumiputera* and the Indian Communities aged between 18 and 65 years. Apart from their loan repayments, each borrower is also encouraged to put some savings into TEKUN, with a minimum value of 5% from their annual repayments. Prior to August 2008 TEKUN charged 8% management fees on the loan which has been reduced to 4% to ease the repayment burden of the microentrepreneurs (Ministry of Finance Malaysia, 2009). The details of TEKUN's loan terms and condition are summarised in Table 3.15.

3.5.3 *Loan achievement and repayment*

TEKUN provides services to the Peninsular and East Malaysia and setup offices according to parliamentary divisions. In August 2009, TEKUN had 150,131 total borrowers with RM1.377 billion value of loans disbursed (see Table 3.16). Over time TEKUN's services reach more small and medium-scale entrepreneurs in Malaysia. As of June 2013, TEKUN's borrowers had increased to 262,497 and value of loans disbursed of RM2.7 billion.

Table 3.15:   TEKUN Loan Terms and Eligibility

Terms	Details
Target borrowers	Male and female, *Bumiputera* (18–65 years) and the Indian community (18–55 years)
Repayment	Weekly, monthly or semi-annually mode; an initial 1 month repayment amount will be deducted from the approved loan
Fees and contribution	4% management fees service charge; flexible grace period according to project; compulsory savings of 5% from annual repayment
Business matters	• Has been operating a business or has potential and viable business venture proposal or plan. • Possess a valid licence/permit/business registration (loans under RM5,000 does not require business registration). • Has a specific business place/location or conducts mobile business. • Involved directly and full-time in business (loans of up to RM5,000 can be considered for applicants conducting part-time business) • Applicants who wish to start a business are required to have their own capital of 20% from the loan/business requirement as a commitment to operate the business (except applications by graduates). • Existing business loan not exceeding RM50,000

Source: Financing Terms & Condition (TEKUN Nasional, 2013b).

Table 3.16:   TEKUN's Achievement (2009–2013)

Achievements	July 2009[a]	June 2013[b]
Total borrowers	150,131	262,497
Total branches	194	n.a.
Total staff	920	n.a.
Total loan disbursed	RM1,377,371,300	RM2,7 billion
Repayment rate	85%	85%

Sources: [a]Mokhtar *et al.* (2012b); [b]Bernama (2013).

However, TEKUN experienced a crisis in their loan repayment collection. As of 2009, TEKUN recorded NPL as high as 15% with a value of RM225 million uncollectible loans that had accumulated since 1999 (Berita Harian, 2009). As a result, TEKUN had difficulty in disbursing loans to new borrowers as they did not have enough capital. Starting on 1 July 2009, TEKUN launched the campaign "Let's Pay Back the Loan" to their borrowers (TEKUN, 2009). Discounts were given as an incentive to the borrowers to repay the loans. Recently, TEKUN management blacklisted defaulters who continued to ignore loan repayment reminders. Despite the campaign, in June 2013 the NPL remained at 15%, indicating no improvement in loan collection management. Mokhtar *et al.* (2012a) reported that TEKUN's NPLs are mostly in male borrowers, borrowers who are involved in lower revenue cycle in agriculture activities (i.e., farming, animal husbandry and fisheries), borrowers who chose weekly instalment mode and borrowers in the age group of 46–55 years. In addition, NPLs are often found in borrowers with no formal religious education, low amount of loan received, borrowers whose business activities are far distance from TEKUN's office, having rare visit of TEKUN's staff to their business premises or having low sales of the business (Nawai & Shariff, 2012).

3.6 Impact of Microcredit in Malaysia

Mokhtar (2011) studied how microcredit loans provided by AIM, YUM and TEKUN affected their borrowers at three levels; microenterprises, households and individual. The three levels impact assessment followed Household Economic Portfolios (HEP) framework proposed by Cohen, Chen & Dunn (1996).

3.6.1 *Impact on the microenterprises*

Microcredit loans may positively affect borrowers' microenterprises but the impact magnitudes may differ across MFIs and vary across enterprise measures (revenue, fixed assets and employment) (see Table 3.17).

Mokhtar reported that 2 years after receiving the microcredit loans the majority of AIM borrowers (74%) exhibited increase in their micro

Table 3.17:   Microcredit Impact on the Borrowers' Microenterprises

Measures	Effect	AIM	YUM	TEKUN
Revenue trends	Increase	**74.0***	**70.2***	**61.3***
	Remain the same	24.0	23.1	37.7
	Decrease	2.0	6.7	1.0
Fixed asset: Tools and equipment	Increase	**61.9***	45.9	52.9
	Remain the same	38.1	51.9	47.1
	Decrease	—	2.2	—
Fixed asset: Land	Increase	20.7	9.0	10.3
	Remain the same	**79.3***	**90.3***	**89.7***
	Decrease	—	0.7	—
Fixed asset: Premises	Increase	17.1	8.2	10.3
	Remain the same	**82.4***	**91.4***	**85.3***
	Decrease	0.5	0.4	4.4
Employment	Increase	39.9	16.8	38.2
	Remain the same	**59.6***	**80.2***	**60.8***
	Decrease	0.5	3.0	1.0

Note: *Indicates the proportion differences are significant at 5% level.
Source: Mokhtar (2011).

businesses' revenue. For YUM borrowers, positive impact was also evident as 70.2% of the borrowers exhibited increase in their microenterprises' revenue after receiving the microcredit loan. Likewise, for TEKUN the proportion of borrowers who experienced increase in their business revenue (61.3%) was significantly higher than those who recorded no changes in revenue from before they received the microcredit. These findings were confirmed by Hamdan & Hussin (2012) who reported positive impact of AIM and TEKUN's loans to their borrowers' microbusinesses revenue.

However, microenterprises' increasing revenue was not necessarily followed by increasing number of employees. In all three MFIs the proportion of borrowers who had generated new employment in their microenterprises (39.9%, 16.8% and 38.2% for AIM, YUM and TEKUN, respectively) were significantly lower than borrowers' microenterprises in which the number of workers remain the same (59.5%, 80.2% and 60.8%

respectively). In other words, microcredit loans had only marginally increased the number of workers in the borrowers' microenterprises in all three MFIs.

Marginal impacts of the microcredit loans were also observed in microenterprises' fixed assets. Only a small proportion of the borrowers had increased their microenterprises' land holdings (20.7%, 9.0%, 10.3% for AIM, YUM and TEKUN borrowers, respectively) after receiving the loans. Likewise, only a small proportion of the borrowers had improved or moved to better business premises (17.1%, 8.2%, 10.3% for AIM, YUM and TEKUN borrowers, respectively) while most of the borrowers operated in the same business premises as before they received the microcredit. A rather significant impact of the microcredit loans on fixed assets were observed in terms of tools and equipment. A large proportion of the AIM borrowers (61.9%) and around half of YUM and TEKUN borrowers reported that their microenterprises used improved tools and equipment after receiving the loans.

3.6.2 *Impact on the household*

Microcredit loans can affect borrowers' households economy through various measures (income, fixed assets, and expenditure on food and children's education) although the magnitudes of the impact may vary among MFIs and differ across the measures (Mokhtar, 2011) (see Table 3.18).

Mokhtar reported that microcredit loans have large impact on the household income of the borrowers. Most of AIM, YUM and TEKUN borrowers (89.8%, 55.6% and 78.4%, respectively) reported higher household income after they received the loans.

The impacts of the microcredit loans on the households' fixed assets, however, are less straightforward for they vary across various types of fixed assets (household's appliances, land, house, farm and livestock). The positive impact of the loans on the borrower's land holdings, farm and livestock were found to be very marginal. Only a small proportion of AIM, YUM and TEKUN's borrowers exhibited improvement in land holdings (14.6%, 7.8% and 6.9%, respectively), farm (5.1%, 19.0% and 1.5%, respectively) and livestock (16.6%, 7.1% and 3.9%, respectively) after receiving the loans. In terms of house, only a small proportion of

Table 3.18:   **Microcredit Impact on the Borrowers' Households**

Measures	Effect	AIM	YUM	TEKUN
Household income trends	Increase	89.8*	55.6*	78.4*
	Remain the Same	9.4	37.3	20.6
	Decrease	0.8	7.1	1.0
Fixed asset: House	Increase	48.6	19.4	22.5
	Remain the Same	51.4	77.2*	73.5*
	Decrease	—	3.4	4.0
Fixed asset: Household's appliances	Increase	67.0*	41.8	46.6
	Remain the Same	30.2	56.0	51.9
	Decrease	2.8	2.2	1.5
Fixed asset: Household's land	Increase	14.6	7.8	6.9
	Remain the Same	85.4*	91.4*	93.1*
	Decrease	—	0.8	—
Fixed assets: Household's farm	Increase	5.1	19.0	1.5
	Remain the Same	94.9*	80.2*	98.5*
	Decrease	—	0.8	—
Fixed assets: Household's livestock	Increase	16.6	7.1	3.9
	Remain the Same	83.4*	88.8*	96.1*
	Decrease	—	4.1	—
Children's education expenditure	Increase	68.0*	33.2	40.2
	Remain the Same	28.4	60.8*	59.8*
	Decrease	3.6	6.0	—
Household's food expenditure	Increase	71.3*	33.9	40.2
	Remain the Same	27.6	64.2*	59.3*
	Decrease	1.0	1.9	0.5

Note: *Indicates the proportion differences are significant at 5% level.
Source: Mokhtar (2011).

YUM and TEKUN borrowers who reported that their houses either increased or improved in size and value (19.4% for YUM and 22.5% for TEKUN) compared to those who reported no change in the condition of their houses after they received the loans. Better house improvement was reported in AIM borrowers where the proportion of borrowers who reported their houses either increased or improved in size and value was almost equal to those who reported no change in their housing condition. However, larger fixed assets improvement were reported in household's appliances among AIM borrowers where a large proportion of borrowers (67%) had improved their household appliances after receiving the loans. For YUM and TEKUN, the proportion of borrowers who reported improvement in their household appliances were almost equal to those who reported no improvement. In other words, microcredit loans have positive but marginal impact on the households' fixed assets of the borrowers except for AIM borrowers who exhibited large improvement in their household appliances.

The rise in borrowers' household income were not necessarily followed by larger expenditure on children's education except for AIM borrowers. A large proportion of AIM borrower (68%) spent more on their children's education after receiving the loan. In other study, Al-Mamun *et al.* (2014) reported that 79.8% of AIM borrowers initiate the discussions with their spouses regarding their children's education and 43.8% reported that their control over the decision regarding children's education were more effective after participating in AIM's microcredit programme. On the contrary, only a small proportion of YUM and TEKUN's borrowers reported that they spent more on their children's education after they received the microcredit (33.2% and 40.2%, respectively).

Similarly, the rise in borrowers' household income were not necessarily followed by higher family food expenditure except for AIM borrowers. A large proportion of AIM borrowers (71.3%) spent more on their family foods after receiving the loans. On the contrary, only a small proportion of YUM and TEKUN's borrowers reported that they spent more on their family food after they participated in microcredit (33.9% and 40.2%, respectively).

3.6.3 *Impact on the individual*

Microcredit loans also affect the individual borrowers' economy but the impact magnitudes vary across individual's economy measures including borrowers' control over business and family decision, self-esteem, personal

Table 3.19: Microcredit Impact on Individual Borrower

Measures	Effect	AIM	YUM	TEKUN
Borrower's control over business decision	Borrower	42.5%*	40.3%	52.4%*
	Borrower and spouse	41.7%	48.9%*	37.3%
	Spouse	13.0%	10.1%	5.9%
	Others	2.8%	0.7%	4.4%
Borrower's control over family decision	Husband	17.6%	13.4%	28.9%
	Wife	15.9%	9.4%	11.3%
	Husband and wife	62.2%*	68.6%*	55.4%*
	Own/single	4.3%	8.6%	4.4%
Microcredit increases a borrower's self-esteem	Agreed	86.2%*	88.1%*	85.8%*
	Disagreed	13.8%	11.9%	14.2%
Microcredit increases a borrower's personal savings	Agreed	91.8%*	77.9%*	90.2%*
	Disagreed	8.2%	22.1%	9.8%
Microcredit has a buoying effect on the borrower's attitude towards future	Agreed	98.2%*	85.4%*	90.7%*
	Disagreed	1.8%	14.6%	9.3%
Microcredit increases the borrower's effectiveness in coping with negative shocks	Agreed	86.2%*	88.1%*	85.8%*
	Disagreed	13.8%	11.9%	14.2%

Note: *Indicates the proportion differences are significant at 5% level.
Source: Mokhtar (2011).

savings, buoying effect on the attitude towards future and effectiveness in coping with negative shocks (Mokhtar, 2011) (see Table 3.19).

One of the way the loan may affect individual borrowers is through the control over resources and income, measured by two types of decisions: the borrowers' control over making a business and family decision. Mokhtar reported that most of the borrowers' business decisions are either made by the borrowers themselves or together with their spouses. TEKUN's borrowers were the most independent where more than half of the borrowers (52.4%) made business decisions by themselves, 37.3% made decisions together with their spouses and only a small number of the borrowers' spouses have a dominant control over the business decision making (5.9%). Likewise, among AIM borrowers most of the business decisions are either made by the borrowers themselves (42.5%) or together with their spouses (41.7%) and only a small number of the borrowers' spouses have a dominant control over the business decision making (13%). A slightly different decision-making power sharing was reported for YUM borrowers where most of the business decisions were made together with their spouses (48.9%) and only 40.3% by the borrowers themselves. However, it is also similar to AIM and TEKUN borrowers in that only a small number of the borrowers' spouses have a dominant control over the business decision making (10.1%). In general, the findings show that many of the women microcredit borrowers have a voice in making business decisions and only a small number of the borrowers' spouses have a dominant control over the business decision making.

Most of AIM, YUM and TEKUN borrowers held equal power with their spouses (62.2%, 68.6% and 55.4%, respectively) when it comes to family decisions. These findings showed that many of the borrowers made family decisions based on collective opinions between the husband and wife. These findings were confirmed by Al-Mamun *et al.* (2014) who reported that more than half of the AIM borrowers made household economic decisions regarding borrowing money, spending money, sale/purchase livestock, repairing or construction of the house and other major spending decisions jointly with their husbands.

Mokhtar further reported that microcredit loans positively affected borrowers' personal savings. Most of the borrowers reported that their personal savings increased after they received the microcredit loans (91.8%, 77.9% and 90.2% for AIM, YUM and TEKUN borrowers, respectively).

The ability to have or increase personal savings in turn affects the borrowers' self-esteem. Most of the borrowers reported that they had higher self-esteem after they received the microcredit loans (86.2%, 88.1% and 85.8% for AIM, YUM and TEKUN, respectively). Three main reasons for increased self-esteem were because the loan enabled them to increase their income, manage their own money and savings and control their own business. Similarly, Al-Mamun *et al.* (2014) reported that microcredit loans enabled most of AIM borrowers to have their own savings and income and contribute to their households' expenditure.

The microcredit loans also affect the borrowers' attitude towards the future. Most of the borrowers agreed that microcredit has a buoyant effect for them to face the future (98.2%, 85.4% and 90.7% for AIM, YUM and TEKUN borrowers, respectively). Three main reasons for the buoyancy were improved business, increase in financial security and confidence in conducting their business.

Finally, the microcredit loans affect the borrowers' effectiveness in coping with negative shocks. Most of the borrowers agreed that microcredit increased their ability to cope with negative shocks (86.2%, 88.1% and 85.8% for AIM, YUM and TEKUN borrowers, respectively). The main negative shocks faced by the borrowers are increasing input goods and fuel prices and increasing business competition. In response to the negative shocks, most of the borrowers from the three MFIs would reduce their expenditures, use savings and engage in other income-earning activities. The borrowers rarely used asset-reducing strategies (liquidation and pawning assets) in response to negative shocks (Mokhtar, 2011). Hence, the borrowers are good at managing strategies to deal with negative shocks because asset-reducing strategies (liquidation and pawning assets) may be harmful and cause long-term productivity losses for the household (Dunn & Arbuckle, 2001). This is partly because of the borrowers' ability to borrow in emergency improve after microcredit participation Al-Mamun *et al.* (2014).

3.7 Conclusions and Implications

This chapter introduces three MFIs in Malaysia, namely AIM, YUM and TEKUN. The establishments of the three MFIs in Malaysia were partly inspired by the success of *the Grameen Bank* in Bangladesh in assisting the poorest member of the society. The poverty and inequality in Malaysia are characterised by the disparity between urban–rural areas, gender, as well as among ethnic groups and states (Economic Planning Unit, 2015b, 2015c).

The three MFIs receive full financial support from the government in terms of grants and soft loans because poverty alleviation has been one of the main goals of Malaysia's economic development. The three MFIs, however, differ in year of establishment, organisation type, lending schemes, service area coverage and target borrowers. AIM is a non-government MFI that applies group lending scheme and targets poor people throughout Malaysia. YUM and TEKUN are government oriented MFIs that apply individual lending scheme but YUM targets poor people mainly in the state of Sabah, while TEKUN targets poor and not-so-poor people throughout Malaysia.

The three MFIs show different performance in loan repayment rate. AIM successfully recorded low NPL (less than 1%), mainly due to the application of group lending scheme, weekly instalment, gradual disbursements and training and education to the borrowers. YUM and TEKUN, however, recorded higher NPL (3.3% and 15%, respectively). The NPLs are mostly found in borrowers with the following characteristics: involved in lower revenue cycle in agriculture, such as farming, animal husbandry and fisheries; chose weekly instalment mode with high weekly repayment amount; had a loan period of less than 1 year; had low amount of loan received; had their business activities rarely visited by MFIs' staff or located far from MFIs' offices; have low sales of the business or used the loan for non-income-generating activities. NPLs are also found to be higher in young borrowers (aged 18–25 years), borrowers in the age group of 46–55 years, male borrowers, borrowers with no formal religious education, borrowers who have low number of gainfully employed members in the household and low number of sources of income in the household.

The three MFIs also differ in the economic impact of their loans on their borrowers. In general the microcredit loans have positive impacts on the economic performance of their borrowers at three levels; individual, households and microenterprises. The magnitudes of the impact, however, vary from marginal to very significant across the three MFIs and across economic performance level/measures. Loans from the three MFIs are found to significantly improve individual borrowers' welfare. After receiving the loans, the borrowers may increase control over their business and family decision, self-esteem, personal savings, buoyancy on the attitude towards future and effectiveness in coping with negative shocks. The loans from the three MFIs significantly increase household income but only marginally increase household assets. In terms of borrower households' expenditure on food and children's education, only AIM loans have significant impact, while YUM and TEKUN loan impacts are marginal.

The loans from the three MFIs are reported to have significant impact on the microenterprises' revenue but only marginally improve the microenterprises' employment. In terms of microenterprises' assets, the impact of the three MFIs loans are marginal, apart from the significant increase of tools and equipment reported by AIM borrowers.

The findings and discussions in this chapter highlight some implications for the MFIs. First, group lending scheme may lead to good loan repayment performance compared with the individual lending. However, the higher repayment rate is not solely because members are committed to repay their weekly loan repayment, but also because of the obligation of the members in the group to repay the loan if other members failed to repay the loan. Hence, while MFIs may consider group lending as more beneficial to the institutions in terms of loan collection (i.e., Cull & Demirgüç-Kunt, 2006; Mersland & Strøm, 2008), they must also consider the burden borne by good group member borrowers who use the loan well and are committed to repay the loan (see de Aghion, 1999).

Second, MFIs should pay greater attention on loans for agriculture activities since agriculture is exposed to climatic factors beyond the borrowers' control. MFIs may develop microinsurance products that not only reduce the burden on the borrowers if their agricultural project failed but also reduce the financial burden on the MFIs from uncollectible loans (see Alip, Navarro & Catibog, 2009). Among the three MFIs, AIM has implemented the welfare and well-being funds for their members whose projects are caused by natural disaster. However, the monetary award under this fund covers only 20% of current loan or outstanding loan.

Borrowers involved in agricultural businesses also need to be given more flexibility in repayment modes and grace periods. Borrowers in agricultural businesses use the loans to buy inputs, such as seed, fertiliser and pesticides and assets, such as farm machinery and livestock. They may need at least 6 months to 1 year to receive the revenue from harvesting the crops. Hence, weekly loan repayments and a few weeks' grace periods simply mismatch the borrowers' revenue cycle and may lead to low repayment rate.

Inexperienced and young graduates are also prone to failure in managing their agriculture projects. Hence, MFIs must closely monitor this group of borrowers to ensure that they have the experience and related skills before granting them loans for agriculture businesses (see Zeller & Meyer, 2002).

Third, MFIs should put more effort to improve borrowers' lack of knowledge in business financial management that can be crucial for the success of their business projects. Trainings on entrepreneurial skills for the borrowers to manage their income and resources efficiently may contribute to the higher repayment rate (see Mokhtar *et al.*, 2012a).

Finally, MFIs should impose a stricter approach to the misuse of microcredit loans (such as the use of microbusiness loans for personal consumption). As a preventive measure, MFIs may place extra conditions on borrowers when they apply in the next microcredit loan cycle. Before a new microcredit loan is given to a borrower, the MFIs may request business records, such as sales performance and the microenterprise's asset status, as proof that their businesses have improved from the use of the previous microcredit loan. A new microcredit loan should not be given in case there is no significant positive achievement in the borrowers' businesses, unless for specific reasons. Moreover, if the microcredit loans misuse is found, the particular borrower needs to be blacklisted from obtaining a microcredit loan from any MFIs in the country. This strategy should reduce morally hazardous behaviour among microfinance borrowers.

The findings and discussions in this chapter also brought some implications for the policy makers. Despite Malaysian government's willingness to continue their financial support (including subsidies) for the microcredit programs because they perceive it as part of their social responsibility (see Siwar & Talib, 2001), the subsidy may contribute to the unsustainability of the microcredit programmes which in turn may affect its performance and outreach. As observed in YUM and TEKUN, subsidised microcredit may lead to higher level of NPL since the MFIs are not really concerned about the low repayment rate of their borrowers. Without self-sufficiency and capital accumulation, microcredit services' sustainability and outreach to the poor people are always constrained.

At least two strategies can be considered if the government is willing to stop or reduce the subsidy given to the MFIs. One way is by lifting the restrictions on MFIs in Malaysia to take deposits from the clients.

Evidence from *the Grameen Bank* in Bangladesh, People's Bank (*Bank Perkreditan Rakyat* — BPR) in Indonesia, Self-Help Groups (SHGs) village banking in India and some other African MFIs show that savings could be a source of funds for lending and in some cases members' savings in the MFIs exceed the credits given so that the MFIs could be sustainable without subsidies and donations (see for example Lafourcade *et al.*, 2005; Mokhtar *et al.*, 2012b; Prahalad, 2005). The safety of the deposits, however, must always be monitored by the Central Bank.

Another way to stop and reduce the government subsidy is by giving investment opportunities to the borrowers as practiced by the BPR in Indonesia (Mokhtar *et al.*, 2012b). This strategy not only reduces the financial burden on the government but also gives the local community a share in the MFIs' branches in their district. This practise can also create borrowers' sense of belonging to the MFIs.

From the Malaysian government's point of view, however, it remains to be seen whether they are willing to stop subsidising the MFIs. The microcredit programmes in Malaysia is the government's favourite project since it may attract political supporters, especially the poor people (Mokhtar, 2011). In case the government insists on continuing subsidising MFIs in the country, an efficient way of subsidising can be proposed. Malaysia can establish a trust fund specifically for the MFIs in the country similar to *the Grameen Trust Fund*. The trust fund could be used to provide funding, management and technical training to the existing MFIs and their new branches (Yunus, 2007). The use of the trust fund, however, should be closely monitored by the government to ensure its sustainability.

References

AIF (2015). *Aiming for Greater Financial Inclusion through Sustainable Development: The story of AIM (Amanah Ikhtiar Malaysia)*. Kuala Lumpur: AIF.

AIM (2010). Yearly Performance Report. Kuala Lumpur: Amanah Ikhtiar Malaysia.

AIM (2013a). Pencapaian Terkini. Retrieved from http://www.aim.gov.my/ informasi/status/status-baki-kini. Accessed on February 21, 2017.

AIM (2013b). Sejarah AIM. Retrieved from http://www.aim.gov.my/kenali-kami/profil/sejarah. Accessed on February 21, 2017.

AIM (2014). Status Terkini. Retrieved from http://www.aim.gov.my/informasi/status/pengeluaran-pembiayaan. Accessed on February 21, 2017.

AIM (2015a). Skim Pembayaran Ikhtiar (SPI). Retrieved from http://www.aim.gov.my/khidmat/skim-pembiayaan-ikhtiar-spi. Accessed on February 21, 2017.

AIM (2015b). Tabung Kebajikan & Kesejahteraan Sahabat. Retrieved from http://www.aim.gov.my/khidmat/tabung-kebajikan. Accessed on February 21, 2017.

AIM Sabah Barat (2012). Produk. Retrieved from http://aimwilayahsabahbarat.blogspot.co.nz/p/produk.html. Accessed on January 26, 2015.

Al-Mamun, A., Wahab, S. A. & Malarvizhi, C. (2011). Empirical investigation on repayment performance of Amanah Ikhtiar Malaysia's hardcore poor clients. *International Journal of Business and Management,* 6(7), 125.

Al-Mamun, A., Wahab, S. A., Mazumder, M. N. H. & Su, Z. (2014). Empirical investigation on the impact of microcredit on women empowerment in urban peninsular Malaysia. *The Journal of Developing Areas,* 48(2), 287–306.

Alip, J., Navarro, E. L. & Catibog, M. M. (2009). Status of microinsurance in Southeast Asia (The case of Cambodia, Philippines and Vietnam). An APRACA FinPower Publication with the Special Sponsorship of the International Fund for Agricultural Development (IFAD).

Amri, S. A. K. (2012). Jana RM2,500 sebulan. *My Metro.* Retrieved from http://www.hmetro.com.my/. Accessed on February 21, 2017.

Berita Harian (2009). Peminjam Tekun gagal jelaskan hutang RM225j. Retrieved from http://www.bharian.com.my/. Accessed on February 21, 2017.

Bernama (2013). Tekun beri dana pinjaman RM600 juta. Sinar Harian. Retrieved from http://www.sinarharian.com.my/mobile/nasional/tekun-beri-dana-pinjaman-rm600-juta-1.181894.

Bourguignon, F. (2004). The poverty-growth-inequality triangle. *Poverty, Inequality and Growth.* Washington, DC: World Bank, p. 69.

Chamhuri, S. & Quinones, B. (2000). Microfinance in Malaysia: Aiming at success. In Auty, R. M., Potter, R. B. & Remenyi, J. (Eds.), *Microfinance and Poverty Alleviation.* New York: Routledge, pp. 180–199.

Chan, S. H. (2010). The influence of leadership expertise and experience on organizational performance: A study of Amanah Ikhtiar Malaysia. *Asia Pacific Business Review,* 16(1–2), 59–77.

Cohen, M., Chen, M. A., & Dunn, E. (1996). *Household Economic Portfolios.* Washington, D.C.: Management Systems International. Retrieved from http://pdf.usaid.gov/pdf_docs/PNABZ077.pdf. Accessed on February 21, 2017.

Conroy, J. D. (2002). Microfinance in Malaysia: Time to rebuild. Retrieved from http://www.bwtp.org. Accessed on November 20, 2007.

Cull, R. & Demirgüç-Kunt, A. (2006). Financial Performance and Outreach: A Global Analysis of Leading Microbanks. World Bank Policy Research Working Paper. No. 3827.

de Aghion, B. A. (1999). On the design of a credit agreement with peer monitoring. *Journal of Development Economics*, 60(1), 79–104.

Dunn, E. & Arbuckle, J. G. J. (2001). *The Impacts of Microcredit: A Case Study from Peru.* New York: AIMS, USAID.

Economic Planning Unit (1991). Second Outline of the Perspective Plan, 1991–2000. Kuala Lumpur. Retrieved from http://www.epu.gov.my/ms/pengurusan-ekonomi/satu-sedutan-sejarah. Accessed on February 21, 2017.

Economic Planning Unit (2013a). *Incidence of Hardcore Poverty by Ethnicity, Strata and State,* Malaysia, 1984–2012.

Economic Planning Unit (2013b). Socio-economic Statistics. Retrieved from http://www.epu.gov.my/en/socio-economic/overview. Accessed on February 21, 2017.

Economic Planning Unit (2015a). Brief Household Income & Poverty Statistics Newsletter, 2012 & 2014. Retrieved from http://www.epu.gov.my/ms/sumber/penerbitan. Accessed on February 21, 2017.

Economic Planning Unit (2015b). *Incidence of Poverty by Ethnicity, Strata and State, Malaysia,* 1970–2014.

Economic Planning Unit (2015c). *Mean Monthly Gross Household Income by Ethnicity, Strata and State, Malaysia,* 1970–2014.

Economic Planning Unit (2015d). Socio-economic Statistics. Retrieved from http://www.epu.gov.my/en/socio-economic/overview. Accessed on February 21, 2017.

Esfahani, H. S. (1994). Lessons from the political economy of privatization and public sector in the Middle East and Southeast Asia. *The Quarterly Review of Economic and Finance,* 34, 301–331.

Hamdan, H. & Hussin, W. S. W. (2012). The importance of monitoring and entrepreneurship concept as future direction of microfinance in Malaysia: Case study in the State of Selangor. *Journal of Global Entrepreneurship,* 3(1), 1–25.

Hashim, S. M. (1998). *Income Inequality and Poverty in Malaysia.* Maryland, USA: Rowman & Littlefield Publishers.

Jamil, A. (2012). Women make better borrowers at Amanah Ikhtiar. *Free Malaysia Today.* Retrieved from http://www.freemalaysiatoday.com/category/business/2012/12/17/women-make-better-borrowers-at-amanah-ikhtiar-says-md/.

Jomo, K. S. (2004). *The New Economic Policy and Interethnic Relations in Malaysia.* New York: United Nations Research Institute for Social Development.

Kasim, S. (2000). Impact of Banking on Rural Poor in Peninsular Malaysia: Final Report of External Impact Evaluation Study on AIM Active Borrowers, Non-Borrowing Members, Dropouts and Non-Participating Poor. Penang: Centre for Policy Research, Universiti Sains Malaysia.

Kosmo (2012). AIM Bantu Tangani Kemiskinan. Retrieved from http://www.kosmo.com.my/kosmo/content.asp?y=2011&dt=0923&pub=Kosmo&sec=Rencana_Utama&pg=ru_02.htm. Accessed on January 24, 2015.

Lafourcade, A., Isern, J., Mwangi, P., & Brown, M. (2005). *Overview of the Outreach and Financial Performance of Microfinance Institutions in Africa.* Washington, D.C.: Microfinance Information Exchange (MIX). Retrieved from http://www.griequity.com/resources/industryandissues.

MacPee, M. (2014). 130 ahli YUM dirai dalam Majlis Makan Malam. *New Sabah Times.* Retrieved from https://www.pressreader.com/malaysia/utusan-borneo-sabah/20161125/281870118039743. Accessed on February 21, 2017.

Malaysian Government (2015). Perkhidmatan Pembayaran Agensi Kepada Komuniti/Syarikat. Retrieved from http://mygov.malaysia.gov.my/. Accessed on February 21, 2017.

McGuire, P. B., Conroy, J. D. & Thapa, G. B. (1998). Getting the framework right: Policy and regulation for microfinance in Asian. Retrieved from www.bwtp.org/knowledgebase_category/books/. Accessed on February 21, 2017.

Menon, J. (2009). Macroeconomic management amid ethnic diversity: Fifty years of Malaysian experience. *Journal of Asian Economics* (20), 25–33.

Mersland, R. & Strøm, R. Ø. (2008). Performance and trade offs in microfinance organisations — Does ownership matter? *Journal of International Development,* 20(5), 598–612.

MicroCapital (2011). Microcapital Brief: Malaysian Microfinance Institution (MFI) Amanah Ikhtiar Malaysia (AIM) to Disburse $164m in Rural Sarawak Region. Retrieved from http://www.microcapital.org/microcapital-brief-malaysian-microfinance-institution-mfi-amanah-ikhtiar-malaysia-aim-to-disburse-164m-in-rural-sarawak-region/. Accessed on January 20, 2015.

Ministry of Finance Malaysia (2009). Economic Report 2008/2009. Retrieved from http://www.treasury.gov.my/. Accessed on February 21, 2017.

Mokhtar, S. H. (2011). Microfinance Performance in Malaysia (Doctoral Thesis). Lincoln University, Lincoln, New Zealand. Retrieved from https://researcharchive.lincoln.ac.nz/.

Mokhtar, S. H., Nartea, G. & Gan, C. (2012a). Determinants of microcredit loans repayment problem among microfinance borrowers in Malaysia. *International Journal of Business and Social Research*, 2(7), 33–45.

Mokhtar, S. H., Nartea, G. & Gan, C. (2012b). The Malaysian microfinance system and a comparison with the Grameen Bank (Bangladesh) and Bank Perkreditan Rakyat (BPR-Indonesia). *Journal of Arts and Humanities*, 1(3), 60–71.

Nawai, N. & Shariff, M. N. M. (2012). Factors affecting repayment performance in microfinance programs in Malaysia. *Procedia*, 62, 806–811.

Prahalad, C. K. (2005). Known problems and systemwide reform. In *The Fortune at the Bottom of the Pyramid: Eradicating Poverty through profits*. Upper Saddle River: Wharton School Publishing, p. 294.

Roslan, A. H. (2006). Microfinance and Poverty: The Malaysian Experience. Paper Presented at the Meeting of the 2nd International Development Conference of the GRES — Which Financing for Which Development?, November 23–26, Bordeaux, France.

Sabah (2015). About Sabah. Retrieved from http://www.sabah.gov.my/main/en-GB/Home/About. Accessed on February 13, 2015.

Siddique, S. & Suryadinata, L. (1981). Bumiputra and Pribumi: Economic nationalism (Indiginism) in Malaysia and Indonesia. *Pacific Affairs*, 54(4), 662–687.

Siwar, C. & Talib, B. A. (2001). Micro-finance capacity assessment for poverty alleviation: Outreach, viability and sustainability. *Humanomics*, 17(1), 116–133.

SMEinfo (2015). TEKUN Financing Scheme. Retrieved from http://www.smeinfo.com.my/index.php?option=com_content&view=article&id=619&Itemid=527. Accessed on February 26, 2015.

TEKUN (2009). *Laporan Prestasi Tahunan*.

TEKUN Nasional (2013a). Background of Establishment. Retrieved from http://www.tekun.gov.my/en/web/guest/latar-belakang-penubuhan. Accessed on February 26, 2015.

TEKUN Nasional (2013b). Financing Terms & Condition. Retrieved from http://www.tekun.gov.my/ms/usahawan-tekun/skim-pembiayaan-tekun-nasional/syarat-syarat/. Accessed on February 21, 2017.

TEKUN Nasional (2013c). Introduction. Retrieved from http://www.tekun.gov.my/en/corporate-info/info/introduction/. Accessed on February 21, 2017.

TEKUN Nasional (2013d). Maklumat & Syarat Pinjaman. Retrieved from http://www.tekun.gov.my/en/tekun-entrepreneur/tekun-nasional-financing-scheme/syarat-syarat-2/. Accessed on February 21, 2017.

TEKUN Nasional (2013e). Repayment Schedule. Retrieved from www.tekun. gov.my/en/tekun-entrepreneur/tekun-nasional-financing-scheme/jadual-bayaran-balik-2/. Accessed on February 21, 2017.

UNDP (2010). Human Development Report 2010. The Real Wealth of Nations: Pathways to Human Development.

UNDP (2015). Human Development Statistical Tables. Retrieved from http://hdr. undp.org/en/data. Accessed on February 15, 2016.

Vieira, S. (2012). *Inequality on the Rise? An Assessment of Current Available Data on Income Inequality, at Global, International and National Levels.* The Department of Economic and Social Affairs, the United Nations Secretariat.

Wahab, S. A., Malarvizhi, C. & Mariapun, S. (2011). Examining the critical factors affecting the repayment of microcredit schemes in Amanah Ikhtiar Malaysia (AIM) in Malaysia. *International Business Research,* 4(2), 93.

World Bank (2015). World Development Indicators, World Databank. Retrieved from http://databank.worldbank.org/data/reports.aspx?Code=NY.GDP.PCAP. CD&id=af3ce82b&report_name=Popular_indicators&populartype=series&is popular=y#. Accessed on February 15, 2016.

World Bank Group (2016). Global Monitoring Report 2015/2016: Development Goals in an Era of Demographic Change. Washington, DC: World Bank.

YUM Sabah (2013). Pengenalan YUM.

YUM Sabah (2014a). Cawangan YUM. Retrieved from http://www.yumsabah. com.my/my/index.php/cawangan-yum/wilayah-barat/tuaran. Accessed on February 11, 2015.

YUM Sabah (2014b). Penyerahan Pinjaman Mengikut Daerah. Retrieved from http://www.yumsabah.com.my/my/index.php/program-dan-pencapaian/peny-erahan-pinjaman. Accessed on February 11, 2015.

YUM Sabah (2014c). Produk Pinjaman. Retrieved from http://www.yumsabah. com.my/my/index.php/produk-dan-perkhidmatan/program-pinjaman. Accessed on February 10, 2015.

YUM Sabah (2014d). Sejarah Ringkas YUM. Retrieved from http://www.yum-sabah.com.my/my/index.php/mengenai-yum/sejarah-ringkas-yum. Accessed on February 13, 2015.

YUM Sabah (2014e). Soalan Lazim (FAQ). Retrieved from http://www.yumsabah. com.my/my/index.php/soalan-lazim-faq. Accessed on February 11, 2015.

YUM Sabah (2014f). Tabung Kecemasan. Retrieved from http://www.yumsabah. com.my/my/index.php/produk-dan-perkhidmatan/tabung-kecemasan. Accessed on February 11, 2015.

Yunus, M. (2007). *Creating a World Without Poverty: Social Business and the Future of Capitalism.* New York: PublicAffairs.

Zeller, M. & Meyer, R. (2002). The triangle of microfinance: Financial sustainability, outreach, and impact. *IFPRI, Food Policy Statement,* 40.

Chapter 4

Credit Market and Microcredit Services in Rural China

Mohamad D. Revindo*,‡ and Christopher Gan†,§

*PhD Candidate, Faculty of Agribusiness and Commerce,
Department of Financial and Business System,
PO Box 85084, Lincoln University, Canterbury, New Zealand

†Professor in Accounting and Finance,
Faculty of Agribusiness and Commerce,
Department of Financial and Business System,
PO Box 85084, Lincoln University, Christchurch, New Zealand

‡Mohamad.Revindo@lincolnuni.ac.nz
§Christopher.Gan@lincoln.ac.nz

Abstract

Gap in credit access to rural poor population in China exists because rural households, especially farmers, are constrained to access credit from formal Rural Financial Institutions (RFIs). The risky nature of agriculture business and the absence of land ownership due to China's village-based communal land-tenure system hinder the farmers from accessing formal credit requiring collateral and force them to resort to informal borrowings that charge exorbitant interest rates. The subsidised-loan programme implemented by the Chinese government in 1986–2000 failed to reduce the credit access gap because it was poorly managed, missed the target borrowers (poor rural households) and was financially unsustainable due to the low repayment rate. Microcredit programme was then introduced in 1994 to bring more effective and sustainable rural poverty eradication. This chapter provides an overview of the rural financial system, rural credit market and the development of microcredit in China. The chapter concludes that microcredit may significantly reduce the gap in the rural credit market and play an important role in rural poverty alleviation provided some reforms are implemented both at RFIs as well as national policy making levels.

Keywords: Rural financial institutions, credit access, credit market, formal credit, informal credit, microcredit, subsidised-loan, China.

4.1 Introduction

China is the world's second largest economy by nominal GDP after United States and the world's largest economy by purchasing power parity (PPP) GDP in 2014 (IMF, 2015). Since its first economic reform in 1978, China has recorded a miraculous 9.81% annual GDP growth rate, enabling the population to enjoy almost 20 times increase in real GDP per capita (World Bank, 2016). However, the income disparity has been widening as indicated by its Gini coefficient that surpassed 0.4 after 1999 as well as decreasing national income share held by the poorest 10% and 20% of the population (World Bank, 2016). The income inequality in China can be partly attributed to urban–rural income gap where in 2014 the urban households earned almost 3 times higher than their rural counterparts (National Bureau of Statistics of China, 2015f).

The rural households in China are mostly characterised by small-scale farmers who are not entitled to the land on which they farm since the government implements a village-based communal land-tenure system (Lin & Zhang, 1998). The absence of land ownership and the risky nature of agriculture business have constrained rural farmers from acquiring formal financial support, credit support in particular and forced them to resort to informal borrowings that charge higher interest rate (Linton, 2007). The limited access to formal credit has hindered rural farmers from production expansion and from improving their living standards, which in turn hampered rural economic growth and poverty alleviation (Cheng & Xu, 2004; Park, Ren & Wang, 2004). To tackle this problem, the government of China initially introduced the subsidised-loan programme in 1986 in order to ease the loan's interest rate burden borne by the poor. However, this programme was not financially sustainable due to high default rates and failed to reach the real poor despite successfully promotes overall regional economic development (Heilig *et al.*, 2006; Park & Ren, 2001). To bridge the persisting gap of credit access for poor households, in the mid-1990s the government launched microcredit programmes that aimed to ameliorate rural poverty in a financially sustainable way (Park *et al.*, 2004).

This chapter provides an overview of credit market and microcredit services for rural households in China. The chapter is organised as follows. Section 4.2 provides the background of economic development and income inequality in China. Sections 4.3 and 4.4 discuss the financial institutions catering rural areas and the gap in credit market for rural households in China, respectively. Section 4.5 gives an overview of the development of microcredit programmes in rural China and highlights the challenges for further microcredit expansion.

4.2 Economic Development, Poverty and Income Inequality in Rural China

4.2.1 *Economic growth and poverty in China*

Prior to 1978 the government of China implemented a centrally planned/command economy in which the state controlled all productive assets (Hu & Khan, 1997). From 1962 to 1977 the economy registered 7.05% average growth but the growth rate fluctuated widely, ranging from a negative growth of –5.7% in 1967 (the lowest) to 19.4% in 1970 (the highest) (see Figure 4.1(a)). In 1978, the government of China initiated economic reform by encouraging the establishments of rural enterprises and private businesses, opening the country to international trade and foreign investment, relaxing price control over some products, developing manufacture industries and investing in workforce education (Hu & Khan, 1997). The economic reform has worked miraculously whereby from 1978 to 2014 the nominal GDP multiplied by almost 70 times from US$148.4 billion to US$10,354.8 billion and recorded 9.81% average annual growth (see Figure 4.1(a)). The economy growth after 1978 was

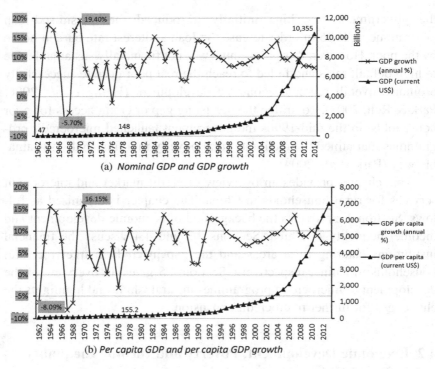

(a) *Nominal GDP and GDP growth*

(b) *Per capita GDP and per capita GDP growth*

Figure 4.1:   China's Economic Growth, 1962–2014

Source: World Development Indicators (World Bank, 2016).

also less volatile than the preceding period and tended to fluctuate narrowly between 5% and 15% (World Bank, 2016).

The rapid and stable economic growth driven by economic reform has also accelerated China's per capita income growth (see Figure 4.1(b)). Prior to the economic reform, China's GDP per capita multiplied 2.21 times in 17 years (1962–1978), while on the contrary after the reform the GDP per capita increased by almost 49 times in 36 years (1978–2014) (World Bank, 2016). In 2014, China recorded GDP per capita of US$10,355 and Gross National Income (GNI) per capita of US$7,400 and was therefore among the upper–middle income country group.[1]

---

[1]The World Bank defines upper–middle-income economies as those with a GNI per capita (calculated using the World Bank Atlas method) of more than $4,125 but less than $12,736 (World Bank, 2016).

Table 4.1: Poverty and Inequality in China, 1984–2013

Indicators	1984	1990	1996	2002	2008	2010	2011	2013
Population, total (million)	1,037	1,135	1,218	1,280	1,325	1,338	1,344	1,357
Number of poor at $1.25 a day (PPP) (millions)	719.9	689.4	455.2	359.3	163.5	122.9	84.1	n.a.
Number of poor at $2 a day (PPP) (millions)	963.3	964.6	806.0	649.5	375.3	310.2	250.1	n.a.
Poverty gap at $1.25 a day (PPP) (%)	25.6	21.0	11.1	8.6	3.1	2.0	1.3	n.a.
Poverty gap at $2 a day (PPP) (%)	47.3	41.2	26.9	20.4	9.5	7.3	5.5	n.a.
Poverty headcount ratio at $1.25 a day (PPP) (% of population)	69.4	60.7	37.4	28.1	12.3	9.2	6.3	n.a.
Poverty headcount ratio at $2 a day (PPP) (% of population)	92.9	85.0	66.2	50.7	28.3	23.2	18.6	n.a.
Rural poverty headcount ratio at national poverty lines (% of rural population)	n.a.	n.a.	n.a.	n.a.	n.a.	17.2	12.7	8.5
Income share held by lowest 10%	3.76	3.49	3.11	2.28	1.77	1.69	n.a.	n.a.
Income share held by lowest 20%	8.85	8.04	7.24	5.47	4.78	4.67	n.a.	n.a.

Source: World Development Indicators (World Bank, 2015).

The steady per capita income growth has brought a remarkable poverty reduction in China. Table 4.1 shows from 1984 to 2011 the number of population lived with less than $1.25 a day declined sharply from 719.9 million to 84.1 million or equivalently from 69.4% to only 6.3% of the population.[2] In the same period, those who lived with less than $2 a day

---

[2] As of October 2015 the World Bank has updated the international poverty line to $3.1 a day and extreme poverty line to $1.9 a day. However, China's poverty data series with the new poverty lines are limited. Hence, in Table 4.1 we still use $2 poverty line and $1.25 extreme poverty line in order to have longer and more consistent data series with the previous years.

declined from 963.3 million to 250.1 million or equivalently down from 92.9% to 18.6% of the population. Further, in 1984 the average income of the poor was 25.6% short of \$1.25 a day and 47.3% short of \$2 a day, while the poor's average income in 2011 was only 1.3% short of \$1.25 a day and 5.5% short of \$2 a day (World Bank, 2015). Looking at these poverty numbers from different angles, however, it means that in 2011 there were still 250.1 million poor people in China, 84.1 million of who lived in extreme poverty. In other words, poverty still exists in the country and the actual number of poor people is still high.

In terms of income equality, from 1984 to 2010 the share of national income held by the poorest 10% of the population continually decreased from 3.76% to 1.69% (see Table 4.1). In the same period, the share of national income held by the poorest 20% of the population also decreased from 8.85% to 4.67%). As a result, income inequality in China exhibited a precarious sign. Figure 4.2 shows that since early 1980s China's Gini coefficient has steadily increased and surpassed the warning threshold of 0.4 in 2002.[3] The World Bank estimated that the Gini coefficient has stayed between 0.4 and 0.45 but China's National Bureau of Statistics estimated that up until 2014 it stayed above 0.45.

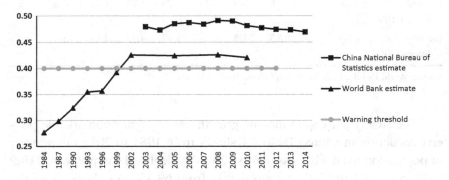

Figure 4.2: China's Gini Coefficient, 1984–2014

Sources: World Development Indicators (World Bank, 2016), National Bureau of Statistics of China, as reported in Global Times (2013) and National Bureau of Statistics of China (2015c).

---

[3]A country with Gini index value above 0.4 is regarded as a country with high inequality or at least medium–high inequality (Bourguignon, 2004; Vieira, 2012).

4.2.2 *Rural and agriculture development in China*

The income inequality may persist across regions, economy sector, employment types and even individuals. In the case of China, the income inequality between urban and rural households is evident and widens over time (see Figure 4.3). When the economic reform began in 1978 the urban and rural households' monthly average income were *Renminbi* (RMB) 343.4 and RMB133.6, respectively.[4] In other words, in 1978 the urban household on average earned a monthly income 2.6 times their rural counterparts and the nominal difference between them was RMB209.8 on average. In contrast, in 2014 the urban households' monthly average income was RMB29,381, almost three times their rural counterparts who earned RMB9,982 and the gap between the two widened to RMB19,489 per month on average. The rural–urban income inequality in China, however, varies across regions. For example, the eastern and southern provinces have a much smaller rural–urban income gap than provinces in Central, Northern and Western China (Heilig *et al.*, 2006).

The slower economic growth in rural China may be attributed, but not limited, to the following causes: (i) shrinking role of agriculture sector in the economy; (ii) insecurity in land-tenure system (Lin & Zhang, 1998); (iii) lack of financial support, especially credit services, for rural

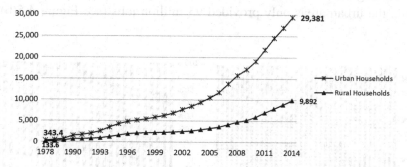

Figure 4.3: Average Monthly Households Income in Urban and Rural Areas in China (in RMB)

Source: Per capita income of urban and rural households (National Bureau of Statistics of China, 2015f).

---

[4]As of February 2016, the exchange rate of Chinese Renminbi was approximately RMB1 = US$0.153 or equivalently US$1 = RMB6.55 (IMF, 2016).

households in general and agriculture activities in particular (Cheng & Xu, 2004; Park *et al.*, 2004).

As experienced in many developing countries, economic development and growth in China has also been characterised by structural transformation that reduced the role of agriculture in the economy. Figure 4.4(a) shows that the contribution of the primary sector to China's GDP steadily decreased from around 30% in 1970s and early 1980s to around 20% in 1992–1996, down to about 10% in 2007–2013, further down to less than 10% in 2014 and is expected to decline further over time. Similarly, Figure 4.2(b) shows that the contribution of agriculture products to China's exports value has shrunk from around 50% in the early of 1980s to 20% in 1992, further down to less than 10% in 2001 and even lower than 5% since 2012.

The decreasing roles of the agriculture sector and rural regions in Chinese economy are also reflected in their contribution to employment provision. From 1978 to 2014 the employment provision had shifted away from the rural regions and agriculture sector (see Figure 4.5). Figure 4.5(a) shows that when the reform began in 1978 the agriculture sector provided around 70% of employments but its provision decreased to only 50% in 2001–2002 and in 2014 only less than 30% of workforce worked in this sector. Region wise, in 1978 the rural areas provided 306 million jobs, while the urban areas only provided 95 million jobs (see Figure 4.5(b)).

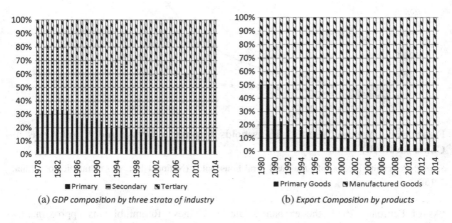

(a) *GDP composition by three strata of industry*   (b) *Export Composition by products*

Figure 4.4:   Contribution of Agriculture Sector in Chinese Economy

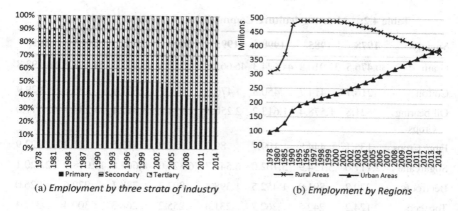

(a) *Employment by three strata of industry*   (b) *Employment by Regions*

Figure 4.5:   Shifts in Employment Provision, by Regions and Sectors

The employment provision in rural areas reached its peak in 1997 (490.4 million) and then steadily decreased over time, both in terms of share of contribution and the real number of job provisions. On the contrary, the job provision in urban areas increased steadily that in 2014 the number of workforce employed in urban areas already exceeded those in rural areas.

The decreasing role of the agriculture sector in Chinese economy does not actually stem from the declining agriculture production level and values. In fact the agriculture production increases over time but it grows at a much lower pace than other sectors in the economy. Table 4.2 summarises the production of several main agriculture commodities from 1978 to 2013. In a span of 35 years Fruits were the only commodity whose production annually grew above 10%. In contrast the production of Tea grew by only 5.8% on average, followed by Oil-bearing Crops (5.6%), Sugarcane (5.29%), Silkworm Cocoons (3.97%), Beetroots (3.58%), Cotton (3.09%), Tobacco (2.9%), Grain (1.96%) and Fibre Crops (4.93%). The agriculture sector, therefore, is not the main driver of China's high average national GDP growth but rather the manufacture and service sectors.

One of the obstacles to restructure the agriculture sector and to boost agriculture productivity is the insecurity in the land-tenure system. China's rural households are predominantly characterised by small-scale farmers who are not entitled to the land on which they farm. Instead, land

Table 4.2:   Main Agriculture Commodities of China (in 10,000 tons)

Variety	1978	1985	1990	1995	2000	2005	2010	2013
Grain	30,476.5	37,910.8	44,624.3	46,661.8	46,217.5	48,402.2	54,647.7	60,193.8
Cotton	216.7	414.7	450.8	476.8	441.7	571.4	596.1	629.9
Oil-bearing Crops	521.8	1,578.4	1,613.2	2,250.3	2,954.8	3,077.1	3,230.1	3,517.0
Fibre Crops	135.1	444.8	109.7	89.7	52.9	110.5	31.7	22.9
Sugarcane	2,111.6	5,154.9	5,762.0	6,541.7	6,828.0	8,663.8	11,078.9	12,820.1
Beetroots	270.2	891.9	1,452.5	1,398.4	807.3	788.1	929.6	926.0
Tobacco	124.2	242.5	262.7	231.4	255.2	268.3	300.4	337.4
Silkworm Cocoons	22.8	37.1	53.4	80.0	54.8	78.0	87.3	89.2
Tea	26.8	43.2	54.0	58.9	68.3	93.5	147.5	192.4
Fruits	657.0	1,163.9	1,874.4	4,214.6	6,225.1	16,120.1	21,401.4	25,093.0

Source: Output of Major Farm Products (National Bureau of Statistics of China, 2014).

is owned by the village (or collective) and is contracted or allocated to rural households. Therefore, the Chinese land-tenure system is actually a village-based communal land-tenure system (Lin & Zhang, 1998). The ownership entity generally retains the rights to reallocate land among households. When the village or collective leaders exercise their rights to reallocate land, rural households risk losing the plots they have farmed and they are neither guaranteed to acquire comparable plots through land reallocation nor fair market compensation. While the reallocation is intended to ensure egalitarian access to land, it also brings significant land-tenure insecurity in rural China.

The insecure land-tenure system discourages farmers from investing in inputs that have a long-term payoff such as organic fertiliser. Moreover, the restrictions on land markets, frequent land reallocation and small-scale landholdings (less than 0.08 hectare per capita) rooted in the Chinese village-based land-tenure system have become the major hindrance to the efficiency of resource allocation and the improvement of agricultural productivity (Huang, Rozelle & Tuan, 1999; Lin & Zhang, 1998). The promulgation of the Land Management Law in 1998 has legally extended the land use contract rights by rural households to 30 years. However, this policy directive has not always been conformed and the dynamics of rural household and village demographics frequently induce local authorities to reallocate land prior to contract expiration. In addition, the Chinese land-tenure system lacks formal rules governing independent land transfers between rural households, which hinders the development of a rural land market (Huang *et al.*, 1999; Prosterman *et al.*, 1998).

The Chinese collective land-ownership system that prevents farmers to have legal title on land has also prevented farmers from accessing traditional credit support from formal financial institutions because farmers cannot use land as collateral which is a necessary requirement in traditional lending. Farmers need financial support, credit support in particular, to expand their production and improve their living conditions. Farmers require credit as an important production input, with which they can invest in high-yielding varieties and purchase fertiliser that is indispensable in agricultural production because of the infertile soils in most of China's impoverished rural areas. In addition, the farmers need credit support to meet their living expenses including the purchase of durable goods, daily consumption, children's education as well as festivals and ceremonies.

Failing to access formal credit, most farmers have to resort to informal borrowings which are typically offered at higher interest rates. While the formal interest rate set by the People's Bank of China (PBC) on short-and medium-term loans is low (less than 6%), interest rates in informal markets generally range from 12% to 30%. For example, in the north-east and north-west areas where the economy is relatively underdeveloped, informal lending rates of 100–200% annually are not unusual (Linton, 2007). Despite the high interest rates charged by the informal lenders, approximately 50–60% of rural households in China still rely on informal credit for their consumption and production (Han, 2004). The high interest on informal loans has increased farmers' indebtedness and further kept most of the household trapped in poverty.

4.3 Financial Institutions and Services in Rural China

The widening gap between rural and urban living standards was brought to the Chinese government attention, partly because it may pose a threat to social and political instability in the countryside (Fan & Sun, 2008).

In that regard, the 1978's economic reform was also followed by rural reforms since the late 1970s.[5] The rural reforms fostered the development of China's rural economy and in turn created a demand for pluralism of investment and financial services in rural areas. The enormous demand for financial services gave an impetus to the formation and expansion of rural financial institutions (RFIs) that led to gradual improvement in the overall rural financial system (Scott & Jun, 2006; Zhang, 2004).

At present, rural financial services in China is catered by both formal (including semi-formal) and informal financial institutions (see Figure 4.6). Figure 4.6 shows that China's rural financial system consists of three kinds of financial institutions including banking institutions, non-banking financial institutions and informal funding organisations. The PBC acts as the central bank implementing a unified monetary policy and supervise

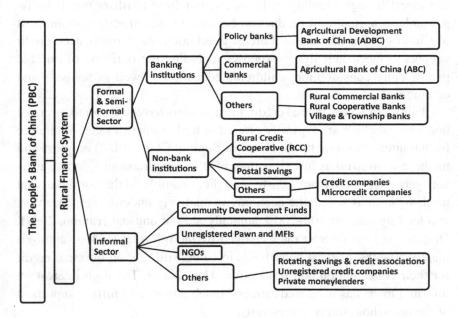

Figure 4.6: Rural Financial System in China

Sources: Feng *et al.* (2014), Li (2010), Zhang (2004).

---

[5]The rural reforms include the raise of state procurement price for major crops, the change from the collective system to the individual household-based-farming system and the greater role given to markets in guiding agriculture production (Lin, 1992).

the overall financial system in the country (Feng, He & Ljungwall, 2014; Ma, 2004; Zhang, 2004).

4.3.1 *Formal financial sector*

The formal financial sector in rural China is characterised as a "three-tier system", comprising a state-owned commercial bank (ABC), government policy-based bank (ADBC) and RCCs. Each of the three RFIs plays a unique role in providing lending support to the agricultural sector and rural households in China.

(1) The ABC

The ABC was founded in 1955 to provide credit support for RCCs. Since then, ABC has undergone several abolishments and re-establishments, mainly re-establishment to implement rural financing policies formulated by the PBC in 1979 and restructured into a commercial bank serving both rural and urban markets after 1994 (Gale & Callender, 2006; IFAD, 2001). The ABC is the largest commercial bank involved in agriculture. Loans from the ABC included specialised agricultural loans (such as comprehensive development and subsidiary businesses in grain, oil and cotton), conventional agricultural loans (such as farming, forestry, livestock, fisheries and the processing of agricultural products), loans for township and village enterprises (TVEs), loans for rural supply and marketing cooperatives (SMCs), and loans for basic rural facilities construction.

Between 1980 and 2001, the cumulative balance of agricultural loans issued by the ABC reached RMB9,449 billion, accounting for 66% of the ABC's total lending (Druschel, 2002; Ma, 2004; Zhang, 2004). However, the ratio of ABC's agricultural loans relative to its total loans steadily declined (Han, 2004). Before the 1990s, more than 98% of the total loans from the ABC were issued to support agricultural development. After the commercialisation reform from the mid-1990s, the ABC's financial resources are no longer restricted to agriculture and more resources have been allocated to rural infrastructure construction such as the rural electricity network, transport and communication. After the 1990s, the ABC gradually withdrew its branches from the countryside and shifted its business focus from agriculture to manufacture industries. Consequently, the share of agricultural lending by the ABC has decreased and the bank lost its dominant position in the rural financial system and market (Dong & Featherstone, 2006; Van Gemert, 2001).

At present, the ABC still provides financial services for agro-related business such as microfinance to farmer households, commodity circulation market construction loan, off-seasons fertilisers reserve loan and SME plant mortgage loan (ABC, 2015). However, agro-related financing is now only one of three types of financial services offered by the bank, with the other two being personal banking and corporate banking services.

(2) The ADBC

The ADBC was founded in 1994 in order to separate the policy-based banking business from the ABC's commercial services. The scope of the ADBC's credit business in the early days of its establishment included loans for the procurement and storage of grain, cotton, oil, sugar and meat; loans for the transfer, marketing and wholesale of grain and oil; loans for grain, cotton and oil processing enterprises; loans for poverty reduction and development, and loans for rural infrastructure construction (Druschel, 2002; He & Guo, 2004; Ma, 2004). However, in the late 1990s, the range of the ADBC's credit business shrank to the supply and management of funds for the procurement of grain, cotton and oil by the state-owned enterprises. The other policy banking businesses such as financing poverty-relief and comprehensive agricultural exploitation were handed over to the ABC (He & Guo, 2004; Ma, 2004).

Due to capital sources insufficiency, it was difficult for the ADBC to assume the heavy burden of China's policy finance (Zhang, 2004). Generally, the main source of the ADBC's capital should be the funds provided by the central government and loan repayment. However, owing to the imbalance between the government revenue and expenditure accumulated over years, the allocation of supplementary funds cannot be guaranteed on time. Instead, the ADBC raises its capital through issuing financial bonds to commercial banks and borrowing from the PBC, which subsequently increases the ADBC's cost of financing (He & Guo, 2004; Zhang, 2004). Over time, the ADBC's scope of business became narrower with only a single function since the bank only acted as a 'purchasing bank' to meet the financing needs of agricultural products procurement and stockpiling by the state-owned enterprises (He & Guo, 2004; Van Gemert, 2001; Zhang, 2004). In this way, ADBC had only limited role in ensuring an efficient supply of agricultural products because it had very limited engagement in issuing policy-related loans to support agricultural production (Van Gemert, 2001).

Nevertheless, at present ADBC has again broadened its services beyond financing the procurement of agricultural products, including loans for agricultural SMEs, agricultural infrastructure, integrated agricultural development and agricultural means of production (ADBC, 2015).

(3) RCCs

Established in the late 1950s, RCCs are financial cooperative organisations with rural labourers as shareholding members. RCCs operate at either the village level or township level: the township-level RCCs can run both savings and credit businesses but the village-level RCCs are only allowed to take in deposits from villagers, plus collecting loan applications and submitting them to township-level RCCs for approval. Since the start-up capital of RCCs comes from farmers (80% or more of RCCs' funding comes from farmers' savings deposits), RCCs have a close relationship with farmers and loans provided by RCCs principally target rural households (Druschel, 2002). Loans issued to rural households are mostly in the form of *microcredit*, giving key support to crop production, fish breeding, raising animals, as well as children's education and daily consumption (PBC, 2001; Zuo, 2001). Operating at county or township level, RCCs are the only formal financial institutions reaching the grassroots of rural society and play a decisive role in providing financial support for agriculture and rural economic development, since other financial institutions such as the ABC withdrew their financial services from rural areas to target more profitable operations in urban areas (Cheng, 2007; Van Empel & Smit, 2004; Zhang, 2004).

Despite the crucial roles played by RCCs in China's rural finance, many problems exist in the way of RCCs' unique roles in rural financing (Scott & Jun, 2006; Van Gemert, 2001). RCCs in China are hampered by ambiguous governance as RCCs are in fact established on the basis of government directives and therefore only 'cooperative' financial institutions in name. Before 1997, RCCs were managed by ABC as affiliates. After separating from ABC in 1997, RCCs began their own business under the direct supervision of the PBC. In addition, RCCs were still partly under the control of local governments, which assigned the supply of capital for agricultural production with little regard to RCCs' institutional sustainability (Dong & Featherstone, 2006; Van Gemert, 2001).

Such ambiguous governance is further complicated by the fact that the China Banking Regulatory Commission (CBRC) has begun to exert both quasi-managerial and supervisory influence on RCCs since 2003 (Scott & Druschel, 2004; Scott & Jun, 2006). RCCs in China are not 'cooperatives' in principle because they fail to meet the requirements of a 'cooperative' such as voluntary participation, democratic management, and mutual risks and benefits (Dong & Featherstone, 2006). Farmers in villages are only theoretical owners of RCCs because they joined RCCs under administrative pressure and have virtually no rights to participate in management and supervision of the operations of RCCs. In addition, the members' share capital is generally in deficit due to the operational losses by many RCCs (Guo & Lei, 2000). Without management rights and bonus incentives, the farmers would rather forego their small shares of capital and are unwilling to bear any responsibility for RCCs' poor performance (Wang, 2004).

In addition to the supervisory imperfection, the legal position of the RCCs in China's financial system is equivocal (Xuechun *et al.*, 2010). China has not enacted specific regulation on cooperative finance and therefore the legal position of the RCCs is defined by the Regulations for the Management of RCCs formulated by the PBC in 1997 (Dong & Featherstone, 2006; Wang, 2004). For daily business, RCCs' legal role is to provide financial services to farmers or rural households; but at the macrolevel RCCs play a dual role of acting as a quasi-policy financial institution to support agriculture and operating as commercial banks to generate profits to maintain their viability. The combination of cooperative, commercial and policy finance in one entity inevitably results in frequent confusion with regard to RCCs' operational roles and behaviours (Druschel, 2002; Wang, 2004). Furthermore, the professional quality of RCCs' staff as well as the management methods and basic facilities still lag far behind those of commercial banks, which makes RCCs less competitive compared to commercial banks (Park *et al.*, 2004).

Problems such as governance ambiguity and unclear legal directives have created disincentives for RCCs to operate effectively to achieve the goal of financial sustainability. In addition, political intervention in lending decisions by local authorities, usually motivated by intentions such as tax collection and employment maintenance, leads to non-recoverable loans made to poorly performing enterprises. This perpetuates weak incentives to implement commercially sustainable lending practices and fosters an unfavourable credit culture within RCCs (Scott & Druschel, 2004). As a result, many RCCs have incurred severe financial losses. At the end of 2000, the accumulative losses of RCCs throughout the country stood at RMB 108.3 billion, accounting for 10% of RCCs' total assets (Han, 2004; Ma, 2004). In spite of the positive response by the PBC to mitigate RCCs' debt burden by writing off bad loans through one-time capital injections, RCCs still have non-performing loans amounting to RMB514.7 billion at the end of 2002, comprising 37% of their total outstanding loans. Only after two forms of financial assistance taken by PBC in 2007 — RMB 168 billion debt-for-bonds swaps and RMB830 million in earmarked loans to assist in deposing bad assets and writing off historical losses — RCCs could enjoy a net profit of RMB23.3 billion and non-performing loan rate of just 5.6% in 2010 (Rehman *et al.*, 2015).

In summary, since the 1978 reform China has enjoyed a relatively stable rural formal financial system that is geared towards meeting the diversified financial needs in rural areas. Within the system, the three major financial institutions (i.e., the ABC, ADBC and RCCs) perform their own functions in regards to commercial, policy and cooperative finance (Van Gemert, 2001; Zhang, 2004). However, there are many criticisms targeted at the rural financing arrangements. China has a much shorter history of using modern financial instruments to support economic and social development compared to developed countries. In addition, the national development strategy implemented in China has long favoured urban areas and industry at the expense of the countryside and agriculture. The contribution of capital to the national economy by the agricultural and rural sectors has been far greater than the capital support received by these two sectors. The rural financing system has been mostly criticised for the functional defects in meeting the basic capital requirements by both the agricultural and rural sectors (Han, 2004; Ma, 2004; Zhang, 2004).

4.3.2 *Informal finance in rural China*

Informal finance refers to all transactions, loans and deposits that occur outside the regulation of a central monetary authority (Atieno, 2001). Informal credit in China includes loans with low interest rates or interest-free obtained from non-commercial sources such as friends, relatives and acquaintances, and loans with high interest rates from private lending and borrowing (PLB) organisations such as professional moneylenders, traders, pawnbrokers and usurers. In rural China, PLBs are the dominant source of informal finance (Cheng & Xu, 2004; Han, 2004).

Informal credit plays an important role in the rural sector in meeting the credit needs of the rural poor. The share of informal credit in the rural sector in developing countries ranges from 30% to more than 80% (Tilakaratna, 1996). In China, informal credit has become the main source of credit among the rural population, accounting for more than 70% of the farmers' total borrowing (Ma, 2004). Informal financing is popular in rural China because it possesses many advantages over formal financing.

(1) Personal relationships with clients

Generally, informal lenders would lend to persons whom they can keep in personal contact and who are part of their social network within which the contracts can be enforced. The close relationships with clients enable informal lenders to have adequate information about the borrowers such as family background and business situation. Such personal knowledge of the borrowers largely releases informal lenders from information constraints, such as the borrowers' creditworthiness, repayment capacity and willingness to repay (Atieno, 2001; Wenner & Proenza, 2000; Zeller & Sharma, 1998). Unlike formal lenders who establish stringent screening criteria such as the requirements of a cosigner and physical collateral to ensure repayment, informal lenders base their transactions on the confidence arising from their relationships with their clients and social sanctions within a community (Atieno, 2001; Qadir, 2005; Wenner & Proenza, 2000; Zeller & Sharma, 1998).

(2) Flexible lending schemes

Most services of informal finance are client-oriented. With intimate knowledge of the borrowers, informal lenders are able to offer flexible arrangements to adjust to different credit demands and changing economic circumstances of the borrowers without serious risk of loss (Atieno, 2001; Zeller & Sharma, 1998). Such flexibility is reflected in the loan amounts, loan repayment schedules and loan purposes. For example, the repayment structure of informal lending is closely related to local production cycles associated with the borrowers' occupations and informal loans can be renegotiated in view of both the lender and borrower respective circumstances (Zeller & Sharma, 1998). In contrast, the rigid lending policies set by formal lenders include prescribed minimum loan amounts, restrictions on credit for specific purposes and strict terms of repayment (Atieno, 2001).

(3) Rapid processing of loan applications

The informality of operations allows informal lenders to process loan applications promptly with little or no paperwork and disburse credit to the borrowers quickly compared to the time taken for technical process and lending procedures of formal lenders (Tilakaratna, 1996).

(4) Low transaction costs for the borrowers

Informal lenders reduce their borrowers' costs of borrowing to a minimum level by applying lending practices which reflect the needs and realities of the borrowers (Islam, 2007). First, they impose little or no costs on borrowers as direct financial charges except explicitly high interest rates. In addition, informal lenders offer a fast and responsive service so that accessibility costs due to delays in loan disbursements are minimised under informal lending (Klein *et al.*, 1999; Qadir, 2005). In contrast, the interest rate charged by formal credit is relatively low but does not cover all transaction costs incurred by the borrowers in securing formal loans, such as opportunity costs resulting from the loss in investment due to the delay in credit delivery, and time and travel costs incurred during the processing of the loan (Atieno, 2001; Islam, 2007).

In short, personal relationships, flexibility, rapidity and low transaction costs comprise the main strengths of informal finance. These superiorities have made informal finance either the exclusive or the preferred credit source in rural areas in China despite high interest rates (between 60% and 240% p.a. charged by PLBs in China) (Cheng & Xu, 2004; Yaron & Mundial, 1992).

However, informal credit also faces several constraints. Lenders' limited resources restrict the extent to which the informal sector can effectively and sustainably satisfy the credit needs of their borrowers (Atieno, 2001). Within informal sector in China the financial intermediation which provides a common clearing house for both borrowers and lenders does not exist. The informal lenders also seldom manage savings deposits, which in turn limit the accumulation and supply of credit (Zeller & Sharma, 1998; Zhang, 2004). The credit shortage within the informal sector is further worsened when natural disasters such as droughts and floods that affect both informal lenders and borrowers simultaneously in the agricultural sector (Zeller & Sharma, 1998). This is mainly because informal lenders are sporadically distributed and have not formed a network of branches across different provinces, which have crippled their ability to diversify risks. As a result, borrowings from informal lenders are usually in small amounts for short periods, which can neither stimulate significant business growth in the microenterprise sectors nor finance long-term investment in assets. Thus, informal finance is generally insufficient for development purposes because it is often for short-term purposes and rarely for capital build-up, usually for traditional rather than innovative activities and mostly for survival needs instead of developmental needs (Tilakaratna, 1996).

To date informal finance remains controversial in China's rural financial construction. On the one hand, there are opponents who traditionally regard informal finance as a violation of normal financial discipline in China despite its contribution to meeting farmers' urgent financial needs. The evidence supporting such argument is that the Chinese government never gives overt recognition to the legal existence of the informal sector and the development of informal credit is generally clandestine and out of the government's supervision (Jia, Heidhues & Zeller, 2007; Zhang, 2004). The opponents also suggest excluding informal credit from rural financial markets by improving the lending operations of formal financial institutions to provide more loans in favour of rural households, which is crucial in establishing a sound rural financial system and maintaining the sustainable development of China's rural economy.

On the other hand, the proponents of informal finance contend that the existence of informal credit in China reflects the imperfections of China's formal rural financing system, which is characterised as the inability to meet the diverse capital demands of the rural households. If no changes are made in the current situation, the persistence of informal credit will be both necessary and rational in view of the credit facilities provided to the farmers (Ayyagari, Demirgüç-Kunt & Maksimovic, 2010; IFAD, 2001).

4.4 Credit Market in Rural China

With a widening gap between rural and urban living standards and the threat of political instability in the countryside, the Chinese government carried out various agriculture-support policies focusing on farmer lending to solve *'three rural problems'*, namely raising rural incomes, improving agricultural production, and developing rural areas (Gale & Callender, 2006; Wu, 2011). To tackle these problems, the Chinese government carried out various agriculture-support policies focusing on farmer lending such as expanding credit access by the rural poor through targeted subsidised-loan programmes during 1986–2000 (Heilig *et al.*, 2006; Meng, 2013).

However, the credit gap still exists in rural China for two reasons. First, at the implementation level the subsidised-loans were not well managed and distributed. Most of the subsidised loans were allocated to the rich household, township enterprises or local government-support industrial projects instead of poor rural households. Second, the subsidised loans were financially unsustainable as indicated by low repayment rates (less than 50%) (Heilig *et al.*, 2006; Park & Ren, 2001).

4.4.1 *Demand for credit by rural households in China*

Credit is important for households engaged in agricultural production because such households need cash during the production cycle. Agriculture production cycle typically lasts for several months including preparation, cultivation and harvesting. During the production cycle cash revenue is seldom earned because cash remuneration is always received some time after the harvest. Hence, the poor farmers need credit to maintain their expenditure and consumption of basic necessities such as foods when there is a shortage of cash during production cycle or after a bad harvest (Diagne & Zeller, 2001; Feder *et al.*, 1990).

In general China's rural households seek credit for at least three purposes (Wang & Liu, 2005). First, they need to spend large sums of money to finance their production, mainly for purchasing production inputs including fertilisers, pesticides, seeds and livestock which they cannot afford without loans. Second, many farmers need capital to diversify their production and expand their business to improve their living conditions as income from agriculture production may be insufficient. Third, poor farmers require credit to support their daily consumption including housebuilding, weddings and funerals as well as expenses for healthcare and children's education that are generally costly in China.

Rural households in China are likely to borrow from different sources of credit for different purposes. There is a strong positive association between formal credit and production loans, and between informal credit and consumption loans (IFAD, 2001), as summarised in Table 4.3. For example, Feder *et al.* (1990) reported that rural households in Jilin Province used formal loans predominantly for the financing of agriculture

Table 4.3: **Major Credit Demand in Rural China**

Source of credit	Activities	Needs
Formal loans	Production	Fertiliser
		Other input for crop production
		Livestock
		Fixed capital
		Self-employment
Informal loans	Consumption	Daily expenses
		Weddings and funerals
		Schooling
		Healthcare
		Housing

Sources: IFAD (2001), Feder *et al.* (1990), Park *et al.* (2004), Chen (2004).

production, while on the contrary obtained informal loans primarily for construction and social expenditures (such as, weddings and funerals). Similarly, Chen (2004) reported that rural households in Sichuan Province borrowed from RCCs largely to support their agricultural production such as purchasing fertilisers and raising livestock (accounting for 52% of the total formal borrowing), while the households borrowed frequently from friends or relatives to supplement their consumption including house building, medical treatment and children's schooling.

It is worth noting that rural households at different wealth levels have different financing objectives and needs. The wealthier households are more likely to borrow for their small businesses and for housing, but less likely for consumption. On the contrary, the poorer households are more inclined to borrow to supplement their daily consumption, especially for medical treatment and children's education (Chen, 2004; IFAD, 2001).

However, the composition of the demand for credit may also change over time as it corresponds to the fast changing structure of economic production. The role of off-farm self-employment activities in China's rural economy tends to increase, while the share of income from traditional agriculture (cropping and livestock) has been declining (Mohapatra, Rozelle & Goodhue, 2007). This in turn affects the composition of demand for credit where a significant increase in credit demand for self-employment has been observed, while credit demand for traditional agriculture inputs such as fertilisers and livestock tends to decline except when large investments are made for economies of scale or growing new input-intensive crops. For example, from 1997 to 2000 the share of loans used for self-employed activities rose from 5.9% to 21.6% (Park *et al.*, 2004) and might increase further as access to credit is crucial to overcome the liquidity constraints faced by new and ongoing small business in rural China (Han & Hare, 2013).

4.4.2 *Supply of credit in rural China*

4.4.2.1 *The role of banks and its limitations*

Banks perceive high default risks in agricultural lending, particularly in lending to small farmers. Agricultural production is seasonal and subject to geographic and climatic conditions beyond farmers' control so that farmers' production and ability to repay the loans can be seriously influenced by natural factors. Lenders also face other specific challenges, such as covariant risks where many or all borrowers are affected simultaneously by market price fluctuations and changes in agricultural policies, which can affect farmers' revenues, bring uncertainty to their loan repayment and in turn severely worsen the quality of lenders' loan portfolios (Carter, 1988; Klein *et al.*, 1999). As a result, banks are frequently reluctant to grant loans to farmers due to high potential financial losses.

Secondly, banks are also unwilling to transact with rural households owing to the high costs incurred from small lending (IFAD, 2001; Islam, 2007; Okurut, Schoombee & Berg, 2005). Due to low population density, the provision of formal financial services to the scattered location of rural households can be costly. The long distances between the villages and underdeveloped rural transportation facilities in many rural areas also greatly raise the costs of loan appraisal, loan monitoring and enforcement of loan repayments. Besides, the banks must bear the fixed cost of loan officers only to cater to irregular intensity of the agricultural lending operations throughout the year (Klein *et al.*, 1999; Okurut *et al.*, 2005). During the periods of high seasonal credit demand, liquidity requirements increase the prices of loanable funds; in times of low demand, however, surplus liquidity has to be invested in low or non-earning assets, which again imposes opportunity costs on the lenders.

On the other hand, poor farmers are also discouraged from borrowing from banks because they often have to confront substantial transaction costs when dealing with banks (Okurut *et al.*, 2005). Other than loan interest, the borrowing costs of farmers in China consist of opportunity cost of time and money spent on travelling and loan applications, gifts and kickbacks to loan officers and membership fees (Cheng & Xu, 2004). Farmers have to visit the bank's branch office several times to conclude redundant loan application procedures which require a long time to process. Earnings foregone during the loan-processing time constitute the major cost encountered by the poor when borrowing from formal institutions (Tilakaratna, 1996). Farmers also have to bear high transportation costs especially when banks are not conveniently located (Klein *et al.*, 1999; Okurut *et al.*, 2005). It is also quite common for loan applicants to invite loan officers to banquets and/or give kickbacks directly to loan officers for loan approvals. In the case of RCCs, farmers have to pay membership fees (usually RMB50–RMB200) to RCCs before they can lodge their loan applications (Xuechun *et al.*, 2010). These non-interest costs can significantly increase the effective interest rates of formal borrowing given the small size of the loans borrowed by the farmers (Tilakaratna, 1996).

In addition to the high borrowing costs, the strict collateral requirement in traditional formal lending also prevents poor farmers from participating in the formal credit market. To address the problems of adverse selection and moral hazard arising from asymmetric information between banks and the borrowers, banks usually attach collateral requirements to loans. Collateral is used to assist in determining creditworthiness, as well as solve the incentive and enforcement problems (Klein *et al.*, 1999). Such collateral requirement becomes even more stringent when the borrower is resource-poor. Lenders always prefer land as form of collateral but farmers in China do not have the ownership of the land on which they farm because farmland is owned by villages and distributed on an egalitarian basis among village members. In some special cases, another acceptable form of collateral is a savings account of equal value to the loan principal, which is unlikely to be provided by poor farmers either. This lack of proper collateral makes formal credit inaccessible by China's poor farmers (Gale & Callender, 2006; Park *et al.*, 2004; Unger, 2002).

4.4.2.2 *Loan subsidy by the government*

Given the failure of formal financial institutions in serving the rural poor and the disadvantages of informal credit due to its exploitative interest rates, China's government has implemented a scheme of providing subsidised credit (poverty loan programme) to the rural poor during 1986–2000. The purpose of providing subsidised credit is to combat poverty by expanding the access to credit to the poor through the easing of interest rates. Providing subsidised loans to the poor is a widely adopted government intervention that many developing countries use to alleviate poverty (Park & Ren, 2001).[6]

---

[6]Besides the subsidised-loan programmes, there are other poverty alleviation programmes implemented in China, such as Food for Work, Agriculture Tax Reduction and Direct Subsidies to Farmers (Grants Programmes). For details see Heilig *et al.* (2006).

Since the launch of the subsidised-credit programme, the government of China has increasingly invested funds in this programme. The annual amount of subsidised-loans increased from RMB2.3 billion in 1986 to RMB8.7 billion in 1997 and the accumulative funding investment accumulated significantly to RMB48.3 billion at the end of 1997 (Rozelle Zhang & Huang, 2003). In addition, the Chinese government has officially designated 592 counties as 'national poor counties' from which the poor households were targeted by the subsidised-loans programmes (Meng, 2013). Most of these counties are concentrated in Heilongjiang, Gansu and Inner Mongolia in the north to Guangxi and Yunnan in the south (Heilig *et al.*, 2006; Rozelle *et al.*, 2003).

Studies show that the subsidised poverty loans in China generally has brought positive impact on the production and income of the borrowers to some degree (Rozelle *et al.*, 2003; Zhang, 1997). However, China's subsidised-credit programme has been heavily criticised for failing to reach the hard core poor (non-targeting issue) and for the high rates of default.[7]

(1) Non-targeting issue

Studies show that the benefit of the subsidised-loan programmes is predominantly enjoyed by the non-poor population and local enterprises. Rozelle *et al.* (2003) indicated that almost all subsidised loans (over 90%) in China in the early 1990s were invested in industrial production instead of agricultural production. Many of the loans did not benefit the poor households but were rather granted to TVEs or county-owned enterprises with the view of raising the revenue base for local governments. This policy failure in targeting the poor can be attributed to several reasons:

(a) The poverty alleviation strategy adopted by the Chinese government is essentially a trickle-down regional economic development strategy. The government carried out a poverty loan policy which expects to

---

[7]The problems of non-targeting and low repayment rates arising from subsidised-credit programmes also exist in other developing countries (see Adams, Graham & Van Pischke, 1984; Klein *et al.*, 1999).

realise income growth of poor households via regional economic development (Heilig *et al.*, 2006; Holcombe & Xu, 1996; IFAD, 2001). Hence, the poverty loan policy is the consequence of a compromise between economic considerations (promoting unity and integrity of the country) and political and moral pressures (reaching the poor). The conflict between the dual roles of the poverty loan programme, with the economic factors being important reason for the introduction of the policy, resulted in the poor targeting of the programme. The local governments who have the authority to select the projects to receive subsidised loans may favour diversion of funds to enterprises and investment in more promising areas rather than lending to the poor in order to generate revenues and boosting overall economic development (Park, Wang & Wu, 2002; Rozelle *et al.*, 2003).

(b) The government's involvement in subsidised loan allocation creates rent-seeking activities which in turn also reduces the targeting incidence of the programme. Rent-seeking arises when the benefits of subsidies primarily goes to those who can pay higher rents, which will certainly preclude most if not all poor households (Klein *et al.*, 1999). In this case the so-called 'iron law of interest rate restriction' is evident, in which the real poor in China have few chances to benefit from the subsidised loan policy despite the low subsidised interest rate (about 2.88%) (Gonzalez-Vega, 1984; Tsai, 2004; Wu, 1997). To tackle this issue, the government has to assume the responsibility to allocate the loans to the target groups. However, the direct involvement of the government in loan allocation, particularly in centrally-controlled planned economy, is confronted by other problems such as the discrete information and uncertainty about the risks posed by the loan applicants.

(c) Profit concerns prevent banks from delivering subsidised-loans to the poor. When implementing the subsidised-credit programmes, banks are required to perform two tasks[8]: (a) pursuing the goal of profit

---

[8]Prior to 1995, the subsidised loans were mainly disbursed by the ABC. Since 1995, the business of issuing poverty loans has been transferred to the ADBC as required by the central government. However, as the ADBC does not have branches in rural areas, it contracts all its credit business to the ABC and therefore the ABC is the actual executor of this programme.

maximisation as enterprises; and (b) execute government policy on delivering subsidised loans to the poor (IFAD, 2001; Rozelle *et al.*, 2003). However, the two objectives often conflict with each other, which is exacerbated by the asymmetric responsibility between the government and banks (Wu, 1997). The government intervenes in the allocation of subsidised loans and influences the selection of projects to receive the loans but leaving all the risks and losses resulting from such intervention to be borne by the banks and letting the wages and bonuses of bank staff closely related to the profits from lending (Holcombe & Xu, 1996; IFAD, 2001). The government does not offer any additional compensation to the banks to cover high costs and great risks of subsidised lending to the poor caused by the lack of collateral as well as to tackle the difficulties in repayment enforcement (Rozelle *et al.*, 2003; Wu, 1997). To reduce losses and risks incurred from providing subsidised loans, banks frequently either lend to the non-poor or TVEs who represent a higher repayment rate and less risk, or put off delivery of the loans to poor clients as a way of earning money from the time delay (Wu, 1997).

(d) The targeting problem is also associated with the difficulty in identifying the real poor. In the absence of reliable household income data, the only way to differentiate the poor from non-poor is principally the instinctive judgement of local officers who often have an obscure and varied understanding of the poverty line set by the government (Wu, 1997).

(2) High default rates

Studies suggest that the average timely loan repayment of China's subsidised-credit programmes are about 50% (Holcombe & Xu, 1996; IFAD, 2001; Park & Ren, 2001). The potential reasons leading to such high default rates include:

(a) There are too many welfare components involved in the poverty loan programmes, thereby the poor tend to treat the subsidised loans as government grants and are not obliged to repay (Park & Ren, 2001;

Wu, 2001). Such misconceptions among the poor lead to the high default rate in the repayment of subsidised loans.

(b) The defects inherent in the construct of poverty loan policy adopted by the Chinese government are likely to distort the behaviour of poor households towards the use of loans, which in turn reduces their ability and willingness to repay loans. For example, the policy stipulates that projects to be financed by the poverty loans should be selected by local governments. The poor households have limited or no voice in decision making in poverty loan utilisation. As a result, without proper monitoring and penalties the households may not use their loan-funded projects in a profitable way, thereby increasing the probability of default. Furthermore, the households can still evade the loan repayment in the case of the failure of loan-funded projects because they are not the main decision maker in the poverty loan utilisation (Park *et al.*, 2002; Wu, 1997).

(c) Households may not be able to repay the loans as the term of the loans might be shorter than the term needed for capital investment returns (IFAD, 2001).

(d) To maintain the operation of the subsidised-loan programmes in some poorer areas, the government has to provide funding support to absorb all or part of the risks in subsidised lending. This unexpectedly promotes the banks' inertia in collecting loans in arrears and further increases loan defaults (Holcombe & Xu, 1996; Wu, 1997).

It can be concluded that the subsidised-credit policy in China is a double-edged sword that has placed the Chinese government in a dilemma. On the one hand, the dual functions of the policy — economic development and social justice — make it difficult to deliver the loans to the real poor. On the other hand, once the poor are targeted as intended by the policy, the programme implementers (including local governments and banks) in China face the problem of high default rates. The high delinquency will substantially impair the financial viability of the programmes, which in turn will reduce the outreach of the programmes to the poor (Holcombe & Xu, 1996; Wu, 1997).

4.4.3 *Gap between credit demand and credit supply in rural China*

RFIs in China tend to restrict farmers' access to formal credit to protect their financial viability due to the high risks and costs in small farmer lending. Failing to access formal credit and microcredit, the majority of poor farmers have to fall back on informal sources to meet their credit needs. The Chinese farmers obtain credit for consumption from their friends and relatives at free of charge and borrow from PLBs with high interest rates for their needs for production (Wang & Liu, 2005). However, despite the strengths of informal credit such as close personal relationships, flexibility and speed, informal lenders are generally ill-equipped to finance substantial, long-term investments since they depend on personal funds (Zeller & Sharma, 1998). The limited credit supply by informal lenders then leads to either severe credit rationing or exploitive interest rates for some borrowers. In short, the access to credit for poor farmers in the formal financial institutions is constrained by the lending terms and conditions, while the access to informal lenders is constrained by limited financial resources (Atieno, 2001). As a result, there is an excess demand for rural credit, leading to the emergence of a credit gap.

The credit gap is further exacerbated by other problems faced by RFIs. First, there is ambiguity of which RFI(s) supposedly provide financial services to the farmers. Although ABC and ADBC serve the rural areas, they do not issue loans to farmers in general because they mainly focus on agricultural product processing companies and large-scale agricultural development projects run by the state government (Ma, 2004; Zhang, 2004). As a result, the RCCs are the only RFI penetrating the grassroots of rural society with the provision of financial services (Van Gemert, 2001). However, there were only about 33,000 RCCs across the country in the early of 2010s, down from 50,000 in the late of 1950s, which credit supply is insufficient to meet the overall credit demand of the enormous number of rural households in China (Zhang & Loubere, 2015).

Second, there has been increasing financial losses of RFIs resulting from the capped lending rates set by the PBC, which have further crippled the RFIs' credit supply. The low lending rates do not generate sufficient revenues for RFIs to make a profit given the high transaction and operational costs incurred in lending to farmers. In the case of RCCs, the maximum lending rate charged is around 8%, with a little flexibility to charge higher lending rates in different areas (Cheng & Xu, 2004). To be profitable, the minimum lending rate for RCCs in major agricultural areas is estimated at 11.5% p.a. and the minimum lending rate in the poor and remote areas at 16% p.a. (Cheng & Xu, 2004).

In addition, unclear governance and inefficient management system have caused further deterioration in RCCs' financial bases and many poorly performing branches had to be closed down (Wang & Liu, 2005). The RFIs in China are part of the national banking system, in which a large proportion of lending (about 42% of total loans) is motivated by government policy objectives (Park & Ren, 2001). This thus leaves less funds for RFIs to undertake commercial lending.

Finally, large amounts of rural funds have flowed from rural to urban areas, driving a growing wedge between the demand for and supply of agricultural credit in China (Cheng & Xu, 2004). The main outflow channels are postal savings and commercial banks. Postal savings take in deposits but do not advance credit to rural households because the deposits absorbed by the postal savings are all redeposited into the PBC. In addition, commercial banks such as the ABC have taken up large amounts of deposits from rural areas but seldom issue loans to the rural households. In particular, after the ABC removed most of its branches from the countryside in the 1990s, fund outflows from rural areas to cities channelled through banks became greater. RCCs also channel funds from rural areas by purchasing bank bonds, issuing loans to urban clients and lending funds to other urban financial institutions (Wang & Liu, 2005). Furthermore, the government control over financial markets has impeded the establishment of new types of RFIs and such control is stricter in rural areas compared with the urban areas. For example, the flow of funds from rural to urban areas is also accelerated when the government gives consent for the establishment of non-governmental banks in the cities but not in the countryside (Ma, 2004).

4.5 The Rise of Microcredit Services in Rural China

The failure of subsidised-credit programmes to efficiently deliver rural credit to poor farmers led to the introduction of microcredit programmes by the Chinese government in 1994, with an aim to achieve poverty alleviation in a financially sustainable manner (Park *et al.*, 2004).

Since then, the development of China's microcredit programme has been going through three stages/phases, each carried out by different organisations (as fund providers) (Li, 2010). The first phase (1994–1996) was an experimental phase intended to explore the feasibility, operating capabilities and policy implications of microcredit in China, during which the microcredit programmes were mainly supported by international donations through the operation of NGOs (Druschel, 2002; Du, 2004, 2005). The second phase (1996–2000) was an expansion phase aimed at poverty alleviation, during which more government agencies such as Poverty Alleviation Offices (PAOs) and financial institutions (the agricultural banks) were involved in the implementation of microcredit besides NGOs (Park *et al.*, 2004; Sun, 2003). The third phase began from 2000 to present with the purpose of expanding credit access in rural areas and characterised by the involvement of formal RFIs (i.e., RCCs) in microcredit implementation. Despite the different types of microcredit programmes operating in different phases, the overwhelming majority of China's microcredit programmes have adopted the *Grameen Bank* model characterised by collateral free, targeting the poor and joint liability (Park & Ren, 2001; Sun, 2003).

4.5.1 *The Experimental stage from 1994 to 1996*

The early microcredit programmes from 1994 to 1996 were experimental projects operated by NGOs or quasi-official institutions in collaboration with international organisations.[9] These pilot practices aimed to investigate the feasibility of *Grameen Bank* methodology, operating modes and policy propositions of microcredit in China, as well as its relevance to poverty alleviation. The outstanding characteristic of this stage is that most projects relied on international donations and soft loans and

---

[9]These international organisations include the World Bank, United Nations Development Programmes (UNDP), Australian Agency for International Development (AusAID), United Nations Children's Fund (UNICEF), United Nations Population Fund (UNFPA), International Fund for Agricultural Development (IFAD), World Food Programme (WFP) and Canadian International Development Agency (CIDA).

scarcely at all on government capital (Druschel, 2002; Du, 2004, 2005; Wu, 2001).

The experimental projects were carried out by two types of institutions. The first type consists of specialised institutions (offices) established to manage projects funded by foreign aid including UNDP, World Bank, UNICEF, AusAID and CIDA, and implement bilateral or multilateral projects in conformity to donors' requirements (Du, 2004). The other institutions are NGOs set up to carry out poverty alleviation. Projects operating in this form of organisational structure included Hong Kong Leshi Association's projects and Funding the Poor Cooperative (FPC) projects which were initiated by the Chinese Academy of Social Sciences (CASS) and supported by the Ford Foundation and *Grameen Trust* (Du, 2004). The experimental microcredit programmes funds stood at RMB90 million at the end of 1996 (Du, 2004).

Previous studies suggest that early NGO microcredit programmes in China performed successfully in three areas: targeting the poor (including poor women), financial sustainability and positive impact on the poor. The NGO programmes effectively targeted poor farmers and poor women by charging a moderate interest rate while also achieved both operational sustainability and financial self-sufficiency (average financial self-sufficiency rate of 95%) (Park & Ren, 2001). The excellence performance of the NGO programmes were also marked by low operating costs, perfect loan repayment (nearly 100%) and a rise in income of the programme participants (Park & Ren, 2001; Wu, 2001).

However, the scale of NGO-led microcredit programmes has significantly diminished since the late 1990s and most programmes failed to institutionalise commercial banking practices that are requisite to maintain sustainable growth (Park *et al.*, 2004). A critical reason for their failure was that the NGOs in China have no legal status to provide any type of financial service and the regulatory restrictions in China have prohibited NGOs from mobilising their own deposits, which has severely reduced the possibilities for expansion (Druschel, 2002; Du, 2005; IFAD, 2001; Park *et al.*, 2004).[10] The ambiguity and the lack of a clear and legal

---

[10] When implementing microcredit programmes, the local governments and donors have to negotiate a temporary legal status for NGOs. The PBC has adopted a compromise method

financial role for the NGO microfinance programmes have undermined the development of China's microfinance to some extent (Lau, 2008).

In addition, poor reporting and information systems and the outdated management practice of many NGO programmes have also impaired their vitality. The majority of the experimental programmes carried out by NGOs did not have sound accounting and financial reporting systems (Du, 2004; Wu, 2001). Consequently, the NGOs had little information about their programmes' performance because they did not have consolidated profit and loss statements or comprehensive loan quality and business progress reports. Moreover, the NGO staffs usually regarded the programmes as development projects or experiments and seldom had personal stakes in the programmes' commercial viability or growth. As a consequence, none of the NGO programmes has institutional potential for widespread expansion and outreach (Du, 2004; Park *et al.*, 2004).

4.5.2 *The expansion stage from 1996 to 2000*

Encouraged by the successful performance of the NGO microcredit programmes in achieving 'win–win' goals (i.e., helping the poor households and maintaining financial sustainability), in 1997 the Chinese government decided to lead rather than follow the microfinance movement by employing the *Grameen Bank* model to disburse loans for its subsidised-loan programme for poverty alleviation (Park & Ren, 2001; Park *et al.*, 2004; Sun, 2003). In October 1998, the Third Plenum of the 15th Central Committee of the Chinese Communist Party passed the *'Resolution of the Central Committee of the Chinese Communist Party on some major problems of agriculture and rural work'*, which proposed that an effective methods of delivering funds to households for poverty reduction, such as microfinance, should be implemented (Du, 2004; Sun, 2003). This was the first confirmation of microfinance as an effective anti-poverty instrument by the central government. In the subsequent working conferences held in 1999 and 2000, the government reiterated the significance of microfinance

---

with regard to the important role played by NGOs in microfinance and their legal limitations, which silently permits the NGOs to provide microcredit for poverty alleviation (Du, 2005).

in combating poverty and emphasised that microfinance programmes should be actively and steadily developed (Du, 2004; Park *et al.*, 2004).

As a result of the policy encouragement, government agencies (e.g., PAOs) and financial institutions (the ABC) began carrying out poverty-focused microcredit programmes on a large scale between 1996 and 2000, in addition to the microcredit programmes led by NGOs (Druschel, 2002). The main funding sources of government-led microcredit programmes were national fiscal funds and subsidised loans from the poverty allevia-tion funds. The main characteristic of the expansion stage was the active involvement of the government with a supply of financial, manpower and organisational resources to ensure the goal of poverty alleviation was achieved (Du, 2004, 2005; IFAD, 2001; Wu, 2001). Following this, prac-titioners began highlighting the necessity of developing China's microfi-nance practice in accordance with international best practice standards (Du, 2004, 2005; Wu, 2001).

The government microfinance programmes were developed to cover 605 counties in 22 provinces nationwide as of August 1998, and issued loans amounting to RMB600 million. The balance of the loans advanced by the government microcredit programmes was then raised to RMB24 billion at the end of 2001 and an outstanding total of 17.2 million impov-erished rural households had been targeted (IFAD, 2001; Park & Ren, 2001; Park *et al.*, 2004).

The rapid expansion of the government-led microcredit programmes almost immediately dwarfed the NGO-led programmes (Park *et al.*, 2004). However, the government-led programmes have been frequently criticised for not targeting the poor effectively and achieving low repay-ment rates (Druschel, 2002; Wu, 2001). The timely repayment rate of microcredit loans from the surveyed government programme was only 64%, much lower than the NGO programmes (98%). Furthermore, while the rich were previously excluded from participating in the NGO pro-grammes, they were more likely to take part in the government pro-gramme mainly due to the higher rents associated with lower interest rates (Park & Ren, 2001).

Hence, in terms of targeting the poor and repayment performance, the government microcredit programmes differed little from the unsuccessful subsidised-credit programmes which they attempted to replace. The failure of the government microcredit programmes resulted both from the rapid expansion without proper preparation and from the inherent incentive conflicts when local governments intervene in the programmes (a similar situation to the subsidised-loan programme) (Du, 2004; Park *et al.*, 2004). In general, there are three problems associated with the implementation of government-run programmes including tight budget and staff constraints, non-professionalisation of government staff in operating credit activities, and frequently, diversion of programme funding by the local governments for purposes other than poverty reduction such as for supporting revenue-generating businesses and/or local industrial development (Zuo, 2001).

The performance of the microcredit programmes administered by government agencies in China is also very disappointing when compared to those in other developing countries such as Indonesia (Park & Ren, 2001).[11] . Druschel (2002) stresses that the monitoring of project funding usage must be strengthened to ensure that the funds are properly invested in microfinance projects. In addition, for the sake of sustainable development some reforms including the provision of strong managerial incentives, fostering professionalism among the programme staff and establishing independent financial accounting systems must be carried out (Du, 2004; Park *et al.*, 2004).

4.5.3 *Year 2000 onwards*

From the end of 2000, formal RFIs such as RCCs gradually became involved in China's microcredit programme to facilitate credit access in rural areas as required by the PBC. In December 2001, the PBC published an '*Opinion on directing the management of microfinance by RCCs to rural households*' that mandated microcredit programmes to be fully implemented by RCCs to solve the problem of 'loan difficulties for rural households' (Du, 2004, 2005). The RCCs' microcredit programme was not solely the means of alleviating poverty but rather a method of increasing

---

[11]The bank-supervised microfinance programme in Indonesia which utilises the village governance structure is a successful example of a government programme in contrast with China's government programme (Llanto & Fukui, 2006).

credit supply in rural China (Druschel, 2002). With the on-lending loans from the PBC as their main funding source, RCCs launched the microcredit programmes on a national scale by the end of 2002 and became the main force in popularising and formalising China's microcredit programmes with their extensive network penetrating the grassroots level (Du, 2004, 2005; Sun, 2003). In 2002 the amount of microcredit loans issued to rural households by RCCs nationwide totalled RMB96.7 billion and around 60 million rural households had been the microcredit recipients. The scale of RCCs' microcredit programme has far surpassed those of both the NGO and government programmes (Druschel, 2002; Du, 2004).

The microcredit loans from RCCs are provided to the rural households who are engaged in land farming and other related business in the agricultural sector. Accordingly, the usage of microcredit includes agricultural production, purchase of small farming machinery, services before, during and after agricultural production, and daily expenditure such as housing, medical services, education and consumption. Moreover, the credit lines of RCCs' microcredit are set by the Rural Credit Unions at county or city level according to the local economic situation, the farmers' income levels and the availability of RCCs' funds, which is finally approved by the PBCs (PBC, 2001).

Compared to the microcredit programmes operated by the NGOs and government agencies, the lending scheme adopted by RCCs' microcredit programme is much more flexible, reflecting the desire of satisfying different credit demands among the rural population. For example, a notable shift in the RCCs' microcredit programme is placing a greater emphasis on individual borrower accountability for loan repayment and less reliance on group-liability (Du, 2004; Sun, 2003; Wu, 2001). Accordingly, RCCs' microcredit programme has two types of loan products including the individual microloan and the group-liability loan for rural households. Individual microloans are issued to individual farmers or households according to their credit limits, which are established by RCCs based on an assessment of the farmers' creditworthiness, i.e., the credit ratings of farmers. The group-liability loan targets clients who have credit needs exceeding their individual credit limits but lack sufficient collateral. Both types of loan products do not require physical collateral provision, except potential social collateral used in the group-liability loan product (Du, 2004; Situ, 2003; Sun, 2003). In addition, while the NGO and government programmes have imposed compulsory savings on the borrowers to be used as a group fund replacing mortgages and guarantees, RCCs' micro-credit programmes encourage rural households to save without linking it to the loans offer. These features of RCCs' microcredit made the access to credit by rural households, especially the poor, much easier (Du, 2004; Wu, 2001).

During this last phase, RCCs as major RFIs serving the rural popula-tion with an extensive network in rural areas have quickly expanded their microcredit activities and took the leading role in popularising and formalising microcredit in China (Du, 2004, 2005). In addition, the PBC promulgated Guidance of Management of RCC's Microcredit Loans in 2001 and Notice on Improvement in Granting Microfinance Loans and Serving Peasants in 2004, which further strengthened the management, systematisation and support of RCC's microcredit programme (Du, 2004, 2005).

The model of RCC microcredit has some advantages over the NGO and government models in terms of financial sustainability and pro-gramme replicability (Zuo, 2001). First, the operational cost of the RCCs' microcredit programme is low since it makes use of existing RCC service outlets and thus reduces the marginal costs for carrying out microcredit programme. Second, unlike the other two types of microcredit pro-grammes which rely heavily on external or government funding, RCCs can mobilise their own programme funds via their saving facility. The low operational costs, combined with the strong capacity to mobilise funds for expansion, leads to the sustainable development of RCCs' pro-grammes. Third, the RCC model can be easily replicated owing to the well-established network of the existing RCC branches throughout the country. Fourth, RCCs' microcredit programmes are supposed to be less financially risky because as a formal financial institution, RCCs are strictly regulated and supervised by financial authorities such as the PBC. This further enables RCCs to easily acquire government support for their programme replication, which is an important condition to operate any programme in China (Wu, 2001; Zuo, 2001). Table 4.4 provides a

Table 4.4: Provision of Microcredit Programmes in China

Characteristics	NGOs	Government	RCCs
Starting time (year)	1994	1997	2000
Loan size (RMB)	400–1,000	1,000–2,000	1,000–20,000
Loan terms	3–12 months	1 year	Ranging from few months to 1 or 2 years
Repayment frequency	1–4 weeks	1–4 weeks	Single repayment at maturity
Lending methods	5-member groups with group funds as collateral	5-member groups with group funds as collateral in rural areas; physical collateral required in urban areas	Individuals; joint-liability groups; no physical collateral required
Savings	Compulsory on members	Compulsory on members	Voluntary
Targeted borrowers	Poor households	Poor households	All households in rural areas
Interest rates	Between 6 and 20% p.a.	Between 2.88 and 7.2% p.a.	Based on bank rates (6 and 7% p.a.)

Source: Li (2010).

comparison of the three types of microcredit programmes implemented in China.

With the implementation of microcredit, China has boosted lending to farmers in recent years. Under the agricultural lending support from the PBC as the main funding source, RCCs have substantially developed their microcredit programmes and evolved as the largest microcredit providers serving the grassroots level in rural China (Sun, 2003). The RCCs' total balance of loans was RMB4.8 billion in 1979, which substantially increased to RMB1,048.9 billion in 2000 and RMB5,300 billion in 2012 (Lucock, 2014). By the end of 2005 there were over 40,000 RCCs nation-wide, 90% of which had been involved in offering microcredit service to 71.3 million rural households, equivalent to 32.31% of the total rural population. In early 2010, the number of RCCs shrank to around 33,000 due to closures but the RCCs' credit had been accessed by 82.42 million rural households, equivalent to 33.5% of 240 million rural households (Han, 2004; Lucock, 2014; Zhang & Loubere, 2015). In the agricultural provinces such as Hubei, Hunan and Sichuan, more than 50% of rural households received loans, and more than 95% of these loans were provided by RCCs in the form of microcredit. Moreover, RCCs' microcredit had achieved a timely repayment rate of 81%, creating a foundation for realising a sound cycle of economic activities (Han, 2004).

Despite the leading role played by RCCs in China's microcredit programmes, RCCs still face many constraints that have impeded the development of their microcredit programmes to a large extent. The most prominent problem is that the interest rates have been regulated and set at artificially low levels by the PBC. The RCCs' interest rates in micro lending can only float within a range around the PBC base interest rate (usually between 0.9 and 2.2 times around the base interest rate). Despite the good intention of ensuring affordable rates for the rural poor, the interest rate ceilings are far from sufficient to cover the high transaction costs arising from lending to the poor (Cheng & Xu, 2004; Du, 2005; Park *et al.*, 2004).

The maximum lending rate charged by RCCs is 7.97% p.a., while Cheng & Xu (2004) suggested that RCCs should at least charge a rate of 15% p.a. to sustain a viable development and in fact the poor farmers in China are able to pay higher rate of interests to access scarce credit. However, the government is reluctant to charge beyond a subsidised rate of interest to the poor borrowers (Holcombe & Xu, 1996). Many RCCs have suffered considerable financial losses due to the interest rate ceiling, resulting in either a decline in credit supply or unwillingness to lend (Cheng & Xu, 2004; Park *et al.*, 2004). Druschel (2002) argues that the elimination of the interest rate ceiling on microcredit would be crucial for the sustainable development of microcredit in China, and market-enforced interest rates should be adopted by China's financial system.

In addition to the interest rate ceiling, weak governance and ambiguous ownership have severely constrained RCCs' ability to expand their microcredit programmes. The imperfection supervision have led to low incentives to implement commercially sustainable lending practices and have fostered a weak credit culture within the RCCs (Park *et al.*, 2004; Scott & Druschel, 2004). In addition, with the lack of farmers' participation, there are no owners with the ability and appropriate incentives to maintain the RCCs' capital stock and accumulation. Instead, managers appointed by the PBC respond to contractual incentives which stress high rates of repayment, deposit mobilisation and profitability. However, the poor governance system, along with inefficient motivations, can easily induce deceptive strategies such as rolling over bad debts, which on paper satisfy the managers' short-term objectives while undermining RCCs' financial viability (Park *et al.*, 2004; Scott & Druschel, 2004). Moreover, limited innovations in financial products and lack of experience and expertise in commercial financial management practices have hindered the expansion of RCCs' microcredit programmes (Dyar *et al.*, 2006; Park *et al.*, 2004).

4.5.4 *Challenges ahead*

In summary, given the relatively short history of microcredit in China compared to other developing countries such as Bangladesh, Indonesia, and India, microcredit in China has developed relatively quickly since its initiation in 1994. The expansion of microcredit programmes in China is attributed to the positive attitude towards and active participation in microcredit programmes by the government (Du, 2004; Park & Ren, 2001; Zuo, 2001). The government has fully recognised the link between microcredit and poverty alleviation and endorsed it as an important part of China's long-standing development strategy. Moreover, China's microcredit programme has evolved from an anti-poverty instrument that only targets the rural poor (such as the NGO-led programmes) to a popular rural financial programme such as RCCs to facilitate credit accessibility to the rural population (Druschel, 2002; Du, 2004).

However, some defects have been exposed during the course of development, which have held back further development of China's microcredit considerably. As far as NGO microcredit programmes are concerned, not being legally recognised as financial institutions has severely limited NGOs and quasi-official organisations in developing microcredit (Druschel, 2002; Lau, 2008; Park *et al.*, 2004). Although the government-led programmes contributed significantly to large-scale aid to the poor, these programmes only aimed at assisting the government's poverty reduction initiatives without a long-term goal of continuing development (Du, 2004; Park & Ren, 2001; Wu, 2001). Finally, the development of RCCs' microcredit programme has been hampered by the capped interest rates, as well as incentive problems and managerial authority limits, which have largely discouraged RCC managers from fostering the necessary motivations to perform profitably with microcredit design features (Cheng & Xu, 2004; Druschel, 2002). In other words, the stagnation of China's microcredit programmes is mainly a consequence of an unfavourable legal and regulatory environment, and therefore microcredit cannot be fully extended without some critical reforms (Park *et al.*, 2004).

4.6 Conclusions and Implications

China recorded outstanding economic growth after the economic reform towards a market economy in 1978. However, the Chinese economy shows a dual urban–rural economic structure where the rural areas develop slower than urban areas. The imbalanced growth can be attributed to the declining role of the agriculture sector and limited financial access for rural households in general and agriculture activities in particular. The rural households in China are mostly characterised by small-scale farmers who are not entitled to the land on which they farm. The absence of land ownership and the risky nature of agriculture business have constrained rural farmers from acquiring formal financial support, especially formal credit requiring collateral, and forced them to resort to informal borrowings that charge exorbitant interest rates.

During 1986–2000, the Chinese government carried out various agriculture-support policies focusing on the expansion of credit access for farmers and rural poor population through targeted subsidised-loan programmes. However, the implementation of the subsidised loans were poorly managed and distributed. Most of the subsidised loans were allocated to the rich household, township enterprises or local government-support industrial projects instead of poor rural households and the subsidised loans were financially unsustainable due to low repayment rates (less than 50%) especially in the rural poor population (see Heilig *et al.*, 2006; Park & Ren, 2001). Hence, despite the success of subsidised loans in promoting overall regional economic development, the credit gap still exists in rural China.

In the mid-1990s the government of China launched microcredit programmes aimed to ameliorate rural poverty in a financially sustainable way. During the experimental stage (1994–1996) the microcredit programme carried out by NGOs or quasi-official institutions in collaboration with international organisations successfully targeted the poor and achieved financial sustainability. However, the weak legal status of NGOs as a financial institution, weak accounting system and the perception of microcredit programmes as experimental projects have restricted fund mobilisation and service expansion. Government agencies and policy banks then led the expansion stage (1996–2000) with the provision of microcredit on a large scale. However, the government-led programmes failed to target the poor and to achieve high repayment rates due to tight budget, staffs incapability and diversion of programme funding by the local governments for purposes other than poverty reduction (see Park *et al.*, 2004; Zuo, 2001). From year 2000 onwards, the microcredit provision in rural areas has been dominated by RCCs. Characterised by flexible lending scheme, RCCs' microcredit has expanded the financial access to farmers and at the same time achieved high timely repayment rate. However, the RCCs microcredit's further expansions are still constrained by the interest rates cap placed by PBC and lack of incentive system that can motivate the managers to perform the microcredit services profitably (see Cheng & Xu, 2004; Scott & Druschel, 2004).

The discussions in this chapter highlight some policy implications with regard to the rural financial system and especially rural microcredit programmes in China. As a bottom line, an integrated approach to reform the Chinese rural financial system is crucial to ensure well-functioning rural financial markets which in turn will improve financial services in rural areas. To achieve this goal, substantial reforms are required in both formal and informal rural financial sectors, at institutional as well as operational levels.

Within the formal rural financial sector, a clear demarcation of the functions between commercial and policy banking is imperative. In particular, the policy financial business such as agricultural development lending carried out by the ABC or RCCs should be shifted to the policy bank (i.e., ADBC), while on the opposite the commercial loans operated by the ADBC should be devolved to the ABC or RCCs. Clarity regarding main responsibilities in rural financing will allow those RFIs to better meet the financial demands of the rural population.

RCCs, currently the main formal microcredit provider in rural China, exhibit ambiguous ownership and managerial supervision. Hence, restructuring RCCs into rural commercial banks with a clear property rights system (shareholding system) can be considered but with caution. The demand for rural financial services varies from province to province because the regional economic development in China is uneven. In remote and impoverished areas, farmers usually require credit in small amounts to maintain simple production and do not have the ability to bear the risks arising from the commercialised operation of the RCCs. Therefore, farmers in these areas need credit cooperatives that offer mutual aid rather than profit-oriented commercial banks. The transformation of RCCs into commercial banks or the overemphasis on pursuing profit will also undermine their microfinance business. Therefore, reform of RCCs should be adapted to local economic circumstances and the actual funding requirements of farmers and rural enterprises.

At the operational level, policy reforms are also required to allow the existing formal RFIs to expand their credit outreach but at the same time increase their sustainability. First, legislation reforms on secured-transactions in rural financial markets should be accelerated, especially regarding collateral. Farmland in China is owned by collectives rather than individuals and thus farmers lack proper collateral for borrowing. Hence, the reforms should highlight the legally acceptable forms of collateral, for example, the use of contractual rights on farmland as collateral by farmers when applying for formal loans. Correspondingly, the reforms of the regulatory and legal system of rural land management must be promoted to increase land tenure security for farmers and formalise land transactions including transfer, rental and leasing. This will provide lenders with formal procedures for claims against property and enforcement of financial contracts, and consequently, increase lenders' willingness to transact with rural people.

Second, new credit policy is required to allow the existing RFIs to provide unsecured loans to potentially productive activities. To minimise the operational risks, group lending methods should be more popularised among RFIs in their unsecured transactions. Group lending is efficient in reducing the high overhead costs associated with small lending (see for example, Besley & Coate, 1995; Hermes, Lensink & Mehrteab, 2005). It also promotes the building-up of good credit culture and helps achieve acceptable loan repayment performance.

Third, agricultural insurance innovations should be promoted in rural areas and among RFIs. Agricultural insurance such as crop insurance provides farmers with a mean of risk management in their production and helps them stabilise their household incomes. On the one hand, it can motivate farmers to demand more capital for expansion of production. On the other hand, it increases RFIs' willingness to lend to farmers because it protects farmers from production losses in case of bad harvests. However, the implementation of conventional crop insurances may be difficult since China's agriculture is characterised by small-scale farming operations which take place in different climatic regions. Alternative insurance instruments, such as index-based weather insurance (IWI) (see Skees, 2008, 2011), can be introduced and popularised. The appealing features of IWI includes simpler information requirements, low administrative costs and flexible contracts tailored to small or microsize business and to farmers' individual weather needs (Turvey, Kong & Belltawn, 2009).

Fourth, microcredit providers should be given freedom in setting microlending rates in accordance with their own business objectives (e.g., reducing poverty or increasing credit supply) and financial performance. For example, the case of *Grameen Bank* in Bangladesh and *Bank Rakyat Indonesia* show that MFIs that set the interest rates based on their own institutional factors and market characteristics are likely to realise both (financial) sustainability and high growth in programme outreach (see Fernando, 2006; Helms & Reille, 2004).

Finally, preferential tax policies (for example, reduction of income tax) could be adopted to decrease the operating costs of microfinance businesses, and hence, enhance the enthusiasm of MFIs in providing microfinance services.

For RCCs in particular, the following reforms at operational level can be considered:

(1) Further simplify lending procedures for their microloan products including documentation requirements and loan-processing time as well as more flexible loan terms and conditions to better suit the diverse needs of the local rural households;

(2) Enhance promotion for its microcredit programme and make poor rural households fully aware of its features (collateral free, flexible terms, etc.) through village meetings (or social gatherings) and mass media such as radio and local newspaper;

(3) Adopt a combination of individual and group lending approaches in its microcredit programme where group loan can be offered to higher risk households (either poor or with blemished credit history). The mixed lending approach would help RCCs expand its microcredit outreach especially to the poor population and at the same time overcome lending security problems created by information asymmetry and control for default risk in the absence of collateral; and

(4) Play a more active role in increasing borrowers' repayment capacity and improving the efficiency of loan use, for example, by providing assistance in loan-supported projects, agricultural technical extension, off-farm business introduction and training in cash flow and risk management.

The rural finance reforms should also address the informal sector. The government should consider to legally permit non-financial institutions (NFIs) including NGOs to provide microcredit services. A formal status will enable NFIs to raise funds for their microfinance businesses from multiple sources such as the public deposits and financing support from the PBC. This will in turn enable NFIs to expand their microfinance services' outreach and achieve sustainable development. The sustainability of NGOs' microfinance programmes may play important parts in realising nationwide poverty reduction because most of the NGO-led microfinance programmes in China concentrates explicitly on poverty alleviation (see Du, 2005; Park *et al.*, 2004).

The reform on formal RFIs and the legalisation of NGOs as a financial service provider, however, will not eliminate the informal financial sector in rural China. Demand for informal microcredit comes from households who fail to obtain financial support through formal channels (including RCCs' microcredit programme) as well as from those who may be able to obtain formal credit but choose to borrow from informal lenders due to the potential merits of informal lenders (i.e., simple loan application and more flexible lending schemes) (see Sagrario Floro & Ray, 1997; Tsai, 2004; Zhang & Fang, 2005). Rather than trying to eliminate informal finance, it would be more appropriate for the government to reinforce the linkages between the formal and informal rural financial sectors in China so that one sector can overcome its own weaknesses by drawing from the other's strengths. For example, banks can make use of the outreach and local knowledge of informal lenders, while informal lenders can benefit from formal lenders' strong resource mobilisation ability and wide networks across the region. Better linkages between the formal and informal sectors will expand microcredit delivery and improve the overall efficiency of the rural financial system, and hence, accelerate poverty eradication and the development of the Chinese rural economy.

References

ABC (2015). Agro-related Business. Retrieved from http://www.abchina.com/en/agro-related-business/. Accessed on June 20, 2015.

Adams, D., Graham, D. & Van Pischke, J. (1984). *Undermining Rural Development with Cheap Credit*. Boulder: Westview Press.

ADBC (2015). Business Scope. Retrieved from http://www.adbc.com.cn/. Accessed on February 22, 2017.

Atieno, R. (2001). *Formal and Informal Institutions' Lending Policies and Access to Credit by Small-Scale Enterprises in Kenya: An Empirical Assessment*, Vol. 111. Nairobi, Kenya: African Economic Research Consortium Nairobi.

Ayyagari, M., Demirgüç-Kunt, A. & Maksimovic, V. (2010). Formal versus informal finance: Evidence from China. *Review of Financial Studies*, 23(8), 3048–3097.

Besley, T. & Coate, S. (1995). Group lending, repayment incentives and social collateral. *Journal of Development Economics*, 46(1), 1–18.

Bourguignon, F. (2003). *The Poverty-Growth-Inequality Triangle?* Paper presented at the AFD-EUDN Conference on Poverty, Inequality and Growth, Paris.

Carter, M. R. (1988). Equilibrium credit rationing of small farm agriculture. *Journal of Development Economics*, 28(1), 83–103.

Chen, F. (2004). *Analysis of the Supply and Demand for Credit Funds for Peasant Households*. Paper presented at the Workshop on Rural Finance and Credit Infrastructure in China (pp. 323–339), Paris: OECD.

Cheng, E. (2007). The demand for microcredit as a determinant for microfinance outreach-evidence from china. *Savings and Development*, 31(3), 307–334.

Cheng, E. & Xu, Z. (2004). Rates of interest, credit supply and China's rural development. *Savings and Development*, 28(2), 131–156.

Diagne, A. & Zeller, M. (2001). *Access to Credit and its Impact on Welfare in Malawi*, Vol. 116. Washington, DC: International Food Policy Research Institute.

Dong, F. & Featherstone, A. M. (2006). Technical and scale efficiencies for chinese rural credit cooperatives: A bootstrapping approach in data envelopment analysis. *Journal of Chinese Economic and Business Studies*, 4(1), 57–75.

Druschel, K. (2002). *Microfinance in China: Building Sustainable Institutions and a Strong Industry*. Massachusetts: American University.

Du, X. (2004). *Attempts to Implement Micro Finance in Rural China*. Paper presented at the workshop on Rural Finance and Credit Infrastructure in China (pp. 271–284), Paris: OECD.

Du, X. (2005). *The Regulatory Environment for Microfinance in China*. Washington, DC: Microfinance Regulation and Supervision Resource Center.

Dyar, C., Harduar, P., Koenig, C. & Reyes, G. (2006). *Microfinance and Gender Inequality in China*. Michigan: International Economic Development Program, Ford School of Public Policy, University of Michigan.

Fan, C. C. & Sun, M. (2008). Regional inequality in China, 1978–2006. *Eurasian Geography and Economics*, 49(1), 1–18.

Feder, G., Lau, L. J., Lin, J. Y. & Luo, X. (1990). The relationship between credit and productivity in Chinese agriculture: A microeconomic model of disequilibrium. *American Journal of Agricultural Economics*, 72(5), 1151–1157.

Feng, X., He, G. & Ljungwall, C. (2014). Rural financial reform in China: Progress made and the path forward. *The Copenhagen Journal of Asian Studies*, 31(1), 62–80.

Fernando, N. A. (2006). *Understanding and Dealing with High Interest Rates on Microcredit*. Manila: Asian Development Bank, p. 13.

Gale, F., & Collender, R. (2006). New directions in China's agricultural lending. *Electronic Outlook Report from the Economic Research Service WRS-06-01*, United States Department of Agriculture. Retrieved from http://usda.mannlib.

cornell.edu/MannUsda/homepage.do;jessionid=BD5F5F8D50AAA33F7AF0 4957583BA2D3. Accessed on February 22, 2017.

Global Times (2013). China's inequality index highlights urgency for distribution reforms. Retrieved from http://www.globaltimes.cn/content/756945. shtml.

Gonzalez-Vega, C. (1984). Credit rationing behavior of agricultural lenders: The iron law of interest rate restrictions. In D. W. Adams, D. H. Graham & J. D. Van Pischke (Eds.), *Undermining Rural Development with Cheap Credit*. Colorado, Boulder: Westview Press.

Guo, X. & Lei, X. (2000). Xindai (Credit). In Xiong, J. (Ed.), Jinru Ershiyi Shiji de Zhongguo Nongcun, (*Into the 21st-century Rural China*). Beijing: Guangming Chubanshe.

Han, J. (2004). The creation of a favourable environment for investment in rural China: Current situation and future prospects. Organisation for Economic Co-operation and Development (OECD), Centre for Co-operation with Non-members, Rural finance and credit infrastructure in China, pp. 23–33.

Han, L. & Hare, D. (2013). The link between credit markets and self-employment choice among households in rural China. *Journal of Asian Economics*, 26, 52–64.

He, G. & Guo, P. (2004). Rational thoughts on the reform of rural policy finance. *Issues in Agricultural Economy*, 3, 1–17.

Heilig, G. K., Zhang, M., Long, H., Li, X. & Wu, X. (2006). Poverty alleviation in China: A lesson for the developing world. *Geographische Rundschau*, 2(2), 4–13.

Helms, B. & Reille, X. (2004). *Interest Rate Ceilings and Microfinance: The Story so Far*. Washington, DC: Consultative Group to Assist the Poorest (CGAP).

Hermes, N., Lensink, R. & Mehrteab, H. T. (2005). Peer monitoring, social ties and moral hazard in group lending programs: Evidence from Eritrea. *World Development*, 33(1), 149–169.

Holcombe, S. H. & Xu, X. (1996). Microfinance and Poverty Alleviation: United Nations Collaboration with Chinese Experiments. Case Study: Credit and Savings Component of the Poverty Alleviation and Sustainable Development Project in Yilong County, Sichuan, Sichuan/China.

Hu, Z. & Khan, M. S. (1997). Why is China growing so fast? *IMF Staff papers*, 44(1), 103–131.

Huang, J., Rozelle, S. & Tuan, F. (1999). *China's Agriculture, Trade, and Productivity in the 21st Century*. Paper presented at the WCC-101 Annual Meeting on Chinese Agriculture and the WTO (pp. 1–30). Seattle, Washington.

IFAD (2001). *People's Republic of China: Thematic Study on Rural Financial Services in China*. Rome: International Fund for Agricultural Development.

IMF (2015). World Economic and Financial Surveys: World Economic Outlook Database. Retrieved, from IMF http://www.imf.org/external/pubs/ft/weo/2015/01/weodata/download.aspx. Accessed on June 25, 2015.

IMF (2016). Exchange Rate Archives. Retrieved from https://www.imf.org/external/np/fin/ert/GUI/Pages/Report.aspx?CT='CHN'&EX=REP&P=MonthToDate&CF=Compressed&CUF=Period&DS=Ascending&DT=Blank. Accessed on February 29, 2016.

Islam, T. (2007). *Microcredit and Poverty Alleviation*. Hampshire, England: Ashgate Publishing, Ltd.

Jia, X., Heidhues, F. & Zeller, M. (2007). Taking the hands off the rural credit market: An evidence from China. *Studies on the Agricultural and Food Sector in Central & Eastern Europe*, 39, 164–180.

Klein, B., Meyer, R., Hannig, A., Burnett, J. & Fiebig, M. (1999). *Better Practices in Agricultural Lending*. Rome: FAO.

Lau, L. (2008). *Poverty and Sustainability Issues of Microfinance in China: A Case Study in Fu'an, Fujian Province*. Lund: Centre for East and South-East Asian Studies, Lund University.

Li, X. (2010). *An Empirical Analysis of Microcredit on China Rural Household* (Doctoral Thesis), Lincoln University, Lincoln, New Zealand. Retrieved from http://researcharchive.lincoln.ac.nz.

Lin, J. Y. (1992). Rural reforms and agricultural growth in China. *The American Economic Review*, 82(1), 34–51.

Lin, J. Y. & Zhang, F. (1998). The Effects of China's Rural Policies on the Sustainability of Agriculture in China Symposium Conducted at the Meeting of the 11th Biannual Workshop on Economy and Environment in Southeast Asia, Singapore.

Linton, K. (2007). Access to capital in China: Competitive conditions for foreign and domestic firms. SSRN Working Paper Series (1031223).

Llanto, G. M. & Fukui, R. (2006). Innovations in Microfinance in Southeast Asia. Philippine Institute for Development Studies Research Paper Series No. 2006-02.

Lucock, D. (2014). *The People's Republic of China: Knowledge Work on Credit Growth in Microfinance and Rural Finance*. Manila: Asian Development Bank.

Ma, X. (2004). *The Difficulties and Policy Reform in China's Rural Finance*. Organisation for Economic Co-operation and Development (OECD) Centre for Co-operation with Non-members.

Meng, L. (2013). Evaluating China's poverty alleviation program: A regression discontinuity approach. *Journal of Public Economics*, 101, 1–11.

Mohapatra, S., Rozelle, S. & Goodhue, R. (2007). The rise of self-employment in rural China: Development or distress? *World Development*, 35(1), 163–181.

National Bureau of Statistics of China (2014). Output of Major Farm Products [China Statistical Yearbook].

National Bureau of Statistics of China (2015a). Exports Value by Category of Goods [China Statistical Yearbook].

National Bureau of Statistics of China (2015b). Gross Domestic Product [China Statistical Yearbook].

National Bureau of Statistics of China (2015c). Indicators on National and Social Development [China Statistical Yearbook].

National Bureau of Statistics of China (2015d). Number of Employed Persons at Year-end by Three Strata of Industry [China Statistical Yearbook].

National Bureau of Statistics of China (2015e). Number of Employed Persons at Year-end in Urban and Rural Areas [China Statistical Yearbook].

National Bureau of Statistics of China (2015f). Per Capita Income of Urban and Rural Households [China Statistical Yearbook].

Okurut, F. N., Schoombee, A. & Berg, S. (2005). Credit demand and credit rationing in the informal financial sector in Uganda. *South African Journal of Economics*, 73(3), 482–497.

Park, A. & Ren, C. (2001). Microfinance with Chinese characteristics. *World Development*, 29(1), 39–62.

Park, A., Ren, C. & Wang, S. (2004). *Micro-finance, Poverty Alleviation, and Financial Reform in China*. Paper presented at the workshop on Rural Finance and Credit Infrastructure in China (pp. 256–270), Paris: OECD.

Park, A., Wang, S. & Wu, G. (2002). Regional poverty targeting in China. *Journal of Public Economics*, 86(1), 123–153.

Prosterman, R. L., Hanstad, T., Schwarzwalder, B. & Ping, L. (1998). *Rural Land Reform in China and the 1998 Land Management Law: Rural Development Institute*.

Qadir, A. (2005). *A Study of Informal Finance Markets in Pakistan*. Islamabad: Pakistan Microfinance Network.

Rehman, A., Jingdong, L., Du, Y. & Zhang, L. (2015). Rural credit cooperatives RCCs financial system and role in economic development of China. *Research Journal of Finance and Accounting*, 6(5), 196–200.

Rozelle, S., Zhang, L. & Huang, J. (2003). China's war on poverty. *How Far Across the River*. Stanford: Standford University Press, p. 235.

Sagrario Floro, M. & Ray, D. (1997). Vertical links between formal and informal financial institutions. *Review of Development Economics*, 1(1), 34–56.

Scott, D. & Druschel, K. (2004). *Institutional Issues and Prerequisites for Efficient Savings Mobilization and Allocation in Rural and Lesser Developed Regions in China.* Paper presented at the Workshop on Rural Finance and Credit Infrastructure in China (pp. 34–50), Paris: OECD.

Scott, D. & Jun, W. (2006). Developments and prospects for rural finance in China. Stanford Center for International Development Working Papers (292).

Situ, P. (2003). *Microfinance in China and Development Opportunities.* Bonn and Eschborn: German Technical Cooperation.

Skees, J. R. (2008). Challenges for use of index-based weather insurance in lower income countries. *Agricultural Finance Review*, 68(1), 197–217.

Skees, J. (2011). Innovations in Index Insurance for the Poor in Low-Income Countries. In R. D. Christy & V. L. Bogan (Eds.), *Financial Inclusion, Innovation, and Investments*: *Biotechnology and Capital Markets Working for the Poor.* Singapore: World Scientific, pp. 73–101.

Sun, R. (2003). *The Development of Microfinance in China Symposium Conducted at the Meeting of the International Workshop on Rural Financial Reforms in China*, Beijing, China.

The People's Bank of China (PBC) (2001). Guidelines on Rural Household Micro-Credit by Rural Credit Cooperatives. Retrieved from http://www. microfinancegateway.org/library. Accessed on February 22, 2017.

Tilakaratna, S. (1996). Credit Schemes for the Rural Poor: Some Conclusions and Lessons from Practice: International Labour Office, Development and Technical Cooperation Department.

Tsai, K. S. (2004). Imperfect substitutes: The local political economy of informal finance and microfinance in rural China and India. *World Development*, 32(9), 1487–1507.

Turvey, C. G., Kong, R. & Belltawn, B. C. (2009). *Weather Risk and the Viability of Weather Insurance in Western China.* Paper presented at the Annual Conference of the American Agricultural Economics Association Milwaukee, Wisconsin. Retrieved from http://citeseerx.ist.psu.edu.

Unger, J. (2002). Poverty, credit and microcredit in rural China. *Development Bulletin*, 57, 23–26.

Van Empel, G., & Smit, L. (2004). *Development of Sustainable Credit Co-operatives in China.* Paper presented at the Workshop on Rural Finance and Credit Infrastructure in China (pp. 97–111), Paris: OECD.

Van Gemert, H. (2001). Financing rural economic development. *World Economy*, 3, 007.

Vieira, S. (2012). Inequality on the rise? An Assessment of Current Available Data on Income Inequality, at Global, International and National Levels, The Department of Economic and Social Affairs, the United Nations Secretariat.

Wang, W. (2004). *The Regulatory Framework for Rural Credit Co-operatives: The Role of Chinese Supervisory Authorities.* Paper presented at the Workshop on Rural Finance and Credit Infrastructure in China (pp. 129–137), Paris: OECD.

Wang, R. & Liu, X. (2005). Problems of China's rural financial system. In Söderlund, L., Sippola, J., Kamijo-Söderlund, M. (Chair), MTT. Symposium conducted at the meeting of the Proceedings SUSDEV-CHINA symposium. Sustainable Agroecosystem Management and Development of Rural-Urban Interaction in Regions and Cities of China.

Wenner, M. & Proenza, F. (2000). Rural finance in Latin America and the Caribbean: Challenges and opportunities. *Inter-American Development Bank Working Paper, March.* Retrieved from http://citeseerx.ist.psu.edu.

World Bank (2015). World Development Indicators [World DataBank].

World Bank (2016). World Development Indicators [World DataBank].

Wu, G. (1997). Policy on subsidized poverty loans in China: A discussion. In. Beijing: Rural Development Institute, Chinese Academy of Social Sciences. Retrieved from http://citeseerx.ist.psu.edu/viewdoc/download;jsessionid=9F D4E557CCD4284978AFFCCD78E62269?doi=10.1.1.509.7592&rep=rep1& type=pdf.

Wu, G. B. (2001). *A Study on China's Microcredit Poverty Reduction (in Chinese).* Beijing: China Economy Press.

Wu, Y. (2011). *A Comparative Analysis of the Operating and Economic Efficiency of China's Microfinance Institutions, Traditional Chinese Agricultural Lenders, and Counterpart Indian Microfinance Institutions.* University of Georgia.

Xuechun, Z., Zhong, X., Minggao, S. & Enjiang, C. (2010). *Rural Finance in Poverty-stricken Areas in the People's Republic of China: Balancing Government and Market.* Manila: Asian Development Bank.

Yaron, J. & Mundial, B. (1992). *Rural Finance in Developing Countries.* Vol. 875. Mumbai: Agriculture and Rural Development Department.

Zeller, M. & Sharma, M. (1998). *Rural Finance and Poverty Alleviation.* Washington: International Food Policy Research Institute (IFPRI).

Zhang, A. (1997). *Poverty Alleviation in China: Commitment, Policies and Expenditures.* New York: UN.

Zhang, H. (2004). The system of Chinese rural financial organisations: Achievements, shortcomings and institutional renewal. Organisation For Economic Co-operation And Development, Centre For Co-operation With Non-Members.

Zhang, L., Huang, J. & Rozelle, S. (2003). China's war on poverty: Assessing targeting and the growth impacts of poverty programs. *Journal of Chinese Economic and Business Studies*, 1(3), 301–317.

Zhang, Y. & Fang, Q. (2005). The reasons why informal finance exists and some suggestions on policy. *Chinese Business Review*, 4(8), 54–57.

Zhang, H. X. & Loubere, N. (2015). Rural finance and development in China. *Rural Livelihoods in China*. London: Routledge, p. 151.

Zuo, X. (2001). Is the RCC Microfinance Model Sustainable and Replicable. PBC–DID Microfinance Project Case Study in Luanping, China, Notebook, 17. Québec, Canada: Dévelopment International Desjardins.

Chapter 5

Microfinance System in Thailand

Satit Aditto

Assistant Professor,
Faculty of Agriculture, Department of Agricultural Economics,
Khon Kaen University, Khon Kaen 40002, Thailand
satit_aditto@hotmail.com

Abstract

Microfinance has been widely discussed as one of the rural development initiatives to distribute credit and financial services to the rural poor in Thailand since the mid-1970s. In 2013, approximately 67.2% of the country's 7.3 million poor resided in the rural areas and nearly half of them lived in north-east region. Most of the poor are smallholder farmers who experience poverty and live below the basic standard of living. Thus, they require to access credit to invest in their farming businesses and for household consumption. The demand for short-term credit plays an important role in the rural households' borrowing that is predominantly supplied by the informal lenders. However, during the past few decades, the proportion of credit from formal financial institutions have grown dramatically to substitute the informal credit in the rural areas. This chapter presents an overview of microfinance in Thailand including the types and characteristics.

Keywords: Rural poor, credit, poverty, agriculture, Thailand.

5.1 Introduction

Like several other developing countries, Thailand's economic development is based on agriculture. Over the recent decades, agriculture has been the mainstay of the Thai economy. In 2013, Thailand's GDP was approximately 12,910,038 million baht with a 0.2% growth rate; agriculture accounts for 11% of the GDP (see Table 5.1) (NESDB, 2015). The proportion of the primary agriculture sector to the GDP has dropped dramatically from 38% in 1951, 27% in 1970 to roughly 11% in 2013. In the late 1980s, the rapid growth and development of the country's economic base came from foreign direct investment in the industrial and service sectors. Thailand developed into a semi-industrial country during that time. This transformation in the country's economic structure affected the GDP. The contribution of the industrial and services sectors to the GDP rose from 62% in 1951 to nearly 90% in 2013. However, agriculture continues to be a major source of raw materials for the industrial sector especially in the agro-industry, industrialised food products and beverages and intermediate products for import substitution and export (Falvey, 2000; Limsombunchai, 2006; Thaiprasert, 2006; Aditto, 2011).

The population of Thailand was estimated at 66.8 million in 2013 and employment in the agriculture sector fell from nearly 53% of the total labour force in 1994 to around 41% in 2013 (NSO, 2015). Since the 1990s, Thailand agriculture has faced a shortage in labour. The huge gap in the wage rate, personal income and employment rate between the agriculture and non-agriculture sector led to an increase in permanent and seasonal rural-to-urban migration and has resulted in rural–urban inequality and rural poverty in Thailand (Fuglie, 2001; Thaiprasert, 2006; Ahmad & Isvilanonda, 2003). NESDB (2015) identified Thailand's Gini coefficient has improved from 0.52 in 1994 to 0.46 in 2013. This shows Thailand is becoming more equal in terms of income distribution. Poverty in Thailand has been reduced from 24.1 million individuals (nearly 42.6%) in 1994 to 7 million individuals (nearly 10.9%) in 2013. The national poverty level was around 30,864 baht/person/year (see Table 5.1). Furthermore, Thailand achieved significant economic development during the past two decades and became an upper–middle-income economy in 2011 (United Nation Development Program, 2015).

Table 5.1: Key Economic and Demographic Indicators of Thailand

Indicator	1994	2000	2006	2009	2013
GDP (million baht)[a]	3,689,090	5,069,823	8,400,655	9,654,016	12,910,038
— Agriculture	318,333	431,082	790,176	945,605	1,459,151
— Non-agriculture	3,370,757	4,638,741	7,610,479	8,708,411	11,450,887
GDP growth rate (%)[a]	3.2	1.6	1.9	2.2	0.2
— Agriculture	7.2	1.2	1.4	0.9	0.1
— Non-agriculture	2.7	1.6	1.9	2.5	0.2
Total population (million people)[b]	56.6	60.9	62.8	66.0	66.8
Employment (million people)[b]	33.2	32.8	36.3	38.4	39.3
— Agriculture	17.6	15.9	15.3	15.9	16.1
— Non-agriculture	15.6	16.9	21.0	22.5	23.2
National poverty line (baht/person/year)[a]	13,884	18,660	23,208	26,088	30,864
Gini coefficient (income inequality)[a]	0.52	0.52	0.51	0.49	0.46
Population living under the national poverty line (million)[a]	24.1	25.8	13.7	11.6	7.3

Source: [a]Office of the National Economic and Social Board (NESDB), 2015.
[b]National Statistic Office (NSO) (2015).

In 2013, approximately 67.2% of the country's 7.3 million poor resided in the rural areas and nearly half of them lived in the north-east region (NESDB, 2015). The majority of Thai farmers experience poverty and are below the basic standard of living, especially smallholder farmers in the rural areas (Krongkaew, 1985). Wattanutchariya and Jitsanguan (1992) argued that smallholder farmers in rural areas, in general, are not able to choose the most efficient type of production to maximise their farm income and the optimal use of resources because of limited farm size. This resulted in inefficient production and lower farm income. Most poor farmers also have insufficient capital and a lack of production technology (Thaiprasert, 2006). In addition, Limsombunchai (2006) argued that smallholder farmers obtained large loans to sustain their farm production, household consumption and investment. However, the large amount of loan can lead to repayment problem among the farmers.

The above discussion strongly demonstrates the importance of agricultural sector to the Thai economy which provided the main source of income and employment for the people who live in rural areas. The incidence of poverty in rural areas of Thailand is also highlighted.

5.2 Microfinance and the Objectives of Microfinance in Thailand

Rural financing system in Thailand has been developed for several decades. The main purpose of microfinance is to help the poor in the rural areas of Thailand, who lack investment funds, cannot access formal credit and depend on informal credit providers (Coleman, 2006; Rafiq, 2013). Microfinance has been widely discussed as one of the rural development initiatives to distribute credit and financial services to the rural poor since the mid-1970s (Fongthong, 2012). Most of the poor are smallholder farmers who lived in the rural areas and they required credit to invest on their farming businesses and for household consumptions. Commercial banks rarely serve the credit needs of the rural poor because of high risk, high transaction costs and lack of collateral deposit from the borrowers (Coleman, 2006; Limsombunchai, 2006).

Table 5.2: Commercial Banks' Credits by Agricultural and Non-agricultural Sectors[a]

Sector	2010	2011	2012	2013
Agricultural sector[b]	331,995 (1.02%)	330,596 (0.87%)	351,953 (0.84%)	431,363 (0.91%)
Non-agricultural sector	32,119,221 (98.98%)	37,276,574 (99.13%)	41,351,540 (99.16%)	46,597,897 (99.09%)
Total loans	32,451,216 (100%)	37,607,170 (100%)	41,703,493 (100%)	47,029,260 (100%)

[a]Consist of Thai commercial banks (without branches aboard) and foreign banks branches, exclude specialised Thai government banks.
[b]Including agriculture, hunting, fisheries and forestry.
Unit: Million baht.
Source: BOT (2015).

According to Bank of Thailand (BOT) (2015), in 2013, commercial banks supplied around 47 billion baht to the credit market. However, only 0.91% of the total commercial loans were distributed to the agricultural sector (see Table 5.2).

Before the mid-1970s, the credit markets in rural areas of Thailand were dominated by informal lenders. The informal lenders charge high interest rate, which causes the farmers to be in debt most of the time and remain in a vicious cycle of poverty. Therefore, the Thai government launched some polices to enlarge rural credit supply; first, they requested all commercial banks to increase agricultural loans by 5% to the rural populations with low interest rates. Second, the Bank for Agriculture and Agricultural Cooperatives (BAAC) was established in 1966 as a specialised government bank to serve institutional loans to replace the informal rural credit market. BAAC's aims not only provide loans with reasonable interest rate designed for the individual farmers, agricultural cooperatives and farmers groups but also improve the quality life of their clients (Isavilanonda, 2002; Menkhoff & Rungruxsirivorn, 2011). The outstanding credit of BAAC has increased dramatically from 577,638 million baht in 2010 to nearly one billion baht in 2013 (see Table 5.3). In 2013, nearly 98% of total loans or 948,983 million baht were allocated to farmers and farmers' institutions, roughly 2% supplied

Table 5.3: **Current Financial Indicators of BAAC**

Item	2010	2011	2012	2013
Total assets (million baht)	899,019	1,055,549	1,191,061	1,338,525
Loans (million baht)	577,683	775,908	874,497	970,630
	(100%)	(100%)	(100%)	(100%)
— Loans to farmers and farmer institutions (million baht)	551,385	689,499	830,645	948,983
	(95.45%)	(88.86%)	(94.98%)	(97.77%)
— Loans to government-secured project (million baht)	2,843	82,121	39,790	17,436
	(0.49%)	(10.58%)	(4.55%)	(1.83%)
— Other loans (million baht)	23,381	4,288	4,062	4,211
	(4.04%)	(0.55%)	(0.46%)	(0.44%)
Deposits (million baht)	726,573	887,259	1,000,857	1,151,619
Loan to deposit ratio	0.79	0.87	0.87	0.84
NPLs (million baht)	37,432	34,258	32,766	38,869
NPLs to loan ratio	6.57	5.34	3.95	4.10
Number of agricultural debtors				
— Individual farmers (person)	4,612,424	4,999,641	5,582,703	5,702,764
— Agricultural cooperatives (group)	1,058	1,123	1,136	1,225
— Farmer associations (group)	30	30	30	38

Source: BAAC (various years).

to government-secured projects and the rest were other loans such as juristic person accounts and housing funds. The number of individual farmers who accepted the loans from BAAC was around 5.7 million persons. These demonstrate the significant share and strong involvement of BAAC in Thailand rural credit market.

In terms of BAAC's financial stability, financial indicators showed that the loan-to-deposit ratio increased slightly from 0.79 in 2010 to 0.84 in 2013. Moreover, the non-performing loans (NPLs) had dropped from 6.57% of total loans in 2010 to 4.10% in 2013. In 2011 and 2012, the BAAC had supported around 82,121 and 39,790 million baht of loans to government-secured policies such as rice pledging scheme, but there was no effect on the financial performance of BAAC.

The high involvement of state-owned bank, including BAAC, with the government populist policies became a hotly contestable debate among

Thai economists because such policies directly increased the risk of fail-ure of the rural credit system. Thai economists also highlighted the house-holds' debt problem, especially rural household in the remote areas. This is because the rural household has a very limited ability to repay their debts. The price of agricultural products in Thailand tends to fluctuate erratically, both seasonally and annually. This affected the variability of farm profitability and farm household incomes. According to Office of Agricultural Economics (OAE), in 2013, the average net farm revenue was 48,470 baht per household which decreased from 57,214 baht per household in 2010. Conversely, the average outstanding debt dramatically increased from 54,061 baht per household in 2010 to 82,572 baht per household in 2013 (see Table 5.4).

The rural financial system in Thailand has undergone a remarkable shift since 2001. The Thai government attempted to reform the rural credit market and help the poor escape from poverty by implementing the Thailand Village and Urban Community Fund (VF), which was one of the

Table 5.4: Average Thailand Farm Household Annual Cash Income, Expenditure and Loan Size, 2010–2013

Item	2010	2011	2012	2013
Income[a]	225,835	242,365	247,743	268,301
— Farm income	137,175	142,039	146,334	148,240
— Off-farm income	88,660	100,326	101,409	120,061
Expenditure[a]	190,125	197,448	207,016	229,955
— Farm expenditure	79,961	84,190	88,709	99,770
— Off-farm expenditure	110,164	113,258	118,307	130,185
Net farm revenue[a]	57,214	57,849	57,625	48,470
Net operating assets[a]	125,618	144,715	121,189	118,730
Average outstanding debt[a]	54,061	59,808	76,697	82,572
Number of farm household (million)	5.871	5.909	5.713	5.715
Average household size (person)	3.94	3.88	4.00	3.96
Average farm size per household (rai)[b]	25.42	25.25	25.28	24.36

[a]Unit: baht/household.
[b]1 rai = 0.16 ha.
Source: OAE (2015).

largest microfinance programmes in the world (Boonperm, Haughton & Khandker, 2013). The Thai government allocated one million baht per community (around US$22,500 at an average exchange rate in 2001, 1US$ = 44.5 baht) broadened to around 77,000 communities, which accounted for 77 billion baht or 1.5% of Thailand's GDP (Menkhoff & Rungruxsirivorn, 2011; Fongthong, 2012). The main purposes of VF were to serve the emergency fund, especially short-term credit, for the unprivileged groups to help them increase investments, job-creation opportunities and social welfare development. The VFs are managed at the national level by the NVFO accompanied by the local committees (comprising 15 members in each committee) at the village level (Fongthong, 2012).

In 2009, Thai government decided to increase the amount of initial working capital (Stage II) to each VF from 200,000 to 600,000 baht with respect to the potential assessment and size of VF.[1] The budget that the government allocated in Stage II was around 19,599.2 million baht. In addition, in Stage III (in 2012), the government supported an additional million baht of working capital to each of Thailand's VF (around 79,255 million baht of the budget). Overall, the total budget that the Thai government maintained in the VF programme since 2001–2014 was approximately 166,895.8 million baht (Thai Parliamentary Budget Office, 2015) The numbers of VFs have been extended to 79,255 communities in 2013 with total members of 12.8 million people. Approximately 44% of the village funds were located in the north-east, the poorest region of the country (see Table 5.5).

However, Chandoevwit & Ashakul (2008) conducted a study to investigate the impact of VF on income, expenditures and the poverty reduction level among rural household in Thailand using a quasi-experiment evaluation technique. The authors' results showed that the VF programme did not help the rural borrowers escape from poverty.

The authors also argued that the amount of loans from the VF programme was inadequate for the rural household to create more

---

[1]The sizes of VF are categorised as Small (S) with 50–150 members, Medium (M) with 151–350 members and Large (L) with more than 351 members. The government had investigated and classified the potential performances of the VF as grade A (very good) and B (good) of around 59,000 out of 79,255 communities, grade C (fair) 12,000 communities and the rest are grade D (need to improve).

Table 5.5: Number of Operating VFs by Region, 2013

Region	Village funds	Urban community funds	Total
North	16,564	582	17,106
North-east	33,102	847	33,949
South	8,641	464	9,105
East	5,354	386	5,740
West	5,572	365	5,937
Central	5,756	1,622	7,378
Total	**74,989**	**4,266**	**79,255**

Source: NVFO (2015).

income and the rural households were more likely to have loan repayment problems. In addition, the VF programme was supposed to reduce poverty and improve rural poor welfare; however, the programme was operated as one of the populist economic policies. This results in high level of indebtedness among the rural poor, where the government attempts to push the loans to the poor without any concern about their repayment capacity.

There is little published empirical evidence about the effect of VF programme in terms of poverty alleviation in rural households of Thailand. Therefore, the pros and cons of VF programme have been widely discussed and debated among the academics, policy makers and politicians in Thailand to this day.

5.3 Types of Microfinance in Thailand

The rural poor household credit transactions are usually associated with short-term loans. This is because most of the rural poor are farmers and they tend to grow annual rather than perennial crops. Moreover, the borrowers fail to meet the formal financial institution collateral requirement. This results in their inability to obtain long-term credit from formal financial institutions. Therefore, the demand for short-term credit plays an important role in the rural households' borrowing that is predominantly supplied by the informal lenders (Siamwalla, 1988).

However, during the past few decades, the proportion of credit from formal financial institutions have grown dramatically to substitute the informal credit in the rural areas (Limsombunchai, 2006). Gine (2011) emphasised that the lower interest rate of the formal institutions was one of the reasons that possibly increased the number of rural poor household borrowers. In addition, the Thai government should reform some of the policies regarding the land title in order for people to own land. This could solve the lack of collateral problem in the formal financial sector for rural poor households.

According to NESDB statistics, the average outstanding debt of a rural poor household in Thailand has continuously increased. The proportion of formal loan has increased from 88% in 2007 to 94% in 2013. In 2013, a rural poor household has an average outstanding debt of approximately 64,006 baht with a large proportion of the loan primarily for agricultural activities, household consumption and purchase of assets. On the other hand, most of the informal loans are spent on household consumption (see Table 5.6).

Similarly, the BOT (2015) reported the notable enhancement of the formal loans that provided for household debtors in domestic credit market. The amount of total formal loans obtained by household borrowers has increased considerably from 24,211,188 million baht in 2010 to 37,709,424 million baht in 2013. Most of the credit supplied were from deposit-taking institutions including commercial banks, state-owned banks and saving cooperatives (see Table 5.7).

The above discussion highlights the importance of loans which impact the development of rural financing system in Thailand. The Banking with the Poor Network (2010) argued that microfinance in Thailand can be divided into three main categories based on the Ministry of Finance (MOF) classification.

5.3.1 Formal microfinance institution

Formal microfinance institutions operate their financial services under the prudential regulations. Formal microfinance plays a critical role in the rural financing system of Thailand including the specialised government banks such as BAAC and Government Savings Bank (GSB). The characteristics and some important projects of BAAC and GSB are described below.

Table 5.6: Average Outstanding Debt of a Rural Poor Household in Thailand (Classified by Sources of Loan and Loan Purposes)

Item	2007	2009	2011	2013
Formal loan	**43,946**	**50,463**	**51,787**	**60,134**
	(88.15%)	**(91.02%)**	**(91.22%)**	**(93.95%)**
— Used for buying or rent house and	4,402	4,646	3,599	4,801
land	(8.83%)	(8.38%)	(6.34%)	(7.50%)
— Used for education	768	893	1,209	1,267
	(1.54%)	(1.61%)	(2.13%)	(1.98%)
— Used for household consumption	14,117	11,676	15,919	14,843
	(28.32%)	(21.06%)	(28.04%)	(23.19%)
— Used for business	1,859	3,859	2,890	2,938
	(3.73%)	(6.96%)	(5.09%)	(4.59%)
— Used for agriculture	21,684	27,743	26,771	35,274
	(43.50%)	(50.04%)	(47.05%)	(55.11%)
— Others	1,112	1,647	1,459	1,011
	(2.23%)	(2.97%)	(2.57%)	(1.58%)
Informal loan	**5,902**	**4,979**	**4,985**	**3,872**
	(11.84%)	**(8.98%)**	**(8.78%)**	**(6.05%)**
— Used for buying or rent house and	543	538	312	160
land	(1.09%)	(0.97%)	(0.55%)	(0.25%)
— Used for education	65	105	193	6
	(0.13%)	(0.19%)	(0.34%)	(0.01%)
— Used for household consumption	2,911	2,694	2,691	1,984
	(5.84%)	(4.86%)	(4.74%)	(3.10%)
— Used for business	842	299	352	435
	(1.69%)	(0.54%)	(0.62%)	(0.68%)
— Used for agriculture	917	820	1,067	960
	(1.84%)	(1.48%)	(1.88%)	(1.50%)
— Others	623	521	369	326
	(1.25%)	(0.94%)	(0.65%)	(0.51%)
Total	**49,848**	**55,442**	**56,772**	**64,006**
	(100%)	**(100%)**	**(100%)**	**(100%)**

Unit: Baht per household.
Source: NESDB (various years).

(I) *BAAC*

BAAC is a state-owned bank with a mission to provide financial assistance for farmers and farmers associations. In terms of credit services,

Table 5.7:   Loans to Household Classified by Type of Financial Institutions[a]

Institution	2010	2011	2012	2013
Deposit-taking institutions	**21,196,451**	**24,787,497**	**28,957,206**	**32,695,470**
— Commercial banks[b]	10,007,834	11,479,788	13,472,040	15,861,753
— Specialised government banks[c]	7,612,132	9,070,731	10,485,941	11,179,742
— Saving cooperatives	3,524,521	4,194,039	4,972,203	5,643,035
— Others	51,964	42,939	27,022	10,940
Other financial institutions	**3,014,737**	**3,289,008**	**4,037,990**	**5,013,954**
— Credit card, leasing and personal loans companies	2,061,462	2,277,410	2,949,344	3,913,975
— Insurance companies	248,928	260,221	279,755	302,463
— Securities companies	105,949	126,060	152,530	204,577
— Asset management companies	390,818	377,943	358,189	296,755
— Pawnshops	181,886	220,607	265,257	249,117
— Others	25,694	26,767	32,915	47,067
Total loans to household	**24,211,188**	**28,076,505**	**32,995,196**	**37,709,424**

[a] Loans in household debtors.
[b] Consist of Thai commercial banks (without branches aboard) and foreign banks branches.
[c] Consist of GSB, BAAC, Government Housing Banks (GHBank), Export-Import Bank of Thailand (EXIM), Islamic Bank of Thailand (IBANK) and Small and Medium Enterprise Development Bank of Thailand (SMEBANK).
Unit: million baht.
Source: BOT (2015).

BAAC has designed a wide range of credits suitable for individual farmers in the rural areas such as the ones listed below (BAAC, 2015a; Limsombunchai, 2006):

(i) *Short-term loans for agricultural production*: This type of loans is aimed to prevent a shortage of working capital for farmers to purchase agricultural inputs to produce annual farm products. The repayment period is usually within 12 months, but in some cases, the repayment period can be expanded to 18 months.
(ii) *Medium-term loans*: The objective of this loan is to purchase livestock, buy farm machinery and/or equipment and for land improvement. This type of loan has to be repaid between 1 and 3 years.

(iii) *Long-term loans*: This type of loan is designed for farmers to invest in fixed farm assets or purchase additional land to expand capacity of their farm production. Moreover, farmers can use long-term loan for reimbursement of their old debts and redemption. The repayment period of long-term loan usually does not exceed 15 years.

Borrower security requirements for short-term credit must be either a written promise by guarantors, or the immoveable properties collateral. On the other hand, for long-term credit, only borrower's assets can be eligible as collateral. The loan interest rate charged for individual farmers is calculated with minimum retail rate (MRR) (see Table 5.8).

BAAC has also provided loans for juristic persons such as farmer associations, agricultural cooperatives, village funds and community enterprises with minimum loan rate (MLR) charged. The purpose of this type of loan is to increase the working capital reserves of rural microfinance institutions.

Besides loan provisions, BAAC also encourages savings mobilisation campaign for rural farmers. Many products and services are recommended for the rural farmers to increase the amount of household savings and develop financially responsible habits. One of the notable successful saving products of BAAC is "Om Sap Taweechoke" saving deposit.

Table 5.8:   Current Deposit and Loan Interest Rate of Selected Banks in Thailand, 2015

Item	BAAC	GSB	Other commercial banks
Deposit (individual)			
— Saving	0.50	0.50	0.05–2.50
— Fixed 3 months period	0.95	0.95	0.25–2.00
— Fixed 12 months period	1.55	1.55	0.25–2.25
— Fixed 24 months period	1.75	1.75	1.30–2.38
Loan			
— MRR	7.00	7.48	8.39
— MLR	5.00	6.70	7.10
— Minimum overdraft rate (MOR)	7.38	7.10	7.92

Unit: Percent per year.
Sources: GSB (2015), BAAC (2015) and BOT (2015).

This product was implemented in 1996 with the aim to increase savings among rural poor clients. The depositors participating in this saving mobilisation programme were entitled to enter into a lucky draw programme which offers durable goods such as a car, motorcycle, gold, television, etc. BAAC (2015a) claimed that in 2007 this programme encouraged more than 3.6 million clients to open saving accounts and the average amount of saving was around 6,200 baht per account.

In addition, Thai government will continue to work closely with BAAC to improve the quality of life of smallholder farmers in the rural areas. In the past, the debt moratorium programme was used many times since 2000 to relieve the repayment problem among farmers who faced production and price risks. The refinancing of old debts scheme is also continually implemented to avoid farmers borrowing from informal lenders. In 2013, around 103,641 farmers registered to participate in the scheme with a total debt of 11,067 million baht (BAAC, 2015a).

(II) *Government Savings Bank*

GSB was established since 1913 with one of the main missions to encourage Thai people to save. GSB's total assets were nearly 2.18 billion baht in 2010 which dramatically increased from 1.46 billion baht in 2010. Moreover, the outstanding credit of GSB has increased from 1.11 billion baht in 2010 to nearly 1.68 billion baht in 2013 (see Table 5.9). 71% of total loans in 2013 were allocated to retail clients for personal and housing loans, roughly 6.2% or 104,055 million baht supplied to grassroots clients using the GSB's loan projects such as "People Bank Loan" and "Rural Community Development Loan" (GSB, 2013).

The People Bank loan project is designed to help small urban poor such as street vendors, who are struggling to maintain working capital for their small businesses, and can access formal crediting rather than using informal creditors. The higher loan limits are not greater than 200,000 baht and the repayment period is usually within 96 months. The security requirements must be either a guarantor's commitment or a borrower's assets. On the other hand, GSB has supplied loans to groups of rural community enterprises, village funds and urban community funds used to increase the amount of reserves among community associations. The borrower security

Table 5.9: **Current Financial Indicators of Government Saving Bank**

Item	2010	2011	2012	2013
Total assets (million baht)	1,461,189	1,772,111	1,962,550	2,177,193
Loans (million baht)	1,111,755	1,351,990	1,585,145	1,678,309
	(100%)	(100%)	(100%)	(100%)
— Loans to retail clients for personal and housing loans (million baht)	768,223	960,183	1,109,601	1,183,208
	(69.1%)	(71.02%)	(70.0%)	(70.5%)
— Loans to grassroots clients (million baht)	40,023	50,429	82,427	104,055
	(3.6%)	(3.73%)	(5.2%)	(6.2%)
— Loans to government and other financial institutions (million baht)	227,910	259,041	305,933	300,417
	(20.5%)	(19.16%)	(19.3%)	(17.9%)
— Loans to business sector (million baht)	74,487	82,336	87,183	90,628
	(6.7%)	(6.09%)	(5.5%)	(5.4%)
Deposits (million baht)	1,180,248	1,525,756	1,679,764	1,879,425
Loan to deposit ratio	0.94	0.88	0.94	0.89
NPLs (million baht)	13,344	12,710	16,752	19,191
NPLs to loan ratio	1.20	0.94	1.06	1.14

Source: GSB (various years).

requirements can be written promises by the steering committees as guarantors of the credit agreement, if the loan is over 3 million baht, the community association's immovable assets are also required as collateral. In this type of loan, the repayment period does not exceed 5 years (GSB, 2013).

5.3.2 *Semi-formal microfinance institution*

Semi-formal microfinance institution is a legitimate institution with a member-based framework and operated under non-prudential regulations. The semi-formal microfinance institutions in Thailand include cooperative organisations, saving for production groups (SPGs) and VFs.

(I) *Cooperative Organisations*

Cooperatives were established in Thailand since 1915 with the main purpose of improving the quality of life of smallholder farmers in the rural areas. Presently, the cooperatives movement in Thailand has exhibited significant growth, which operated under the Cooperative Act 1968 and is supervised by the Cooperatives Promotion Department (CPD) and Cooperative Auditing Department (CAD). The cooperatives in Thailand are divided into 7 types including agricultural, land settlement, fisheries, consumer, saving and credit, service and credit union cooperatives (The Cooperative League of Thailand, 2015). According to CPD, there are 7,134 cooperatives in Thailand in 2013. More than half of the cooperatives are agricultural cooperatives followed by saving and credit cooperatives. Both types of cooperatives serve over 9 million registered members. Moreover, CPD (2015) pointed out that the volume of the cooperative businesses was originally from credit business with the volume of 1,233,843 million baht in 2013 (see Table 5.10).

The agricultural cooperatives aim to help farmer members access production loans, provide input supplies, selling members' products at market prices and provide agricultural extension services. Similarly, the

Table 5.10:   Number of Cooperatives, Members and Businesses Volume in Thailand (2010–2013)

Items	2010	2011	2012	2013
Number of cooperatives	6,962	6,963	7,018	7,134
— Agricultural cooperatives	3,850	3,777	3,768	3,812
— Saving and credit cooperatives	1,366	1,373	1,383	1,393
— Credit union cooperatives	420	440	466	496
— Others	1,326	1,373	1,867	1,433
Number of members	10,342,347	10,563,375	10,827,490	11,111,117
— Agricultural cooperatives	5,968,358	6,116,121	6,224,230	6,338,691
— Saving and credit cooperatives	2,618,501	2,638,641	2,640,664	2,727,637
— Credit union cooperatives	431,325	494,067	585,607	647,638
— Others	1,324,163	1,318,546	1,376,989	1,397,151
Businesses volume classified by business activities of cooperatives (million baht)	1,712,277	2,049,063	2,073,803	2,040,788
— Deposit	469,560	559,809	648,747	587,217
— Loan	1,067,218	1,249,763	1,194,494	1,233,843
— Input supplies business	61,530	71,419	83,201	85,365
— Others	113,969	168,072	147,361	134,363

Source: CPD (2015).

saving and credit cooperatives aim to promote savings and provide loans to the members who are in the same occupation or same community areas (The Federation of Saving and Credit Cooperatives of Thailand Limited (FSCT), 2015). There are three types of loans that saving and credit cooperatives provide to their members (FSCT, 2015):

(i) *Emergency loans*: The member can access this type of loan without any collateral whenever they are faced with a life crisis. The amount of emergency loan may be up to half of the member's monthly income and the repayment must be done in two payment installments.

(ii) *Ordinary loans*: The amount of the loan depends on the members' monthly income that ranges between 40,000 and 300,000 baht and the repayment period between 24 and 72 installments. In all cases, at least one member guarantor is needed for this type of loan.

(iii) *Special loans*: The member can borrow special loans to purchase land, building and for improvement or other permanent investment. Collateral is required for this type of loan and the repayment period is between 10 and 15 years.

The deposit and credit interest rates of each saving and credit cooperatives are different. Usually, the deposit interest rate of the cooperatives is slightly higher and the loan rate is slightly lower than other commercial banks. For example, in 2015, the Khon Kean University Savings Cooperative announced the savings rate at 2% per year. Emergency and ordinary loan rates are charged at 6.50% and special loan rate at 5% per year.

(II) *Savings for Production Group*

The SPG was initiated with the dual aims to develop sustainable human capital and solve the lack of credit accessibility problem of members in rural community (see Figure 5.1). The members in each rural SPG gathered together and regularly save their money in the group cash funds. The amount of savings among the members is constant in certain period of time, such as 1 baht per day, 10 baht per week, etc. This type of accumulated savings is called "Sajja savings". The members elected the committees to manage the group funds and manage others activities. When the group funds multiply, it can generate more economic activities such as

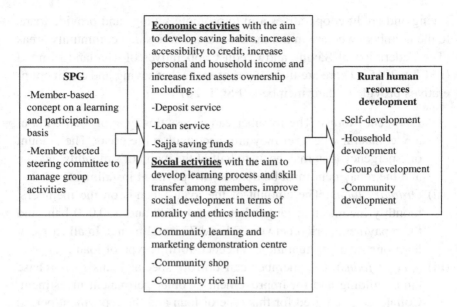

Figure 5.1: Conceptual Framework for Operating the SPG in Thailand

Source: Adapted from Luxchaigul (2014).

saving service to improve the welfare and loan service to help other members who lack business investment. In addition, SPG builds up social networking activities among group members, such as community learning and marketing demonstration centre, community shop, community rice mill, etc. These social networking activities help improve the learning process and knowledge sharing which can enhance sustainable human capital development of the rural SPG members (Luxchaigul, 2014).

In 2013, the numbers of SPGs were approximately 44,944 groups and serve over 6.7 million members all over the country with a total amount of Sajja funds around 58,374 million baht. A total of 19,385 SPGs are located in north-east region followed by northern and central regions, respectively (Community Development Department, 2015).

(III) *Village Fund*

The VF was introduced to Thailand's rural financial system in 2001. This scheme is operated under the supervision of the National Village and

Urban Community Funds Office (NVFO) which is responsible for developing and implementing various policies, rules and regulations concerning monitoring and management of funds at the national level.

According to Menkhoff & Rungruxsirivorn (2011) and Chandoevwit & Ashakul (2008), the considerable requirements to establish the VF in the villages include villagers forming a 10–15 person committee that should be elected from the village members. Subsequently, the draft regulations and guidance such as the lending policies and procedures, interest rate charged, the borrower's qualifications and the policies and procedures for collecting loans and punishment are documented by the committee which can differ from one VF to another. Each VF must meet the requirements of law referred to the Regulation on Establishment and Management of the National Village and Urban Community Fund (B.E.2544). This would guarantee that each VF conducts its operations under the same standards.

The draft regulations and guidance in the establishment of the VF are approved by the NVFO. One million baht of working capital will then be transferred from the government directly to each VF's bank account using the BAAC or GSB banks (Menkhoff & Rungruxsirivorn, 2011). The members who are willing to borrow from the VF can submit loan application to the local VF committee. Once the application has been considered and approved by the committee, the entire loan will be transferred to borrower's individual account. Later when the loan is due, the borrowers can repay the principal and interest charged to the VF's bank account and will receive the documents from BAAC or GSB banks to prove as evidence of repayment (see Figure 5.2). This process showed that the local VF committees do not need to hold cash in hand. Moreover, the BAAC and GSB banks work closely with the local VF committees as auditors to monitor the VF funds account (Menkhoff & Rungruxsirivorn, 2011).

The amount of VF loan may not exceed 20,000 baht per person and the repayment period is within 1 year. However, in some cases, the amount of loan can be extended to 50,000 baht which depends on the decision of the local VF committee.

5.3.3 *Informal microfinance institution*

The Banking with the Poor Network (2010) emphasised the informal microfinance institution in Thailand such as independent lenders and

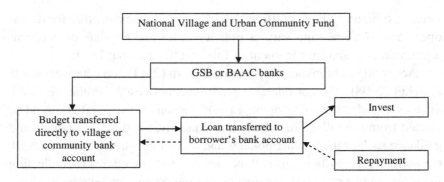

Figure 5.2:   VFS Administration Process
Source: Chandoevwit & Ashakul (2008).

community-based organisation with support from NGOs, local govern-ment agencies and monks. Meagher (2013) argued that the informal microfinance institutions have grown significantly in the past few years. However, the institutions face more default risks since they are not legalised. This means financial services of the informal microfinance institutions are not under regulation and supervision of the government. Recently, the Thai policy makers attempted to relax some financial regula-tions to encourage informal microfinance institutions to register and be recognised by the government agencies. This enables the government to collect more taxes from financial transaction of informal microfinance institutions and to prevent the poor borrowers from being exploited by informal lenders.

Informal microfinance institutions are more likely to provide credit services to low-income citizen groups in both rural and urban areas of Thailand. The lending interest rate is much higher than those of formal lenders, and some borrowers revealed that the independent lenders charged around 2% per day of loan interest and used force in debt collec-tion (Rural debt in Thailand, 2013). In addition, Meagher (2013) sug-gested the alternative ways to solve the informal microfinance institution illegality problems in Thailand is for the government to implement a comprehensive credit information system that raises the awareness of consumer rights and consumer protection, enhances financial literacy, and use of legal mechanisms to protect the poor.

5.4 Traditional Credit and the New Approach to Microenterprise Finance

In the past few years, the Thai government has intervened both directly and indirectly in the development of the microfinance sector. The government provided several microfinance programmes with the purpose of expanding the access and use of financial services opportunities to the rural poor. Some of the microfinance programmes that were launched recently by the government are discussed next.

5.4.1 *Nano-finance scheme*

Launched in 2015, the "Nano-finance" scheme was approved by the MOF and BOT. The nano-finance scheme aimed to facilitate non-banking financial institutions to supply loans to grassroots citizens who have limited opportunities to access capital to invest and increase their income. Therefore, several parts of the financial regulations were relaxed by the MOF and BOT. The government permits 18 new entry investors (with a minimum of 50 million baht in registered capital) to operate nano-finance business in Thailand. The maximum loan amount of 100,000 baht without any collateral, at an interest rate of 30–36% per year, is offered to grassroots clients under nano-finance scheme. However, the loan considerations depend on the loan purpose and the borrower's repayment capacity (MOF, 2015; Parpart, 2014, 2015a).

The Thai government believed that the development of nano-finance would expand the microcredit market. The government also argued that the nano-finance scheme can reduce the demand for informal money lending among the poor. This is because all the operation of nano-finance is under the supervision of government agencies and the borrowers are protected by the law (Parpart, 2014). On the other hand, some policy makers still worried that the nano-finance scheme may increase the level of poor household debt and the amount of NPLs.

5.4.2 *Capital injection to the village funds*

By the end of 2015, the Thai government planned to inject an additional one million baht into the VF. The GSB and BAAC will provide 30 billion baht each to activate this government project worth around 60 billion baht.

Grades A and B of VF are selected from the NVFO performance report to get one million baht loan from GSB or BAAC. The important loan conditions include the repayment period up to 7 years with no interest charge for the first 2 years and no more than 4% interest charge for the remaining 5 years (Parpart, 2015b). In addition, this injection of funds illustrates that the Thai government still focuses on the VF mechanism which stimulates development in the rural areas.

5.4.3 *BAAC debt-relief measurement*

In 2015, the government approved the debt-relief measures of the BAAC which aimed to help more than 800,000 farmers who are in debts. The BAAC provided the budget of around 116 billion baht for this scheme using debt forgiveness and debt restructuring measurements.

This scheme applied to target farmers that were separated into three groups: (i) the farmers who lacked the ability to repay their debt, (ii) the farmers who have low repayment potential and (iii) the farmers who have ability to repay but are faced with seasonal production and/or marketing risks. The debt forgiveness measure will be applied to the first target group which comprises and 28,000 farmers accounted to around 4 billion baht. For the second group of 400,000 farmers, the BAAC will waive repayment of the principal for three years, but the farmers are still required to repay interest charges. The cost of debt restructuring measure applied to the second group of target farmers is around 48 billion baht. In the third group, the BAAC will determine how to extend the repayment period of those 450,000 farmers with a budget of 64 billion baht (BAAC, 2015b; Debt-relief measures, 2015).

The government and BAAC expect these series of measures will increase the debt-repayment capacity of the farmers and encourage the growth of the microfinance sector as a whole.

5.5 Characteristics of Successful Microfinance

Although the rural finance system in Thailand remains considerably active, the system faces several factors that affect the success and failure of the microfinance institutions. The factors include the following (Limsombunchai, 2006; The Banking with the Poor Network, 2010; Meagher, 2013):

1. *Level of indebtedness*

The relatively high level of indebtedness among rural poor is one of the main problems that distorts the efficiency of the rural financing system in Thailand. In the past few decades, several programmes have been launched by the Thai government to solve the high level of indebtedness problem such as a debt moratorium programme. The government spent millions of baht to subsidise these programmes so as to restructure the rural poor debt and increase their debt-repayment capacity. These programmes directly affected the growth of the microfinance sector. Thus, the policy impact assessment should be considered carefully if new measures are to benefit all stakeholders in the rural financing system.

The use of loan without any desire and its intended purposes primarily influence the loan repayment problem, especially among smallholder farmers in the rural areas of Thailand (Huayhongtong, Aditto & Pakdee, 2015). Therefore, the Thai government should promote the appropriate financial literacy and farm accounting knowledge to increase the financial management capabilities and reduce the level of indebtedness of the rural poor.

2. *Loan interest rate charged*

There is a wide range of opinions among policy makers regarding the optimal loan interest rate charge by microfinance institutions to the rural poor in Thailand. The Thai government plays an important role in providing low interest credit to the microfinance sector via the state-owned banks such as BAAC and GSB. However, due to the lack of collateral problem, some of the rural poor may not be able to access the lower interest rate loan from the formal institutions (Meagher, 2013).

Informal and semi-formal microfinance institutions tend to charge their borrowers high interest rates to replace the high cost of funds and risk of default on their debt. Therefore, a reasonable and sustainable loan interest rate must be carefully planned among the microfinance institutions. Recently, the government's attempt to reform property rights and land title helped the smallholder farmers in remote areas to access formal credit (Limsombunchai, 2006).

3. *Lack of legal mechanism*

Appropriate regulatory measures are an important component of strategies to monitor and control financial services of microfinance institutions. Bird *et al.* (2011) argued that the current laws in Thailand are unfavourable for investors to participate in microfinance market such as the interest rate ceilings for non-banking financial institutions, restrictions on license to operate microfinance business and the government credit subsidised programmes. Therefore, the MOF and BOT should establish new regulations or lighten up some existing financial regulations to support microfinance players to enable them to operate their business efficiently.

4. *Fund management strategies*

Fund management is one of the key factors affecting success or failure of microfinance operations, especially semiformal and informal institutions. It can be clearly seen that the ability to expand on borrowed fund of microfinance institutions is limited. This is due to the small size of the funds and high risks in defaults (The Banking with the Poor Network, 2010). Therefore, strengthening microfinance fund management with transformation strategies should be considered as part of the development and growth of microfinance operations in Thailand.

5.6 Conclusion

There has been significant growth in the microfinance sector over the recent decades. The remarkable shift in the rural financing system in Thailand started in 2001, when the government launched the Thailand VF which was one of the largest microfinance programmes in the world. However, the pros and cons of the VF programme in terms of poverty alleviation in rural households in Thailand have been widely debated to this day. The VF program is supposed to reduce poverty and improve rural poor welfare but resulted in high level of indebtedness and NPLs among the rural poor.

The Thai government intervention plays an essential role in providing low interest credit to the rural poor households and operated several microfinance schemes via the state-owned banks such as BAAC and GSB.

The purposes of those measures are to ease the problem of access to formal credits and to increase debt-repayment capacity among the rural poor households. Further, those measures directly affected the growth and development of the microfinance sector. Policy makers should therefore recognise that any changes in major policies without taking the rural household into consideration could negatively impact the operational efficiency of stakeholders in rural financial system.

Government agencies such as MOF and BOT should reform appropriate legal mechanisms and supervision measurements to attract new investors into the microfinance industry. This can result in competition in the microfinance industry to enhance the growth and development of the rural financial system and reduce poverty of rural poor households in the near future.

5.7 Policy Implication

The development and reform of the regulatory framework for microfinance institutions should be one of the Thai government's priorities. The frameworks may include (i) restructuring the licensing restrictions and supervision regulatory on microfinance business, and (ii) legislating appropriate interest rate ceiling to sustain the microfinance sector. It is hoped that some modified regulatory and supervisory frameworks will be a magnet for new investors into the microfinance sector (The Banking with the Poor Network, 2010; Meagher, 2013).

Meagher (2013) also argued that the Thai government should consider setting up an independent microfinance regulatory agency which is free from political power or domination. Theoretically, this should be an efficient institution to administer licensed microfinance institutions. Moreover, incentives should be provided to commercial banks in order to initiate financial services which are specific for rural poor. In terms of microfinance subsidies programmes, policy makers have to carefully generate any new programmes that are economically reasonable for all stakeholders in the rural financial system.

Alternatively, the government agencies such as MOF, NVFO and BAAC should try to find solutions that would improve the performance of the village funds nationwide. This is because the village funds have been one of the key mechanisms that the government applied to provide access to credit among the rural poor. The local village fund committees should pay more attention to strengthening their knowledge regarding financial management practices, lending strategies, credit appraisal and internal audit process. Therefore, appropriate short training courses should be considered as a priority to introduce that information to the local village fund committees nationwide.

The government should transfer knowledge of accounting and basic financial literacy to the rural poor. This may result in an increase in financial management capabilities and reduce the level of indebtedness of the rural poor.

References

Aditto, S. (2011). *Risk Analysis of Smallholder Farmers in Central and North-East Thailand.* Doctoral thesis, Lincoln University, Lincoln, New Zealand.

Ahmad, A. & Isvilanonda, S. (2003). Rural poverty and agricultural diversification in Thailand. Working Papers No. 2003:19. Department of Economics, Lund University. Retrieved from http://EconPapers.repec.org/RePEc:hhs:lunewp:2003_019.

Bank for Agriculture and Agricultural Cooperatives [BAAC] (2015a). Annual Report (in Thai). Retrieved from http://www.baac.or.th/content-report.php?content_group_sub=3. Accessed on February 10, 2015.

Bank for Agriculture and Agricultural Cooperatives [BAAC] (2015b). Press Release News 1/2558 (in Thai). Retrieved from http://www.baac.or.th/file-upload/13000-1.

Bank of Thailand [BOT] (2015). Thailand Key Economic Indicators. Retrieved from https://www.bot.or.th/English/Statistics/Pages/default.aspx. Accessed on March 22, 2015.

Bird, K., Hattel, K., Sasaki, E. & Attapich, L. (2011). Poverty, Income Inequality and Microfinance in Thailand. Asian Development Bank Southeast Asia Working Paper Series No. 6. Retrieved from https://www.adb.org/sites/default/files/publication/29271/poverty-income-inequality-microfinance-thailand.pdf.

Boonperm, J., Haughton., J. & Khandker, S. R. (2013). Does the village fund matter in Thailand? Evaluating the impact on incomes and spending. *Journal of Asian Economics,* 25, 3–16.

Chandoevwit, W. & Ashakul, B. (2008). The impact of the village fund on rural households. *TDRI Quarterly Review,* 23(2), 9–16.

Coleman, B. E. (2006). Microfinance in Northeast Thailand: Who benefits and how much? *World Development*, 34(9), 1612–1638.

Community Development Department [CDD] (2015). Community Database Report (in Thai). Retrieved from http://203.114.112.233/CDDCENTER/cdd_report/com_rpt1.php.

Cooperatives Promotion Department [CPD] (2015). Cooperatives Statistics (in Thai). Retrieved from http://www.cpd.go.th/ewt_dl_link.php?nid=2446&filename=Cooperative_Infor_Statistics.

Debt-Relief Measures to Waive Four Billion Owed by Farmers. (2015). *The Nation*. Retrieved from http://www.nationmultimedia.com/national/Debt-relief-measures-to-waive-Bt4-billion-owed-by--30257228.html.

Falvey, J. L. (2000). *Thai Agriculture: Golden Cradle of Millennia*. Bangkok: Kasetsart University Press.

Fongthong, S. (2012). Determinants of loan sizes of microcredit for villages and communities in Thailand. *International Journal of Intelligent Technologies and Applied Statistics,* 5(2), 121–142.

Fuglie, K. O. (2001). Agricultural development in Thailand. In Pray, C. E. & Fuglie, K. O. (Eds.), *Private Investment in Agricultural Research and International Technology Transfer in Asia* (pp. 76–98): USDA Economic Research Service. Retrieved from http://www.ageconsearch.umn.edu/bitstream/33927/1ae010805.pdf.

Gine, X. (2011). Access to capital in rural Thailand: An estimated model of formal vs. informal credit. *Journal of Development Economics*, 96(2011), 16–29.

Government Savings Bank [GSB] (2013). Annual Report (in Thai). Retrieved from http://www.gsb.or.th/getattachment/57a54b07-35dc-4ce6-b27b-a1f13345383c/img-report-2556.aspx. Accessed on March 25, 2015

Huayhongtong, P., Aditto, S. & Pakdee, P. (2015). The factors affecting the loan repayment of borrowers of Bank of Agriculture and Agricultural Cooperatives, Kong district, Nakornratchasima province, Thailand (in Thai). *Khon Kaen Agriculture Journal*, 1, 755–758.

Isvilanonda, S. (2002). Rice supply and demand in Thailand: Recent trends and future outlook. In Sombilla, M., Hossain, M. & Hardy, B. (Eds.), *Development in the Asian Rice Economy* (pp. 211–238). International Rice Research Institute. Retrieved from http://irri.org/resources/publications/books/item/developments-in-the-asian-rice-economy.

Krongkaew, M. (1985). Agricultural development, rural poverty, and income distribution in Thailand. *The Developing Economies*, 23(4), 325–346.

Limsombunchai, V. (2006). *Rural Financing in Thailand*. Doctoral thesis, Lincoln University, Lincoln, New Zealand.

Luxchaigul, N. (2014). The effectiveness of sustainable development of the saving for production groups in Northeast of Thailand. *Environment Management and Sustainable Development*, 3(1), 168–180.

Meagher, P. (2013). Microfinance regulation and supervision recommendations report in Thailand. ADB technical assistant consultant's report. Retrieved from https://www.adb.org/sites/default/files/project-document/80373/45128-001-tacr-03.pdf.

Menkhoff, L. & Rungruxsirivorn, O. (2011). Do village funds improve access to finance? Evidence from Thailand. *World Development*, 39(1), 110–122.

Ministry of Finance [MOF]. (2015). Nano-Finance Scheme Descriptions (in Thai). Retrieved from http://www.mof.go.th/home/.../58-07-01-NanoFinance.pdf.

National Statistical Office of Thailand [NSO]. (2015). Thailand population statistics. Retrieved from http://www.nso.go.th. Accessed on January 26, 2015.

Office of Agricultural Economics [OAE] (2015). Agricultural Statistics of Thailand. Retrieved from http://www.oae.go.th.

Office of the National Economic and Social Development Board [NESDB] (2015). Macroeconomics statistics of Thailand (in Thai). Retrieved from http://www.nesdb.go.th/Default.aspx?tabid=433. Accessed on February 20, 2015.

Parpart, E. (2014). BOT considers 'nano-financing' for grass-roots people. *The Nation*. Retrieved from http://www.nationmultimedia.com/business/BOT-considers-nano-financing-for-grass-roots-peopl-30246202.html.

Parpart, E. (2015a). Nano-finance Regulations Approved. *The Nation*. Retrieved from http://www.nationmultimedia.com/business/Nano-finance-regulations-approved-30252792.html.

Parpart, E. (2015b). GSB says it can meet the Village Fund Loan Target. *The Nation*. Retrieved from http://www.nationmultimedia.com/business/GSB-says-it-can-meet-the-Village-Fund-loan-target-30268079.html.

Rafiq, S. (2013). The effect of microfinance on human capital formation: Evidence from rural Thailand. *The Michigan Journal of Business*, 6(2), 69–116.

Rural debt in Thailand: Turning the tide (September 19, 2013). *The Economist*. Retrieved from http://www.economist.com/blogs/schumpeter/2013/09/rural-debt-thailand.

Siamwala, A. (1988). Rural credit markets in Thailand. *TDRI Quarterly Newsletter*, 3(4), 9–11.

Thai Parliamentary Budget Office (2015). Village and Urban Community Funds (in Thai). Retrieved from http://www.parliament.go.th/ewtadmin/ewt/parbudget/ewt_dl_link.php?nid=105.

Thaiprasert, N. (2006). Rethinking the role of agriculture and agro-Industry in the economic development of Thailand: Input-Output and CGE analyses. PhD

Dissertation, Graduate School of International Development, Nagoya University, Japan.

The Banking with the Poor Network (2010). Microfinance Industry Report: Thailand. Retrieved from http://www.microfinancegateway.org/library/microfinance-industry-report-thailand.

The Cooperative League of Thailand (2015). The Historical Movement of Cooperatives in Thailand. Retrieved from http://eng.clt.or.th/index/.

The Federation of Saving and Credit Cooperatives of Thailand Limited [FSCT]. (2015). Cooperatives in Thailand. Retrieved from http://www.fsct.com/english/index.php?f1=menu1.8.html.

United Nation Development Program [UNDP] (2015). About Thailand. Retrieved from http://www.th.undp.org/content/thailand/en/home/countryinfo.html.

Wattanutchariya, S. & Jitsanguan, T. (1992). Increasing the scale of small-farm operations in Thailand. Retrieved from http://www.agnet.org/library.php?func=view&id=20110726143050.

Chapter 6

Rural Financial Markets and Credit Delivery System in the Philippines

Salvador P. Catelo,* Maria Angeles O. Catelo†
and Ceptryl S. Mina‡

Professor, Department of Agricultural and Applied Economics,
Associate Professor, Department of Economics,
Research Assistant, Department of Agricultural and Applied
Economics, College of Economics and Management,
University of the Philippines Los Baños, Laguna, Philippines

*spcatelo@up.edu.ph
†mocatelo@up.edu.ph
‡cepmina03@gmail.com

Abstract

The growth in the microfinance industry in the Philippines as a potential 'financial inclusion' innovation is a welcome development. Micro, small and medium enterprises (MSMEs) and low-income clients are able to increase their economic activity and income, build up assets, prepare against emergencies and invest in education, health and housing services.

But despite the many benefits and growing importance of micro-finance, there remain social and financial performance issues as well as impact concerns that continue to challenge the industry. Central to its success is a strong link between rural finance and other components of development like access to basic infrastructure, appropriate technology and improved marketing infrastructure that are necessary conditions for competitive and sustainable economic activities. The inclusion of the private sector in financial intermediation must be reinforced by microfinance institutions (MFIs) and other channels of government funds that have the required competence, network, carrying capacity as well as infrastructure to minimise, if not totally eliminate, credit pollution and defaults. Regular access and proper use of credit ultimately leads to increase in total income, the springboard of the two long-standing development objectives of poverty alleviation and food security.

The chapter discusses the role of microfinance in rural development in the Philippines. It particularly identifies the effects of microcredit on input use, productivity and income in the context of Philippine agriculture. The chapter concludes with an overview of the success of microfinance in the Philippines followed by policy directions.

Keywords: Agriculture, credit, rural finance, microfinance, poverty, the Philippines.

6.1 Introduction

The importance of rural financial market and credit delivery system in the Philippines cannot be overemphasised. The country's historical policy reforms have focused on the modernisation of the agriculture and fisheries sector in the pursuit of two long-standing development objectives: poverty alleviation and food security. To accelerate agricultural and rural development in order to achieve these twin goals, a necessary condition is a well-functioning agricultural credit and delivery programme.

While it is recognised that policies have, to a large extent, addressed the *hardware* requisites (e.g., infrastructure, production, processing and trade facilities), the *software* needs (e.g., knowledge management and capacity building) and the *orgware* essentials (e.g., risk management, stakeholder network and consortium building) (Smits, 2002) and the persistent production and market problems that are oftentimes deeply rooted on poor rural financial markets and credit delivery system have rendered the attainment of poverty alleviation and food security more complex and more challenging to handle.

Just like most emerging countries in rural Asia, the Philippines has an evolving experience in the provision of agricultural credit through the development of rural financial markets. In recent years, microfinance has also taken center stage in the country as a potential 'financial inclusion' innovation as it is commonly associated with poverty alleviation through banking. But as Manos, Gueyie & Yaron (2013) posit, despite the many benefits and the growing importance of microfinance in providing financial service to low-income clients, there remain social and financial performance issues as well as impact concerns that continue to challenge the industry.

This chapter offers more light into the microfinance story in the Philippines. Section 6.2 discusses agricultural credit and microfinance policies in the Philippines. Section 6.3 explains the credit sources and microfinance institutions (MFIs) for Philippine agriculture, while Section 6.4 provides an overview of the problem in rural/agricultural credit and elucidates on where microfinance lies in rural development. Section 6.5 identifies the effects of microfinance credit on input use, production, productivity, and income. Section 6.6 concludes the chapter by looking at successful agricultural credit and microfinance systems and drawing lessons and policy directions.

6.2 Agricultural Credit and Microfinance Policies in the Philippines

6.2.1 *Evolution of rural credit policies*

This section traces the history of various credit programmes that were implemented in order to provide Filipino farmers with access to formal credit. Table 6.1 summarises the salient provisions of these major financial market reforms and legislations.

As early as the 1960s, rural banks and cooperatives started the concept and practice of servicing small loans. In fact, the Philippines adopted a 'supply-led approach' where different credit programmes such as low-cost rediscount facility for agricultural lending, input and credit subsidies, and

Table 6.1:   Salient Provisions of Rural Credit Policies in the Philippines, 1960–2009

Year/Period	Credit policy/Legislation	Salient provisions	Source
1960s	Supply-led approach policies were used Rural Bank Law in 1952[a] Agricultural Credit Cooperative and Farmers' Association (ACCFA),[b] Masagana 99[c] and PD 717[d]	— Provided low-cost rediscount facility for agricultural lending, input and credit subsidies — Imposed allocation for agricultural credit — Adopted regulatory schemes like credit quotas, deposit retention and subsidised loans from the Central Bank	Llanto (1993); Geron & Casuga (2012)
1970s to mid-1980s	DCPs	— Rural banks, development banks and other GFIs were mobilised to provide highly subsidised credit to the rural poor	Llanto (2004); Micu (2010)
	Grameen Bank Approach	— Implemented by NGOs — Provided small loans for micro entrepreneurial activities	Llanto (2004); Micu (2010)
Mid-1980s to 1990s	CALF (E.O. 113)	— provided credit to the Philippine Crop Insurance Corporation (PCIC),[e] Quedan Rural Credit and Guarantee Corporation (QUEDANCOR)[f] and Guarantee Fund for Small and Medium Enterprises (GFSME)[g]	Llanto (1993)
	Financial market reforms and liberalisation	— Deregulation of interest rates by removal of interest rate ceilings on all deposits and loans — Termination of the Central Bank's subsidised rediscounting facility for agriculture — and Implementation of mandatory increase of the minimum capital requirements for banks	Llanto (1993, 1994); Poliquit (2006)

	AMCFP	— Market-based financial and credit policies for the agriculture sector were adopted — Provided the enabling policy environment for increased private sector participation in the provision of agricultural credit — Credit programs were rationalised and subsidies reduced — Lowered costs of intermediation to allow other banks, financial institutions and NGOs to operate and provide credit in rural areas	(Lamberte *et al.*, 1994) The ADB helped in improving the formal credit system
1997 (enacted in 2004)	AFMA	— Initiated the AMCFP, the current agriculture, fisheries and agrarian reform credit and financing system of the country	Corpuz & Kraft (2005)
2000	GBL	— Recognised microfinance as a legitimate banking activity BSP set rules and regulations to make banks more microfinance-friendly	Llanto (2004); Micu (2010); BSP (2013)
2002	BMBEs Act (R.A. 9178)	— Integrated micro enterprises of the informal sector into mainstream economy — Microfinance credit windows were made available to service financial needs of BMBEs	MSME Development Plan (2011–2016)

(Continued)

Table 6.1: *(Continued)*

Year/Period	Credit policy/Legislation	Salient provisions	Source
2008	CISA (R.A. 9510)	— Created the Credit Information Corporation (CIC) that receives and consolidates basic data on credit history and financial condition of borrowers to lower the credit risks of financial institutions	BSP (2013)
2009	Agri–Agra Reform Credit Act of 2009 (R.A. 10000)	— Amended PD 717 — Provides agriculture, fisheries and agrarian reform credit, insurance and financing system to enhance the productivity of the agriculture and fisheries sectors	Aquino, Anil & Correa (2014)

[a]Permits establishment of family-owned rural banks, in which the government provided 50% government equity, access to preferential rediscount rates, tax exemption and technical assistance (Geron & Casuga, 2012).

[b]Established in 1952 to develop cooperatives for small farmers to serve as channels of small production credit and marketing loans to farmers (Geron & Casuga, 2012).

[c]Package of production incentives to farmers that includes low cost production credit, fertiliser subsidy, technical assistance and other agricultural support services (Esguerra, 1981).

[d]Enacted in 1975, also known as Agri–Agra Law that mandated banks to extend at least 25% of their loanable funds for agricultural credit in general, of which at least 10% of the loanable funds shall be made available for agrarian reform credit.

[e]Used by CALF to guarantee the production credit of small farmers.

[f]Provides a guarantee cover to inventory financing.

[g]Provides credit guarantee to small and medium-sized firms/enterprises.

an imposed allocation for agricultural credit are included (Geron & Casuga, 2012). Regulatory schemes such as credit quotas, deposit retention and subsidised loans from the Central Bank were also part of this approach (Llanto, 1993).

Moreover, from the 1970s until the mid-1980s, rural banks, development banks and other government financial institutions (GFIs) were mobilised to provide highly subsidised credit to the rural poor through Directed Credit Programs (DCPs). However, the 'supply-led approach' was plagued by serious default problems resulting in weak financial performance of most financial institutions, particularly the rural banks which were used as conduits of cheap government funds (Geron & Casuga, 2012).

With the failure of the 'supply-led approach' of credit programs, the government then ventured into implementing financial reforms in the mid-1980s. The Grameen Bank Approach[1] was adopted by non-government organisations (NGOs) to provide the much-needed small loans for micro-entrepreneurial activities. Ahon sa Hirap Inc. (ASHI) is the first serious replication of Grameen Bank in the Philippines in 1989 that also accepted the challenge of becoming an agent of change among poor women. The common goal of this MFI is the reduction of poverty through the provision of financial services to poor women (http://www.ashi.org.ph). The implementation of Ahon sa Hirap Programme did not only create economic benefits but also empowerment, increased respect and a greater sense of self-worth among women. Increases in income from being ASHI benefactors were reported (Sulit, 1990; Jaldon, 1999; Capuyan, 2011). The increase in income led to increased food expenditure, higher loan repayments and household expenditures.

Other financial market reforms such as the deregulation of interest rates on all deposits and loans, termination of the Central Bank's subsidised rediscounting facility for agriculture, and the mandatory increase in the minimum capital requirements for banks were also implemented. The lending programmes of non-financial government agencies and 20

---

[1]A banking approach originated in Bangladesh in 1976 with collateral from the client. The banking system is based on mutual trust, accountability and participation lending only to groups rather than individuals to enable them to start up income-generating activities (IFAD, 2003).

agriculture credit programmes were then terminated and consolidated into the Comprehensive Agricultural Loan Fund (CALF) (Llanto, 1993).

However, the financial market reforms of the mid-'80s to the 1990s suffered from poor programme management, large default rates, political intervention and inefficient program operations resulting in high intermediation and government costs [National Credit Council (NCC)[2] (1999a, 1999b, 1999c)].

The Agriculture and Fisheries Modernisation Act (AFMA) was subsequently passed in 1997. AFMA adopted the market-based interest rates and mobilisation of GFIs as wholesalers of funds (Llanto, 2004; Micu, 2010). Philippine microfinance has then become a social development initiative to alleviate poverty. Microfinance is the provision of a broad range of financial services that include money transfers, loans, deposits, payment services and insurance aimed at empowering the poor and financially incapable people. It assists borrowers in increasing their income or in giving them a source of income. Microfinance also offers technical support through seminars and trainings. Microcredit is an extremely small loan given by microfinance and is essential for any microbusiness or microenterprise to withstand irregularities of their finances.

At the same time, further market-based financial and credit policies for the agriculture sector were adopted under the Agro-Industry Modernisation Credit and Financing Program (AMCFP) which provided the enabling policy environment for increased private sector participation in the provision of agricultural credit. Credit programs were rationalised and subsidies substantially reduced (Lamberte *et al.*, 1994). The Asian Development Bank helped in improving the formal credit system by reducing the costs of intermediation, allowing other banks and financial institutions to operate in the rural areas, removing credit subsidies and encouraging NGOs to play a greater role in providing credit (Poliquit, 2006).

In 2000, the General Banking Law (GBL) recognised microfinance as a legitimate banking activity. The BSP was mandated to set the rules and

---

[2]The National Credit Council was created under AO No. 86 in 1993 and comprises representatives from both the government and the private sector with the main mandate of rationalising the implementation of all government DCPs and of developing viable and sustainable alternative mechanisms for providing the poor access to credit.

regulations which made the banking sector more microfinance-friendly (Llanto, 2004; Micu, 2010; BSP, 2013). Other key legislation includes the Barangay Microbusiness Enterprise Act (BMBE), the MSME Law, the Credit Information Systems Act (CISA) and the Amendment of the Cooperative Code of the Philippines.

In particular, Republic Act No. 9178, otherwise known as BMBE Act of 2002 and the National Small and Medium Enterprises Development Plan (NSMEDP) of the Department of Trade and Industry-National Capital Region (DTI-NCR) are only two of the microfinancing measures that provide assistance to the poor. BMBE Act of 2002 is an act that promotes the establishment of BMBEs, provides incentives and benefits and encourages the formation and growth of BMBEs. Any business enterprise engaged in production, processing or manufacturing of products, including agro-processing, as well as trading services, with total assets not more than PHP3 million may qualify as beneficiaries of BMBE. Being a beneficiary of BMBE means exemption from paying taxes emerging from the business. However, aspiring entrepreneurs who want to apply in BMBE do not include professionals like accountants, lawyers and the like.

NSMEDP is another government initiative that prioritises strategically the development of the Small and Medium Enterprise (SME) sector. Having almost the same goals with the BMBE, the NSMEDP was launched to help micro and small enterprises to develop higher levels of business undertakings by upgrading their productivity and value-added capabilities. It has five elements: (1) financing; (2) human resource development/entrepreneurship training; (3) market development; (4) product development and (5) advocacy for enabling environment.

6.2.2 *Current policies and programmes*

6.2.2.1 *Republic Act 8435: AFMA*

AFMA was passed in 1997, enacted on 2004 and extended until December 2015. AFMA aims to help increase the agriculture sector's productivity and competitiveness in order to enable farmers and fisherfolk to meet the challenges of globalisation. It covers the many elements critical to agriculture modernisation, such as research and development (R&D), infrastructure, training, marketing and credit, among others. AFMA initiated the AMCFP,

Table 6.2: Borrowing by Major Source of Loans (in %), Philippines, 1996–2005

Source (%)	1996–1997	1999–2000	2001–2002	2004–2005
All borrowers	100	100	100	100
Formal institutions	24	38.6	34.4	49.4
Informal lenders	76	61.3	60.3	50.6
Formal and informal lenders			5.3	

Source: ACPC Small Farmer and Fisherfolk Credit Accessibility Surveys (Llanto, 2008 as cited by SEPO, 2009).

which is the current agriculture, fisheries and agrarian reform credit and financing system of the country. AMCFP terminated all government DCPs to agriculture and adopted a national strategy of a wholesale lending programme.

Initial assessments of the AMCFP showed that the credit policy reforms introduced by the AFMA as well as the mainstreaming of microfinance principles (through the adoption of a National Strategy for Microfinance) have shown some promise, encouraging more private sector participation in rural credit markets, while increasing the access of small farmers to formal financing. Surveys conducted by the Agricultural Credit Policy Council (ACPC) have shown an increase in borrowing from more formal credit sources. From only 24% of small farmers borrowing from formal institutions in 1997, this jumped to 49% in 2005 (see Table 6.2).

6.2.2.2 *Republic Act 10000: Agri–Agra Reform Credit Act of 2009*

The Agri–Agra Reform Credit Act is the amended PD 717 that aims to provide the agriculture, fisheries and agrarian reform sectors with credit, insurance and financing system to enhance their productivity as stipulated under the AFMA and the Agrarian Reform Code of the Philippines (Aquino *et al.*, 2014).

Presidential Decree 717, otherwise known as the Agri/Agra Law, mandates that all banks set aside 25% of their net loanable funds for agricultural lending, of which 10% is to be lent to agrarian reform beneficiaries and 15% for agricultural lending. While minimum lending requirements have been easily exceeded for the latter client group given the good number of creditworthy agribusinesses, compliance has not historically been met in terms of lending to the agrarian reform beneficiaries. The main reason is that banks are not structured to manage profitably the provision of small loans to widely dispersed beneficiaries.

The Agri–Agra Reform Credit Act of 2009 provided increased access to credit and financial support to farmers, fisherfolk and agrarian reform beneficiaries and is viewed to cater to their need for financial capital to support production and consumption requirements.

6.2.3 *Other policy initiatives*

The ACPC designs innovative financing schemes to address the particular requirement of marginalised farmers and fisherfolk who cannot meet the collateral requirements of banks. Likewise, in cooperation with both government and private training institutions, the ACPC provides grants to farmer organisations for institutional capacity building activities such as: capital and savings mobilisation; development of management information systems; social preparation for small farmers and fisherfolk; management training; credit risk management; and organisation, establishment and strengthening of cooperative banks and other farmer-owned financial institutions (Corpuz & Kraft, 2005).

6.3 Microfinance and Credit Institutions for Philippine Agriculture: Boon or Bane

Figure 6.1 shows the major players that comprise the rural financial market in the Philippines. Formal credit channels consist of banking and non-banking institutions, while informal credit channels include all credit sources that are not under the umbrella of the banking system.

6.3.1 *The formal credit institutions*

Formal financial institutions are owned, controlled and regulated by the government. Heidhues & Schrieder (1999) identified five formal intermediaries of the rural financial market which include the commercial and development banks, specialised agricultural financial institutions, cooperatives and NGOs.

Formal financial institutions are assigned to provide interventions that were formulated by governments to encourage farmers to adopt

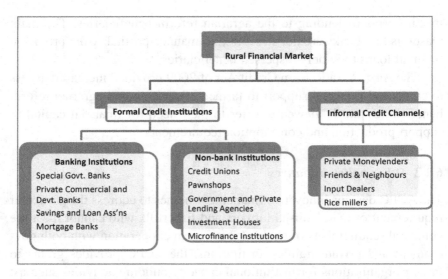

Figure 6.1:   Schematic Diagram of the Rural Financial Market in the Philippines

technologies and have access to funds (in the form of credit) at "more reasonable interest rates than available from informal sources (Llanto *et al.*, 2007). Subsidised-credit programs to stimulate the rapid adoption of the new technology (e.g., seeds, fertiliser and chemicals for production) are also offered in formal credit institutions (Llanto *et al.*, 2007).

The government implemented interventions that aimed to address the problem of rural financing such as the introduction of loan quotas, subsidised interest rates and DCPs, among others. Unfortunately, it was observed that the outcomes of these programmes have been minimal at best (SEPO, 2009). The distortions that were introduced in the financial markets by these programmes weakened the financial discipline and rendered these DCPs unsustainable which forced the government to look into alternative methods of providing rural finance.

The performance of formal credit financial institutions proved to be disappointing (Heidhues & Schrieder, 1999) for several reasons. Commercial and development banks had limited knowledge on agriculture and showed little interest in lending to farmers. NGO's, on the other hand, were able to extend credit *albeit* to a limited clientele only. Expectedly, small farmers were generally considered to be non-creditworthy because of the fact that agriculture activity is a very risky venture. Moreover, formal financial institutions also required voluminous basic documents and collateral, and loan procedures were long and complicated and all these factors drove farmers to rely on informal credit sources instead, despite the relatively higher interest rates charged by informal lenders (SEPO, 2009). Clearly, there is market failure in the form of information asymmetry particularly from the viewpoint of formal credit institutions whose little knowledge about the borrower characteristics limited their assurance of guaranteed repayment (Poliquit, 2006).

On the other hand, MFIs granting small loans at market rates without collateral have been established in order to reach small-scale clientele such as non-farm enterprises and microenterprises. Thrift, rural and cooperative banks are BSP-regulated banks that are involved in the provision of microfinance services in the low-income sector.

However, there are also institutions that are non-regulated and non-supervised by the BSP that play significant roles in microfinance. These are the credit and multipurpose cooperatives and microfinance NGOs. They are discussed in more detail in the following sub-section.

6.3.2 *Rural banks*

Rural banks are government partners in countryside development and play a crucial role in promoting and expanding the rural economy by providing basic financial services to rural communities that are not served to any significant extent by other banks (Aragon, Kakinaka & Kim 2011). The establishment of rural banks has been promoted by the government since the early 1950s, primarily to serve as a conduit for its credit program across the countryside.

Rural banks are ideally suited to the provision of commercial microfinance and they offer both savings and credit facilities to their clients. Unlike commercial banks, rural banks are locally managed on a continuing basis with the same staff to keep information costs low in selecting micro and small-scale clients (Charitonenko, 2003). Compared to microfinance NGOs and cooperatives, rural banks can accommodate a wider range of clients with higher loan balance but only a few of them provide group loans to clients. Most rural banks that are engaged in microfinance provide individual loans.

Table 6.3:   Snapshot of Microfinance Exposure of Banks in the Philippines (December 2012)

Banks	No. of banks	Outstanding loans (in million pesos)	No. of borrowers
Microfinance-oriented thrift banks	3	186	21,378
Microfinance-oriented rural banks	6	2,669	444,583
Microfinance-engaged rural banks	138	3,585	500,175
Microfinance-engaged cooperative banks	22	653	63,062
Microfinance-engaged thrift banks	19	766	71,579
Microfinance-engaged universal bank	1	1.5	41
Microfinance-engaged regular commercial-bank	1	61	4,636
TOTAL	190	7,922	1,105,454

Note: The Inclusive Finance Advocacy Staff of the BSP provides the distinction between microfinance oriented banks (MOBs) from microfinance engaged banks. Are licensed under Circular 273 series of 2001 where at least 50% of the gross loan portfolio consists of microfinance loans at all times as defined under BSP regulations. On the other hand, microfinance engaged banks do not have license to do microfinance but have some level of microfinance operations, and their gross loan portfolio may be less or greater than the 50% cap provided under Circular 273.
Source: Bangko Sentral ng Pilipinas.

Table 6.3 shows that rural banks are the major sources of microfinance loans, having the highest number of branches (144 out of 190 as of December 2012) spread in various regions. Outstanding loans accounted for close to 80% of the total microfinance loan exposure or about PHP6.3 billion as of December 2012 (BSP, 2012). These rural banks were able to service 944,758 borrowers or about 86% of the total.

Given this strategic significance, the failure of rural banks would be a major concern. Between 1970 and 2007, there were about 400 rural bank failures recorded due to various factors such as misguided government policies and programmes that subsidised credit initiatives. The absence of a network was also a constraint to rural bank operation of microfinance programmes because in an increasingly competitive environment, it constituted a disadvantage that was linked to the institutional structure of a rural bank. Furthermore, rural banks did not have access to crucial support services due to their inherent nature as a unit-based structure. Thus, developing new microfinance products and services, training their staff and effectively enforcing the auditing and control mechanisms proved costly and difficult on their own. Rural banks need support services for them to compete over the long term.

Given the challenges that rural banks faced in the past, government instituted reforms to strengthen their performance and these reforms started with more stringent minimum capital regulation coupled with a buffer that was sufficient to protect bank depositors in the event of adversities and reversals (Aragon *et al.*, 2011). Establishing strategic alliances with other financial institutions to branch out aggressively was perceived as the only solution to gain access to regional markets.

6.3.3 *Cooperatives*

Similar to rural banks, cooperatives are established close to their communities to provide them good access to important information about their members. Member-clients also have a stake in the continued financial success of their cooperative and this mutual stake-taking helps to reinforce discipline in the management and operations of cooperatives.

In the microfinance sector, cooperatives reach significantly more individuals and families than do other financial institutions. This makes them the actors who are truly responsible for improving access to financial services by all, thereby contributing to increasing local economic growth and reducing poverty (ICA, 2015). Credit cooperatives are registered, regulated and supervised by the Cooperative Development Authority (CDA) of the Philippines. Cooperatives perform similar functions as those of recognised financial institutions. For instance, the credit cooperatives are legally permitted to offer loans and take deposits from their members even if they are not licensed banks (BSP, 2011).

The member-borrower's capacity to pay and his/her cash-flows are usually not used by the cooperatives in determining creditworthiness and repayment terms (Microfinance Council of the Philippines, 2012). In recent years, a number of cooperatives have shifted towards cash-flow based lending to avoid high default rates. Microfinance services offered by cooperatives mostly include microenterprise loans and savings.

Cooperatives provide loans on both individual and group lending basis. Some cooperatives require compulsory savings through loan retention. These savings are then used to build members' capital to eventually be able to meet the required member share capital for regular members. Interest rates charged by cooperatives on their microfinance loans are usually higher than the regular loans offered to the regular members (Microfinance Council of the Philippines, 2012).

The NCC in coordination with the CDA and major credit cooperatives had released the Standard Chart of Accounts and its accompanying Manual of Accounts, as well as the COOP (Compliance to administrative and legal requirements, Organisational structure, Operation and management, and Plans and programs) (COOP) administrative standards and Portfolio quality, Efficiency, Stability, Operations, and Structure of Assets (PESOS) financial standards to transform cooperatives from a purely developmental entity to an effective regulatory agency (Charitonenko, 2003). The remaining challenge lies in their widespread adoption and use.

6.3.4 *Microfinance NGOs*

NGOs have emerged as key players in the microcredit industry. Microfinance NGOs are not regulated by the BSP but they have been playing the role of intermediary in various dimensions (Charitonenko, 2003). They are also registered with the Securities and Exchange Commission.

Microfinance NGOs provide credit services to their client members but unlike cooperatives, they are not allowed to take deposits from the public nor from their members. Resources and tools were developed by these NGOs for communities and microcredit organisations to monitor progress and identify good practices. But while these NGOs also created opportunities to learn about the principles and practice of microcredit through publications, workshops and seminars and training programmes, some of them have weak ownership and governance structures with board members that lack background in finance and banking and thus, are less equipped to overcome financial challenges. Furthermore, majority of small microfinance NGOs do not provide adequate attention or commitment to sustaining the organisation (Charitonenko, 2003).

Another issue on microfinance NGOs is that they are small weak institutions and dependent on subsidised funds for their survival (Charitonenko, 2013). This curtailment in growth is perceived to be rooted in insufficient management information systems and the lack of capacity to undertake market research. Aggravating this situation is the poor access of Microfinance NGOs to appropriate systems and support services (Microfinance Council of the Philippines, 2012).

Lastly, the lack of transparency has historically been an important issue of these NGOs in mobilising deposits and placing client savings at risk by lending them out. Though NGOs are not legally authorised to mobilise deposits, unfortunately, many do so as a way to substitute donor funds to fund their loan portfolios (Charitonenko, 2003).

6.3.5 *Informal financial institutions*

The ADB (1989) as cited by Floro & Yotoupolos (1991) identified four broad categories of informal credit; direct lending, united lending, tied lending and group/mutual finance. Direct lending are loans extended by friends and relatives. United credit involves lenders that lend and operate with self-generating funds or from borrowed money. Tied credit refers to credit that is tied-up with other transactions that serve as collateral, such as the purchase of harvest (Floro & Yotoupolos, 1991). Group or mutual finance is composed of individuals that lend or save money on a rotating or non-rotating basis.

The failure of farmers to form organisations such as cooperatives shaped the credit-marketing tie-up mode where farmers eventually developed heavy reliance on traders to buy their produce and sell them to consumers. The credit-marketing tie-up of farmers with the traders is believed to be the end result of farmers' lack of access to the formal credit market or the farmer's inability to repay their loans. The financial advances provided by traders allow the farmers to smooth out their consumption pattern despite the seasonality of production (Llanto, 2005).

Among the informal sources of credit, input–output traders are the most common. These traders provide the inputs and at the same time serve as market for the borrowers' produce (Peñalba, Paunlagi & Elazegui, 2012).

Cash loans are sometimes provided by traders for the food and other necessities of the borrower household prior to harvesting time. In spite of the loan services that formal lenders offer, informal sources prevail due to accessibility and flexibility in favour of borrowers. There is no collateral requirement, cumbersome documentation, processing and bookkeeping requirements. Informal moneylenders are more liberal and more willing to deal with transactions even in small absolute amounts.

On the downside, these informal credit sources are noted for usury and exploitation of borrowers. This was evident in the high interest rates charged on their credits that are often over 100% a year (Madamba, 2005). The high interest rates compensate the high risks in granting credit to less credible borrowers (Castillo, 2005). Loans from immediate relatives and friends which are generally small and of short duration may not even be available to borrowers in time of needs as they, too, may have their own economic needs. Nevertheless, they perform an important contribution in rural areas in the absence of any other alternative source of credit.

The case of farmers' resort to informal credit is worsened by the occurrence of random shocks on assets such as crop loss, and medical emergencies, which households are typically vulnerable under credit crunch (Peñalba *et al.*, 2012). For instance, farmers who could not access formal credit sources due to their inability to meet the latter's requirements can find it less cumbersome to borrow from informal credit sources. There is, however, no assurance that the terms and conditions of the informal credit sources are better than the formal sources.

While the informal credit system may fill the gap as far as lending to small-scale farmers is concerned, there is no assurance that farmers would be better off under the usurious terms and conditions (Peñalba *et al.*, 2012). What makes them better off than borrowing from the formal credit system, though, is the timeliness of available credit especially for the much needed capital for production purposes (Peñalba *et al.*, 2012).

However, the emergence of informal credit system that offers high interest rates and low product prices that are detrimental to farmers' welfare prodded policy makers to review existing credit policies. Hence, the Credit Act of 2009 was created to provide credit and financing system for agriculture and agrarian reform at cheaper rates and costs through banking institutions.

6.4 Where Lies Microfinance in Philippine Rural Development

Philippine agriculture remains to be an important economic pillar. From 2004 to 2010, it contributed an average of 18.4% to the Gross Domestic Product and accounted for a considerable share of total export earnings. It also provided employment to about one-third or 11.8 million people of the country's labour force (BAS, 2014).

However, the majority of people in the agricultural sector reside in the rural areas. The rural sector accounts for over 70% of the total poor, with poverty incidence highest among fishermen and farmers at 39% and 38%, respectively (PSA, 2014). Why is there massive poverty among the rural population? Poliquit (2006) explains that rural poverty is the result of poor productivity growth in agriculture, under-investment in rural infra-structure, unequal land and income distribution, high population growth, and the low quality of social services. This is aggravated by other factors such as natural disasters the risks associated with volatile markets, lack of access to financial services (Tayag, 2011) and information (Charitonenko, 2003; ACPC, 2014) which can disrupt growth and further increase poverty levels.

Thus, reducing rural poverty has far-reaching welfare and develop-ment implications and assumes even greater importance especially when food prices soar as an offshoot of low production and imbalance in the food supply. This is because the poor and the vulnerable are hit the hardest and their already perilous quandary is worsened when these events occur.

As the Philippines prepares for the Association of Southeast Asian Nations (ASEAN) regional cooperation, it has to fortify its economic pil-lars to effectively coalesce and share the responsibility of strengthening the economic and social stability of the region. Hence, competitiveness and food security remain top priority of the government. As most studies would show, the need for well-functioning and effective financial markets that could provide credit especially to small farmers is key (Heidhues & Schrieder, 1999) to improving agricultural productivity.

Microfinance and agricultural credit can be an effective solution to the so-called "vicious circle of low capital formation". As expounded on by the Asian Development Bank (2000), the primary function of the financial system is to facilitate resource allocation across space and time in an uncertain environment. When it functions well, it contributes to economic growth through two channels: capital accumulation and technological innovation. The factors that affect capital formation include per capita income, savings rate, investment rate and productivity. Access to rural credit can ultimately lead to increase in total income via productivity gain and incremental income from more IGAs. In turn, increased income can infuse additional household savings and capital for farming aside from the enhancement of farmers' liquidity management and risk carrying capacities.

The Philippines is a staunch supporter of microfinance and agricultural credit to accelerate rural and agricultural development. Formal credit institutions in the rural areas are deemed important in improving the income and livelihood strategies of small farmers (Geron & Casuga, 2012). Financial institutions such as the Philippine National Bank (PNB), the Development Bank of the Philippines (DBP) and the Land Bank of the Philippines (LBP) were established to provide financing specifically to the agriculture sector. The PNB concentrated on financing the needs of the sugar sector, while the DBP provided funds to agri-based processing industries such as rice milling, coconut and livestock. The LBP catered mostly to land reform beneficiaries.

However, while several policy reforms[3] were designed to develop a viable and sustainable rural financial market to make credit more accessible and available to small farmers, bank lending to agriculture was kept small and access to formal credit institutions and loan availment rates remained low for rural households (Llanto, 1993; Corpuz & Paguia, 2008; Peñalba *et al.*, 2012; Aquino *et al.*, 2014).

The Agricultural Credit and Policy Council (ACPC, 2014) noted that the limited access to credit by small farmers and fisherfolk, despite the banking sector's reported large amount of funds available for lending, was due to certain transaction costs and information asymmetry

---

[3]Issuance and enactment of the National Strategy for Microfinance in 1997; the Social Reform and Poverty Alleviation Act of 1997; the AFMA; the Executive Order (EO) 138 which directed the government agencies to implement credit programmes to adopt the NCC Credit Policy Guidelines; the AMCFP; General Banking Act (GBA) of 2000; the Agri–Agra Reform Credit Act of 2009; and, GBA which includes provisions mandating the Bangko Sentral ng Pilipinas (BSP) to recognise the unique nature of microfinance.

such as: (a) the lack of track record among farmers; (b) lack of knowledge on accessing formal or bank financing, particularly putting together the required documents; (c) lack of acceptable collateral and/or delayed release of loans; and (d) other documents that formal lending institutions required from farmers upon commencement of transactions. On the part of the banks, moral hazard and adverse selection issues such as aversion to high-risk and low-income agricultural projects and poor repayment performance of agricultural loans, plus the absence of economies of scale in administering small loans served as deterrents to the provision of credit to farmers and fisherfolk (NEDA, 2013).

The foregoing issues and constraints pertaining to the provision and availability of formal credit to the agricultural sector ultimately gave birth to the adoption of the Microfinance[4] innovation in the Philippines. The introduction of microfinance in the Philippines as an innovative micro-lending technique was enhanced by the enabling environment brought about by the enactment of the GBA in 2000 (Pabuayon *et al.*, 2013). This law included provisions mandating the Bangko Sentral ng Pilipinas (BSP) to formulate policy guidelines for the microfinancing implementation (Llanto and Laviña, 2006).

Drawing from the experiences in other developing countries, microfinance is deemed to have solved, in more ways than one, the puzzle of profitably lending funds to microenterprises and the poor. For one, microfinance has come to play a major role in development because of its direct relationship to both poverty alleviation and women. It overcame barriers such as collateral requirements, male or salaried guarantor requirements, documentation requirements, cultural barriers, limited mobility and literacy that have traditionally kept women from accessing formal financial services. As of June 2014, there are a total of 183 banks with microfinance operations serving about 1.2 million clients with outstanding loans amounting to PHP9.3 billion. The number of borrowers between 2008 and 2014 grew at a significant rate of 31% over the 7-year period (see Table 6.4).

---

[4]Microfinance or microcredits are small loans such as deposits, loans, payment services, money transfers and insurance products granted to the poor and low-income households and their microenterprises that enable them to raise their living standards and income levels (BSP, 2013).

Table 6.4: Outstanding Loans and Number of Borrowers of Microfinance-related Banks, Philippines, 2008–2014

Year	Outstanding loans (in billion PHP)	No. of borrowers
2008	6.4	878,322
2009	6.7	880,000
2010	6.9	930,000
2011	7.2	980,000
2012	7.9	1,137,813
2013	8.1	1,017,351
2014	9.3	1,155,282

Source: BSP (2014).

Thrift, rural and cooperative banks are presently involved in the provision of microfinance services in the form of savings, loans, payment and money transfer for the low-income sector. The BSP (BSP, 2011) classifies these banks into MOB and Banks Engaged in Microfinance Operations (BEMO). MOBs are banks with microfinance loans that are at least 50% of their gross loan portfolio. Meanwhile, BEMO are banks whose microfinance portfolio is less than 50% of the total loan portfolio. In 2013, 82% of the microfinance loans released was used by microenterprises and small businesses, while the rest were allotted for micro-agri loans and housing.

MFIs are now becoming more familiar with the needs and demands of clients such that the range of products and services offered have diversified. Aside from the usual microenterprise and agri-loan products, MFIs have begun to offer microinsurance, housing microfinance, and microsavings or microdeposits to their clients. The Microenterprise Access to Banking Services (MABS) Project[5] shows an increasing number of MABS participating banks providing these nontraditional products and services (see Table 6.5).

---

[5]MABS is a USAID program designed to accelerate national economic transformation by encouraging the Philippine rural banking industry to significantly expand access to microfinance services (http://www.rbapmabs.org/).

Table 6.5: Products and Services of MABS Participating Banks, 2004–2011

Microenterprise loan	2004	2005	2006	2007	2008	2009	2010	2011
Microenterprise loan								
Total no. of participating banks	72	82	87	90	91	90	90	95
No. of Participating bank units	204	264	320	358	529	573	584	625
Housing microfinance								
No. of banks with housing microfinance product	...	...	...	...	3	4	6	9
No. of participating bank units	...	...	...	...	6	40	56	72
Micro-agricultural loan								
No. of banks with micro-agricultural loan products	4	8	10	17	18	18	18	20
No. of participating bank units	5	16	25	41	49	55	58	61
Mobile phone banking[b]								
No. of banks with mobile banking services	...	...	...	...	46	60	67	72
No. of participating bank units	...	...	...	...	413	885	974	1,165
Microinsurance								
No. of bank units with microinsurance products	...	...	...	...	70	74	155	128

Notes: ... Data not available, MABS = Microenterprise Access to Banking Services, No. = number.
[a]Data is only for MABS participating banks and do not represent the entire rural banking sector.
[b]Data for mobile phone banks are as of end-November 2011. Bank units refer to branches and other banking offices.
Source: MABS Project.

6.4.1 *Microinsurance*

Microinsurance in the Philippines is offered by three major providers: (i) the commercial insurance companies; (ii) MBAs and (iii) cooperatives. Formal microinsurance refers to products provided by institutions that are regulated by the Insurance Commission and have the required license to sell insurance policies. On the other hand, informal microinsurance is offered by institutions that may or may not be legally registered with the Insurance Commission and do not have a license to sell insurance policies.

It is often provided by NGO-MFIs and cooperatives through mutual fund schemes, where members contribute a pre-determined amount to the fund on a regular basis and are assured of a guaranteed amount of benefits when a risk event takes place (GTZ–MIPSS, 2007).

As of 2015, the Department of Finance (DOF, 2015) reported that the Philippines has the highest microinsurance coverage among Asia-Pacific Economic Cooperation (APEC) member economies. It is recorded at 28% in 2014 from 20% in 2012. It covers 28 million individuals with an annual growth of 18.4%. There are more than 50 licensed insurance entities such as banks, cooperatives and microfinance NGOs that provide microinsurance products. Moreover, 23 micromutual benefit associations, 18 life insurance companies, 24 non-life insurance companies, 42 rural/cooperative bank agents and around 100 microinsurance agents are engaged in the provision of microinsurance products.

An example of a microinsurance institution is the Center for Agriculture and Rural Development, Inc. (CARD). CARD's microinsurance programme started in April 1994 as CARD Members' Mutual Fund (MMF) that aimed to provide benefit to members in case of death. The CARD MMF also covers death, disability and pension benefits. On 29 October 1999, the MMF was registered with the Securities and Exchange Commission as CARD MBA. CARD MBA has three major products: life insurance programme, loan redemption and retirement savings fund. As of June 2015, CARD MBA reported a total of 11,631,625 insured individuals (CARD, 2015).

Microinsurance works not only for the protection of the most vulnerable, but also for sustainability and inclusive growth. According to Portula & Vergara (2013), available microinsurance products today also provide benefits against flood, crop loss, fire, hospitalisation and earthquake. The importance of microinsurance as a potent tool for rehabilitation in times of economic shocks (ISEA, 2014) was highlighted after Typhoon Haiyan inflicted damages on farmlands and fisheries estimated at PHP32 billion (Department of Agriculture, 2014). The government, through MFIs set up a PHP2 billion fund that helped 416,000 entrepreneurs and their small businesses to cheap financing to enable them to recoup their operation, create new jobs and revive the economies of affected areas. In addition, 129,786 families reportedly took out new microinsurance policies after the typhoon (DOF, 2015).

6.4.2 *Housing microfinance*

Housing microfinance products are non-mortgage loans intended 'to finance renovations, improvements and expansion and are characterised by common elements of microfinance, such as small loan amounts, short terms, market-based pricing and non-mortgage guarantees' (CGAP, 2004). They do not require collateral and documentary requirements and are much simpler. Hence, the usual barriers that the poor face in accessing housing finance are addressed (BSP, 2008). The housing microfinance provision is also perceived as one modality to improve the living conditions of the enterprising poor and the low-income households and to contribute to better health, productivity and quality of life.

An increasing number of microentrepreneurs now use their homes as productive assets in generating income because the home can be a venue for 'producing goods, storing inventory and conducting business' (CGAP, 2004). Thus, providing financial assistance through home loan products would certainly pave the way for increasing the productivity of micro enterprises.

On a different note, the housing problem in the Philippines is serious, a largely urban phenomenon as reported in the National Urban Development and Housing Framework (NUDHF) 2009–2016. It is estimated that in 2016, the magnitude of housing needs will reach about 5.8 million housing units (HUDCC, 2015) with close to half a million backlog projected for Metro Manila alone.

To address the housing needs and gaps in basic services, especially for the poor and the marginalised, the NUDHF plans to stimulate housing microfinance for end-user financing. The BSP approved the housing microloan product in February 2008 to spur economic activity and create employment through the multiplier effects generated in the downstream industries. Housing microfinance loans are granted for the purpose of home improvement, house construction and the acquisition of house and/or lot (BSP, 2013).

Bank units offering housing microfinance in MABS-participating banks increased from only 3 in 2008 to 9 in 2011 (BSP, 2015). Table 6.6 shows various microfinance loan products that include micro housing. An example of a MFI that offer housing microfinance is the Tulay sa Pag-Unlad, Inc. (TSPI) which established a partnership with Habitat for

Table 6.6: Microfinance Loans Classified by Purpose, June 2012, (in million PHP)

Particulars	Total	Micro-enterprises and small businesses	Micro-enterprise loan plus/ Microfinance plus[a]	Micro-agri loan	Micro housing	Others
Microfinance-oriented thrift banks	213	188	6	19	0	0
Microfinance-oriented rural banks	2,536	2,219	0	209	108	1
Subtotal	2,750	2,407	6	227	108	1
Microfinance-engaged rural banks	3,332	2,443	44	286	40	519
Microfinance-engaged cooperative banks	691	646	0	9	11	25
Microfinance-engaged thrift banks	786	605	8	28	10	135
Microfinance-engaged universal bank	1	1	0	0	0	0
Microfinance-engaged regular commercial banks	64	63	2	0	0	0
Subtotal	4,875	3,758	54	322	62	678
Grand total	**7,624**	**6,165**	**60**	**549**	**170**	**679**

Note: [a]Per BSP Circular 744 defined as loan products ranging from PHP150,001 to PHP300,000 catering to the growing businesses of microfinance clients. Microfinance-oriented banks are banks with microfinance loans that are at least 50% of their gross loan portfolio. Microfinance-engaged banks' microfinance portfolio is less than 50% of the total loan portfolio.
Source: BSP.

Humanity Philippines (HFHP) in 2006. TSPI's housing microfinance loan started as a loyalty programme for their long-time clients and has expanded to 75% of TSPI branches throughout the country. TSPI quickly realised that it could reach thousands of poor Filipinos seeking to improve their shelter by offering a loan that responds to the demand of their clients. In 2012, TSPI also partnered with Lafarge and launched its microfinance programme for affordable housing. The objective of the programme is to develop a service that meets local market needs and improves the housing conditions of low-income communities. The programme has helped more than 400 microcredit recipients and as of July 2012, TSPI's housing products has disbursed 11,000 housing microfinance loans worth US$7 million since 2006.

6.4.3 *Microsavings* (*Microdeposits*)

The BSP defines microdeposits as "microfinance savings accounts that cater to the needs of the basic sectors and low-income clients and those that are unserved or underserved by the financial system".[6] The minimum maintaining balance for microsavings accounts must not exceed PHP100 or just about US$2.12[7]; they are not subject to dormancy charges and the average daily balance account should not exceed PHP15,000 or approximately US$319.

The very low minimum balance and ease of opening microsavings accounts aims to serve as an incentive to low-income individuals and families to store funds for future use (Babajide, Taiwo & Isibor, 2015). Microsavings are innovative products that are envisioned to increase the overall impact of microfinance on poverty reduction as they could help the poor to manage their risks and enable them to smooth out their consumption and create financial assets by themselves (Ashraf *et al.*, 2003).

The BSP (2014) shows evidence of an improving access to microfinance savings by clients at the national level. The number of banks offering microdeposit accounts increased by 19% from 58 banks in 2012 to 69 banks in 2013. The growing number of banks offering microdeposits also resulted in a noticeable growth with regards to volume and value of the accounts. In terms of volume, the total number of microdeposit accounts surged by 36% to 1.5 million accounts in 2013 from 1.1 million accounts in 2012. On the other hand, the total value of microdeposit accounts went up by 27% from PHP2.33 billion in 2012 to PHP296 billion in 2013. The

---

[6]The BSP issued Circular 694 in 2010 which provided notes on microfinance products that include microdeposits.

[7]The average monthly exchange rate of US$1: PHP47 for November 2015 .

upward trend in the number and value of microdeposit accounts suggests increasing acceptance of the low-income market for a deposit product.

At the local level, the data from the Micro Banking Bulletin revealed that in terms of the total number of depositors, CARD Bank Inc. recorded the largest number of clients in 2014 with 1,016,867 members. In terms of total deposits, however, the 1st Valley Bank tops the list. Moreover, the average annual deposit per member of the 1st Valley Bank amounted to about PHP30,000 or an estimated US$638 as against CARD's average deposit of only PHP3,461 or US$74 (See Table 6.7).

Traditional commitment savings account is one of the strategies of MFIs in the Philippines that encourage savings behavior by restricting withdrawals until a pre-set savings goal is reached. Ashraf, Karlan & Yin (2006) designed a commitment savings product for a Philippine bank and conducted a baseline survey on 1,777 existing or former clients of the same bank. Using a randomised control methodology, the savings product that was intended for individuals who want to commit to restrict access to their savings was implemented. After a month, the commitment product was offered to a subset of 710 clients who were randomly chosen and 202 (28.4%) accepted the offer and opened the account. Their findings revealed that women who potentially have a preference for commitment

Table 6.7: Top MFIs' Total Deposits and Number of Depositors, Philippines, 2014

MFIs	Deposits (PHP millions)	Number of depositors
1st Valley Bank	3,757	122,465
CARD Bank	3,520	1,016,867
ASA Philippines	2,158	849,232
GM Bank of Luzon	1,890	117,434
Bangko Kabayan	1,754	49,173
Bangko Mabuhay	1,009	34,750
RB Camalig	668	31,857
TSKI	436	319,777
NWTF	434	216,819
Pagasa	348	193,363

Source: http://www.themixmarket.org/(2015).

as exhibited by their marginal rates of time preference, were more likely to open the commitment savings account. After 1 year, clients in the treatment group had average savings balances that rose by 81% points relative to those in the control group. They concluded that the 'savings response represents a lasting change in savings, and not merely a short-term response to a new product'.

Building from Ashraf *et al.*'s (2006) research, the Innovations for Poverty Action (IPA) designed the commitment savings product with fixed instalments in 2013. The result showed that demand for commitment is high, even in a low-income population with little previous bank exposure (John, 2015). The findings indicated that the take-up rates were 27% for the Regular Saver (RS) product and 42% for the Withdrawal-restriction (WR) product, even though all individuals were given a is free standard savings account' just before they were offered the commitment products. John (2015) concluded that offering the RS product is highly effective at increasing savings because the RS clients saved PHP1,928 (US$41) and the WR clients saved PHP324 (US$6.9) more than the control group. Moreover, the RS product clients were more likely to buy the expenditure item using their regular savings instead of borrowing.

6.4.4 *Challenges in microinsurance, housing microfinance, and microsavings or microdeposits*

6.4.4.1 *Microinsurances*

Portula & Vergara (2013) cited the low purchase of insurance[8] and product development as challenges of the microinsurance industry in the country. The lack of a strong insurance culture among the people was mentioned as a primary reason for low purchase of insurance in the country. The authors revealed that majority of the population in the country did not appreciate the benefits and importance of insurance and only few were

---

[8]In microfinance, take-up rates refer to the ratio of persons who join a programme to the number of persons in a larger population. Participation may be in the form of borrowing in the last few years, having an active loan, opening a savings account, signing-up for an insurance contract, etc. In this ratio, the denominator is typically the more difficult to measure and may result in varying calculations (Karlan *et al.*, 2010)

willing to part with their hard earned money for guaranteed benefits for contingent events. The Filipino culture usually relies on fate and this makes insurance a hard-to-sell product in the country. To increase insurance penetration, Portula & Vergara (2013) suggest that the low-income market segment should be tapped. There is a need for the people to be informed about the advantages and benefits of insurance products. Educating the low-income markets to overcome their bias against insurance and implementing a comprehensive financial education programme that teaches clients to become proactive money managers was suggested by ADB (2013a).

Another challenge in microinsurance posed by the ADB (2013b) is affordability and accessibility. Low-income clients do not usually obtain insurance because of the cost they might incur. Maintaining low cost of administration and distribution is important for microinsurance to be able to offer affordable and accessible insurance to the low-income market. In a study conducted by GTZ–MIPSS (2007), accessibility is found to be the deciding factor for availing of insurance. The survey revealed that the number of insurance users is directly proportional to the level of awareness of the product. The relationship between enrolment and affiliation with organised groups or MFIs is strong. Most availed of the insurance services through the MFI they were affiliated with.

The use of institutions, associations and points of sale in proximity to the clients play an important role in expanding the outreach of microinsurance. To ensure that these delivery channels facilitate trust in the insurance system, ADB (2013a) suggests that the Insurance Commission must develop appropriate rules and guidelines in facilitating delivery of microinsurance. An organised group like an MFI was suggested by GTZ–MIPSS (2007) to serve as a vital channel for access to information and insurance services for the people since they are present locally and have gained the trust of the community, which is important in accessing insurance services.

6.4.4.2 *Housing microfinance*

Housing microfinance offered by MFIs tends to be short term, usually a year or less. CGAP (2004) also noted that while some housing microfinance providers capture savings, they rarely collect enough to cover the demand for housing loans. Adequate funding instruments were also suggested by CGAP (2004) that would allow institutions to expand their portfolios and avoid a mismatch between the sources and uses of funds.

The poor in the Philippines can access some of the government's social housing projects. However, the supply of such projects continues to be insufficient to meet the demand. Despite high demand for housing improvement, renovation and repairs, this market is underserved by the housing finance sector (Habitat.org). The threat of natural disasters also affects the increase in demand for housing microfinance. Since the Philippines is usually hit by typhoons, communities have to rebuild their houses because these houses are not resilient enough to strong winds.

Given the foregoing support that the country has been extending to the development of microfinance services, the Economist Intelligence Unit (EIU) named the Philippines as the 3rd country in the world which has the most conducive environment for microfinance business in 2013 (see Table 6.8). Peru held the top position in the Global Microscope 2014 for the seventh consecutive year, followed closely by Colombia. The study revealed that countries with enabling environments for microfinance tend to have favourable conditions for financial inclusion. As a result, the Philippines has been recognised for providing a business environment within which MFIs thrive.

Table 6.8:   Overall Microfinance Business Environment Ranking, Philippines 2013

Rank	Country	Score
1	Peru	87
2	Columbia	85
3	**Philippines**	**79**
4	Chile	66
5–6	India	61
5–6	Mexico	61

Note: Weighted sum of category scores (0–100 where 100 = most favourable).
Source: The EIU Limited (2014).

6.4.4.3 *Microsavings (Microdeposits)*

This section presents the challenges of CARD Bank Inc., in particular, in offering the microsavings product.[9] The main challenges are related to accessibility to microsavings, absence of communication infrastructure and affordability of microsavings service. These challenges are not necessarily unique to CARD Bank, Inc., as a MFI.

c.1 Access to microsavings

In the past, CARD had tried to collect more voluntary savings, but the efforts were inadequate. Grameen Foundation's Microsavings supported CARD Bank with market research and product design, marketing and financial literacy, information technology, human resources, financial risk management and social performance management to help create a more robust savings programme.

The market research results showed that accessibility is the highest priority for a savings account. For instance, *"Matapat"* is a CARD pilot product that was designed to give the greatest microsavings accessibility to customers. Grameen Foundation's Microsavings assisted in the implementation of this ATM-based savings product, along with a mobile financial services solution to reach rural customers of the bank. The combination of these two technologies enabled the bank to meet its customers' needs.

To make this microsavings product convenient for clients, CARD provided services to customers to pick up their deposits. ATMs were put at some CARD branches and in other banks throughout the country to give the clients access to their funds outside branch hours.

c.2 Absence of Communication Infrastructure in Some Rural Areas

The most popular feature of the *"Matapat"* *microsavings* account is the use of ATM because of the convenience of withdrawal at any time of the day. Confirmation of deposits and account balance through SMS also adds a feeling of security for the client. However, there is still the absence of communication infrastructure in some rural areas that makes it not conducive to provide such services.

---

[9]From CARD Bank, Inc. Annual Report 2013.

While technology such as ATMs and SMS texting services can be used to make a product more accessible and convenient, it must be implemented carefully to ensure that clients are comfortable with the technology and trust that it is reliable. There is also a need to ensure that communication facilities are available in the area concerned.

c.3 Affordability of microsavings service

The market research identified affordability (low opening balance) as one of the top three desired attributes for CARD's savings product. The minimum balance at PHP500 (US$10.6), consistent with CARD's existing savings products and competitors' products was initially introduced. It was raised to PHP1,000 but because the initial take-up of the product turned out to be much slower than projected, the initial deposit was lowered to PHP100 and the minimum balance for earning interest to PHP500. The impact of this change was the doubling of the number of accounts opened in just 1 month following the change. A low opening balance appeared to be extremely important to the clients.

Despite the aforementioned challenges to providing microsavings, evidence shows that microfinance clients have transformed into net savers and are now attaining a certain level of financial independence (BSP, 2013). In May 2013, BSP issued Circular 796 which amended the general features of microdeposits to further encourage the microfinance clients to build up their savings. Based on June 2013 data, there are 186 banks with microfinance operations reaching more than million clients. The savings of microfinance clients have reached PHP8.87 billion, higher than the total amount of outstanding microfinance loans (PHP8.04 billion).

However, while the country is at the forefront of creating an enabling environment for microfinance, EIU (2014) believes that the delivery and implementation is still a challenge for the country. An archipelagic setup of the country gives security and logistical challenges in reaching the poor. The findings of various studies give credence to this claim (Microfinance Council of the Philippines (MCPI, 2012; BWTP, 2015; BSP, 2014; Charitonenko, 2003; Micu, 2010; Corales & Cuevas, 1987): (a) the developing preferential markets of MFIs resulted in an imbalanced supply of concentration of financial services where there is multiple supply in some communities, while leaving others un-served; (b) the level of penetration by MFIs in more than 42,000 (65%) barangays has saturated and over saturated levels[10] which means that there may be more than one borrower in a household or a client may have taken more than one loan from different MFIs; (c) microfinance services were delivered to only one-third of the total poor households in the country due to the absence of banking offices in some of the municipalities and the relative concentration of microfinance facilities in the urban areas; (d) poor infrastructure and transportation system, cultural and social barriers, lack of education, and absence of bookkeeping as basis of cash flow made microfinance a high risk and (e) more than 50% of banking presence remained concentrated in highly urbanised countries such as Metro Manila, Central Luzon and Southern Luzon. Economic opportunities, infrastructure and communication facilities, peace and order conditions and policies affected branching and establishment of small rural-based unit banks and non-bank institutions.[11]

Similar to the findings of Manos *et al.* (2013), the effect of agricultural rural credit (microfinance in particular) on rural development of emerging countries like the Philippines is rather mixed or ambiguous. Transaction costs and information asymmetry issues such as moral hazard and adverse selection could limit the ability of the poor to participate in and benefit from development opportunities and income-generating activities that microfinance can offer.

6.5 Effects of Credit and Microfinance on Input Use, Production, Productivity and Income

Most small farmers face inadequate cash flow to avail of important inputs such as fertilisers and pesticides (Sial, Awan & Waqas, 2011) which typically account for 20–30% of production cost (BAS, 2014). Thus, access to credit is undeniably necessary.

---

[10]Market penetration by MFIs can mean the 'ratio of current to potential low-income earners' in a geographical area. Saturation implies over-indebtedness of households who borrow from MFIs because there is too much available credit from different MFIs who may be targeting the same household clients in a geographical area.

[11]Includes credit unions and pawnshops.

The poor performance of the Philippine agricultural sector over the decades was associated to the failures and shortcomings in the policy and institutional environment in this sector, especially access to credit (Habito & Briones, 2005). Habito and Briones reiterated that the failure to provide adequate quantity and quality of investments in irrigation, rural roads and ports, and research & development (R&D) significantly raised the costs of rural credit.

Compounding the fact is that access to credit has been constrained by a number of supply- and demand-related limitations. Corpuz & Paguia (2008) identified supply-related constraints that include, among others: (1) poor credit standing of many farmers; (2) inherent risks in agricultural projects; (3) high transactions costs and interest rates and (4) limited low-cost funds to support the credit needs of the agri-fishery sector. On the demand side, access to credit is constrained by (1) farmers' reluctance to borrow from banks because of stringent requirements such as collateral; (2) farmers' continuing dependence on traders/informal lenders for financing needs and (3) lack of government agri-support fund for indigenous people, among others.

The proportion of agricultural credit to non-agricultural credit over time supports the hypothesised relationship between credit, GDP and performance of the agriculture sector. The proportion of agricultural loans to total bank loans continued to shrink over the years (see Table 6.9). In the late 1970's, agricultural production loans were high at 8%. It was the period when the government provided credit subsidies (Llanto, 1993). However, from 1999 to 2010, the proportion of agricultural production loans were down to only a little over 1%. Geron & Casuga (2012) claimed that it was the period when AFMA and the market-based policies in agricultural lending were implemented and they argued that the market-based approach encouraged financial institutions to finance not just production loans. Thus, as a result, financial institutions moved away from financing agricultural production to financing non-production related agricultural activities. The share of agricultural production loans to total bank loans and the declining ratio of agricultural production loans to the gross value added in agriculture (GVA) also lend support to this claim (see Tables 6.9 and 6.10).

Nevertheless, agricultural production depends on the inputs that are transformed into outputs, enabling the rural household to balance its budget

Table 6.9: Agricultural Loans Granted (in Million PHP), Philippines, 1978–2010

Commodities	1978–1990	1991	1992	1993	1994	1995	1996	1997	1998	1999	2000
Total Agri Prodn. Loan	17,090	46,160	56,110	67,780	74,340	82,570	564.720	376.240	115.080	170.480	114.507
Total Agri Loans Granted							620.900	403.660	299.040	401.880	335.311
Agri Prodn. Loan to Output (Gva) Ratio (%)											21.65
Total Loans (Million Peso at Current Price)	196,290	941,470	1,241,070	3,669,290	4,615,270	6,262,830	10,636,250	10,141,480	8,650,830	9,901,130	9,464,726
Agri Prodn. Loan to Total Loans Granted Ratio (%)	8.7	4.9	4.5	1.8	1.6	1.3	5.3	3.7	1.3	1.7	1.2
Agricultural Loan to Total Loans Granted Ratio (%)							5.8	4	3.5	4.1	3.5

Commodities	2001	2002	2003	2004	2005	2006	2007	2008	2009	2010	Average
Total Agri Prodn. Loan	122,596	123,460	135,158	163,887	108,936	932,28	153,832	193,056	227,862	239,681	193,515
Total Agri Loans Granted	414,275	326,995	341,661	467,822	476,145	302,162	386,070	463,165	606,610	624,542	431,349
Agri Prodn. Loan to Output (Gva) Ratio (%)	22.33	20.62	21.39	22.32	14	10.92	16.3	17.51	20.01	20.27	18.85
Total Loans (Million Peso at Current Price)	7,090,020	14,362,960	15,397,729	16,183,184	11,935,642	17,479,544	17,459,080	21,083,347	24,727,476	25,08,0624	14,639,601
Agri Prodn. Loan to Total Loans Granted Ratio (%)	1.7	0.9	0.9	1	0.9	0.5	0.9	0.9	0.9	1	2.2
Agricultural Loan to Total Loans Granted Ratio (%)	5.8	2.3	2.2	2.9	4	1.7	2.2	2.2	2.5	2.5	3.3

Source: ACPC.

Table 6.10: Ratio of Agriculture Production Loans to GVA in Agriculture, Annual Average in Various Periods, Philippines, 1978–2008

Item	1978–1980	1981–2000	2000–2008
Agriculture production loans to GVA ratio, %	41.34	39.36	22.10

Source: ACPC (in Geron and Casuga, 2012).

during the season of high expenditures due to input and consumption purchases coupled with low incomes (Dong, Lu & Featherstone, 2010). The absence of or limited access to credit can become a constraint to agricultural production because the optimal combinations of inputs may not be employed by farmers and this will also tend to limit their optimal production and consumption choices.

Thus, the growth in the microfinance industry in the Philippines is a welcome development. Empirical evidence and success stories abound which demonstrate microfinance as an effective tool for economic development. Microfinance has been playing a pivotal role in reducing poverty by increasing people's consumption capacity and income levels (Khan, 2014). This bears significance for the Philippines where 944,897 MSMEs make up 99.58% of our total industries. Of the total number of MSMEs, 89.78% (844,764) are micro enterprises and the rest are SMEs (DTI n.d.).

The development of rural microenterprises is a key element in the government's economic strategy. Without access to financial services, these microenterprises will be forced to rely more on the informal credit sector. Hence, microfinance can have a direct contribution and impact on economic development and poverty alleviation only if it will be accessible to MSMEs. Besides allowing MSMEs to increase their economic activity and income, build up assets, prepare against emergencies and invest in education, health and housing services, microfinance can also make microbusinesses generate the much needed employment and increase the overall economic activity in local economies.

However, the limited access to microfinance services is still a key constraint identified by the World Bank (2013) to the new entry and further expansion of SMEs in the Philippines. It is also a main obstacle to rural development. A large number of these enterprises are involved in adding value to primary crops but they are constrained by low-productivity technologies that hardly meet the emerging standards for quality and food safety required by the domestic market and foreign importers. Only about a fourth of these enterprises have access to reliable sources of credit such as rural banks, credit unions, cooperatives and non-profit MFIs. Similar to the plight of small-scale farmers, SMEs often lack the acceptable forms of collateral and transparent accounting practices and are considered risky ventures.

Karlan & Zinman (2010) evaluated the access of microcredit loans in the Philippines focusing on micro entrepreneurs. Their study revealed that subjective well-being of borrowers slightly declined, access to credit did not increase investment of the business and the overall number of business activities and employees. But access to credit helped borrowers cope with risk, strengthened their community ties and increased their access to informal credit. Karlan & Zinman (2010) conclude that microcredit can work, but through channels different from those often hypothesised by its proponents. They also recommended to start with improving the welfare of the household rather than that of the business.

Corpuz & Paguia (2008), on the other hand, also underscore the prerequisite of a wide network/or extensive outreach of credit retailers. Accordingly, credit programmes can only be as effective as the extent of their reach, making this factor as among the most critical for a programme's success. A wide network also provides more opportunity for supervised lending and lesser transaction cost.

6.6 Conclusion: Lessons and Policy Directions

6.6.1 *Lessons learned from different credit and microfinance policies*

The Philippine government has adopted policy measures to enhance small farmers' access to credit (Corpuz & Kraft, 2005). Before the policy reforms in 1986, the rural credit policy adopted by the government was the supply-led approach with emphasis on DCPs and interest rate subsidies (Llanto, 2005). Studies, however, have shown that many rural banks that participated in the government's subsidised-credit programmes collapsed because of high arrearages and low loan recovery (Peñalba *et al.*, 2012).

Realising the failure of such a supply-led approach, the government abolished the implementation of subsidised DCPs. Thus, the government adopted and implemented the market-based credit policies to enhance access to credit. The NCC, with the assistance of the Credit Policy Improvement Program (CPIP), was able to pursue and implement market-based credit policies and rationalise the implementation of subsidised DCPs. These reforms were geared towards the development of a viable and sustainable rural and microfinance market (Peñalba *et al.*, 2012).

To eliminate or minimise unintended credit subsidies (in the form of default subsidies), it is important to make sure that the channel of government funds have the required competence, network, as well as infrastructure to minimise defaults. Supervision and monitoring of an independent third party (e.g., the BSP) is key to ensuring that the necessary systems and procedures for effective and efficient lending are in place. The LBP, a GFI, also qualifies for the role (Geron & Casuga, 2012).

6.6.2 *Microfinance credit and its effect to input use, income, production and productivity*

Llanto (1993) underscored the presence of a good credit service for rural people since credit is an essential part of production and consumption in the rural areas. Majority of the rural households have very low or no-surplus production, thus they tend to borrow, even at very high interest rates for survival (Chowdhury & Garcia, 1993). A wide scope loan purposes covering production, consumption and for other non-farm activities should be included in the offers of the financial institutions (Chowdhury & Garcia, 1993). In order to address the needs of rural households, various institutional set-ups of rural banking should be effectively conducted in the rural areas (Desai & Mellor, 1993).

The use of modern technology, improved inputs and credit supervision may further improve the agricultural productivity of small farmers. Credit provision for small or landless farmers can prove a better option to move out of poverty (Mohsin, Ahmad & Anwar, 2011).

There is nothing new in saying that agricultural credit is an important financial support that a small farmer can get in order to bridge the gap between his income and expenditure on the field. It is an important instrument that enables farmers to have command over the use of working capital for enhancing their productivity and income. Thus, agricultural credit is an essential ingredient in the growth strategy of this sector (Mohsin *et al.*, 2011).

The success of agricultural policy depends on linkages between rural finance and other components of development like access to inputs, markets and marketing infrastructure, land and appropriate technology. The government must assess the capacity of the targeted households to utilise financial services to raise their productivity and enable them to repay loans and ensure full beneficiary participation (IFAD, 2014).

6.6.3 *Microfinance credit access instead of funding costly activities*

There is still a need to increase the amount of financing that is made available to the rural sector as well as further improve access of small farmers to these funds. The provision of government services like basic infrastructure, appropriate technology and improved market information for farmers would eliminate/minimise the inherent risks in the agricultural sector which would still be the best solution to bringing in rural finance.

Agricultural support policies should specialise in expanding credit access and providing extension (Habito & Briones, 2005). Unfortunately, scarce resources have funded costly activities such as the provision of post-harvest facilities, marketing and credit subsidies, which are probably better off left to the market (Tolentino *et al.*, 2001). Failure to provide credit access can affect the provision of adequate quantity and quality of investments in irrigation, rural roads and ports and R&D that can significantly raise the costs of rural access.

6.6.4 *Inclusion of private sector*

Since there are unintended credit subsidies (default subsidies) when there is a provision of government funds for agricultural lending, the government may rethink the use of public funds. Some studies and recent evidence have revealed that the private sector has the necessary liquidity and is willing to provide the much needed credit resources to viable economic activities. Thus, subsidy to agriculture may be better provided in improving the viability of economic activities in the agriculture sector which could be achieved through other means in a more transparent manner (e.g., farm to market roads, irrigation, post-harvest facilities). This will increase economic activity in the rural areas and increase income, thereby directing or encouraging private financial institutions to provide the needed credit resources to the sector (Geron & Casuga, 2012).

The government may also look for other support services that would make agriculture lending less risky thereby encouraging greater private sector participation in financial intermediation. The use of weather-based insurance index may be considered by the government to minimise risks in agriculture. The cost of weather-based insurance is relatively high but the government may want to look more closely on how the cost may be reduced since the benefits from the insurance tend to be high (Geron & Casuga, 2012).

6.6.5 *Strengthening the microfinance sector*

6.6.5.1 *Developing/strengthening credit information bureau*

Strengthening the access to credit information by creating a credit information bureau can make the information system more transparent to improve credit process of MFIs (Charitonenko, 2003). With the increasing need for microfinance as a potential tool to reduce poverty to support the development of small enterprises and microenterprises, the number of microfinance players is also increasing. The rise in the number of microfinance players, however, may cause credit pollution wherein clients become multiple borrowers. A client is considered as a multiple borrower if found to be indebted simultaneously to two or more MFIs. Chua & Tiongson (2012) discovered that 85% of all multiple borrowers have outstanding loans from only two MFIs. About 15% of all multiple borrowers have three or more existing loans. The main results of their study suggest that, on average, 14% of active MFI clients borrow from more than one MFI.

MFIs must implement strategies to protect clients especially from over indebtedness. Policies on maximum debt exposure levels should be developed to be able to assess the repayment capacity of the borrowers. More careful screening of loan applications is important, especially in areas where many MFIs compete for the same type of clients. MFIs should monitor multiple borrowing among clients and align their systems and processes to be able to help clients in financial distress and keep other clients from falling into the debt trap (Diaz & Ledesma, 2011).

The Bankers Association of the Philippines (BAP) is a private, national credit bureau that is in operation since 1990. As of May 2015, it has an accumulated 840,210 record of corporate and individual borrowers. However, records are accessible only to the members of the association. The CISA was created in 2008 to envision a CIC that will act as a database repository for all credit information pertaining to the creditworthiness of individuals and corporations. However, to date, the implementation and operations of the Credit Registry are still hampered by the lack of budgetary appropriations from the national government for the initial capitalisation requirement of the bureau (BSP, 2015).

In 2012, a private credit bureau dedicated for microfinance borrowers was formed. The Microfinance Data Sharing System (MiDAS) is a pilot credit bureau that allows participating MFIs to submit reports, send inquiries and retrieve information on borrower information. This credit bureau operates on the reciprocity of information wherein only the contributing MFIs can use the platform.

Considering that there is already an enabling law for the establishment of a central credit information system, this concern should be given importance not just by the government but also by the network of MFIs looking after the viability of the sector and the welfare of the MFI clients.

6.6.5.2 *Boost links among microfinance networks*

Links among banking and microfinance networks (rural banks, cooperatives, microfinance NGOs and commercial banks) are important to provide credit services to rural households and microenterprises to expand sustainability of microfinance. MFIs that operate locally and near the borrowers usually have better credit information about the clients and microentrepreneurs. However, they are constrained with funds to expand their services. On the other hand, commercial banks have more funds but less information and knowledge about the farmers and microentrepreneurs. Thus, a strategic link between the commercial banks and local MFIs would be useful in serving the credit needs of farmers, microenterprises and small enterprises.

Regulatory policies must also be reviewed and re-established to protect small-scale farmers from fraudulent lenders. Peñalba *et al.* (2012) and Llanto & Vogel (2005) suggest that Congress should pass an act that will establish a comprehensive credit information system in the country to better understand the role of informal finance in addressing credit gaps in the rural areas and to find out the extent of the complementary role between informal and formal finance.

6.6.5.3 *Strengthen microfinance technical capacity*

The BSP has included microfinance in the Basic Rural and Thrift Banking Courses. There are also several private institutions that provide training for microfinance, such as (1) PUNLA sa Tao Foundation which has an affiliation with Ateneo University and the Asian Institute of Management (AIM), (2) CARD Training Center, (3) TSPI Training Center and (4) Microfinance Council of the Philippines which provide some select courses. The Rural Bank Association of the Philippines–Microenterprise Access to Banking Services (RBAP–MABS) for rural banks, and the Credit Union and Environment Services (CUES) specifically for Cooperatives also provide microfinance technical assistance. However, there is no institution that provides a regular schedule and affordable technical courses on microfinance programme management and operation. The AIM Center for Development Management and the Asian Center for Entrepreneurship offer advanced training and certificate programmes in project management, social development and entrepreneurship but have not yet designed public training programmes for MFI managers that exclusively address microfinance issues.

Finally, the microfinance industry needs to further build its technical capacity for enhanced professionalisation and commercialisation. Increased attention should be given to human resources in order to strengthen their financial analysis and banking knowledge to be able to manage and operate the MFIs in ways that will result in greater outreach to target clientele.

Acknowledgement

The authors would like to acknowledge the comments provided by Dr. Generoso G. Octavio on the initial draft of this chapter.

References

Agricultural Credit and Policy Council (ACPC) Website (2014). Retrieved from http://www.acpc.da.gov.ph.

Agriculture and Fisheries Modernization Act of 1997 (AFMA). Retrieved from http://www.lawphil.net.

Aquino, A. P., Ani, P. A. & Correa, A. B. (2014). Republic Act No. 10000: Providing Agricultural and Agrarian Reform Credit. Retrieved from http://ap.fftc.agnet.org.

Aragon, J., Kakinaka, M. & Kim, D. (2011). Capital requirements of Rural Banks in the Philippines. Bangko Sentral Review 2011. Retrieved from http://www.bsp.gov.ph.

Ashraf, N., Gons, N., Karlan, D. & Yin, W. (2003). A Review of Commitment Savings Products in Developing Countries. A project sponsored by the Asian Development Bank. Retrieved from http://www.adb.org/publications/review-commitment-savings-products-development-countries.

Ashraf, N., Karlan, D. & Yin, W. (2006). Tying Odysseus to the mast: Evidence from a commitment savings product in the Philippines. *Quartely Journal Economics*, 121(2), 635–672.

Asian Development Bank (ADB) (2000). *Rural Asia: Beyond the Green Revolution*. Manila: ADB.

Asian Development Bank (ADB) (2012). Philippines: Microfinance Development Program–Performance Evaluation Report.

Asian Development Bank (ADB) (2013a). Assessment of Micro Insurance as Emerging Microfinance Service for the Poor: The Case of the Philippines. Retrieved from http://www.adb.org.

Asian Development Bank (ADB) (2013b). Philippines: Microfinance Development Program. Retrieved from http://www.adb.org.

Babajide, A. A., Taiwo, J. N. & Isibor, J. A. (2015). microsavings mobilization innovations and poverty alleviation in Nigeria. *Journal of Social*

Sciences, 6(4), 375–387, http://www.mcser.org/journal/index.PHP/mjss/article/view/6942.

Banking With the Poor Network (BWTP) Website. (2015). Philippines: Country Profile. Retrieved from http://www.bwtp.org.

Bangko Sentral ng Pilipinas (BSP) (2008). Housing Microfinance Product Launch. Speech delivered by BSP Governor Amando Tetangco, jr. at the BSP Executive Business Center on 13 May 2008. Retrieved from www.bsp.gov.ph/publications/speeches.asp?id=317&year=2008.

Bangko Sentral ng Pilipinas (BSP) (2011). BSP Releases Guidelines to Implement New Agri-Agra Law. Retrieved from http://bsp.gov.ph.

Bangko Sentral ng Pilipinas (BSP) (2012). Report on the State of Financial Inclusion in the Philippines 2011. Inclusive Finance Advocacy Staff, Supervision and Examination Sector. Retrieved from http://bsp.gov.ph.

Bangko Sentral ng Pilipinas (BSP) (2013). Report on the State of Financial Inclusion in the Philippines. Retrieved from http://bsp.gov.ph.

Bangko Sentral ng Pilipinas (BSP) (2014). Financial Inclusion Initiatives. Retrieved from http://bsp.gov.ph.

Bangko Sentral ng Pilipinas (BSP) (2015). Report on the State of Financial Inclusion in the Philippines. Retrieved from http://bsp.gov.ph.

Bureau of Agricultural Statistics (BAS) Website (2014). Retrieved from http://www.bas.gov.ph.

Capuyan, K. L. (2011). Effects of Ahon Sa Hirap Inc. (Ashi) on Income and Socio Economic Status of Women Borrowers in Calamba City, 2010. Unpublished Undergraduate Thesis. Department of Agricultural Economics, College of Economics and Management, University of the Philippines Los Baños.

Castillo, C. Q. (2005). Impact of Agricultural Credit of the Land Bank of the Philippines on the Income of Backyard Poultry Farmers in Malolos, Bulacan. Unpublished Undergraduate Thesis. Department of Agricultural Economics, College of Economics and Management, University of the Philippines Los Baños.

Center for Agriculture and Rural Development (CARD) (2013). Keeping the Spirit. Card Bank Inc. Annual Report 2013. Retrieved from http://www.card-bank.com.

Center for Agriculture and Rural Development (CARD) (2015). Microfinance Institutions Continue to Provide Health Services to the Poor Communities. Retrieved from http://www.cardmri.com/.

Charitonenko, S. (2003). Asian Development Bank (ADB) report on commercialization of microfinance in the Philippines.

Chowdhury, A. H. M. N & Garcia, M. C. (1993). Rural Institutional Finance in Bangladesh and Nepal: Review and Agenda for Reforms. Retrieved from https://openaccess.adb.org/ handle/ 11540/3175.

Chua, R. T. & Tiongson, E. R. (2012). Philippine Microfinance Discussion Papers: multiple borrowing in the Philippines: A Pilot Area Study Based on Branch Client Data. Retrieved from http://www.microfinancecouncil.org/.

Consultative Group to Assist the Poor (CGAP) 2004. Helping to Improve Donor Effectiveness in Microfinance. Housing Microfinance. Retrieved from http://www.cgap.org and http://www-wds.worldbank.org/external/default/WDS ContentServer/WDSP/IB/2005/11/16/000011823_20051116174843/ Rendered/INDEX/342400ENGLISH0DonorBrief120.txt.

Corales, C. I. & Cuevas, C. E. (1987). Cost of Agricultural Credit in the Philippines: The Short-Run Effects of Interest Rate Deregulation.

Corpuz, J. & Kraft, N. (2005). Policy Options in Agricultural & Rural Finance: The Experience of the Philippines and Other Asian Countries. In *Asia-Pacific Rural and Agricultural Credit Association Planning Workshop on Integrating Training Interventions with other APRACA Development Initiatives*, Manila, Philippines.

Corpuz, J. M. & Paguia, F. (2008). Rural Credit Success Stories: The Case of the Philippines and Selected APRACA Member Countries. Paper presented during the Regional Consultation on World Development Report and Preparation for the 2008 IFAP. World Farmers Congress, April 16, AIM Conference Center, Makati City, Philippines.

Department of Agriculture (DA) Website. (2014). Retrieved from http://da.gov.ph.

Department of Trade and Industry (DTI) (n.d.). Retrieved from http://www.dti. gov.ph/ dti/index.PHP/ resources/sme-resources/sme-statistics.

Department of Finance (DOF) (2015). Microfinance Institutions continue to provide health services to the poor communities: Philippines Leads the Way on Microinsurance. Retrieved from http://www.dof.gov.ph.

Desai, B. & Mellor, J. (1993). *Institutional Finance for Agricultural Development: An Analytical Survey of Critical Issues, Food Policy Review*. Washington: International Food Policy Research Institute.

Diaz, J. N. & Ledesma, J. M. (2011). MicroSave Briefing Note # 114: A Closer Look at Multiple Borrowing in the Philippines.

Dong, F., Lu, J. & Featherstone, A. M. (2010). *Effects of Credit Constraints on Productivity and Rural Household Income in China*. Ames, Iowa: Center for Agricultural and Rural Development Iowa State University.

Esguerra, E. (1981). An Assessment of the Masagana 99 Credit Subsidy as an Equity Measure. Philippine Review of Economics and Business. Volume XVIII, Number 3&4, September and December 1981.

Floro, S. & Yotopoulos, P. (1991). *Informal Credit Markets and the New Institutional Economics: The Case of Philippine Agriculture.* Boulder: West-view Press.

German Technical Cooperation–Microinsurance Program for Social Security (GTZ–MIPSS). (2007). Demand study of microinsurance in the Philippines. Retrieved from http://www.microinsurance.ph/.

Geron, M. P. & Casuga, M. (2012). Credit Subsidy in Philippine Agriculture. Philippine Institute of Development Studies (PIDS) Discussion Paper Series No. 2012-28. Retrieved from http://dirp3.pids.gov.ph.

Habito, C. & Briones, R. (2005). Philippine Agriculture Over the Years: Performance, Policies and Pitfalls. Retrieved from http://siteresources.world-bank.org.

Heidhues, F. & Schriender, G. (1999). Rural Financial Market Development: Supply Response Within the Farming System. Retrieved from http://www.uclouvain.be/cps/ucl/doc/ecru/documents/TF5M3D07.pdf.

Housing and Urban Development Coordinating Council (HUDCC) (2015). 2014 Housing Sector Year End Report. Retrieved from http://www.hudcc.gov.ph/.

International Cooperative Alliance (ICA) Website (2015). Retrieved from http://ica.coop.

Investing in Rural People (IFAD) Website (2003). Replicating Grameen in the Philippines: A Winning Development Strategy? Retrieved from http://www.ifad.org.

IFAD Website (2014). Livestock and Rural Finance. Retrieved from http://www.ifad.org.

Institute for Social Entrepreneurship in Asia (ISEA) (2014). Reconstruction Initiative through Social Enterprise: A Poverty Sector-Focused, Post-Yolanda Response in the Philippines.

Jaldon, M. D. J. (1999). Evaluation of the operation and impact of Ahon sa Hirap program in Los Baños.Laguna. Unpublished Undergraduate Thesis. Department of Agricultural Economics, College of Economics and Management, University of the Philippines Los Baños.

John, A. (2015). When Commitment Fails — Evidence from a Regular Saver Product in the Philippines. Retrieved from http://www.poverty-action.org/sites/default/files/publications/ When_Commitment_ Fails.pdf.

Karlan, D., Morduch, J. & Mullainathan, S. (2010). Take Up: Why Microfinance Take Up Rates are Low and Why It Matters. Retrieved from http://www.microfinancegateway.org/sites/default/files/mfg-en-paper-take-up-why-microfinance-take-up-rates-are-low-why-it-matters-jun-2010.pdf.

Karlan, D. & Zinman, J. (2010). Expanding credit access: Using randomized supply decisions to estimate the impacts. *The Review of Financial Studies*, 23(1), 433–464. Retrieved from http://www.jstor.org/stable/40468313.

Khan, N. (2014). The impact of micro finance on the household income and consumption level in Danyore, Gilgit–Baltistan Pakistan. *International Journal of Academic Research in Economics and Management Sciences*. 3(1).

Lamberte, M., Llanto, G., Meyer, R. & Graham, D. (1994). *Dynamics of Rural Development*. Makati City, Philippines: Philippine Institute for Development Studies.

Lamberte, M., Llanto, G., Meyer, R. & Graham, D. (1997). Microfinance institutions in poverty alleviation: A case of the blind leading the blind? Publication at Philippine Institute for Development Studies.

Lamberte, M., Llanto, G., Meyer, R. & Graham, D. (2004). *Is the Promise being Fulfilled? Microfinance in the Philippines: Status, issues and challenges, PIDS Policy Notes No. 2004-10*. Makati City: Philippine Institute for Development Studies.

Lamberte, M., Llanto, G., Meyer, R. & Graham, D. (2007). Overcoming Obstacles to Agricultural Microfinance: Looking at Broader Issues. *Asian Journal of Agriculture and Development*. 4(2). Retrieved from http://ageconsearch.umn.edu.

Lamberte, M., Llanto, G., Meyer, R. & Graham, D. (2008). Credit. In R. Dy, L. Gonzales, M. Bonifacio, W. David, J. P. De Vera, F. Lantican, G. Llanto, L. Martinez & E. Tan (Eds.), *Modernizing Philippine Agriculture and Fisheries: The AFMA Implementation Experience*. Metro Manila: University of Asia and the Pacific.

Llanto, G. (1993). Agricultural Credit and Banking in the Philippines: Efficiency and Access Issues. Working Paper Series No. 93–02. Philippine Institute for Development Studies.

Llanto, G. (1994). The Financial Structure and Performance of Philippine Credit Cooperatives. Discussion Paper Series No. 94-04. Philippine Institute for Development Studies.

Llanto, G. (2004). Rural Finance and Developments in Philippine Rural Financial Markets: Issues and Policy Research Challenges. Discussion Paper Series No. 2004-18. Philippine Institute for Development Studies.

Llanto, G. (2005). Rural Finance in the Philippines: Issues and Policy Challenges. Philippines: Agricultural Credit Policy Council and Philippine Institute for Development Studies. Retrieved from http://dirp3.pids.gov.ph/ris/books/pidsbk05-ruralfinance.pdf.

Llanto, G. M. & Laviña, G. R. (2006). Innovations as Response to Failures in Rural Financial Markets. Discussion paper Series No. 2006–24. Philippine Institute for Development Studies.

Llanto, G. M. & Vogel, R. C. (2005). Philippine Rural Finance: Apparent and Real Problems, with Some Possible Solutions. First Draft. Credit Policy Improvement Program Department of Finance — National Credit Council.

Madamba, A. C. T. (2005). Impact of SIKAP BIDANI Credit Program on Member Borrowers in Los Baños, Laguna. Unpublished Undergraduate Thesis. Department of Agricultural Economics, College of Economics and Management, University of the Philippines Los Baños.

Manos, R. Gueyie, J.-P. & Yaron, J. (2013). Dilemmas and Directions in Microfinance Research. In Gueyie, Manos & Yaron, (Eds), *Microfinance in Developing Countries: Issues, Policies and Performance Evaluation*. London: Palgrave Macmillan.

Microfinance Council of the Philippines, Inc (MCPI). The 2012 Microfinance Client Mapping: The State of market saturation and inclusion in the Philippines. Retrieved from http://www.microfinancecouncil.org.

Micu, N. (2010). State of the art of microfinance: A narrative. Pinoy Me Foundation, Ninoy and Cory Aquino Foundation, and Hanns Seidel Foundation. Retrieved from http://www.hss.de.

Mohsin, A.Q., Ahmad, S. & Anwar, A. (2011). Impact of supervised agricultural credit on farm income in the Barani Areas of Punjab. *Pakistan Journal of Social Sciences*. 31(2), pp. 241–250.

National Credit Council Policy Notes 99-2, Policy Framework for Rationalizing Directed Credit Programs, July, (1999a).

National Credit Council Policy Notes 99-3, The Agro-Industry Modernization Credit and Financing Program: An Alternative to Directed Credit Programs in Agriculture, August (1999b).

National Credit Council Policy Notes 99-4, Executive Order No. 138: Towards Sustainable Financial and Credit Policies, September, (1999c).

National Economic and Development Authority (NEDA). (2013). Philippine Development Plan 2011–2016: Competitive & Sustainable Agriculture & Fisheries Sector. Retrieved from http://www.neda.gov.ph.

Pabuayon, I. M., Catelo, S. P., Rola, A. C. & Paris, Jr., T. B. (2013). *Agricultural Policy: Perspectives from the Philippines and Other Developing Countries*. Metro Manila: The University of the Philippines Press (ISBN 978-971-542-715-9).

Peñalba, L. M., Paunlagui, M. M. & Elazegui, D. D. (2012). The Role of the Informal Credit System in the Agricultural Innovation Promotion Chain. Center for Strategic Planning and Policy Studies, College of Public Affairs and Development, University of the Philippines Los Baños, Philippines. Working Paper No. 2012-02. Retrieved from http://cpaf.uplb.edu.ph.

Philippine Statistics Authority Website (2014). Retrieved from http://www.psa. gov.ph.

Poliquit, L. Y. (2006). Accessibility of Rural Credit Among Small Farmers in the Philippines. Thesis presented to the Massey University, Palmerston North, New Zealand. Retrieved from http://mro.massey.ac.nz.

Portula, D. O. & Vergara, R. (2013). Case Study. The Philippine Experience on Microinsurance Market Development. Retrieved from https://a2ii.org.

Senate Economic Planning Office (SEPO) 2009.

Sial, M. H., Awan, M. S. & Waqas, M. (2011). *Role of Institutional Credit on Agricultural Production: A Time Series Analysis of Pakistan.* Pakistan: University of Sargodha.

Smits, R. (2002). Innovation studies in the 21st century: Questions from a user's perspective. *Technological Forecasting and Social Change*, 69(9), 861–883.

Sulit, T. R. (1990). Effects of the Ahon Sa Hirap Project in Alleviating Poverty Among Women-Borrowers and Their Household in Selected Villages in Laguna. Unpublished Undergraduate Thesis. Department of Agricultural Economics, College of Economics and Management, University of the Philippines Los Baños.

Tayag, P. (2011). A Corporate Strategy to Develop a More Inclusive Financial System. In *The Fletcher School Leadership Program for Financial Inclusion.* Policy Memoranda 2011. Retrieved from http://fletcher.tufts.edu/~/media/ Fletcher/Microsites/CEME/pubs/papers/MEMOS% 20Final.pdf.

Tolentino, B., David, C., Balisacan, A. & Intal, P. (2001). Strategic Actions to Rapidly Ensure Food Security and Rural Growth in the Philippines. In *Yellow Paper II: The Post-Erap Reform Agenda.*

World Bank Website (2013). Philippine Economic Update. Retrieved from http:// www.worldbank.org.

Chapter 7

Islamic Microfinance in Indonesia

Bayu Arie Fianto*,‡ and Christopher Gan†,§

*PhD Candidate, Faculty of Agribusiness and Commerce,
Department of Financial and Business System,
PO Box 85084, Lincoln University, Canterbury, New Zealand
†Professor in Accounting and Finance, Faculty of Agribusiness
and Commerce, Department of Financial and Business System,
PO Box 85084, Lincoln University, Christchurch, New Zealand
‡BayuArie.Fianto@lincolnuni.ac.nz
§Christopher.Gan@lincoln.ac.nz

Abstract

Indonesia is an agricultural country with the world's largest Muslim population. Islamic microfinance institutions can play a significant role in poverty alleviation in the rural sector predominantly dominated by agricultural activities and poor farmers. The institutions offer unique financial products that cater to the needs of traditional farmers and rural households based on the risk-sharing concept in Indonesia. Islamic microfinance institutions operate cooperatively on equity financing and debt-based financing. Islamic finance provide products and services that parallel with Muslim clients' religious beliefs. The chapter begins with a historical overview and landscape of Islamic microfinance in Indonesia followed by the principles of Islamic values in Islamic microfinance and the factors that influence Islamic Microfinance Institutions' performance.

Keywords: Islamic microfinance institutions, poverty, rural household, Indonesia.

7.1 Microfinance Institutions in Indonesia

Microfinance, in general, is a tool that can create financial inclusion and especially help the poor, improve household welfare and reduce poverty (Berhane & Gardebroek, 2011; Li, Gan & Hu, 2011; Littlefield, Morduch & Hashemi, 2003; Widiarto & Emrouznejad, 2015). Microfinance Institutions (MFIs), are institutions that provide financial access for everyone because their objective is to minimise financial exclusion (Lapenu & Pierret, 2006). MFIs come in many forms, from project, non-profit organisations (NGOs), cooperatives, to private companies. The institutions can be part of the private, public or non-profit sectors (Lapenu & Pierret, 2006).

Indonesia microfinance has a long history. Microfinance in Indonesia started in the late 19th century, initially with banks in rural areas. On 16 December 1895, R. Bei Aria Wiraatmadja established the *Hulp-en Spaar Bank der Indlandsche Bestuurs Ambtenaren* or Bank for Civil Servants in Purwokerto, Central Java, Indonesia. This rural bank is known as Bank Rakyat Indonesia (BRI) (BRI, 2015b; Shodiq, 2014).

Indonesia has the most differentiated microfinance and banking sector of any developing country in the world (Seibel & Dwi Agung, 2006). In December 2014, there were 119 commercial banks with 19,948 offices and 1,643 rural banks with 4,895 offices (see Table 7.1). Based on data from the Ministry of Cooperatives and Micro and Small Medium Enterprises (MoCMSMEs) of Republic of Indonesia, there were 38,083 formal savings and loan cooperatives under its supervision in 2005 (OJK, 2014a; MoCMSMEs Republic of Indonesia, 2005).

Besides conventional financial institutions, Indonesia also has institutions that adopt Islamic principles in their operations. In 2014, Islamic financial institutions in Indonesia consisted of 12 Islamic commercial banks with 2,151 offices; 163 Islamic rural banks with 439 offices (see Table 7.2) and based on data in 2012, there were 4,117 formal Islamic

Table 7.1: Indonesia Conventional Financial Institutions in 2014

Types	Total institutions	Total offices network
Commercial bank	119	19,948
Rural banks	1,643	4,895
Cooperatives	38,083*	NA

Sources: Indonesia Financial Services Authority (OJK) (2014a); MoCMSMES (2005).
*2005

Table 7.2: Indonesia Islamic Financial Institutions in 2014

Types	Total institutions	Total offices network
Islamic commercial bank	12	2,151
Conventional bank with Islamic business unit	22	320
Islamic rural banks	163	439
Islamic cooperatives	4,117*	NA

Sources: OJK (2014a); MoCMSMES Republic of Indonesia (2005); Sugianto (2012).
*2012

financial cooperatives under the supervision of MoCMSMEs (OJK, 2014a; Sugianto, 2012).

There are three categories of MFIs in Indonesia: formal, semiformal and informal. Based on the financial authorities and international recognition, formal financial institutions that offer microfinance services include units of the BRI Microbanking Division and the rural bank (BPR). MFIs not supervised by Otoritas Jasa Keuangan (OJK) are categorised as semiformal institutions while microfinance-like channelling groups and rotating savings and credit associations (ROSCAs) are classified under the informal category (Seibel & Dwi Agung, 2006).

7.1.1 *Formal MFIs in Indonesia*

Formal MFIs are institutions supervised by financial authorities (e.g., OJK). According to Seibel & Dwi Agung (2006), formal MFIs in Indonesia include units of the BRI, BPR.

(1) BRI

BRI, which started operation in 1895, is a state-owned bank involved in microlending. BRI has a large number of customers with 50 million deposit accounts in 2014. Approximately 31.25% of its lending caters for micro, small and medium enterprises (SMEs) through its microbanking division. As of December 2014, BRI's total assets were over RP800 trillion; there were over 8,000 offices in the microbanking division that served over 7 million microclients (BRI, 2014, 2015a; Gallardo, 2001; OJK, 2014a).

Table 7.3 shows the history of PT. BRI (persero) Tbk development. The milestones history of BRI began in 1895 under the name *De Poerwokertosche Hulp en Spaarbank der Inlandsche Hoofden*. The institution began managing trust funds from society and was a mosque-based association. The funds were redistributed to the society in a simple scheme. In 1912, the institution changed its name to *Centrale Kas Voor Volkscredietwezen*; under the Japanese colonisation in 1942 it changed to *Syomin Ginko*; and in 1946 it was nationalised by the Indonesian government and changed its name to BRI. In 1960, the Indonesian government changed its name to BKTN and in 1968 changed its name back to BRI. Finally, in 1992, BRI changed its legal status to a limited liability company or perseroan terbatas, and the official name became PT BRI (BRI, 2016).

In 1969, the Indonesian government appointed BRI to distribute credit to Indonesians through BIMAS, then, in 1984, BRI started to manage its own commercial microbusiness through its most successful division, the microbanking division, with its own BRI units known as BRI Unit Desa. The BRI Unit Desa reached break-even point within 18 months and earned a profit of over US$25 million in 1989. During 1984–1990, BRI Unit Desa distributed 7.9 million loans, valued at US$614.5 million with an average US$340 per loan to low level income households who live in rural areas in Indonesia (Boomgard & Angell, 1990; Seibel, 2005).

BRI wanted to expand its business and become a more successful state-owned company, therefore, in 2003, BRI listed on the Jakarta stock exchange (now Indonesia stock exchange); the Indonesian government owned 56.75% whereas 43.25% of shares were owned by the public. Its performance after going public increased significantly; the value of its

Table 7.3: **History of BRI**

Year	Milestones	Description
1895	Company founded under the name of De Poerwokertosche Hulp en Spaarbank der Inlandsche Hoofden	• Initially an institution that managed mosque funds distributed to society • In 1912 changed its name to *Centrale Kas Voor Volksscredietwezen* • Under Japanese colonisation, the name changed to *Syomin Ginko* (1942–1945)
1946	Nationalised by Indonesian government and changed its name to BRI	• The government of Indonesia changed the bank's name from *Syomin Ginko* to through the government regulation no. 1/1946 • The main aim of at that time was to support Indonesia's development
1960	Indonesian government changed its name to Bank Koperasi Tani Nelayan (BKTN)	NA
1968	The Indonesian government changed its name back to BRI	• Based on regulation No. 21/1968, the bank's name changed back to BRI • The government of Indonesia designated BRI as a state commercial bank
1969	The Indonesian government appointed BRI to distribute credit to Indonesian society through "Bimbingan Massal (BIMAS)"	• BIMAS is an agricultural diversification programme from the government that includes a rural credit component with the aim to provide small loans to farmers at below market rates • BRI started to establish BRI units
1984	BRI managed its own commercial microbusiness and channelled it through BRI units	• This is after the Indonesian government stopped the BIMAS programme
1992	The government of Indonesia changed the legal entity of BRI to a limited liability company or perusahaan perseroan (persero)	• This was based on government regulation No. 21/1992

(Continued)

Table 7.3:   (*Continued*)

Year	Milestones	Description
2003	BRI listed on the Jakarta stock exchange (now Indonesia stock exchange)	• In November 10, 2003 BRI started to sell its shares through IPO with the ticker "BBRI" • BBRI now incorporated in LQ-45 or blue chip shares on the Indonesia stock exchange (BEI)
2007	BRI established its subsidiary Bank BRI Syariah	• BRI acquired Bank Jasa Artha and then converted into PT. Bank BRI Syariah (BRI's Islamic bank)
2009	BRI started its real-time online interconnection for its whole network	• BRI involved 6,480 work units in this event
2013	BRI started its Hybrid banking service	• BRI's Hybrid banking is self-service banking • This service was the first in Indonesia
2014	BRI is a bank that has the most automated teller machines (ATM) and has the biggest electronic data capture (EDC) network in Indonesia	• ATM: 20,792 units • EDC: 131,204 units • BRI has 50 million customers • In April 28, 2014 BRI signed a contract with Space System/Loral (SSL) and Arianespace to launch its own satellite named Satelit BRI (BRIsat)

Sources: BRI (2014); World Bank (2012).

stock increased approximately 30 times from 2003 to 2014 and its profit reached trillion rupiahs.

In 2014, BRI had 10,413 offices and served 50 million accounts of corporate, retail and microcustomers. In order to upgrade its communication network and achieve integrated banking, BRI planned to launch its own satellite (BRIsat) in 2016. The satellite allows BRI to connect its office network from its headquarter to Teras BRI (mobile) effectively. Most of BRI's offices are in rural areas and difficult to reach with conventional telecommunication technology. Satellite technology will enable BRI to connect all of its offices to become a one-stop service bank in Indonesia (BRI, 2014; Fahlevi, 2015).

BRI has various types of office networks across Indonesia. It has a headquarter office, regional offices, branch offices, subsidiary branch offices, cash offices, BRI units, Teras BRI, Teras BRI (mobile) and inspection offices. This office network covers all provinces in Indonesia from Aceh to Papua (BRI, 2014). The various types of offices means the bank covers different areas, for instance, branch offices are usually placed in cities, while BRI units in rural areas. The most extraordinary offices are the BRI units that are considered by USAID as one of the most successful financial institutions in the world serving rural borrowers and savers in developing countries (Boomgard & Angell, 1990).

BRI's office network has increased gradually from 7,000 in 2010 to 10,000 offices in 2013. In 2014, BRI had over 10,000 offices across the archipelago (see Table 7.4). This makes BRI the bank with the biggest office network in Indonesia. BRI believes that there is a large opportunity in microbanking business in Indonesia, especially in remote areas. This is because, according to the MoCMSMEs, in 2012, there are more than 55 million micro, SMEs in Indonesia. Based on this figure, about 98.83% (over 54 million) are microenterprises, 1.09% (about 602.195) are small enterprises and 0.08% are medium enterprises. Based on the history, microenterprises tend to be more resilient in financial crises. This makes microenterprises and microcredit a magnet for the banking industry especially in Indonesia (BRI, 2014; Sutaryono, 2015).

Table 7.4:   BRI Office Network (2010–2014)

Type	2010	2011	2012	2013	2014
Headquarters	1	1	1	1	1
Regional offices	18	18	18	18	19
Branch offices	413	431	446	453	461
Subsidiary branch offices	470	502	545	565	585
Cash offices	822	870	914	950	971
BRI units	4,649	4,849	5,000	5,144	5,293
Teras BRI	617	1,304	1,778	2,212	2,457
Teras BRI (mobile)	—	100	350	465	610
Inspection offices	14	14	16	17	17
Total	**7,004**	**8,089**	**9,068**	**9,825**	**10,413**

Source: BRI (2014).

Table 7.5:   BRI Subsidiary Companies

Company name	Type	Dates of shares subscription from BRI	BRI's shares (%)	Commencement date
PT. Bank BRI Syariah	Islamic commercial bank	19 December 2007	99.99	16 October 2008
PT. Agroniaga Tbk (BRIAGRO).	Commercial bank (private)	3 March 2011	80.43	8 February 1990
BRIngin Remittance Co. Ltd.	Remittance company	16 December 2011	100	7 April 2005

Source: BRI (2014).

Three subsidiary companies are owned by BRI. They are PT. Bank BRISyariah; BRIAGRO; and BRIngin Remittance Co. Ltd (BRC) (see Table 7.5). All three subsidiary companies are important and support BRI in some ways. As the third biggest Islamic bank in Indonesia, Bank BRISyariah is important for BRI to expand its business into the Islamic banking market. By utilising BRI's office network across Indonesia, BRISyariah can develop its Islamic banking business easily and compete with other Islamic banks (IBs). In December 2013, BRISyariah was appointed by the Indonesian government as one of the IBs that can receive and manage the Hajj fund or Bank Penerima Setoran Biaya Penyelenggaraan Ibadah Haji (BPS BPIH). This allows BRISyariah to have greater opportunity to increase its Muslim customers, especially those planning to perform a hajj.[1]

BRIARGO is important for BRI because its focus is on the agribusiness sector. BRIAGRO has a unique market in providing financial services to this sector. PT Perkebunan Nusantara, a stated-owned enterprise, is an example of BRIAGRO's clients. Other main clients are PT Shang Hyang Seri, PT Pertani, PT Pupuk Nusantara, RNI and Perum Perhutani. BRIAGRO has a collaboration agreement with BRI especially on funding products, for example, all BRIAGRO customers can easily make

---

[1] Hajj is important for Muslim and one of the pillars of Islam. Muslims are obligated to take at least once in their lifetime if they are able (The British Museum, 2012).

transactions on BRI's ATMs across Indonesia. Another example of collaboration between BRI and BRIAGRO is the integrated promotion programme, which covers product promotion, building network, and regular training for the sales force. Finally, BRC is also important for BRI to provide a competitive advantage especially on remittance business for Indonesian labour in Hong Kong. BRC has implemented the BRIFAST online system from BRI, which is integrated with BRI's office network in Indonesia (Bank BRI Agro, 2014; BRI Remittance, 2013).

Bank BRISyariah started its official operation on 16 October 2008. This company was initially Bank Jasa Artha acquired by BRI in 2007, which was converted to Bank BRISyariah to serve customers with *shari'ah* banking preferences. BRISyariah also focusses on microbusiness; the total microfinancing business in 2014 increased by 31% from RP2.45 trillion in 2013 to RP3.21 trillion. In 2014, there were 311 *shari'ah* microunits across Indonesia, an increase of 6.87% from 2013 (291 unit). In order to maintain its excellent service to microbusiness, BRISyariah focuses on improving its speed, convenience, comfort, sustainability and *shari'ah* compliance in all of its products (BRI Syariah, 2014).

BRIAGRO started operations on 8 February 1990 and was acquired by BRI on 3 March 2011. In 2012, the bank changed its name to PT. Bank Rakyat Indonesia Agroniaga Tbk or BRIAGRO. In 2014, it had a total office network of 35 offices, 3 cash offices, 1 payment point, 42 ATMs and 785 officers focusing on agriculture and the agribusiness sector in Indonesia. In terms of shareholders, 80.42% of shares are held by BRI, Dana Pensiun Perkebunan (pension fund) 14.03% and 5.55% held by the public (Bank BRI Agro, 2014). BRIAGRO exhibits good performance in 2014 with a significant increase in profit from RP52 billion in 2013 to RP62 billion (18.23%). The increased in profit was due to increase in credit, 26.93% higher than 2013 (Bank BRI Agro, 2014).

As a bank that focuses its business to support agribusiness, most credit from BRIAGRO is distributed in this sector. Since its first establishment, BRIAGRO has distributed 60–75% of total credit in the agribusiness sector. The clients of BRIAGRO include PT Perkebunan Nusantara, PT Shang Hyang Seri, PT Pertani, PT Pupuk Nusantara, and Perum Perhutani which are engaged in agribusiness. BRIAGRO's financing focuses on off and on farm agribusiness. An example of on farm financing is financing to palm oil, coffee and cocoa plantations which are competitive commodities in the market. An example of off farm financing is working capital financing agribusiness companies (Bank BRI Agro, 2014).

BRC operated as a subsidiary of BRI since 16 December 2011. In October 2012, the financial institution changed its name to BRI Remittance or BRC. BRC is based in Causeway Bay, Hong Kong. In Hong Kong, BRC offers services to transfer money to Indonesia named BRIFast, which is linked to the BRI network in Indonesia; customers can withdraw from 9,000 BRI offices across Indonesia. BRC also sets up savings accounts in Hong Kong for its customers called BRItAma (Bloomberg, 2015; BRI Remittance, 2013). BRC benefits Indonesia especially as a source of foreign exchange. By the end of 2014, total remittances of the Indonesian working force or Tenaga Kerja Indonesia (TKI), which remit money via BRC to Indonesia, were RP13.65 trillion (3.5 million transactions) (Kusuma, 2015).

The microbanking division of BRI is called BRI unit, Teras BRI and Teras BRI (mobile) are sub-outlets of BRI unit and part of the microbanking division. In 2014, the total network of BRI's microbanking division was 8,360 offices. In 2014, BRI's microbanking division office network consisted of 5,293 offices of BRI unit, 2,457 offices of Teras BRI and 610 unit of mobile Teras BRI (see Table 7.4).

Total loans disbursed by the microbanking division in 2014 was over RP150 trillion covering over 7.3 million microcustomers. The BRI's microcredit in 2014 increased to RP21.1 trillion or 15.99% in 2013. This increase is due to the strategies adopted by BRI in 2014. One of the strategy was to expand the main unit of the microbanking division, Teras BRI. In 2014, BRI added 251 new Teras BRI and 145 new Teras BRI (mobile) offices generating a total of 3,067 Teras BRI units. This expansion was followed by an increase in productivity. In 2014, the total productivity of each Teras BRI increases because credit increased from RP3.7 billion in 2013 to RP4.4 billion, and savings increased from RP1.9 billion in 2013 to RP2 billion in 2014. BRI's market share of microbusiness is around 50%, which makes BRI a leader in the Indonesian microbusiness market (BRI, 2013, 2014).

Based on BRI's financial summary from 2010 to 2014 (see Table 7.6), all financial indicators experienced significant growth with total assets

Table 7.6: BRI Financial Summary (in billion RP)

Description	2010	2011	2012	2013	2014
Total asset	404,286	469,899	551,337	626,183	801,955
Total earning asset	379,696	432,647	499,042	568,546	728,094
Third party fund	333,652	384,264	450,166	504,281	622,322
Net income for the year	11,472	15,088	18,687	21,354	24,254

Source: BRI (2014).

Table 7.7: BRI Financial Performance (in percentage)

Description	2010	2011	2012	2013	2014
ROA	4.64	4.93	5.15	5.03	4.74
ROE	43.83	42.49	38.66	34.11	31.22
NIM	10.77	9.58	8.42	8.55	8.51
OER	70.86	66.69	59.93	60.58	65.37
LDR	75.17	76.20	79.85	88.54	81.86
NPL (gross)	2.78	2.30	1.78	1.55	1.69

Source: BRI (2014).

increased from RP404 trillion[2] in 2010 to Rp801 trillion in 2014. Total earning assets increased from RP379 trillion in 2010 to RP728 trillion in 2014. The third party fund increased from RP333 trillion in 2010 to RP622 trillion in 2014. Net income increased from RP11 trillion in 2010 to RP24 trillion in 2014 (BRI, 2014).

Based on BRI's financial performance from 2010 to 2014 (see Table 7.7), ROA, ROE, NIM and OER fluctuated during the period. In 2014, BRI's ROA decreased from 5.03% in 2013 to 4.74%. This is because of increased on liquidity, especially in BRI's securities. On the other hand, ROE decreased from 34.11% in 2013 to 31.22% in 2014, because of the increased on cost of funds. The operational efficiency ratio (OER) increased from 60.58% in 2013 to 65.37% in 2014. This was due to the high inflation rate in 2014 (8.36%). NIM decreased slightly from

---

[2]US$1 = RP13,876 (Bloomberg Business, 2015).

8.55% in 2013 to 8.51% in 2014. This was because of the dynamic macroeconomic conditions in Indonesia; during 2014, the central bank rate increased to 7.75% and this led to an increase in banks' interest rate. LDR decreased from 88.54% in 2013 to 81.86% in 2014 whereas NPL increased from 1.55% in 2013 to 1.69% in 2014. This was because of the macro conditions and political instability in Indonesia during 2014 (general and presidential election year). In 2014, because of the impact of global economic downturn, the banking industry could not reached its credit target. Indonesia economic growth grew only 5.01%, much lower than the previous year of 5.6%. This condition led to a decrease in BRI's LDR, an increase in NPL and, finally, a decrease its NIM (Bank BRI Agro, 2014; BRI, 2014).

(2) BPR

BPR, the people's credit bank, is Indonesia's rural bank, which started business in the early 1990. BPR's business focuses on providing financial services in rural areas; this parallels its mission since the first establishment of the institution, which provides financial services to SMEs and households in rural areas in Indonesia. OJK, as regulator, encourages BPR to focus its business in rural areas because urban areas are served by commercial banks (Neraca, 2015). Since the banking reform and implementation of the law Paket Kebijakan Oktober (PAKTO 27) in 1988, which was designed to promote the establishment of new commercial banks in Indonesia, BPR may be owned by individuals. This regulation led to an increase in the private banking sector in Indonesia especially for BPR. Based on OJK's regulations, the legal entity of BPR consists of limited liability company, cooperative, or local-state enterprise. Therefore, if individuals want to establish a BPR, they have to choose among the three legal entities and obtain permission from OJK (OJK, 2014c; Seibel, 2005; Seibel & Ozaki, 2009; Tambunan, 2015).

In December 2014, there were 1,643 BPRs with 4,895 offices in Indonesia (see Table 7.8). Total assets were RP89 trillion and the bank served over 13 million clients. Based on this figures, 62% of BPRs and 74% of its offices are concentrated in Java. The number of BPR rural banks slightly decreased during 2010–2014. However, the total bank offices experienced significant growth during the same period (see Table 7.8). This

Table 7.8:   Growth of BPR (Rural Bank)

Description	2010	2011	2012	2013	2014
Total rural banks	1,706	1,669	1,653	1,635	1,643
Total bank offices	3,910	4,172	4,425	4,678	4,895

Source: OJK (2014a).

Table 7.9:   BPR Financial Performance (in percentage)

Description	2010	2011	2012	2013	2014
ROA	3.16	3.32	3.46	3.44	2.98
ROE	26.71	29.46	32.63	32.41	27.89
LDR	79.02	78.54	76.63	84.34	79.79
NPL	6.12	5.22	4.75	4.41	4.75

Source: OJK (2014a).

is because some BPRs have merged into a bigger bank, e.g., BPR Jatim. A small number of other BPRs have had their licence revoked by the central bank of Indonesia (BI) because of poor performance. However, there is no significant impact on the whole industry (Praditya, 2013a).

Based on BPR's financial performance data from 2010 to 2013, the bank's ROA and ROE increased. However, in 2014, the ROA and ROE of BPR decreased to 2.98% and 27.89%, respectively (see Table 7.9). The decrease in ROA and ROE in 2014 was due to the instability of the macroeconomic conditions such as rise in oil prices and high inflation that impacted the banking industry in Indonesia (Syariah, 2014; Neraca, 2015). Other indicators such as LDR and NPL fluctuated during the 2010–2014; in 2014, the LDR decreased from 83.34% in 2013 to 79.79% and the NPL increased from 4.41% in 2013 to 4.75% in 2014. The decrease in LDR means there is excess of liquidity and a need to disburse more finance whereas an increase in NPL means that banks must allocate more reserve funds for non-performing loans (OJK, 2014a).

Based on law No. 21/2011, starting from 31 December 2013, the regulatory and monitoring function for banks was undertaken by OJK from the BI. BI focuses only on managing inflation and is responsible for monetary stability. OJK is responsible for monitoring all financial institutions in Indonesia including BPR; every June BPRs have to submit an annual report to OJK (BI, 2015; Gallardo, 2001; Gera, 2013; OJK, 2014a, 2014c).

7.1.2 Semi-formal MFIs in Indonesia

According to Seibel & Dwi Agung (2006), semi-formal MFIs in Indonesia include various types of cooperatives and so-called village banks (bank desa). Semi-formal MFIs in Indonesia are outside the regulation and supervision of the financial authorities. Some financial cooperatives in Indonesia may be registered and supervised under the MoCMSMEs and some may be unregistered. Financial cooperatives registered under the MoCMSMEs are considered more "formal" than unregistered ones.

There are two types of financial cooperatives registered under the MoCMSMEs. The first types are Koperasi Simpan Pinjam (KSP) and Unit Simpan Pinjam (USP) that operate within the conventional system (non-Islamic). In 2005, there were 38,083 units of KSP and USP in Indonesia serving over 16 million clients (see Table 7.10). The second type are Koperasi Jasa Keuangan Syariah (KJKS) and Unit Jasa Keuangan Syariah (UJKS) that operate within the *shari'ah* system (Islamic).

KJKS and UJKS provide financial services to their members that are *shari'ah* compliant. As a cooperative institution, members of KJKS and UJKS can apply for Islamic financing e.g., *murabahah* (cost plus mark-up), *mudarabah* (trustee financing), *musharakah* (equity participation). However, members must pay primary, compulsory saving to join these cooperatives (Choudhury & Dusuki, 2008; Ministry of Cooperatives and Micro and Small, 2007; Obaidullah & Khan, 2009). Members also have

Table 7.10:   Financial Cooperatives Registered under MoCMSMEs

Types	Total institutions	No of clients
KSP/USP savings and loan cooperatives	38,083[a]	16,871,000[a]
KJKS/UJKS Islamic financial services cooperatives	4,117[b]	762,000[b]

Sources: MoCMSMEs of Republic of Indonesia (2005); Sugianto (2012).
[a]Year 2005; [b]Year 2012.

an opportunity to profit sharing in the cooperative at the end of the year. In 2012, there were 4,117 units of KJKS and UJKS in Indonesia serving over 700,000 clients (see Table 7.10).

The financial cooperatives are regularly monitored and supervised by the MoCMSMEs. At the end of each year, all cooperatives have to arrange an annual member meeting to report on all activities as well as distribute the cooperative's profits to members. Financial and activities reports have to be submitted to the MoCMSMEs after the annual meeting (OJK, 2015b; Ministry of Cooperatives and Micro and Small, 2007).

The Indonesian government, through OJK, issued regulations to MFIs in Indonesia. First, there are only two legal statuses of "formal" MFIs in Indonesia, as a cooperative or a limited liability company. This means that only registered MFIs and under the supervision of the government are eligible for official assistance. Second, all MFIs under the government supervision should get their business licence from OJK or a deed of incorporation of the cooperative from the MoCMSMEs. Third, every 4 months, all MFIs except cooperatives, are required to submit a financial report to OJK (OJK, 2015b).

7.1.3 *Informal MFIs in Indonesia*

Informal MFIs in Indonesia have a long history and include a wide variety of self-help groups (SHG), channelling groups and ROSCAs or in Indonesia called "arisan". (Seibel, 2005; Seibel & Dwi Agung, 2006). SHGs in Indonesia are established and managed by government, and community organisation that is still linked to government programmes, or NGOs. Other SHGs operate with *shari'ah* principle.

Meanwhile, arisan is a traditional group, an Indonesian version of ROSCA and a social gathering as well. Arisans generally have a fixed interval meeting (every month or year) and are held in a member's house. Each member in the group is paid a certain amount of money agreed within the group. Members that get rota (drawn by lot) will receive all the money. However, he/she is then responsible to hold the next Arisan meeting and provides food for the meeting (Conroy, 2003). As an informal group, arisans do not have specific rules for its members. Most rules are decided and managed based on consensus. The main products of this type of microfinance services are savings and credits for members (Conroy, 2003).

Informal Islamic MFIs comprise Baitul Maal Wat Tamwil (BMT), which follows the regulations of cooperatives or SHG. If a BMT operates under the cooperative rules, it will be regulated under the cooperative law (Cooperative Act No. 25/1992), supervised by MoCMSMEs and considered as semi-formal Islamic MFIs. However, if a BMT is established as an SHG there will be no rules regulating it; it is formed by a group of people and considered as an informal Islamic MFI. The products and services offered by BMT are similar to KJKS and UJKS, it is only the legal entity that is different.

In Indonesia, there is a wide variety of SHG called Kelompok Swadaya Masyarakat (KSM). An example of an SHG is PHBK under the Bank Indonesia's Program Linking Banks and SHG. PHBK is a financing scheme from a regional/local bank to SMEs. In the PHBK scheme, SMEs also receive assistance from local government after they obtain finance from the bank. The aim of PHBK is to give financial access to local SMEs in order to develop their business.

In the context of Islamic MFIs terms, there are various names (see Table 7.11). First BMT, which may have a semi-formal or informal legal

Table 7.11:   Informal MFIs in Indonesia

Types	Description
SHG/KSM	Some BMT are in the form of SHGs or KSMs and others such as KJKS and UJKS are under the MoCMSMEs
Channelling groups	In 2003, there were around 800,000 channelling groups in Indonesia
ROSCAs, Arisan	There are millions of ROSCAs in Indonesia known as Arisan from indigenous origins
BMT	Most BMTs are under the guidance of the Centre for microenterprise incubation Pusat Inkubasi Bisnis Usaha Kecil (PINBUK) or associated with Induk Koperasi Syariah BMT (Inkopsyah BMT)
Baitul Tamwil Muhammadiyah (BTM)	These comprise 5% of Islamic cooperatives, guided by Muhammadiyah since 1999
Baitul Qirad (BQ)	Term used in the Aceh province to denote Islamic cooperatives or BMTs

Sources: Seibel & Dwi Agung (2006); Imady & Seibel (2006); Adnan & Ajija (2015).

status. Semi-formal Islamic MFIs follow the form of a cooperative and are registered under MoCMSMEs (known as KJKS and UJKS), whereas informal Islamic MFIs are established as SHGs. If the legal status of BMT is a SHG, they will receive guidance from Pusat Inkubasi Bisnis Usaha Kecil (PINBUK) or can be associated with Induk Koperasi Syariah (Inkopsyah) BMT (Seibel & Dwi Agung, 2006; Zain *et al.*, 2006). Second BTM, an Islamic MFIs guided by Muhammadiyah, the second-largest Islamic mass organisation in Indonesia (Adnan & Ajija, 2015; Imady & Seibel, 2006). Finally, BQ is a term for Islamic cooperatives in Aceh province. The implication of BMT, BTM and BQ is that they follow a cooperative form, receive formal assistance from and are monitor by the government. However, BMT, BTM and BQ that follow the SHG form will not receive any formal assistance from and monitor by the government but receive assistance only from PINBUK or Inkopsyah BMT. This is because they are not registered under the government (Adnan & Ajija, 2015; Imady & Seibel, 2006).

BMT is an Islamic MFI that mixes commercial and social attributes in their business products, for example, BMT can generate profit from Profit and Loss Sharing (PLS) or get a margin/fee from a non-PLS mechanism and can also collect zakah,[3] *infaq*[4] and *sadaqat*[5] or *waqf*[6] and distribute it for social purposes (Imady & Seibel, 2006). According to Hassan (2010), the integration of social dimensions such as *zakah* and *waqf* with commercial products such as *mudarabah* and *musharakah* in Islamic MFIs will benefit the poorest better. This is because Islamic MFIs can use *zakah* fund to fulfil the basic consumption of its clients and *waqf* funds can be used as working capital for microbusiness (Hassan, 2010). Islamic MFIs can use *mudarabah* or *murabahah* schemes to develop their clients' business.

---

[3]Compulsory charity for Muslims (if their wealth exceeds the condition (*nisab*)), equal to 85 grams of gold and hold it for a year (*Haul*). It is more for consumption purposes and there are certain rules of *zakah* in Islam such as from whom *zakah* is collected, at what rate, and who can benefit from *zakah* (Ahmed, 2007; Obaidullah, 2008a).
[4]Charitable spending (Obaidullah, 2008a).
[5]Optional charity can be used for productive activities (Ahmed, 2007).
[6]*Sadaqah jariyah* or continuous *sadaqah*. The *waqf* is created when somebody gives away an asset for the benefit of society. The concept of cash *waqf* can be used in order to benefit society (Ahmed, 2007).

7.2 History and Development of Islamic MFIs

Islamic finance has experienced rapid, significant growth over the past four decades. A major reason is Muslims comprise over 21% of the world's population with US$1 trillion of assets to invest. Islamic finance is a promising financial industry and the industry's assets are expected to reach US$2 trillion in 2015. With this estimate, the compounded asset growth rate will be 17.3% (Azmat, Skully & Brown, 2014, 2015; Chong & Liu, 2009; El-Komi & Croson, 2013; Ibrahim, 2015; Sumarti, Fitriyani & Damayanti, 2014).

Islamic MFIs follow Islamic law or parallel Muslim beliefs. Islamic MFIs' products and services must be free from certain elements[7] forbidden in Islam (Obaidullah, 2008a). Based on a survey conducted by CGAP in 19 Muslim countries in 2007 cited in El-Komi & Croson (2013), 20–40% of poor Muslims rejected receiving loans from conventional MFIs for religious reasons. Since one-third of the world's poor are Muslim, this means that not all Muslims can take advantage of existing microfinance products which are not parallel with their religious beliefs (El-Komi & Croson, 2013). The history of Islamic MFIs cannot be separated from the history and development of Islamic finance and MFIs. The global success of Islamic finance has influenced the establishment of other industries including Islamic MFIs (Nasdaq OMX, 2012). The popularity and rapid development of MFIs has led to the combination of this financing vehicle with Islamic finance (Karim, Tarazi & Reille, 2008).

According to Ainley *et al.* (2007) and Huda (2012), the development of Islamic finance institutions in the modern era started with the establishment of an Islamic bank in the Middle East in the 1960s. The combination of Islamic finance and microfinance was first discussed and elaborated in depth by Rahul and Sapcanin in 1998 (Akhter, Akhtar & Jaffri, 2009). Based on a study by Abdouli (1991) cited in Dhumale & Sapcanin (1999), there are three basic financing schemes of Islamic finance that could combine with MFIs to build a successful microfinance programme: *mudarabah* (trustee financing), *musharakah* (equity participation) and *murabahah* (cost plus mark-up).

---

[7]It must be free from *riba* (interest), free from *gharar* (uncertainty/lack of information disclosure), *qimar* (gambling) and *mysir* (games of chance involving deception) (Obaidullah, 2008a; Sumarti *et al.*, 2014).

Mudarabah is a profit-sharing agreement in which Islamic financial institutions provide the entire capital for specific project and customers provide their expertise and labour. The profit will be shared based on pre-agreed basis and losses will borne by the Islamic financial institution as long as there is no negligence by the customers. *Musharakah* is similar to a joint venture agreement in which Islamic financial institutions and their customers contribute capital to a specific project. This is a profit and loss sharing agreement; any profit and loss from the project will be shared by both parties on a pre-agreed basis (Chong & Liu, 2009). *Murabahah* is a financing scheme under the debt-based financing mechanism in which Islamic financial institutions will purchase goods desired by their customers and sell the goods to them at an agreed price (mark-up price) with payment settled on an agreed time frame; it may be by instalments or a lump sum (Obaidullah, 2008b).

7.2.1 *Islamic finance in Indonesia*

Indonesia has over 250 million of people with 56 million households and 87.21% of the population is Muslim (approximately 218 million people) (Masyita & Ahmed, 2011; Ministry of Religious Affairs of the Republic of Indonesia, 2013; Statistics Indonesia, 2014). Based on those statistics, the availability of Islamic financial institutions in Indonesia is crucial. This is because Muslims have some restrictions on conventional finance, particularly they are prohibited from involvement in transactions that contain *riba* (interest).

There was no specific legal foundation for Islamic financial institutions especially Islamic bank, at that time; they were just accommodated in law No. 7/ 1992 in one sentence "bank with profit and loss sharing system". In 1998, the Indonesian government implemented a dual banking system in Indonesia, conventional and Islamic, into law No. 10/1998. More specific legal foundation for Islamic banks (IBs) in Indonesia are regulated in law No. 21/2008. This law led to a boost in the number of full IBs in Indonesia from 5 to 11 in less than 2 years (2009–2010) (OJK, 2015a; Seibel, 2008).

Table 7.12 shows the development of Islamic finance in Indonesia. Islamic finance started to evolve in 1990, mainly through the initiative of Islamic scholars and Islamic organisations in Indonesia. The first Islamic financial institution in Indonesia was Islamic cooperative followed by an

Table 7.12:   **Highlights of Islamic Finance Development in Indonesia**

Year	Milestones	Description
1990	Islamic finance started to develop in Indonesia	• Due to the initiatives from Islamic scholars and organisations • Initially started with Islamic cooperative
1991	Islamic rural bank/Bank Pembiayaan Rakyat Syariah (BPRS) initial growth	• Experienced 12% average growth per year • The four BPRS were licensed, three in Bandung (west java province) and one in Aceh • Until 1996 there was a gradual expansion of BPRS
1992	The establishment of first Islamic commercial bank in Indonesia	• Approval of the first Islamic commercial bank in Indonesia, named Bank Muamalat Indonesia (BMI) • Establishment of Indonesia Islamic bank association/Asosiasi Bank Islam Indonesia (Asbisindo)
1999	Second Islamic commercial bank established	• Bank Syariah Mandiri (BSM) was the second Islamic commercial bank in Indonesia • The first sharia unit of a conventional commercial bank was also established in 1999 • 1999 was a stagnant period for BPRS, however, the Islamic bank started its gradual expansion until 2003
2010	Indonesian government issued regular *sukuk* (Islamic bonds)	• Regular rupiah *sukuk* was issued once every 2 weeks • Most of Indonesia's *sukuk* are short term (less than a year)
2014	Indonesia ranks 7th in the Global Islamic Finance Report for the Islamic Finance Country Index (IFCI)	• 12 Islamic commercial banks • 22 Islamic business units in conventional banks • 163 Islamic rural banks • 4,117[a] units of Islamic cooperatives or KJKS and UJKS under MoCMSMEs • Indonesia is a member of Islamic Development Bank (IDB), Islamic Financial Services Board (IFSB), the International Islamic Financial Market (IIFM), and the International Islamic Liquidity Management Corporation IILM • Indonesia adopted the regulations of IFSB and the Accounting and Auditing organisation for Islamic Financial Institutions (AAOIFI)

Note[a]: Year 2012.

Sources: Lawrence (2014); Seibel (2008); Seibel & Dwi Agung (2006); Global Islamic Finance Report (2014); Sugianto (2012).

Islamic rural bank in 1991 and an Islamic commercial bank in 1992. The Indonesian government started to issue regular *sukuk* (Islamic bonds) in 2010 (Lawrence, 2014; Seibel, 2008; Seibel & Dwi Agung, 2006). According to the Global Islamic Finance Report (2014), Indonesia achieved 7th rank in 2014 for the IFCI.

Besides the development of Islamic financial institutions, there are also many associations concerned with Islamic economic development in Indonesia. Some of the associations are Pusat Komunikasi Ekonomi Syariah (PKES); Dewan Syariah Nasional — Majelis Ulama Indonesia (DSN-MUI); Masyarakat Ekonomi Syariah (MES); Ikatan Ahli Ekonomi Islam Indonesia (IAEI); Asosiasi Bank Syariah Indonesia (Asbisindo); Asosiasi Asuransi Syariah Indonesia (AASI); Asosiasi Perusahaan Penjaminan Indonesia (Asippindo); Badan Amil Zakat Nasional (Baznas); Badan Wakaf Indonesia (BWI); Forum Zakat; Ikatan Saudagar Muslim Indonesia (ISMI); and Himpunan Ilmuwan dan Sarjana Syariah Indonesia (HISSI). In August 2013, these 12 associations signed a mutual agreement named the Sharia Economic Movement or Gerakan Ekonomi Syariah (GRES). The aim of this movement is to increase the awareness of Indonesians about sharia economics.

This movement is also a campaign programme to accelerate Islamic economic growth in Indonesia. All Islamic economics' stakeholders from regulators, practitioners, academicians and other parties concerned with Islamic economic development in Indonesia supported this campaign. There have been many events in this campaign such as expos, seminars, focus group discussions, held not only in Jakarta but also in other main cities across Indonesia (Ministry of Religious Affairs of the Republic of Indonesia, 2013; Praditya, 2013b).

Some of these associations or organisations also have important roles and contributions to enhance Islamic economic development in Indonesia. Majelis Ulama Indonesia or the Council of Indonesia Ulama (DSN-MUI), for example, is responsible for the *shari'ah* compliance of all Islamic financial institutions' products and services in Indonesia (The Council of Indonesian Ulama, 2013). Meanwhile, IAEI and MES were established in Indonesia in order to accommodate Islamic economics scholars and to accelerate Islamic economic development, respectively. The aim of PKES is to provide socialisation and education about Islamic economics to Indonesians. Baznas is a government organisation with the objective to collect and distribute *zakah*, *infaq* and *sadaqat* at the national level. BWI is also a government organisation with the aim of managing *waqf*, especially educating the *nazhir*[8] and ensuring the *waqfs'* assets are managed properly (BAZNAS, 2016; BWI, 2012; IAEI, 2013; MES, 2008; PKES, 2013; The Council of Indonesian Ulama, 2013).

7.2.2 *Islamic financial institutions in Indonesia*

Indonesia has several types of Islamic financial institutions, such as IBs, Islamic rural banks, Islamic insurance, Islamic MFIs, etc. Education and awareness of Islamic finance in Indonesia is conducted regularly either by the government or by the associations.

In December 2014, there were 12 full Islamic commercial banks in Indonesia. In addition, there were 22 Islamic business units of conventional banks (see Table 7.13). The market share of IBs in August 2014 was

Table 7.13:   Islamic Financial Institutions in Indonesia in December 2014

Types	No of units	No of offices
Islamic commercial bank	12	2,151
Islamic business unit (from conventional bank)	22	320
Islamic rural bank (BPRS)	163	439
Islamic insurance	5	N/A
Islamic insurance unit	44	N/A
Islamic financing institution	3	N/A
Islamic financing unit	41	N/A
Islamic venture capital	4	N/A
Islamic credit insurance	2	N/A
Islamic credit insurance unit	1	N/A
Islamic financial services cooperatives (KJKS/UJKS)	4,117[a]	N/A
BMT	5,000[a]	22,000 [a]
BTM	330[b]	N/A
BQ	32[a]	N/A

Note: [a]Year 2012; [b]Year 2013.
Sources: OJK (2014a); OJK (2014b); Sugianto (2012); Fauzia (2013); Marhiansyah (2012).

---

[8]Nazhir or Mutawalli is a *waqf's* asset manager (Hassan, 2010).

5.5% or equal to RP198.98 trillion. There is still a huge opportunity for IBs to evolve in Indonesia. There are Islamic rural banks, Islamic insurance companies, Islamic financing institutions, Islamic venture capital and Islamic credit insurance to support the Islamic banking sector. In the microsector, Indonesia has KJKS and UJKS supervised by the MoCMSMEs and in informal sector these are BMT, BTM and BQ (Dwiantika, 2014; OJK, 2014a, 2014b).

7.2.3 *Islamic MFIs in Indonesia*

The CGAP survey cited in Nasdaq OMX (2012) on Islamic MFIs worldwide revealed that there is still a gap between demand and supply. Based on that survey, Islamic MFIs comprise 0.005% of global MFIs and are mainly concentrated in Indonesia, Bangladesh and Pakistan. Islamic MFIs operate globally in about 32 countries across 6 continents, North Africa, Sub-Saharan Africa, the Middle East, Central Asia, South Asia and Southeast Asia (Nasdaq OMX, 2012).

The establishment of Islamic financial institutions in Indonesia was initiated by Islamic MFIs. The concept of an Islamic bank in Indonesia was trialled first in a limited scale through Islamic MFIs named Bait At-Tamwil Salman ITB in Bandung and the Ridho Gusti cooperative. This is why Islamic MFIs are key for developing Islamic financial institutions in Indonesia. Islamic MFIs can play a decisive role in Indonesia; based on the Bank Indonesia report, 49% of rural households in East Java would prefer to bank with Islamic financial institutions rather than conventional to avoid the use of interest in their financial transactions (OJK, 2015a; Karim *et al.*, 2008; Seibel & Dwi Agung, 2006).

The first Islamic cooperative in Indonesia, Ridho Gusti, was established in 1990 in Bandung. In 1995, PINBUK started promoting Islamic cooperatives under the new name BMT (Seibel & Dwi Agung, 2006). There are different types of Islamic MFIs in Indonesia with several kinds of legal entity. Most Islamic MFIs in Indonesia follow the cooperative form to run their business.

Significant growth of Islamic MFIs in Indonesia started from 1996 with the help from the non-government organisation (NGO) named the PINBUK. During the financial crisis in 1998 and 1999, the number of

Table 7.14:   Islamic MFIs in Indonesia

Type	Status	Description
KJKS/UJKS Islamic financial services cooperatives	Semi-formal	Receive guidance and supervision from MoCMSMEs
BMT	Informal	Most of the BMTs are not registered with MoCMSMEs. They only receive guidance from the PINBUK or are associated with Inkopsyah BMT
BTM	Informal	Guided by Muhammadiyah is the second-largest Islamic mass organisation in Indonesia, and receive informal supervision from Muhammadiyah economic development centre or Pusat Pengembangan Ekonomi Muhamamdiyah (PPEM)
BQ	Informal	A uniquely Acehnese term for Islamic MFIs

Sources: Seibel (2008); Seibel & Dwi Agung (2006).

Islamic MFIs was around 3,000. This figure reduced to 2,900 in 2003 because of the lack of regulation and supervision led to dormancy and bankruptcy of some MFIs (Masyita & Ahmed, 2011; Seibel, 2008).

Table 7.14 lists some examples of Islamic MFIs in Indonesia such as KJKS/UJKS, BMT, BTM and BQ. KJKS and UJKS are Islamic cooperatives registered under the MoCMSMEs and regulated by the Cooperative Law: Cooperative Act No. 25/1992, especially Act No. 91/Kep/M. KUKM/IX/2004 about the implementation guidelines of KJKS and UJKS (Ministry of Cooperatives and Micro and Small, 2007). Simple and less complicated requirements are the advantages of KJKS and UJKS which help people in rural areas to access credits. Islamic MFIs have more advantages because they operate with *shari'ah* principles, which provide more options to clients who are concerned with their religion. Another advantage is that Islamic MFIs products are based on the PLS mechanism, which allows clients to share in profits and losses based on their business performance.

The establishment of BMT is certified by a notary and the institution can request a business certificate from PINBUK. BMT sources of funds are derived from founding members, compulsory and voluntary contributions, donations and loans (Adnan & Ajija, 2015). BMT must have their own *shari'ah* supervisory board to ensure their products and services follow the guidance set by DSN-MUI. For instance, BMT At-Taqwa has four members of the *shari'ah* supervisory board who meet monthly with its management, and internal control board. Another example is BMT Latanza, which has a *shari'ah* supervisory board of three; members of the *shari'ah* supervisory board are responsible for *shari'ah* compliance in their respective BMT (Seibel & Dwi Agung, 2006).

Islamic MFIs in Indonesia still face several challenges. There is still a lack of prudential regulation and effective supervision of Islamic financial cooperatives, as a consequence, some Islamic cooperatives are technically bankrupt or dormant (Seibel & Dwi Agung, 2006). Islamic MFIs in Indonesia also suffer from unsystematic recording because most are not registered with MoCMSMEs. They need support from the government in order to create healthy Islamic financial cooperatives. This challenge is not only for the Islamic financial cooperatives but also for all financial cooperatives in Indonesia.

7.2.4 *Impact of Islamic microfinance on rural households*

Previous studies identified several ways to measure the impact of Islamic and conventional MFIs' financing of rural households. Kotir & Obeng-Odoom (2009) investigate the impact of conventional MFIs on rural household through (1) the use of credit; (2) improvement in productive capacity; (3) improvement in income; (4) improvement in household welfare; (5) Improvement of life; (6) improvement in household saving behaviour; and (7) the contribution to community development. Kotir & Obeng-Odoom (2009) study reveals that microfinance programme has a moderate impact on household welfare and modest impact on rural community development.

The popular technique to measure the causal effect of programmes or treatments used by Li *et al.* (2011) and Kondo *et al.* (2008) is called the difference-in-difference (DD) method. Li *et al.* (2011) use the following variables (1) household annual income; (2) household annual consumption; (3) age of household head; (4) number of children of school-age; (5) household size; (6) number of income earners; (7) total loan borrowed;

(8) programme participation and (9) a year indicator to measure the welfare impact of microcredit on rural households in China. Kondo *et al*. (2008) use (1) household outcome of interest; (2) household characteristics; (3) village characteristics (4) membership status; and (5) treatment area to measure the impact of MFIs on rural households in the Philippines. Li *et al*'s. (2011) study reveals that microcredit programme helps improve households' welfare especially income and consumption. Similarly, Kondo *et al*. (2008) study reveals a positive impact of programme loans on households' income and expenditure. However, the study also reveals a negative and insignificant impact for poorer households.

Samer *et al*'s. (2015) study measures the impact of Malaysian microfinance, Amanah Ikhtiar Malaysia (AIM) on household income. The finding of their multinomial logit analysis reveals a positive impact of microfinance on household income especially for old clients. Financing from AIM also has a positive impact on poverty reduction, especially in rural areas.

However, there are only a few studies that measure the impact of Islamic MFIs on rural households. Rahman (2010b) measures the impact of Islamic microfinance programme in Bangladesh on rural poverty alleviation. Rahman study shows the clients' family income increased over 33%, their religious activities increased by 21%, and their business knowledge and communication skills increased by 72% and 79%, respectively.

Based on the Rahman (2010b) study, several factors influence income-generating activities in Islamic MFI such as (1) age, (2) education, (3) asset holdings, (4) land size, (5) family labour, (6) rural infrastructure, (7) skill-building training and (8) morality and ethics. Rahman (2010b) uses ordinary least squares (OLS) and logit regression to estimate the impact of Islamic microfinance programme on various economic outcomes in Bangladesh. The logit model predicts the probability of increasing the welfare level of Islamic MFIs' clients. The study not only measured the improvement in economic welfare but also moral and ethical principles. The study reveals that the Islamic microfinance programme improves clients' religious behaviour such as praying and fasting, and it also increased household income, productivity of crops and livestock, expenditure and employment.

Rahman (2010a) believes that moral and Islamic values in Islamic MFI schemes can effectively boost the motivation of microentrepreneurs to develop their business. Islamic MFIs used ethical principles to encourage their clients to keep up to date with their payments. Before implementing the Islamic MFI scheme and values in practice, Islamic MFIs have to ensure that their products agree with Islamic ethical principles. There are four basic tenets in Islamic finance ethical systems: (1) unity (*tawhid*[9]); (2) equilibrium (*al-adl wa'l ihsan*[10]); (3) free will (*Ikhtiyar*[11]); and (4) responsibility (*Fard*[12]) (Naqvi & Qadir, 1997) as cited in (Rahman, 2010a).

Another study on the impact of Islamic MFIs financing on rural households was by Adnan & Ajija (2015). Their study focused on the effectiveness of Islamic MFIs' financing in reducing poverty in Indonesia. Their sample comprises clients from Islamic MFI, namely BMT MMU Sidogiri, in East Java, Indonesia. Poverty measurement indicators such as headcount index, GINI index, Sen index and Foster–Greer–Ihorbecke index were used to measure the impact of financing on clients' welfare. Their study conclude that most clients can increase their income after receiving financing (*mudarabah*) from Islamic MFIs.

7.2.5 *Values and schemes of Islamic MFIs*

The important value of Islamic finance is the commitment to avoid the practice of usury or *riba*[13] in transactions (Dhumale & Sapcanin, 1999). *Riba* is prohibited in Islam and taking profit from lending money is considered *haram*[14] (Dhumale & Sapcanin, 1999).

---

[9]This axiom means that behaviour should be guided by ethical principles; it is a vertical dimension and a unifier for every individual as an integral part of all aspects of life.

[10]It means a horizontal dimension which requires balance and fairness in society. Every individual should maintain this ethical principle.

[11]It is the opportunity to give maximum effort in all aspects of life. Every person has the freedom to change himself/herself with changing times.

[12]Every person is required to be responsible, especially when it comes to public goods. It is also about the responsibility towards society.

[13]*Riba* is translated as any excess which is added into the loan. It is also known as interest and can be found in conventional financing or lending schemes. The additional amount, pre-determined before the transaction, is called *riba* (Dhumale & Sapcanin, 1999).

[14]It is forbidden in Islamic beliefs.

In the *shari'ah*, *riba* technically refers to the premium that must be paid by the borrower to the lender together with the principal amount as a condition for the loan or for an extension in its maturity (Chapra, 2006). In other words, *riba* is the pre-determined return on the use of money. *Shari'ah* bans *riba* and there is now a general consensus among Muslim economists that *riba* is not restricted to usury but also encompasses interest. There two major forms of *riba* defined in Islam. They are *riba al-qarud/qard*, which relates to usury involving loans, and *riba al-Buyu*, which relates to usury of trade. *Riba al-qarud* involves a charge on a loan arising from the passage of time, in other words a loan with interest. It arises when a borrower, in any form, enters a contract to repay to a lender a pre-agreed amount in addition to the principal that was borrowed.

Meanwhile, *riba al-buyu* comprises *riba al-fadl* or *riba al-nasa/nasiah*. *Riba al-fadl* involves an exchange of unequal qualities or quantities of the same commodity simultaneously and could therefore be described as the usury of surplus. *Riba al-nasa* involves the non-simultaneous exchange of equal qualities and quantities of the same commodity and does not involve a surplus but only a difference in the timing of exchange (Aichbichler, 2009).

Thus, in the Islamic economic concept, an important, though not the only, element of such a strategy is the abolition of interest. This would necessitate the reorganisation of financial intermediation on the basis of equity and profit-and-loss sharing thus making the financier share in the risks as well as the rewards of business, and not assuring him/her of a pre-determined rate of return whatever the ultimate outcome of business (Sufian, 2007).

Most conventional MFIs' products do not fulfil the needs of Muslim clients. Many Muslims prefer products from Islamic MFIs because conventional MFI products contradict their religious beliefs (Akhter *et al.*, 2009). The practice of Islamic finance emphasises a profit and risk-sharing mechanism. For instance, Islamic MFIs' products such as *mudarabah*,[15]

---

[15]Under a *mudarabah* contract, one party provides all the capital needed while the entrepreneurs give their effort and time to the project. The profits are shared in a fixed ratio and losses are borne by the financial institution (Dhumale & Sapcanin, 1999).

musharakah,[16] *muzara'ah,*[17] and *muzaqat*[18] are more concerned with cooperation between funders and entrepreneurs (Akhter *et al.*, 2009; Dhumale & Sapcanin, 1999). According to Chowdhry (2006), Islamic finance provides a good mechanism to empower the poor and can convert potential capital into profit under the PLS scheme. The PLS mechanism offers reward- and risk-sharing for both parties, the financial institutions and the clients (Abdul-Rahman *et al.*, 2014).

Figure 7.1 shows two main contracts under Islamic finance: PLS and non-PLS contracts. PLS contracts are riskier than non-PLS

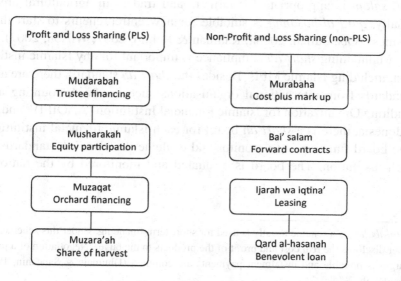

Figure 7.1: Types of Islamic Finance Contracts

Sources: Iqbal & Mirakhor (1987); Kazarian (1993) as cited in (Dhumale & Sapcanin, 1999); (Obaidullah & Khan, 2009); Hassan (2010).

---

[16]Under a *musharakah* contract, two or more parties contribute their equity to a project and profits are shared based on an agreement whereas losses are shared based on equity participation. It is similar to a joint venture agreement (Chong & Liu, 2009; Dhumale & Sapcanin, 1999).

[17]*Muzara'ah* is a *mudarabah* contract in the agricultural sector; one party provides the land or funds and the other party contributes his/her effort. Both parties share the harvest based on the agreement (Dhumale & Sapcanin, 1999).

[18]*Muzaqat* is a *musharakah* contract in the orchard sector where the harvest is shared based on equity participation (Dhumale & Sapcanin, 1999).

contracts because of the possibility of asymmetric information that may occur in these contracts (e.g., *musharakah* and *mudarabah*). However, there are opportunities to implement the PLS mechanism in rural areas because of the honesty of rural communities (Dhumale & Sapcanin, 1999; Shahinpoor, 2009).

Non-PLS contracts include *murabahah,*[19] *bai'salam,*[20] *ijarah wa iqtina'*[21] and *qard al-hasanah.*[22] *Murabahah*, for instance, can be used to purchase and resell commodities in rural areas (Wilson, 2007). *Ijarah wa iqtina* can be applied to the lease of equipment or fields for a rural client. *Bai' salam* is appropriate for farmers and traders in agricultural areas. Finally, *qard al-hasanah* is suitable for new entrepreneurs to start their business (Obaidullah, 2008a; Rahman & Rahim, 2007; Wilson, 2007).

Maintaining *shari'ah* compliance is important for any Islamic institution, including Islamic MFIs. Besides the *shari'ah* standard, there are also standards from international organisations such as the Accounting and Auditing Organization for Islamic Financial Institution (AAOIFI)[23] and, in Indonesia, there is a *shari'ah* board for each Islamic financial institution. The board function is to monitor and evaluate the *shari'ah* standards of each institution. The board is evaluated and monitored by the national

---

[19] *Murabahah* is a scheme usually is used for short-term financing. Under this scheme, the seller discloses the real cost and profit of the products to the buyer. Negotiation of a profit margin is possible and instalment payments are common (Dhumale & Sapcanin, 1999; Obaidullah, 2008a).

[20] *Bai' salam* is a scheme similar to forward contracts. Under this scheme, the seller and the buyer agree to the future transaction where the buyer pays the full amount of the price and the seller promises to deliver the goods. Quality, quantity, price, and time of delivery are determined at the time of the contract (Dhumale & Sapcanin, 1999).

[21] *Ijarah wa iqtina'* is a leasing transaction consisting of *ijarah* (pure leasing) and *Ijarah wa iqtina'* (lease and purchase). In a lease and purchase scheme, a portion of each regular payment is applied to the purchase of the goods where the goods are transferred to the buyer at the end of the period (Dhumale & Sapcanin, 1999; Obaidullah, 2008a).

[22] *Qard al hasanah* is the only loan permissible under Islamic finance concepts. This scheme is a zero return loan. However, administration and transaction costs are permissible (so long as there is no relationship with the maturity and amount of the loan) (Dhumale & Sapcanin, 1999).

[23] Available at http://aaoifi.com/en/about-aaoifi/about-aaoifi.html.

shari'ah board of Indonesia.[24] Islamic MFIs products and services should also follow the rules/*fatwa* from the national *shari'ah* board of Indonesia or DSN-MUI (OJK, 2015b).

7.2.6 *Measuring the impact of Islamic financing mechanisms*

Based on the literature, there are two models of contract in Islamic finance, PLS and non-PLS contracts. However, there are few studies that discuss these two models of contract in Islamic MFIs (see Table 7.15).

According to Aggarwal & Yousef (2000), Dusuki & Abdullah (2006) and Asutay (2007), the common model of financing in Islamic financial institutions is the non-PLS model, especially debt-like instruments (e.g., *murabaha* and *ijarah wa iqtina'*). There is a debate among scholars about which is the better model, PLS or non-PLS. However, according to Dusuki & Abdullah (2006), the ideal model for Islamic financial institutions is a PLS contract. This is because PLS contracts represent the true spirit of the Islamic finance concept, which differs significantly from the conventional or interest based system (Dusuki & Abdullah, 2006).

In addition, Asutay (2007) argues that PLS contracts are the solution to achieve justice and equality and meet not only the *maqasid al-shari'ah* (objective of shari'ah),[25] but also the objectives of Islam. PLS contracts are also important in distinguishing Islamic financial institutions from conventional financial institutions; it is a unique feature of Islamic finance (Azmat *et al.*, 2015; Chong & Liu, 2009; Ibrahim & Mirakhor, 2014). PLS contracts can be implemented in most Islamic financial institutions including Islamic MFIs. In Islamic MFIs, the implementation of PLS contracts can be found in savings and financing products. An example of a PLS contract is *mudarabah* financing through which Islamic MFIs provide capital and the clients provide their effort for a certain project (Hassan, 2010).

However, Farooq (2007) challenges why Islamic financial institutions avoid PLS contracts and use non-PLS contracts overwhelmingly. Farooq (2007) study reveals that: (1) PLS contracts are vulnerable to the agency problem because the clients have disincentives to put in effort and

---

[24] Available at http://mui.or.id/mui/category/tentang-mui/lembaga/dewan-syariah-nasional.
[25] *Maqasid* of *shari'ah*: protection of faith (*Din*), life (*Nafs*), posterity (*Nasl*), property (*Mal*) and reason (*'Aql*) (Abdul-Rahman *et al.*, 2014).

Table 7.15: **PLS and Non-PLS Studies in Islamic Finance**

Sources	Focus of Studies	Methods	Results
Dusuki & Abdullah (2006)	The ideal structure in Islamic banks, especially the PLS mechanism	• Explanatory research • Survey on Islamic banks' stakeholders' perceptions and attitude in Malaysia (Kelantan, Johor, Penang, Kuala Lumpur)	• Islamic banks (IB) should balance profit-orientation and social-welfare commitment • Products and services should be *shari'ah* compliant and IB should emphasise the PLS mechanism more
Aggarwal & Yousef (2000)	Financial instruments used by Islamic banks (between PLS and non-PLS)	• Descriptive statistics (data from International association of Islamic banks and annual report) • Investment and capital structure model based on incomplete contracts (this model is modified from Hart & Moore (1997) Bolton & Scharfstein (1990))	• Most IBs rely heavily on non-profit and loss sharing (non-PLS) mechanisms • Agency problem in PLS makes decreases the optimality of this mechanism followed by domination of debt-based contracts (non-PLS); • Moral hazard problem leads to non-PLS financing (debt-like instrument) in IB
Azmat et al. (2015)	Attempt to explain why debt-based contract (non-PLS) is dominant in IB. Focus on asymmetric information, moral hazard, and adverse selection issues	• Asymmetric information model for PLS financing • Moral hazard model in PLS financing; • Long-term relationships and legal punishment model • Risk averse bank depositors model	• Borrower can get higher profit through non-PLS mechanism, this is why non-PLS dominant in IB • Presence of asymmetric information alone cannot explain the absence of PLS mechanism in IB • Changes in depositors' attitudes might influence the increase of PLS financing schemes in IB

Chong & Liu (2009)	Comparative study between Islamic and conventional banks especially on deposit rates issues	• Engle-Granger error correction method used to study the long-term and short-term dynamics between Islamic investment rates and conventional deposit rates	• Rapid growth in IB is more likely because of Islamic resurgence worldwide rather than the uniqueness of PLS mechanism in IB • Changes in conventional deposit rates causes Islamic investment (PLS mechanism) rates to change, but not vice versa • Islamic deposits, in practice, are not very different from conventional deposits
Farooq (2007)	Arguments and rationale why Islamic financial institutions avoid PLS mechanism	• Theoretical study (describing arguments from Islamic scholars about PLS mechanism)	• Avoiding PLS financing mechanism is normal and rational behaviour of individuals or business organisations
Sumarti et al. (2014)	Mathematical model to find an optimal portion of profit share from PLS mechanism in microcredit based on real financing data	• Mathematical model for PLS scheme • Moral hazard model in PLS financing	• Average rate of return for the PLS investments is around 17.7%–23.1% • Borrowers and lenders benefit from PLS schemes

incentives to report less profit; (2) Islamic financial institutions offer a relatively less risky mode of financing, such as the non-PLS model, because they have to compete with conventional financial institutions that are already established and competitive and (3) PLS contracts are not appropriate to fund short-term projects because of their high degree of risk, hence Islamic financial institutions rely heavily on non-PLS contracts.

Based on a study by Paul & Presley (1999) as cited in Chong & Liu (2009), Islamic financial institutions do not adopt PLS contracts because of moral hazard problem associated with the *ex-post* information asymmetry, which is more likely to occur in this mode of contract. The entrepreneur (the borrower) has an incentive to manipulate the profit report (reduce their profit). Second, the moral hazard problem can also occur in a *mudarabah* (profit sharing) contract because the entrepreneur can undertake high risk projects whereby they gain profit and bear no losses from the business (Chong & Liu, 2009). This problem can occur in most types of Islamic financial institutions including Islamic MFIs.

7.2.7 *Models for government intervention*

Studies on government intervention in Islamic MFIs by Seibel (2008), Seibel & Dwi Agung (2006), Karim *et al.* (2008), Dusuki (2008), Obaidullah (2008a) and Obaidullah & Khan (2009) show that a supporting financial system (soft loans from donors), clear regulation, funding and monitoring are important for the sustainability of Islamic MFIs. However, some programmes are ineffective.

The first factor to consider is the source of funding, government or donors. Funding from the government provides some benefits but also weaknesses. According to Obaidullah (2008a), the government's main responsibility is to establish a sound, strong and competitive financial environment. The author found that funding from government is usually regarded as a reward (or gift) that leads to moral hazard behaviour and is less likely to be returned. This culture is common in countries with a history of forgiveness programmes for agricultural or other lending. For instance, there are high default rates in subsidised rural credit programmes in some countries such as India (50%), Bangladesh (71%) and Malaysia and Nepal (40%). The implementation of low interest rates in government funding programmes also means that financial institutions cannot cover their costs and will require continuous government subsidies in order to survive (Helms & Reille, 2004; Obaidullah & Khan, 2009).

Second, the government should develop an appropriate system to monitor and evaluate the sustainability of Islamic MFIs. Based on Seibel & Dwi Agung (2006) study, only formal Islamic MFIs are recorded by the government; the government should record all types of Islamic MFIs and supervise and monitor their performance (Seibel & Dwi Agung, 2006). This is because formal Islamic MFIs, such as KJKS and UJKS, are registered under the government via MoCMSMEs and regularly report their activities to the MoCMSMEs. However, from 2013, all MFIs are required to obtain business license as a formal MFI from the OJK and they obliged to submit financial report to OJK every 4 months (OJK, 2015b).

Based on a pilot study conducted by the Bank Indonesia (BI), Islamic MFIs' clients in Indonesia received three types of assistance either from Islamic MFIs or from the government. The study divided clients into three groups based on the type of assistance they received: (1) clients with financial assistance only; (2) clients with financial and technical assistance and (3) clients with financial, technical assistance and spiritual treatment. The study reveals the third group outperformed the two other groups. Based on finding of this pilot study, BI will develop a model for microfinance that includes spiritual treatment (Obaidullah & Khan, 2009).

7.3 Conclusion

Indonesia is a country with the most differentiated microfinance institutions in the world. There are three categories of MFIs in Indonesia: formal, semi-formal and informal. There are over 55 million micro, SMEs in Indonesia. About 98% are microenterprises and most need support from financial institutions, especially MFIs. The MFIs in Indonesia adopt Islamic principles in their operation. Indonesia is the largest Muslim country in the world. The Muslims in Indonesia face some constraints from conventional finance, especially on *riba* (interest) and prefer to use financial products and services that parallel with their religious belief. The main challenges for MFIs in Indonesia are the lack of prudential regulation, ineffective supervision and unsystematic recording, which has to be solved by the Indonesian government.

7.4 Policy Implications

The various types of MFIs imply several challenges for policy makers in Indonesia. The first challenge is to obtain a complete database of MFIs in Indonesia. At present there is no complete database of MFIs. A complete database is important in order to manage information and to make decision or policy efficiently and effectively. Most MFIs in Indonesia are unregistered and are considered as informal financial institutions. The authorities, especially the OJK, have taken some steps to obtain a complete database of MFIs in Indonesia. The first step is to mandate all MFIs (both conventional and Islamic) to register with the relevant authorities. Second, all MFIs in Indonesia have to choose their legal status, either a cooperative or a limited liability company. If MFIs choose a cooperative, they must register with MoCMSMEs and follow the rules and regulations of this ministry. However, if MFIs choose a limited liability company, they have to register and gain a business license from OJK.

The second challenge involves monitoring and supervising of the MFIs by OJK and MoCMSMEs in order to avoid fraud and maintain stability and safety of MFIs. This issue is common in MFIs especially with cooperative status; monitoring and supervision is low and the MFIs are required to submit financial reports only once a year. Monitoring of MFIs also means that the authorities must guarantee that the MFIs follow and comply with regulations, which is an ongoing challenge for these institutions because of the large numbers of MFIs in the country.

The Indonesian government should also maximise the opportunity to develop Islamic financial institutions in Indonesia. As a country with the largest Muslim population in the world, Indonesia can become a centre and barometer of Islamic finance. However, the current market share of IBs is only 5% and even there is no detailed market share data available for Islamic MFIs. Related organisations, such as the Council of Indonesian Ulama (DSN-MUI), must continue their roles to ensure Islamic financial institutions' products in Indonesia comply with Islamic law, while organisations like Indonesia Islamic Bank Association (Asbisindo) and *Shari'ah*

Economic Society (MES), which play their role in terms of socialisation and education of the public in order to improve people's knowledge of Islamic finance.

Finally, government assistance for MFIs is important, especially in difficult situations such as a financial crisis. The government must ensure that MFIs can survive through a crisis; the most important assistance is to secure the depositors' funds. Another form of assistance, such as upgrading MFIs' staff skills, upgrading MFI's office software and other assistance from the authorities should continue in order to improve the MFIs' performances.

References

Abdouli, A. (1991). Access to finance and collaterals: Islamic versus western banking. *Islamic Economics,* 3(1), 59–80.

Abdul-Rahman, A., Latif, R. A., Muda, R. & Abdullah, M. A. (2014). Failure and potential of profit-loss sharing contracts: A perspective of New Institutional, Economic (NIE) Theory. *Pacific-Basin Finance Journal,* 28, 136–151.

Adnan, M. A. & Ajija, S. R. (2015). The effectiveness of Baitul Maal wat Tamwil in reducing poverty. *Humanomics,* 31(2), 160–182.

Aggarwal, R. K. & Yousef, T. (2000). Islamic banks and investment financing. *Journal of Money, Credit and Banking,* 32(1), 93–120.

Ahmed, H. (2007). *Waqf-based Microfinance: Realizing the Social Role of Islamic Finance.* Washington, DC: World Bank.

Aichbichler, E. (2009). *Islamic Banking in Germany and Switzerland.* Uniwien.

Ainley, M., Mashayekhi, A., Hicks, R., Rahman, A. & Ravalia, A. (2007). *Islamic Finance in the UK: Regulation and Challenges.* London: Financial Services Authority.

Akhter, W., Akhtar, N. & Jaffri, S. K. A. (2009). Islamic Micro-Finance And Poverty Alleviation: A Case of Pakistan. *2nd CBRC.* Lahore, Pakistan.

Asutay, M. (2007). Conceptualisation of the second best solution in overcoming the social failure of Islamic banking and finance: Examining the overpowering of homoislamicus by homoeconomicus. *International Journal of Economics, Management and Accounting,* 15(2).

Azmat, S., Skully, M. & Brown, K. (2014). The Shariah compliance challenge in Islamic bond markets. *Pacific-Basin Finance Journal,* 28, 47–57.

Azmat, S., Skully, M. & Brown, K. (2015). Can Islamic banking ever become Islamic? *Pacific-Basin Finance Journal,* 34, 253–272.

Badan Amil Zakat Nasional (2016). Visi dan Misi. Retrieved from http://pusat. baznas.go.id/visi-misi/ Accessed on January 15, 2016.

Badan Wakaf Indonesia (2012). Sekilas Badan Wakaf Indonesia. Retrieved from http://bwi.or.id/index.php/in/tentang-bwi/sekilas-bwi.html. Accessed on January 15, 2016.

Bank BRI Agro (2014). Annual Report. Jakarta, Indonesia: Bank BRI Agro.

Bank Rakyat Indonesia (BRI). (2013). Ini Dia 4 Keunggulan BRI. Retrieved from https://edwinarieframdhani.wordpress.com/2014/04/18/ini-ida-4-keunggulan-bri/. Accessed on February 4, 2016.

Bank Rakyat Indonesia (BRI) (2014). Annual Report. Jakarta, Indonesia: Bank Rakyat Indonesia.

Bank Rakyat Indonesia (BRI) (2015a). BRI, Menuju Bank Terbesar di Indonesia. Retrieved from http://www.bumn.go.id/bri/berita/98/BRI.Menuju.Bank. Terbesar.di.Indonesia. Accessed on July 23, 2015.

Bank Rakyat Indonesia (BRI) (2015b). Sejarah BRI. Retrieved from http://www. bri.co.id/subpage?id=14. Accessed on August 12, 2015.

Bank Rakyat Indonesia (BRI) (2016). Corporate Profile. Retrieved from http:// ir-bri.com. Accessed on January 4, 2016.

Bank Rakyat Indonesia Syariah (2014). Annual Report. Jakarta, Indonesia: Bank Rakyat Indonesia Syariah.

Berhane, G. & Gardebroek, C. (2011). Does microfinance reduce rural poverty? Evidence based on household panel data from northern Ethiopia. *American Journal of Agricultural Economics*, 93(1), 43–55.

Bloomberg (2015). Company Overview of BRI Remittance Company Limited, *Bloomberg Business*. Retrieved from http://www.bloomberg.com/research/ stocks/private/snapshot.asp?privcapid=227936401.

Bloomberg Business (2015). Spot Exchange Rate. Retrieved from http://www. bloomberg.com/quote/USDIDR:CUR. Accessed on January 28, 2016.

Bolton, P. & Scharfstein, D. S. (1990). A theory of predation based on agency problems in financial contracting. *The American Economic Review*, 93–106.

Boomgard, J. J. & Angell, K. J. (1990). *Developing Financial Services for Microenterprises: An Evaluation of USAID Assistance to the BRI Unit Desa System in Indonesia*. Bethesda: Development Alternatives Inc.

BRI Remittance (2013). BRI Remittance Services. Retrieved from BRI Remittance http://briremittance.com/en/services/. Accessed on October 22.

Central Bank of Indonesia (BI) (2015). Indonesia Banking Statistics. Jakarta, Central Bank of Indonesia. Retrieved from http://www.bi.go.id/id/statistik/ seki/terkini/moneter/Contents/Default.aspx.

Chapra, M. U. (2006). The nature of riba in Islam. *The Journal of Islamic Economics and Finance, 2,* 7–25.

Chong, B. S. & Liu, M.-H. (2009). Islamic banking: Interest-free or interest-based? *Pacific-Basin Finance Journal,* 17(1), 125–144.

Chowdhry, S. (2006). *Creating an Islamic Microfinance Model — The Missing Dimension.* Retrieved from http://www.sa-dhan.net.

Choudhury, A. M. & Dusuki, W. A. (2008). Banking for the poor: The role of Islamic banking in microfinance initiatives. *Humanomics,* 24(1), 49–66.

Conroy, J. D. (2003). *The Challenges of Microfinancing in Southeast Asia.* Melbourne: Foundation for Development Cooperation.

Dhumale, R. & Sapcanin, A. (1999). An application of Islamic banking principles to microfinance. Technical Note, A study by the Regional Bureau for Arab States, UNDP, in cooperation with the Middle East and North Africa Region, World Bank.

Dusuki, A. W. (2008). Banking for the poor: The role of Islamic banking in microfinance initiatives. *Humanomics,* 24(1), 49–66.

Dusuki, W. & Abdullah, I. (2006). The ideal of Islamic banking: Chasing a Mirage Symposium conducted at the meeting of the INCEIF Islamic Banking and Finance Educational Colloquium, Kuala Lumpur, 3rd–5th April.

Dwiantika, N. (November 6, 2014). Bank Indonesia ingin Pangsa Pasar Perbankan Syariah Tembus 30%. *Tribunnews.com.* Retrieved from http://www.tribunnews.com/bisnis/2014/11/06/bank-indonesia-ingin-pangsa-pasar-perbankan-syariah-tembus-30.

El-Komi, M. & Croson, R. (2013). Experiments in Islamic microfinance. *Journal of Economic Behavior & Organization, 95(0),* 252–269.

Fahlevi, F. (April 23, 2015). BRI Jadi Contoh BUMN Go Public yang Sukses. *Tribunnews.* Retrieved from http://www.tribunnews.com/bisnis/2015/04/23/brijadi-contoh-bumn-go-public-yang-sukses.

Farooq, M. O. (2007). Partnership, equity-financing and Islamic finance: Whither profit-loss sharing? *Review of Islamic Economics, 11,* 67–88.

Fauzia, A. (2013). *Faith and the State: A History of Islamic Philantrophy in Indonesia.* Leiden, The Netherlands: Koninklijke Brill NV.

Gallardo, J. (2001). *A Framework for Regulating Microfinance Institutions: The Experience in Ghana and the Philippines.* Washington, DC: The World Bank.

Gera, I. (2013). OJK Resmi Ambil Alih Tugas Pengawasan Perbankan dari BI. Retrieved from Voice of America http://www.voaindonesia.com/a/ojk-resmi-ambil-alih-tugas-pengawasan-perbankan-dari-bi/1820703.html. Accessed on January 16.

Global Islamic Finance Report (2014). Islamic Finance Country Index. Retrieved from http://www.gifr.net/publications/gifr2014/ifci.pdf. Accessed on January 16.

Hart, O. & Moore, J. (1997). *Default and Renegotiation: A Dynamic Model of Debt.* Cambridge: National Bureau of Economic Research.

Hassan, M. K. (2010). An integrated poverty alleviation model combining zakat, awqaf and microfinance. *Symposium conducted at the meeting of the Seventh International Conference — The Tawhidi Epistemology.* Zakat and Waqf Economy, Bangi, Malaysia.

Helms, B. & Reille, X. (2004). *Interest Rate Ceilings and Microfinance: The Story so Far.* Washington, DC: Consultative Group to Assist the Poorest (CGAP).

Huda, A. N. (2012). The development of Islamic financing scheme for SMEs in a Developing Country: The Indonesian case. *Procedia-Social and Behavioral Sciences,* 52, 179–186.

Ibrahim, M. H. (2015). Issues in Islamic banking and finance: Islamic banks, Shari'ah-compliant investment and sukuk. *Pacific-Basin Finance Journal,* 34, 185–191.

Ibrahim, M. H. & Mirakhor, A. (2014). Islamic finance: An overview. *Pacific-Basin Finance Journal,* 28, 2–6.

Ikatan Ahli Ekonomi Islam Indonesia (2013). Profile. Retrieved from http://www.iaei-pusat.org/id/page/profil. Accessed on January 15, 2016.

Imady, O. & Seibel, H. D. (2006). Principles and Products of Islamic Finance. University of Cologne Development Research Center, 2, 2006–2001.

Indonesia Financial Services Authority (OJK) (2014a). Indonesia Banking Statistics. Accessed on July 23, 2015.

Indonesia Financial Services Authority (OJK) (2014b). Other Financial Services Institutions. Jakarta, Indonesia.

Indonesia Financial Services Authority (2014c). *Peraturan Otoritas Jasa Keuangan tentang BPR (Regulation for BPR).* Jakarta, Indonesia: Indonesia Financial Services Authority. Retrieved from http://www.certif.or.id/files/POJK%2020%20BPR%202015.pdf.

Indonesia Financial Services Authority (OJK) (2015a). The History of Islamic Bank. Retrieved from http://www.ojk.go.id/id/kanal/syariah/tentang-syariah/Pages/Perbankan-Syariah.aspx. Accessed on January 14, 2016.

Indonesia Financial Services Authority (OJK) (2015b). Microfinance Institutions. Retrieved from http://www.ojk.go.id/en/kanal/iknb/Pages/Microfinance-institutions.aspx. Accessed on June 19, 2015.

Iqbal, Z. & Mirakhor, A. (1987). *Islamic Banking* Vol. 49. Washington, DC: International Monetary Fund.

Karim, N., Tarazi, M. & Reille, X. (2008). *Islamic Microfinance: An Emerging Market Niche.* Washington DC USA: CGAP.

Kazarian, E. G. (1993). *Islamic versus Traditional Banking*: *Financial Innovations in Egypt*. Boulder, CO: Westview Press.

Kondo, T., Orbeta, A., Dingcong, C. & Infantado, C. (2008). Impact of microfinance on rural households in the Philippines. *IDS Bulletin*, 39(1), 51–70.

Kotir, J. H. & Obeng-Odoom, F. (2009). Microfinance and rural household development a Ghanaian perspective. *Journal of Developing Societies*, 25(1), 85–105.

Kusuma, D. R. (2015). BRI Perluas Kerjasama Bisnis Perbankan di Malaysia. *Detik*. Retrieved from http://finance.detik.com/read/2015/06/02/154354/2931 499/5/bri-perluas-kerjasama-bisnis-perbankan-di-malaysia.

Lapenu, C. & Pierret, D. (2006). *Handbook for the Analysis of the Governance of Microfinance Institutions*. Washington D.C.: The World Bank.

Lawrence, J. (2014). Islamic Finance in Indonesia: Past, Present, and Future. Retrieved from http://www.klgates.com/islamic_finance_in_indonesia/. Accessed on November 25, 2015.

Li, X., Gan, C. & Hu, B. (2011). The welfare impact of microcredit on rural households in China. *The Journal of Socio-Economics*, 40(4), 404–411.

Littlefield, E., Morduch, J. & Hashemi, S. (2003). Is microfinance an effective strategy to reach the Millennium Development Goals? *Focus Note*, 24, 1–11.

Marhiansyah (2012). Pinbuk Aceh: LKMS BI-nya Baitul Qiradh. Harian Aceh. Co. Retrieved from http://www.slideshare.net/dasepbux/profil-pinbuk-lengka-pok.

Masyarakat Ekonomi Syariah (2008). Sejarah. Retrieved from http://www.ekono-misyariah.org/tentang-mes/sejarah/

Masyita, D. & Ahmed, H. (2011). Why is Growth of Islamic Microfinance Lower than Conventional? A Comparative Study of the Preferences and Perceptions of the Clients of Islamic and Conventional Microfinance Institutions' in *Indonesia Symposium conducted at the meeting of the Eighth International Conference on Islamic Economics and Finance*, Doha, Qatar

Ministry of Cooperatives and Micro and SMEs of Republic of Indonesia (2007). Standard Operating Procedure KJKS and UJKS: Ministry of Cooperatives and Micro and Small, and Medium Enterprise of Republic of Indonesia.

Ministry of Cooperatives and Micro and SMEs' of Republic of Indonesia (2005). Cooperation Data. Accessed on July 23, 2015.

Ministry of Religious Affairs of the Republic of Indonesia (2013). The Annual Report of Religious Life in Indonesia. Jakarta, Indonesia, Ministry of Religious Affairs of the Republic of Indonesia.

Naqvi, S. N. H. & Qadir, A. (1997). The dimensions of an Islamic economic model. *Islamic Economic Studies*, 4(2), 1–24.

Nasdaq OMX (2012). Global Islamic Microfinance Landscape. Retrieved from Nasdaq OMX Sharia indexes http://www.gifr.net/gifr2012/ch_25.pdf.

Neraca (2015, June 05). OJK Minta BPR Salurkan Pembiayaan ke Pedesaan Harian Ekonomi Neraca. Retrieved from http://www.neraca.co.id/article/54670/ojk-minta-bpr-salurkan-pembiayaan-ke-pedesaan.

Obaidullah, M. (2008a). Introduction to Islamic microfinance. *Mohammed Obaidullah, Introduction to Islamic Microfinance.* New Delhi: IBF Net Limited.

Obaidullah, M. (2008b). Role of Microfinance in Poverty Alleviation: Lessons from Experiences in Selected IDB Member Countries. *Mohammed Obaidullah, Role of Microfinance in Poverty Alleviation: Lessons from Experiences in Selected IDB Member Countries.* Jeddah: Islamic Development Bank.

Obaidullah, M. & Khan, T. (2008). *Islamic Microfinance Development: Challenges and Initiatives.* Jeddah: Islamic Development Bank.

Obaidullah, M. & Khan, T. (2009). *Islamic Microfinance Development: Challenges and Initiatives.* Jeddah: Islamic Development Bank.

Paul, S. & Presley, J. R. (1999). *Islamic Finance: Theory and Practice.* Macmillan.

Praditya, I. I. (2013a). Jumlah BPR Makin Menciut. Jakarta, Retrieved from Liputan6 http://bisnis.liputan6.com/read/674995/jumlah-bpr-makin-menciut. Accessed on January 16.

Praditya, I. I. (2013b). *Luncurkan Gres, BI Jor-joran Pacu Ekonomi Syariah RI.* Jakarta, Retrieved from http://bisnis.liputan6.com/read/613210/luncurkan-gres-bi-ijor-jorani-pacu-ekonomi-syariah-ri. Accessed on January 11, 2016.

Pusat Komunikasi Ekonomi Syariah (2013). Retrieved from http://keuanganlsm.com/pusat-komunikasi-ekonomi-syariah-pkes-interaktif/. Accessed on January 15, 2016.

Rahman, A. R. A. (2010a). Islamic microfinance: An ethical alternative to poverty alleviation. *Humanomics*, 26(4), 284–295.

Rahman, M. M. (2010b). Islamic micro-finance programme and its impact on rural poverty alleviation. *International Journal of Banking and Finance*, 7(1), 7.

Rahman, A. R. A. & Rahim, A. (2007). Islamic microfinance: A missing component in Islamic banking. *Kyoto Bulletin of Islamic Area Studies*, 1(2), 38–53.

Samer, S., Majid, I., Rizal, S., Muhamad, M. & Rashid, N. (2015). The impact of microfinance on poverty reduction: Empirical evidence from Malaysian perspective. *Procedia-Social and Behavioral Sciences*, 195, 721–728.

Seibel, H. D. (2005). The Microbanking Division of Bank Rakyat Indonesia: A flagship of Rural Microfinance in Asia, Working paper/University of Cologne, Development Research Center.

Seibel, H. D. (2008). Islamic microfinance in Indonesia: The challenge of institutional diversity, regulation, and supervision. *SOJOURN*, 23(1), 86–103.

Seibel, H. D. & Dwi Agung, W. (2006). Islamic Microfinance in Indonesia, Working paper/University of Cologne, Development Research Center.

Seibel, H. D. & Ozaki, M. (2009). *Restructuring of State-owned Financial Institutions: Lessons from Bank Rakyat Indonesia.* Manila, Philippines: ADB.

Shahinpoor, N. (2009). The link between Islamic banking and microfinancing. *International Journal of Social Economics,* 36(10), 996–1007.

Shodiq, M. (2014, September 11). Next generation of microfinance: Leveraging Indonesian experience. *The Jakarta Post.* Retrieved from http://www.thejakartapost.com/news/2014/09/11/next-generation-microfinance-leveraging-indonesian-experience.html.

Statistics Indonesia (2014). Monthly Report of Socio-Economic Data December 2014, Statistics Indonesia. Retrieved from http://www.academia.edu/11386648/Berita_Resmi_BPS_2015.

Sufian, F. (2007). The efficiency of Islamic banking industry: A non-parametric analysis with non-discretionary input variable. *Islamic Economic Studies,* 14(1–2), 53–78.

Sugianto (2012). Denyut Koperasi Syariah. Retrieved from http://www2.depkop.go.id/index.php?option=com_content&view=article&id=948:denyut-koperasi-syariah&catid=54:bind-berita-kementerian&Itemid=98.

Sumarti, N., Fitriyani, V. & Damayanti, M. (2014). A mathematical model of the Profit–loss sharing (PLS) scheme. *Procedia-Social and Behavioral Sciences,* 115, 131–137.

Sutaryono, P. (2015). Prospek Perbankan 2015. Koran Sindo. Retrieved from http://nasional.sindonews.com/read/945516/18/prospek-perbankan-2015-1420264059.

Tambunan, T. (2015). Financial Inclusion, Financial Education, and Financial Regulation: A Story from Indonesia, ADBI Working Paper Series.

The British Museum (2012). Hajj: Journey to the Heart of Islam. Retrieved from http://www.britishmuseum.org/about_us/news_and_press/press_releases/2011/hajj_exhibition.aspx.

The Council of Indonesian Ulama (2013). Fatwa DSN-MUI. Retrieved from http://mui.or.id/. Accessed on January 15, 2016.

The World Bank (2012). KUPEDES: Indonesia's Model Small Credit Program. Retrieved from http://lnweb90.worldbank.org/oed/oeddoclib.nsf/DocUNIDViewForJavaSearch/7DBBAC3B636F7FDC852567F5005D8AD3.

Widiarto, I. & Emrouznejad, A. (2015). Social and financial efficiency of Islamic microfinance institutions: A data envelopment analysis application. *Socio-Economic Planning Sciences,* 50, 1–17.

Wilson, R. (2007). Making development assistance sustainable through Islamic microfinance. *International Journal of Economics, Management and Accounting,* 15(2), 197–217.

Zain, Y., Fattah, S., Djauhariah S. L., Siawadharma, B., Mustari, B. & Tadjibu, J. (2006). Skema Pembiayaan Perbankan Daerah Menurut Karakteristik UMKM pada Sektor Ekonomi Unggulan di Sulawesi Selatan, Bank Indonesia. Retrieved from http://www.bi.go.id/id/publikasi/perbankan-dan-stabilitas/ arsitektur/Documents/7709a1620def439da1081d6eece8d3b4SkemaPembiaya anPerbankanDaerahMenurutKarakteristik.pdf.

Chapter 8

Microfinance Market in Bangladesh

Mohammad Monirul Hasan[*,‡]
and Mohammad Abdul Malek[†,§]

[*]PhD Researcher, Center for Development Research (ZEF),
University of Bonn, Bonn and is also affiliated with Institute
for Inclusive Finance and Development (InM) at Dhaka

[†]Senior Research Fellow at BRAC Research and Evaluation Division
(RED), Dhaka and is also affiliated with Faculty of Economics,
University of Tokyo and Centre
for Development Research (ZEF), University of Bonn

[‡]mhasan@uni-bonn.de
[§]malekr25@gmail.com

Abstract

This chapter gives an overview on the microfinance market in Bangladesh, often known as the hub of microfinance institutions (MFIs) in the globe. The development of microfinance is based on the principle of financial inclusion of the poor on one hand and the sustainability of the institute on the other hand. The outreach-sustainability trade off could successfully be achieved by proper targeting and better designing of the microfinance products. The positive impact of microcredit has been widely documented and it produced a momentum in the rural economy which could have been lost if there are no microcredit operations.

This chapter explores the evolution and present status of the microfinance market in Bangladesh, supply and demand factors, opportunities for further research and innovations and policy recommendations.

Keywords: Microfinance, poverty, sustainability, risk, Bangladesh.

8.1 Introduction

Bangladesh is called the hub of microfinance institutions (MFIs) and many countries across the globe have replicated the model to extend financial inclusion in their respective countries (Hossain & Bayes, 2015). The microfinance market in Bangladesh has gained tremendous exposure in last three decades and it has proved that poor people are credit worthy and they repay loans regularly. The market which was basically credit service only to the poor has added other financial services such as savings, insurance, financial transfers, etc. and established itself a dominant institution which works as an alternative to the costly informal credits and fill up gaps in the formal credit sector. The development of microfinance was based on the principle of financial inclusion of the poor on one hand and the sustainability of the institute on the other hand. These dual objectives of reaching credit operations to the hard-to-reach households and making the MFI financially viable put the market in a challenging position such as lower operational self-sufficiency (OSS) (Wahid, Hasan & Rabbani, 2015). However, the outreach-sustainability trade off could successfully be achieved by proper targeting and better designing of the microfinance products. Banking with the poor requires proper targeting and risk mitigating strategies. In the beginning of the microcredit programme in Bangladesh, many lending methodologies were tried and later on the group-based approach was mostly successful. The main reasons for the success of the group-based approach were the risk reduction from the adverse selection of the households and the moral hazard problem of the incumbent borrowers (Armendáriz de Aghion & Morduch, 2005). Apart from proper targeting by the MFIs, the peer effect from the group members and weekly group meeting of members prevented them from becoming loan defaulters. Additionally, the members also could follow the practice of others and could successfully repay the instalment of the loans. The economics of microfinance remains in the nexus of consumption smoothening and improving the individual and household opportunities in employment, income, assets, health and capacity development. Despite its positive impact, microfinance has been criticised recently almost all over the world mainly by the policy makers because of its higher interest rate than formal banking which contributes to higher indebtedness of borrowers and facing peer pressure of loan collection (Duvendack *et al.*, 2011). So it is worth elaborating to get an overview of the microfinance sector in Bangladesh.

8.2 Rural Credit Market: Emergence and Revolution of Non-government Organisation-microfinance Institutions (NGO-MFIs)

Rural credit market comprises formal, quasi-formal and informal credit market. Formal credit market is credit from the commercial banks both public and privately owned and informal credit market is credit from friends, families, local businessman or traders and traditional moneylenders. Quasi-formal credit market is operated by the MFIs, which works as formal credit in a different outfit than the formal credit.

8.2.1 *Informal rural credit market*

The operation of microfinance is not a new term in the rural credit market. It evolved in the form of informal credit to mitigate the needs of the rural inhabitants such as consumption smoothening, medical treatment, festival, education, serving small and medium enterprises, agricultural activities, etc. The informal source of credit comprises relatives, friends, neighbours, shopkeepers and traditional moneylenders (Hollis *et al.*, 1997; Spooner, 1846). Because of the absence of formal credit market or lack of access to formal credit, these money lenders charge very high interest rates which adversely impact the welfare of the borrowers. The popularity of informal credit still prevails because of the easy loan from relatives (form of social networking) and unmet demand for credit from formal credit market. The excess demand for credit and the rigidity of repayment of the formal credit fuelled the sustainability of the informal credit in the economy with high very interest rate ranges from 100% to 120% per annum (Berg, Emran & Shilpi, 2014).

The formal supply of finance in the rural economy is limited and credit is only available to the rich portion of rural inhabitants. In rural financial market, the non-institutional structure enables the transfer of fund and financial assets through localised transactions in credit and goods and services among the agent of the rural economy such as household, farms, traders, landlords, money lenders, etc. These financial transactions are mostly without paper and written regulation face numerous problem of repayment, fraudulence, commitments that sometimes drive them into acute poverty (Mudahar & Ahmed, 2010). There is always a demand for formal credit market in the rural economy but commercial banks do not expand their activities in rural areas because of screening and high default problem. The classical economic problem of adverse selection and moral hazard constrained formal lenders to operationalise formal rural finance in Bangladesh. The problem of screening and also the fear of loan default specially when there is no collateral drive such lenders out of rural credit operation and only concentrate in urban credit market (Armendáriz de Aghion & Morduch, 2005).

8.2.1.1 *Formal rural finance*

Formal financing in Bengal was started during the British colonisation and first Bengal bank was established in 1784 offering credit in many parts of Bangladesh (Shah, Rao & Shankar, 2007). However, this chapter will concentrate mostly on the last few decades especially after independence (1971) of Bangladesh to learn more about the recent credit history.

8.2.1.2 *Exclusion of poor from financial inclusion*

There were only two financial institutions — Bangladesh Krishi Bank (BKB) and the cooperatives that offered agricultural credit between 1971 and 1976. To increase the outreach of credit to the agricultural sector, the Bangladesh government introduced Nationalised Commercial Banks (NCB) in 1976 to cater seasonal crop loans but the operation was limited in many aspects. NCBs targeted the traders and the businesses who could offer collateral against the loan. Many NCBs projects in agricultural loans to the farmers failed due to institutional flaws. They excluded the poor intentionally under their umbrella (Faruqee & Badruddoza, 2011a). Private banks did not extend their loan policy targeting the poor people. There were 844 branches of BKB and 301 branches of Rajshahi Krishi Unnayan Bank (RAKUB) assisting farmers in the rural areas but credit was only given to farmers who offered land as mortgage (Alamgir, 2010). Apart from these two institutions, other organisations such as Bangladesh Samabaya Bank Limited (BSBL), cooperatives land mortgage banks, central sugarcane growers association and thana(sub-district)-cooperative societies, etc. provide rural finance. The financial performance of these banks was poor and mostly excluded the poor and hard-core poor (Ferrari, 2008). Despite the substantial increase in the agricultural credit in the last decades, public banks such as NCB, BKB and RAKUB together serve only 50% of the total agricultural credit at present. Before the introduction of Grameen Bank's (GB) operation all national and commercial banks operated at some scale in rural finance but mostly targeting the non-poor entrepreneurs who had collateral.

In the rural development initiative in Bangladesh, Akhter Hameed Khan, a development practitioner and social scientist, in 1959 launched a programme named "Comilla Model" where he involved grass root cooperative participation by the people to stimulate rural development. Mr. Khan found that for rapid development to take place, the region infrastructure especially roads, drainage and irrigation have to be developed which can be maintained by the people themselves. After the tenure of Mr. Khan, the model failed for many reasons. One of the reasons was the inability to continue the movement under the leadership of Mr. Khan (Alamgir, 2010). Ineffective internal and external control and also the lack of donor fund caused it to fall down drastically.

Although "Comilla Model" failed, it provided some lessons for the practitioners. Muhammad Yunus of GB and Fazle Hasan Abed of BRAC (Bangladesh Rehabilitation Assistance Committee) tested this model and they understood that the cooperative model would not work in rural Bangladesh. Following this, the GB targeted the poor directly with collateral free loan. The failure of credit operative in rural Bangladesh was mainly due to the large size of the group with heterogeneous economic groups where more affluent members populate the organisation (Dowla & Barua, 2006). By 1990s, GB and BRAC along with other MFIs dropped the Comilla model and developed a more centralised control and service delivery structure.

8.2.2 *Emergence of GB*

The breakthrough of GB involved redesigning the traditional system of credit delivery by the national and commercial organisations which only provided credit. However, GB broke away from the existing credit delivery system and developed a new organisation, which served the poor with financial services (Alamgir, 2010). The GB (Grameen means village in local language) is a result of an action research project of Professor Muhammad Yunus in 1976 when he was trying to adopt a model where poor people can get credit without collateral. The research successfully tested the credit delivery system which was first implemented in "Jobra village" and adjacent villages during 1976–1979. With the help of the central bank and other NCB, the pilot project was extended to "Tangail district" in 1979 and became successful. Later on the project was extended to other districts. In October 1983, the GB project was institutionalised as an Independent Bank by government legislation (Alamgir, 2010). Currently, GB is mostly owned by rural poor members. In 2006, GB and Professor Muhammad Yunus were awarded the Nobel Peace Prize for its contribution to economics and social development for the poor.

The GB approach is quite different from the traditional banking in Bangladesh. GB implemented some critical steps such as (Alamgir, 2010):

(1) GB targeted poor women who mostly bear the burden of poverty. They select their members from those who had less than 0.5 acre of land and excluded the rich for getting the financial service from GB. The rationale for targeting women was that women repay their loans regularly, invest borrowed fund on productive projects and spend most part of their income on improving the quality of life of family members. Women become empowered by this kind of economic activity and play a vital role in the society.

(2) Instead of providing loans to individual women, GB formed a group of 5 persons and a center of 6 to 10 groups where they based their loan activity.

(3) GB offered collateral free loans but distributed the liability among the group members. The peer effect among the group members stimulates members to repay more successfully which was the major success of GB.
(4) GB offered small loans manageable by the women and the repayment of weekly instalment with interest rates.
(5) Members do not need to visit the banks rather the banks take the financial services to the poor. Bank staffs visit the members' house on a weekly basis and conduct the necessary financial services to the poor similar to a commercial bank. They made the banking procedure simple and easy to understand for the illiterate poor women. Transactions are mainly done in public to keep the credibility and possibility of corruption. Strong monitoring system is developed among the bank staff members of the bank.

The Grameen approach in reaching the poor with simple methodology attracted many development practitioners (mostly credit operating NGOs) to replicate the model (Alamgir, 2010). The dual objectives of the programme such as reaching out to the poor as well as making the institution sustainable attracted many NGOs who were already operating many social programmes such as education, health, relief and rehabilitation, capacity development to introduce microcredit operations to make their existing programmes sustainable. Instead of copying the Grameen formula, they initiated some variations in the model in terms of interest rate, savings operations, loan ceiling, group size, repayment systems, etc. Rather than being restricted to 5 persons group, some offered larger group such as 20 to 50 persons with some flexibility in the repayment schedules. Savings operations in some cases were tied to the loans and there were some savings threshold before disbarment of the loans, but many NGOs relaxed or tightened those options for their own benefits. Loan policy became diverse with different types of loans, different size of loans, successive loans, instalment time and grace repayment periods of the loans (Faruqee & Badruddoza, 2011a). Within two decades the NGO-MFIs followed Grameen model with few changes in the modalities and occupied the nation with their many financial services including differentiated products.

8.2.2.1 *Emergence of Bangladesh Rural Advancement Committee*

BRAC (originally established in 1972 based in Bangladesh as Bangladesh Rehabilitation Assistance Committee, latter termed as Bangladesh Rural Advancement Committee), founded by Sir Fazle Hasasn Abed, has developed into one of the world's largest non-governmental development organisation (BRAC, 2016b). BRAC vision is a world free from all forms of exploitation and discrimination where everyone has the opportunity to realise their potential with the mission of empowering people and communities with regards to poverty, illiteracy, disease and social injustice. BRAC interventions aim to achieve large scale, positive changes through economic and social programmes that enable men and women to realise their potential. BRAC believes that the underlying causes of poverty are manifold and interlinked. BRAC developed support services in the areas of human rights and social empowerment, education and health, economic empowerment and enterprise development, livelihood training, environmental sustainability and disaster preparedness. It operates social enterprises that are strategically connected to development programmes, and form crucial value chain linkages, which increase the productivity of members' assets and labour, and reduce risks of their enterprises. To ensure that BRAC continue to be innovative and that its work remains relevant, BRAC has put in place training, research and monitoring systems across all activities and financial checks and balances in the form of audits (BRAC, 2016b). BRAC has extended its development activities in 12 different countries in Asia and Africa including one (Haiti) in South America.

8.2.2.2 *Emergence of Association for Social Advancement*

Association for Social Advancement (ASA) founded by Md. Shafiqual Haque Choudhury in 1978 initially served poor people to organise and empower themselves for their political and social rights (Alamgir, 2010). ASA undertook numerous programmes including awareness development for social actions, legal aid programme, training programme, communication support programme, training of rural journalists, etc. ASA conducted operations in health, nutrition, education, sanitation and financial service to the poor people. ASA offered a complete package of microfinance comprising of credit, savings and mini-life insurance for securing the income of the poor people. ASA has international operation in few countries in Asia and Africa.

8.2.2.3 *Growth of NGO-MFIs in Bangladesh — Microcredit Regulatory Authority in operation*

Several hundred of NGO-MFIs are currently operating in Bangladesh (see Figure 8.1 and Table 8.2 shows number of NGO-MFIs). However, the exact figures are unknown. Many small NGOs operate social activities; disburse loans and deposit saving from their clients. There are many NGO-MFIs without formal licences. MFIs collects savings and invest the money elsewhere and sometimes may disappear without notice and trace. They also charge high interest rates. This because of monitoring. The Bangladesh Government enacted the Microcredit Regulatory Authority (MRA) Act in 2006 and the MRA was established in the same year to monitor the microfinance sector in Bangladesh.

The numbers of NGO-MFIs were growing fast from 1996 to 2003 and then remained constant for a year and then declined to some extent (see Figure 8.1). According to the 2009 Bangladesh Microfinance Statistics, the number of NGO-MFIs in Bangladesh was 745. MRA adopts some cut off point to provide licences to NGO-MFIs with a minimum of 1,000

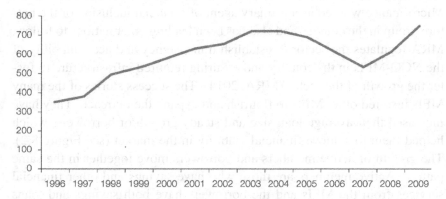

Figure 8.1:   Number of NGO-MFIs in Bangladesh from 1996 to 2009

Source: Bangladesh Microfinance Statistics, adapted from Faruqee & Badruddoza (2011a).

members and minimum of 4 million taka in loan outstanding. Many NGOs do not meet this criterion and may face extinction in the near future (Faruqee & Badruddoza, 2011a).

8.2.2.4   *Role of Palli Karma-Sahayak Foundation*

The Palli Karma-Sahayak Foundation (PKSF), an apex organisation for wholesale selling of microfinance established by the government, started its operation in Bangladesh in 1990 with the aim to alleviate poverty with employment creation by providing subsidised funds to MFIs (http://pksf-bd.org/portal/). PKSF disburses funds to MFIs whom they call Partner Organisations (PO). At present there are 257 POs in PKSF, which offer subsidised wholesale credit to conduct financial services among the poor in the rural areas as well as in the urban areas. Among many other specialised programme of PKSF, Rural Microcredit (RMC), Urban Microcredit (UMC), Microcredit for Entrepreneurship (ME), Microcredit for Ultra-poor (UPP), Agriculture Sector Microcredit (ASM), Seasonal Loans (SL), etc. are the prominent operations.

8.2.3   *Size of the market and operations*

The microfinance movement in the last three decades gained most vibrant and effective strength for financial inclusion of the excluded poor. Microfinance worked as a primary agent of financial inclusion of the bottom group in the country and also has been leading other nations to follow. MRA regulates the sector to establish transparency and accountability of the NGO-MFIs in the country and ensuring required infrastructure to foster the growth of the sector (MRA, 2014). The success stories of the many MFIs inspired other MFIs to flourish and expand the outreach. They have increased their average loan size and steady growth of borrowers, which helped them to achieve financial viability in the market (see Figure 8.2). The growth of active members and borrowers move together in the same pattern. Active members are those who have savings and other financial services from the MFIs and the borrowers have both savings and loans from the MFIs. After 2001, there is a sharp increase in both memberships and borrowings. Steep increase in the number of active members and

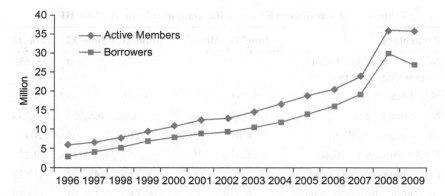

Figure 8.2: Number of NGO-MFIs in Bangladesh (1996 to 2009)

Source: Bangladesh Microfinance Statistics, adapted from Faruqee & Badruddoza (2011a).

borrowers has been observed in 2007 and 2008 (see Figure 8.2). From 1999 to 2009, microcredit member increases from 11.79 million to 35.71 million. In the same period, borrowers increased from 9.25 million to 27.05 million which implies a healthy growth rate (MRA, 2011).

The 20 MFIs constitute 90% of the microfinance sector (MRA, 2014). Table 8.1 shows the characteristics of the microfinance sector in Bangladesh. Until 2013, a total of 650 NGO-MFIs were registered with MRA. There are 14,674 branches of NGO-MFIs in operation as of 2013 and almost 110,734 employees work directly in the sector (see Table 8.1), which serves a total of 24.6 million clients throughout the country. The growth of loan disbursement is quite impressive until 2012 although it declined in 2013. Previous microcredit loan disbursement was limited mainly to small-scale non-farm business activities and thus there was no evidence of providing agriculture loan by NGO-MFIs which has increase in recent years. The members' savings play a vital role in mobilising rural credit, which contributes almost 37% of the loan outstanding in 2013 (MRA, 2014). The loan recovery rate is very impressive over the years which close to 98% in 2013 (see Table 8.1).

Figure 8.3 shows a declining trend in members and borrowers from 2010 to 2012. After 2012, there is a sharp increase in both members and borrowers. The number of borrowers in 2012–2013 boosted the loan out-standing by almost 50%, which is an excellent growth (see Figure 8.4).

Table 8.1: Microfinance Sector in Bangladesh (Licenced NGO-MFIs)

Particulars	June'09	June'10	June'11	June'12	June'13
No. of licenced NGO-MFIs (provided valid data)	419	516	576	590	650
No. of branches	16,851	17,252	18,066	17,977	14,674
No. of employees	107,175	109,597	111,828	108,654	110,734
No. of clients (million)	24.85	25.28	26.08	24.64	24.6
Total borrowers (million)	18.89	19.21	20.65	19.31	19.27
Loan disbursement (Tk. billion)	261.18	306.72	303.18	456.02	432.28
Agricultural loan disbursement (Tk. billion)	—	—	93.63	110.84	131.98
Amount of loan outstanding (Tk. billion)	143.13	145.02	173.79	211.32	257.01
Agricultural loan outstanding (Tk. billion)	—	—	59.36	66.71	89.05
Amount of savings (Tk. billion)	50.61	51.36	63.3	75.25	93.99
Loan recovery (Tk. billion)	—	280.78	271.83	314.11	375.07
Recovery rate (%)	97.93	97.35	95.52	97.74	97.69

Source: MRA–MIS database 2013, adapted from MRA (2014).

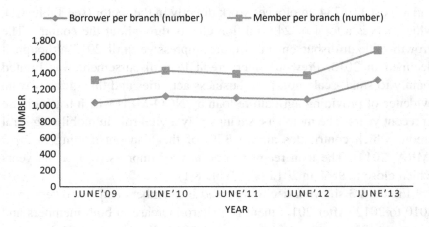

Figure 8.3: Growth of Members and Borrowers (per branch)

Source: MRA–MIS database 2013, adapted from MRA (2014).

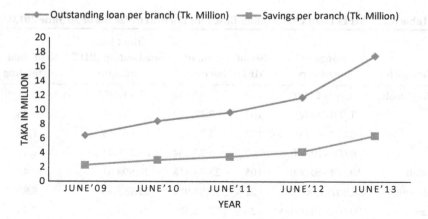

Figure 8.4:   Growth of Loan Outstanding and Savings (per branch)

Source: MRA–MIS database 2013, adapted from MRA (2014).

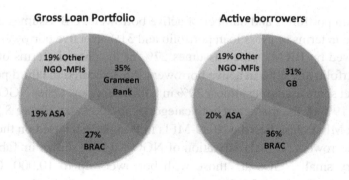

Figure 8.5:   Market Share of MFIs in Bangladesh in 2009

Note: Figures based on the data mixed market of 28 largest MFIs that covers more than 90% of the microfinance market.

Source: Adapted from Faruqee & Badruddoza (2011a).

The savings rate also increased which also fuelled the loans to grow further (MRA, 2014).

MFIs such as GB, BRAC and ASA occupy 81% of Bangladesh microfinance market share. These institutes started their operation pretty early and still dominate the microfinance market (Alamgir, 2010). They have both the most loan portfolios and borrowers. Figure 8.5 shows the percentage of market share the large MFIs hold in Bangladesh in terms of

Table 8.2:　MFIs Loan Outstanding Based on Borrower Size (as of 30 June 2013)

Categories	Range of borrowers	No. of MFIs	No. of borrowers	Total loan outstanding (BDT million)	% of total outstanding
Very small	Up to 1,000	171	1,35,130	1,831.37	0.71
	1,001–2,000	165	2,32,729	1,955.97	0.76
	2,001–6,000	123	4,36,916	3,962.65	1.54
	6,001–10,000	42	3,22,254	3,765.44	1.47
Small	10,001–50,000	105	23,74,418	26,809.01	10.43
Medium	50,001–1,00,000	22	15,88,952	22,735.43	8.85
Large	1,00,001–10,00,000	20	57,22,781	71,403.24	27.78
Very large	10,00,001–Above	2	84,52,815	124,546.89	48.46
Total		**650**	**19,265,995**	**257,010.00**	**100**

Source: MRA–MIS database 2013, adapted from MRA (2014).

gross loan portfolios and number of active borrowers. GB assumes 35% of the share in terms of gross loan portfolio and 31% in active borrowers. This is followed by BRAC which assumes 27% of the share in terms of gross loan portfolio and 30% in active borrowers. ASA secured the third position in market share assuming almost 20% in both categories. Other NGO-MFIs assume 19% of the market in both categories in 2009 (see Figure 8.5).

The MRA classified the NGO-MFIs in Bangladesh based on the number of borrowers. The classification of NGO-MFIs is shown in Table 8.2. The very small NGOs are those with borrowers up to 10,000. On the contrary, the very large MFIs are those with borrowers more than one million. The large NGO-MFIs constitute almost 76% of total loan outstanding of the market in 2013 (see Table 8.2).

Apart from the GB, the top 20 MFIs play the lead role in microfinance market in Bangladesh. BRAC has the highest cumulative loan disbursement followed by ASA (see Table 8.3). Buro Bangladesh, TMSS, JCF and SSS are also large MFIs with major cumulative loan disbursement.

8.3. Supply Side: Innovation in the Sector Over Time

Since the last three decades, the microfinance sector in Bangladesh has been continuously innovating new products for the members. The MFIs compete with each other to capture more shares in the market and

Table 8.3: Cumulative Loan Disbursement of Top 20 MFIs in Bangladesh (in billion taka)

Name of MFIs	2009	2010	2011	2012	2013
BRAC	394.35	469.46	544.39	642.12	754.77
ASA	305.08	377.49	454.96	549.58	645.76
Buro Bangladesh	23.6	33.38	44.87	58.14	80.25
TMSS	31.11	38.71	48.45	60.3	74.94
JCF	12.77	17.29	25.29	34.65	45.73
SSS	19.23	24.78	32.01	41.48	53.88
Shakti foundation	13.2	18.33	26.93	29.24	34.27
Uddipan	9.27	13.15	17.76	23.5	30.36
Padakhep	8.34	11.1	14.62	20.04	24.71
RDRS	8.82	10.79	13.48	16.65	20.06
PMK	7.67	9.77	12.31	15.27	18.83
Caritas	10.38	11.72	13.91	16.42	19.16
CDIP	3.72	5.44	7.97	11.22	15.11
Sajida foundation	4.9	6.85	9.11	12.34	16.1
CSS	2.92	4.18	6.99	8.58	11.4
RRF	7.05	8.59	10.82	13.17	15.76
RIC	4.25	5.66	8.26	11.01	14.1
POPI	5.89	8.28	9.21	11.32	13.76
DSK	5.26	6.31	8.24	10.56	14.46
Total	**918.86**	**1124.35**	**1354.64**	**1632.93**	**1953.03**

Source: MRA–MIS database 2013, adapted from MRA (2014).

attempts to achieve sustainability in the long run (PKSF, 2014). The competition is in three areas — location, product and price. Almost all MFIs have several products in the market, which are almost homogenous. The modalities and model are very close to each other but differ in terms of target group, repayment schedule, repayment grace period (flexibility), loan size, loan purpose, interest rate and savings products (Faruqee & Badruddoza, 2011a). The MFIs segment the market in terms of poverty and occupational groups and designed the loan and savings products to reasonably meet the demand of different groups. The segmentation of the market is based on demand driven financial products, for example, loans, savings, insurances, etc. keeping the demand of the target group in mind. For instance, in designing a product for the hard core poor or ultra-poor the MFI keeps in mind that the money is required for personal consumption first and then they use parts of the loan amount to income-generating activities. They do not save regularly and they withdraw their savings at any time. Thus, an MFI should design the product such as (1) no minimum savings amount; (2) savings can be deposited and withdrawn at any point of time; (3) loan is not tied to savings and (4) loan repayment should start after few weeks later than the regular loan repayment dates (Alamgir, 2010). Thus, MFIs segment the market based on the needs of the target group. Besides the variations in the credit products, MFIs also offer credit plus services to the members such as health services, capacity development training, technical services, total development projects, etc.

The variation in the MFIs products also differs in terms of selecting target groups, loan modalities, loan ceilings, purpose of loan, loan repayment schedules, flexibility in repayment grace period, innovations in the saving products, etc. In addition, many specialised programmes [such as Programmed Initiatives for Monga Eradication (PRIME)] which are offered by the multinational donors or international research institutions are also carried out by the NGO-MFIs in Bangladesh (PKSF, 2014). As a result, the microfinance market in Bangladesh is diverse and consistently comes up with new innovations. Table 8.4 shows the basic products are offered by most NGO-MFIs. For example, Table 8.4 shows PKSF's POs implemented the entire core products over the years. Most MFIs target hard core poor or moderate poor in selling their loans. POs get wholesale loan from PKSF with subsidised price and then distribute those loans to their members/clients with higher interest rate between 10% and 15% annually (effectively almost 30% per annum) (Rashid, 2011). The effective interest rate (EIR) is 30% because MFIs use a flat rate calculation, not declining balance method. Following MRA regulated policies, the MFIs calculate their loans based on the declining balance method because this method produces effective lower interest which helps the borrowers in regards to their repayment capacity (MRA, 2014). PRIME and Learning and Innovation Fund to Test New Ideas (LIFT) are the two kinds of specialised program mainly funded by donors designed for ultra-poor households.

Table 8.4: Mainstream Programs Conducted by Various MFIs of PKSF in Bangladesh

Name of product	Modalities	Target group	Loan amount (BDT)	Year of inception by PKSF
Ultra-poor programme	Group	hard core poor	500–5,000	2004–2005
Regular microcredit	Group	Moderate poor	5,000–30,000	1990–1991
Urban microcredit	Group	Moderate poor	5,000–30,000	1998–1999
Microenterprise programme	Group/ individual	Moderate poor	25,000–500,000	2004–2005
Agricultural SL	Group	Marginal farmers	10,000–50,000	2006–2007
PRIME	Group	Hard-core poor	2,000–10,000	2006–2007
LIFT	Group	Hard-core poor and Moderate poor	2,000–50,000	2006–2007

Source: PKSF Annual Report, 2014 (PKSF, 2014).

Besides the regular program of PKSF by the POs, Table 8.4 also shows other specialised programs such as:

- SUFOLON–ASM started in 2008–2009.
- Finance for Enterprise Development and Employment Creation (FEDEC) Project started in 2008–2009.
- Enhancing Resources and Increasing Capacities of the Poor Households towards Elimination of their Poverty (ENRICH) started in 2009–2010.
- Developing Inclusive Insurance Sector Project (DIISP) started in 2010–2011.
- Bangladesh Climate Change Trust Fund (MCCTF), started in 2012–2013.
- Livestock Unit and Agriculture Unit started in 2013–2014.
- Social Advocacy & Knowledge Dissemination Unit started in 2013–2014.
- Results-Based Monitoring (RBM) Unit started in 2013–2014.

Compared to other microfinance providers in Bangladesh, BRAC seeks to understand the heterogeneous needs of the poor and design microfinance services accordingly. BRAC's microfinance programme offers diversified financial services to poor people who are unable to access mainstream banking services. It uses its wealth of expertise in other areas of rural development, for example, agriculture, education and health to innovate financial services that meet the specific needs of different groups. These include products tailored for rural poor and urban women, landless and land-holding farmers, migrant workers and small entrepreneurs (BRAC, 2016c). One such loan product is microcredit for tenant farmers with customised credit programme aimed to develop lives and livelihoods of the tenant farmers, who were neglected by formal banking and mainstream NGO-MFIs for many years and to contribute to the country's agricultural farm productivity and food security status (Malek *et al.*, 2015).

With BRAC, clients are able to access savings products and loans from between USD 100–10,000. BRAC seeks to ensure that clients can get the most out of its products. To support borrowers, BRAC has invested in supply chains and marketing infrastructure so that supply of products from microenterprises can reach the market (BRAC, 2016c). In addition, each microfinance product integrates a set of financial education and client protection measures into its services to help safeguard against risks for the clients. BRAC is committed to a stringent monitoring and evaluation process. All BRAC microfinance projects are piloted, evaluated and revised before being presented to more than 2,000 branches in all 64 districts in Bangladesh. Since BRAC is a social impact-driven organisation, the success of its microfinance programme is measured according to the effectiveness of its projects in delivering social goods. Financial sustainability of BRAC microfinance products enables it to deliver more effective products and services, and offers more benefits to the clients. BRAC believes that financial services are not enough to achieve sustainable poverty reduction. BRAC's microfinance programme represents one component of BRAC's holistic approach to development. It is designed to complement other interventions such as education, healthcare and legal aid, and all microfinance clients are encouraged to make use of these services. BRAC also successfully innovates microfinance products that are not suitable for everyone especially for the ultra-poor. Therefore, it operates a separate programme 'Targeting the Ultra Poor programme (TUP)' for the most vulnerable which comprises asset transfer, training and follow-up, known as BRAC graduation approach, which is now a globally accepted model for the upliftment of ultra-poor (Banerjee *et al.*, 2015b).

Like BRAC, ASA and other NGO-MFIs in Bangladesh exhibit almost the similar kind of products in the market but with different names. These products differ in terms of target groups, loan amount, credit plus financial services. There are competitions among the NGO-MFIs in terms of differentiated products so that each MFI can obtain maximum share from its operation. These differentiated products can be classified into main four domains where MFIs operate. These are financial services, non-financial services, capacity building and management and product quality improvement and marketing (PKSF, 2014). Table 8.5 shows the classified products under these four domains.

Table 8.5: Innovations in Microfinance Sector in Bangladesh

Financial services	Non-financial services	Capacity building and management	Product quality improvement and marketing
— Emergency loan — Flexible microcredit — Disaster management credit — Savings product — Microinsurance product — Remittance transfer	— Group formation — Primary healthcare services — Public health campaign — Technical assistance program for IGA — Education programme — Scholarships for education — Training center facilities — Remittance transfer — Advocacy for new technology adaptation — Advocacy for women empowerment — Advocacy for legal assistance — Climate change adaptation & awareness — Disaster management services — Cash for work to mitigate seasonal hunger	— Skill and vocational training of members for both farm and non-farming activities — Workshops for income-generating activities — Disaster management training	— Promotion of their own products — Promotion of new agricultural technology — Promotion of solar energy — Value chain development services

Source: (PKSF, 2014).

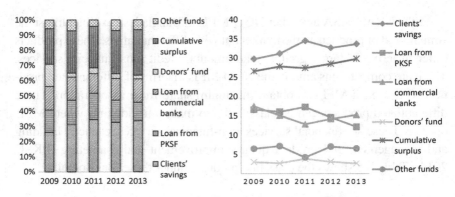

Figure 8.6:   MFIs Sources of Funds in Bangladesh (2009–2013)

Source: MRA–MIS database 2013, adapted from MRA (2014).

8.3.1 *Funding of MFIs*

Source of funding is a critical issue for MFIs because it involves financial sustainability of the institutions. Heavy dependence on donor funds for a lengthy period affects the sustainability of MFIs. Although most MFIs depended on donor funds with a subsidised rate, the dependence is reduced greatly. Today donors' fund contribute only 2.64% of the total funding on average. Figure 8.6 shows that donor funds has been on a decline every year. This include loans from PKSF. The sector is now becoming more financially sustainable because the main source of fund comes from their cumulative surplus and from clients' savings. Funding from commercial banks and other sources of funds now play a constant role for financing MFIs in Bangladesh in last 5 years (MRA, 2014).

8.3.2 *OSS*

Financial sustainability is an important for MFIs to operate in a competitive market. To ensure the sustainability of MFIs, most MFIs try to remain viable in their operations in terms of OSS and financial self-sufficiency (FSS). OSS measures the MFIs ability to cover the operation and financial cost from their operating incomes. On the contrary FSS is the measure of MFIs' ability to cover operating cost from their income after adjusting for all types of subsidy, loan loss provision and inflation (Wahid

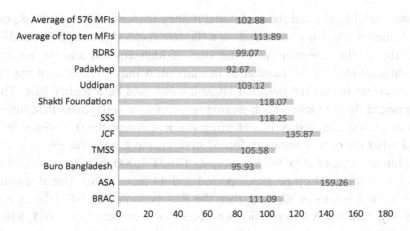

Figure 8.7:   OSS of Major MFIs in Bangladesh (in percentage)
Source: MRA–MIS Database 2011, adapted from MRA (2011).

et al., 2015). As MFIs in Bangladesh become more self-financed and the dependency of subsidy is reduced to a great extent, we concentrate our analysis only on OSS. OSS is the ratio of operating income and cost where operating income is the sum of loans and investments. Costs comprise operating cost, loan loss provisions and financial costs. OSS is measured with a reference value of 100% where cost equals income and the MFIs are operationally self-sufficient. But if the values are less than 100% then it is not operationally self-sufficient meaning the operating cost is higher than income (Wahid *et al.*, 2015). Figure 8.7 shows the OSS of major MFIs in Bangladesh and the average top ten MFIs. Some major MFIs in Bangladesh such as Buro Bangladesh, Padakhep and RDRS exhibit OSS with less than 100%. The sectoral average (based on 576 MFIs) is 102.88%, which implies that the MFIs in Bangladesh are operationally self-sufficient. This is also true for the top 10 MFIs showing OSS at 113.89%.

8.3.3 *EIRs of MFIs*

Interest rates of microfinance sector are being criticised since the start of the sector. NGO-MFIs started their operations to fill the gaps between the commercial banks and the traditional money lenders who served the poor with higher interest rates based on a flat rate method (Faruqee & Khalily, 2011b). A flat rate method is the sum of loan amount and the interest amount divided by the number of instalment. A major problem of the flat rate system is that the nominal interest rate could be a higher EIR. This happened due to factors such as frequency of loan repayment instalment, grace period (flexibility of deferring the instalment date), various fees, and other charges (insurance, forced savings, etc.). For example, a nominal interest rate of 10% for a principal of BDT 1,000, generates an EIR of 25.1% conditional on no grace period and 44 instalments. But if a grace period of 4 weeks is allowed, then the EIR becomes 22.3%. (Faruqee & Khalily, 2011b). A commission consisting of members from InM, MRA and PKSF proposed some regulations for setting EIR which were recently approved by the monitoring agency, MRA. The regulations include (Faruqee & Khalily, 2011b):

- Maximum EIR set at 27% annually and the calculation of interest rate should be based on a declining balance method.
- The minimum number of instalment week for loan repayment must be 46 weeks for general loans.
- A minimum grace period of 15 days to be applied between loan disbursement and the first instalment.

Higher EIR is not only a problem in for MFIs in Bangladesh but also globally. Most MFIs claim that they have to cover costs to reach areas where the ultra-poor risk is high. Thus, doing business with the poor requires higher returns on their loan assets. However, with competition in the market and regulation from the monitoring agencies MFIs are forced to lower their interest rates to some extent (Islam, 2012). Figure 8.8 shows the annual EIR of 25 POs of PKSF in different products. The urban and RMC programme including microenterprise have EIR greater than 30%. A major reason is that the number of instalments is changed to monthly rather than weekly. If the number of instalment is 48 or 52 weeks, then the EIR is higher but if 12 then it is lower. When the loan products interest rate is set monthly or semi-annually the EIR declines sharply. The lowest EIR is 23.91% for the ultra-poor programme (see Figure 8.8).

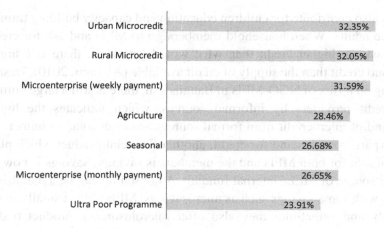

Urban Microcredit	32.35%
Rural Microcredit	32.05%
Microenterprise (weekly payment)	31.59%
Agriculture	28.46%
Seasonal	26.68%
Microenterprise (monthly payment)	26.65%
Ultra Poor Programme	23.91%

Figure 8.8:   EIR charged by 25 POs of PKSF in 2011
Source: PKSF (2014).

8.4 Demand Side: Credit Utilisation, Determinants Influencing Accessibility of Microcredit by Rural Households in Bangladesh and Impact on Rural Lives and the Economy

8.4.1 *Demand for credit*

The demand for credit by people is to smoothen their consumption by borrowing and pay back when there is surplus. Credit demand in the rural households is mainly to support their income-generating activities such as farming, non-farm activities, small business, etc. In addition, households need credit to support their consumption during a crisis period, to finance the extra expenditures such as marriage, rituals and health related shocks. Both covariate and idiosyncratic shocks deviate the households from their regular consumption pattern requiring more financial and non-financial assistances (Hasan, 2014). Mostly friends and relatives help in this regards. However, the assistance from kinships is inadequate and hence the demand for credit is an inevitable part of most households. As discussed earlier the commercial banks could not provide loans for many reasons and the advent of microfinance played a vital role for the poor people. The MFIs in the rural economy contributes a significant portion to the national economy. MFIs help to reduce poverty and empower women.

MFIs also contribute for children education and capacity building training for the adults. When household members go to MFIs and ask for credit, they ask for higher credit than what would get. Thus, there is a higher demand credit than the supply of credit available (Alamgir, 2010). Despite having an influx of NGO-MFIs in Bangladesh, there is still a large number of credit providers by informal sources, which indicates the higher demand of microcredit from formal sources are inadequate or unmet.

Apart from demand for credit, another financial product which plays a vital role for both MFIs and the members is savings. Savings is now the major source of MFIs' internal funding. A household can be a member of MFIs with some savings such as microsavings. MFIs collect small savings weekly and sometimes they also offer microinsurance product tied to loans. Previous studies show that poor households can also save even if they have very limited amount of money for consumption (Islam, 2012).

8.4.2 *Multiple borrowing of microcredit*

Households demand for credit is not from one MFI but from several MFIs. Although MFIs strive to increase their business most often they fail to assess the loan application of incumbent borrowers (who also take loans from multiple MFIs) which adversely affect the quality of their loan portfolio. This is because the borrowers put themselves in the risk of higher defaulters. Many borrowers borrow from multiple sources where loans are misdirected. Sometimes borrowers do not use the borrowed amount for the stated purpose. Misused of loans together with loans from informal sources put the borrower into a debt trap. Thus, multiple borrowing is not encouraged by MFIs because the borrowers cannot pay back some of the loans from multiple sources (Khalily & Faridi, 2011a). The main reasons for multiple borrowings are due to loan ceiling for specific loan purpose from MFIs, higher enterprise loan demand from the borrowers, and different interest rates for different loan products. Sometimes MFIs also induced members to take loans in the name of other members of the family just to increase their business. Figure 8.9 shows the rate of multiple borrowing overtime by households as well as the individual member of households in Bangladesh. In recent years the rate varies from some 40% to 50%.

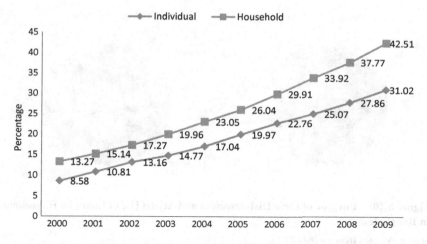

Figure 8.9: **Multiple Borrowing in Microfinance Sector in Bangladesh**
Source: Adapted from Khalily & Faridi (2011a).

8.4.3 *Credit utilisation*

Loans should be spent on the stated purpose(s) by the households but most often that does not happen. There are many reasons behind this such as higher demand for consumption loan, emergency loan and some extra expenditure such as health, marriage, rituals and bribes, etc. MFI documents the intended purpose of the loan but most often they are unable to trace where the money is spent (Rashid, 2011). As money is fungible in nature it is quite impossible to trace which money is spent on a specific purpose. Critics say that MFIs mainly target functionally landless households (having 50 decimals of land) and thus credit is mostly used for non-farm activities. However, using Mahabub Hossain (MH) 62 village panel dataset, Hossain & Bayes (2015) find that microcredit is also being channelled to pursue agricultural activities. One recent study by Malek *et al.* (2015) find that the customised microcredit program for the tenant farmers' loan has been used mostly for agricultural purpose (about 60%).

Based on the 2009 Bangladesh Microfinance Statistics, it is recorded that a substantial amount of money is under "other category", which comprises consumption loan and other diversified loan purpose which varies among MFIs. The second large category is the small business and farming

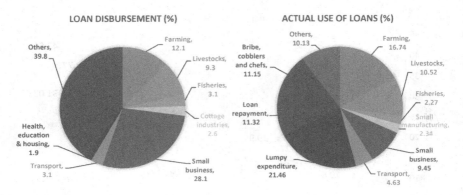

Figure 8.10:   Purpose of Loan Disbursement and Actual Use of Loans by Households in Bangladesh

Source: Adapted from Rashid (2011).

loans (see Figure 8.10). The actual use of loans by the households' shows that most loan amount is being spent on lumpy expenditure (21.46%) and farming (16.74%). Small business, livestock, loan repayment, bribes and others exhibit the same amount (almost 10%) in the total use of MFIs loans (see Figure 8.10).

8.4.4 *Determinants of MFIs participations*

Microfinance products in Bangladesh are diverse and different microfinance products target different income group ranges from ultra-poor to middle income entrepreneurs. Different products have different eligibility criteria for access to that particular credit. For example, for ultra-poor programme the eligibility criteria is household having less than 50 decimal of land or household is a day labourer or household earns less than BDT 3,000 (PKSF, 2014). Thus, any household having any of these criteria are eligible to get credit from MFIs. Other products such as regular microcredit and other products also assess the required eligibility criteria for providing loans.

8.4.5 *Impact of microfinance*

Microfinance plays an important role in rural economy especially it involves the fund of rural savings and loans which add values to the rural

GDP as well as the national income. Besides, MFIs impacts on many aspects of rural lives such as (1) financial inclusion; (2) poverty alleviation; (3) promotion of savings and investments; (4) women empowerment; and 5) human capital formation (Rashid, 2011).

(a) *Financial inclusion*

Microfinance enables the excluded poor to access financial services. The poor are capable of handling financial services from MFIs. In Bangladesh almost 77% of the households have access to some kind of financial services such as credit, savings or insurances and 43.23% of the household have access to MFI services (Khalily & Khaleque, 2011b).

(b) *Poverty alleviation*

Poverty is multidimensional and the role of microfinance in poverty alleviation only works through the channels of household and individual characteristics. Employment creation, income generation, asset accumulations, education and capacity development and production of health are the main contributing factors by microfinance. Hossain (1988) used GB microcredit borrowing households and counterfactual households to test the income differences and found that microcredit participants have 28% higher income than the non-participants in the same village. Using the same kind of methodology Khandker (1998) uses 1991–1992 World Bank–BIDS survey data found that households located in the microcredit programme villages could increase their average production over 50%. Similar result was found by Kerr (2009) which showed that microcredit participation could increase output per unit of labour for non-farm enterprises. The positive effect of microcredit on entrepreneurships and employment among the individuals and households are documented in the literature. For example, credit given to female participants in Grameen Bank raise the household labour supply significantly (Pitt & Khandker, 1998). Women productivity in work has increased because of credit plus services such as training and other technical assistance service provided by the MFIs (McKernan, 2002; Nussbaum, 1999; Zaman, 1998b). Studies have found that microcredit could mitigate the root causes of vulnerability (Zaman, 1998a). It is important to use the loan amount in productive purposes (Khandker, 1998; Roodman & Morduch, 2009). Even taking loans for consumption purpose could help households by reducing the distress sale of assets during crisis time (Osmani, 2011).

(c) *Promotion of savings and investment*

MFIs collect savings and give loans and the impact of savings is huge for both the MFIs and borrowers. MFIs could reduce the dependency on informal credit market through the accumulation of rural savings and enabling households to borrow from this quasi-formal market. Khandker and Chowdhury (1996) using data from GB, BRAC and BRDB showed that microfinance could generate positive impact on savings and assets accumulation. Current savings of participants are significantly higher than the non-participants. Household spend the accumulated savings in investment especially in housing, transportations and livestocks. Rahman (1996) showed that the higher the number of loans taken from MFIs the higher the capital assets the borrower has.

(d) *Women empowerment*

Major role of microfinance lies in the empowerment of women through some income-generating activities and plays as a vital agent for theory of change. Microfinance recipients are mostly women (above 90%) in Bangladesh who brings both material and non-material changes to households as well as to the society. Previous literature on microcredit criticises that women borrow but men control (Goetz & Gupta, 1996) however, Malek *et al.* (2015) challenges this proposition by explaining the control of women over how loans are invested, as demonstrated in a number of cases in the evaluation of a targeted credit programme for the women tenant farmers in Bangladesh. The impact of microfinance on women empowerment has also been analysed in numerous studies and found that access to credit could raise women's power inside the households (Hashemi, Schuler & Riley, 1996; Zaman, 1998b). It is also found that the prevalence of domestic violence against women in the microcredit borrowing households tend to decrease with the length of the women membership with microcredit

(e) *Impacts on human capital formation*

MFIs have major roles in human capital formation through enhancing productivity in Bangladesh. Some MFIs provides non-formal primary education to children of the poor households. Many MFIs offer training and workshops in income-generating activities besides technical assistance programmes. The role of MFIs in formation of human capital is documented in studies such as Rahman (1996), Hossain (1998) and Khandker (1998). These studies discussed the increase in school enrolment, child immunisation, use of sanitary latrines and contraceptive prevalence. However, Islam & Choe (2013) find that household participation in a microcredit program may increase child labour and reduce school enrolment this may be due to additional pressure on households to earn additional income for paying regular instalment of microcredit.

8.5 Conclusion and Way Forward

MFIs can be found in almost every place in Bangladesh. Besides MFIs, nationalised commercial banks and commercial banks are also providing microcredit. MFIs have additional roles in disseminating microfinance and credit plus services. The new terminology "Financial Inclusion" is popular in recent microfinance literature. Today, MFIs target poor people with not only credit but also credit plus services which could enable them to manage their credit and lift them out of poverty. Although there are innovations in product designs and modalities in microfinance, still many households are not targeted and they depend upon informal lending. Poor households sometimes do not like microcredit because of their rigidity in repayment schedules. More innovation is required in this regard. It is necessary to know how much credit can change the fate of poor people and how to avoid becoming defaulters. Therefore, designing appropriate products with different target groups is the key to further success in this sector.

Although the microfinance market in Bangladesh and the world has attained impressive progress in providing financial services to rural poor, the real impact of microfinance is somewhat questionable. This is mainly because of methodological issues (Bunting, 2011). The rationale behind this logic is that the participants in microfinance are self-selected and the programme is introduced in a specific area based on the needs. Thus, the results of most of the empirical studies and quasi-experimental studies suffer from selection bias. However, the recent experimental evidence regarding microcredit programmes, such as Banerjee, Karlan & Zinman (2015a), Angelucci, Karlan & Zinman (2015), Crépon *et al.* (2015),

Augsburg *et al.* (2015), Angelucci *et al.* (2015) and Attanasio *et al.* (2015) found no impact or little impact on poverty in the short run. The main reason might be the small credit could help the poor to start their business but they need to sustain the business with higher amount of enterprise loans to make visible changes and therefore, they need longer exposure to microcredit (Islam, 2012). But randomised control trial (RCT) analysis with long exposure is not cost-effective and also difficult to implement. Thus, the long run impact of microfinance is inconclusive in the microfinance literature.

Nevertheless, the empirical studies show statistically significant result of microcredit on poverty reduction, employment generation, asset accumulations, women empowerment, mobility of household members, reduced vulnerability and also increase total consumption. But these studies cannot truly measure the extent of the impact that is generated by the microcredit itself. However, the positive impact of microcredit is widely accepted and it produced a momentum in the rural economy which could have been lost if there were no microcredit operations. Osmani (2014) categorically made two strong conclusions: firstly, there is hardly any other intervention that has been able to bring 1 out of 10 beneficiaries out of poverty anywhere in the world. Secondly, the benefit of microcredit goes well beyond the number of people it manages to pull above the poverty line. The discourse on microcredit should move forward. Instead of taking rigid positions on the efficacy of microcredit in general, the protagonists should focus attention on the details of how microcredit can be made more useful for the poor. Apart from that, it is important to see the impact of microfinance in comparison with government assisted programmes and the financial components of MFIs themselves. As the product of MFIs are diverse and they also offer credit plus services such as training, technical assistance programme, primary healthcare services, etc. it is a very difficult task to isolate each of these components to identify the impact. It would be also interesting to see some synergies and trade off among the financial services that are offered by the MFIs. Besides, cross country analysis of microfinance is also important to test replication of success stories. Research on MFIs sustainability and financial viability is extremely important. As of now in Bangladesh, MFIs are tax exempted but if government introduces tax on MFIs then what impact it has on MFIs performance remains a topic for the policy makers.

8.6 Policy Recommendations

Although the microfinance program in Bangladesh exhibits impressive progress, this sector should address some key concerns and create some favourable socio-political environments for its expansion. Among the key concerns are the high interest rates, multiple borrowing (overlapping loans) and indebtedness of the poor. For the further development of the sector, special emphasis should be placed on creating a socio-political environment, easing loan repayment using ICT, flexibility in loan recovery, ensuring sustainability of MFIs, scaling up microfinance, add-on remittance services and microinsurance, linking with formal financial system and strengthening the regulation and supervision of MFIs. (Faruqee & Badruddoza, 2011a).

Interest rate is an important factor for the microfinance sector as well as the policy makers. It should legitimately cover operating cost in an efficient way. Transparency and uniformity in the interest rate calculation such as declining balance method is highly desirable. Regulators should also be aware of those MFIs who charge very high interest rates and take necessary steps to address this issue. Besides interest rate, multiple borrowing is a critical issue which is caused by several reasons such as inherent terms and condition of the loan, repaying existing loans, excess demand for loan for managing projects, etc. Multiple borrowing of loans sometimes put the households over indebtedness and become loan defaulters. Several innovative steps can reduce the extent of multiple borrowing such as establishing credit bureau/data base, harnessing the credit policies, restructuring the loan amount and repayment methods and a proper information system to screen the application. With regards to the problem of indebtedness, MFIs should scrutinise the credit application and the credit records of the incumbent borrower based on his or her ability to repay the loan. Pro-active measures should be taken into account to tackle this issue.

National policies of financial liberalisation are important for sustaining the evolution of the microfinance sector. The principles should be such that credit decisions must be made without political interferences. Ensuring property rights, legal administrative support for securing the transaction are needed for the benefit of the financial sector. An independent bank regulatory and supervisory authority should strongly monitor the sector.

At present the microfinance sector in Bangladesh is practicing inadequate use of information technology. It is important to upgrade the financial accounting system to internet-based system and the MIS software should be available at the rural branch level. To efficiently manage and report to the regulatory authority it is important to use management software at the local level. Borrowers should also be exposed to mobile banking and repayment of loan through mobile banking system so as to reduce transaction costs. It will also ensure the proper documentation and credibility between the borrowers and the MFIs. Apart from loan repayment, mobile phone applications could be used for deposit savings, premium for microinsurances and remittance services.

Ensuring sustainability of MFIs is important for the financial sector of any country. Financial sustainability depends on several issues such as management efficiency, portfolio quality, lower operating cost, etc. MFIs should mobilise their own resources efficiently rather than depend heavily on donor funds. Besides, scaling up the microfinance sector could help attain financial sustainability because of economies of scale. Catering to the needs of the poor should be given the priority. Innovation for designing new products should be the rule of the game for the microfinance sector.

The microfinance sector is not recognised as a formal financial system and only target the low-income people, particularly the rural poor. It becomes a complex situation when commercial banks and state-owned banks provide microfinancing the people. Instead of having two credit systems operating separately, it would be better to integrate the two systems for proper managing and monitoring of credit allocation. Strengthening the supervisory body such as MRA can facilitate and supervise the sector efficiently.

Financial inclusion is the new era of economic and social development. MFIs should not concentrate only on operating loans and savings but also on other financial services such as differentiated savings accounts, microinsurance, enterprise development assistance and enabling support services such as training and marketing, welfare support such as basic literacy, health services, gender and social awareness training and disaster management training. Group platform, for example, village organisation, needs to be more functional to coordinate all grass root level activities.

References

Alamgir, D. H. (2010). State of Microfinance in Bangladesh. Dhaka. Retrieved from http://www.inm.org.bd/publication/state_of_micro/Bangladesh.pdf.

Armendáriz de Aghion, B. & Morduch, J. (2005). *The Economics of Microfinance*. Massachusetts, London: The MIT Press Cambridge.

Angelucci, M., Karlan, D. & Zinman, J. (2015). Microcredit impacts: Evidence from a randomized microcredit program placement experiment by compartamosBanco, *American Economic Journal*, 7(1), 151–182.

Attanasio, O., Augsburg, B., De Haas, D., Fitzsimons, E. & Harmgart, H. (2015). Estimating the impact of microcredit on those who take it up: Evidence from a randomized experiment in Morocco. *American Economic Journal*, 7(1), 90–122.

Augsburg, B., De Haas, R., Harmgart, H. & Meghir, C. (2015). The impacts of microcredit: Evidence from Bosnia and Herzegovina. *American Economic Journal*, 7(1), 183–203.

Banerjee, A., Karlan, D. & Zinman, J. (2015a). Six randomized evaluations of microcredit: Introduction and further steps. *American Economic Journal*, 7(1), 1–21.

Banerjee, A., Duflo, E., Glennerster, R. & Kinnan, C. (2015b). The miracle of microfinance? Evidence from a randomized evaluation. *American Economic Journal*, 7(1), 22–53.

Berg, C., Emran, M. S. & Shilpi, F. (2014). Microfinance and Moneylenders: Long-run Effects of MFIs on Informal Credit Market in Bangladesh (No. 25). Dhaka, Bangladesh.

BRAC (2016a). BRAC at a Glance. Retrieved from http://www.brac.net/partnership. Accessed on March 17, 2016.

BRAC (2016b). BRAC Approach. Retrieved from http://www.brac.net/our-approach. Accessed on March 17, 2016.

BRAC (2016c). BRAC Microfinance Program Overview. Retrieved from http://brac.net/microfinance-programme/item/855-overview. Accessed on March 17, 2016.

Bunting, M. (2011). Microfinance's Sober Reckoning. Poverty Matter's Blog, *The Guardian* 2011. Retrieved from http://www.guardian.co.uk/global-development/poverty-matters/2011/aug/18/microfinance-sober-reckoning-studies-question.

Crepon, B., Devoto, F., Duflo, E. & Pariente, W. (2015). Estimating the impact of microcredit on those who take it up: Evidence from a randomized experiment in morocco. *American Economic Journal*, 7(1), 123–150.

Dowla, A. & Barua, D. (2006). *The Poor Always Pay Back: The Grameen II Story*. Bloomfield, Connecticut: Kumarian Press Inc.

Duvendack, M., Palmer-Jones, R., Copestake, J. G., Hooper, L., Loke, Y. & Rao, N. (2011). *What is the Evidence of the Impact of Microfinance on the Well-being of Poor People?* London: EPPI-center, Social Science Research Unit, Institute of Education, University of London.

Faruqee, R. & Badruddoza, S. (2011a). Microfinance in Bangladesh: Past, Present and Future. Dhaka: Institute of Microfinance (InM). Retrieved from http://inm.org.bd/publication/occasionalpaper/Occasional paper-2.pdf.

Faruqee, R. & Khalily, M. A. B. (2011b). *Interest Rates in Bangladesh Microcredit Market*. Dhaka: Institute of Microfinance.

Ferrari, A. (2008). *Increasing Access to Rural Finance in Bangladesh: The "Missing Middle."* Washington, D.C.: The World Bank.

Goetz, A. M. & Gupta, R. S. (1996). Who takes the credit? Gender, power, and control over loan use in rural credit programmes in Bangladesh. *World Development*, 24(1), 45–63.

Hasan, M. M. (2014). Climate change induced marginality: Households' vulnerability in the meal consumption frequencies. *American Journal of Environmental Protection*, 3(3), 103–112.

Hashemi, S. M., Schuler, S. R. & Riley, A. P. (1996). Rural credit programs and women's empowerment in Bangladesh. *World Development*, 24(4), 635–653.

Hollis, A., Sweetman, A., Emery, H., Feeny, D., Mokyr, J., Connor, G. O. & Gr, C. (1997). Complementarity, Competition and Institutional Development: The Irish Loan Funds through Three Centuries. Microfinance Gateway. Retrieved from: microfinancegateway.org.

Hossain, M. (1988). *Credit for Alleviation of Rural Poverty: The Grameen Bank of Bangladesh*. Washington D.C: IFPRI.

Hossain, M. & Bayes, A. (2015). Rural credit market. In Hossain, M. & Bayes, A. (Eds.), *Leading Issues in Rural Development: Bangladesh Perspectives*. Dhaka, Bangladesh: AH Development Publishing House.

Islam, N. (2012). Thoughts on Microfinance and All That. Research & Publications Cell Palli Karma-Sahayak Foundation (PKSF), Dhaka, Bangladesh. Retrieved from: http://intranet.ifpri.org:8090/COM/IFPRIpurchasedarticles/Thoughts on Microfinance and All That-Final Print.pdf.

Islam, A. & Choe, C. (2013). Child labour and schooling responses to access to microcredit in rural Bangladesh. *Economic Inquiry*, 51(1), 46–61.

Kerr, E. (2009). *Micro-Credit and Household Productivity: Evidence from Bangladesh.* Waco: Baylor University.

Khalily, B. & Faridi, R. (2011a). *Multiple Memberships (Overlapping) in Microcredit Markets of Bangladesh.* Dhaka, Bangladesh: Institute of Microfinance (InM).

Khalily, B. & Khaleque, A. (2011b). *Access to Financial Services in Bangladesh.* Dhaka, Bangladesh: Institute of Microfinance (InM).

Khandker, S. R. & Osman H. C. (1996). Targeted Credit Programs and Rural Poverty in Bangladesh. World Bank Discussion Paper 336. Washington, D.C.

Khandker, S. R. (1998). *Fighting Poverty with Microcredit Experience in Bangladesh.* New York: Oxford University Press.

Malek, M. A., Ahasan, A., Hossain, M. A., Ahmed, M. S., Hossain, M. & Reza, M. H. (2015). Impact assessment of credit programme for the tenant farmers in Bangladesh, 3ie Grantee Final Report. New Delhi: International Initiative for Impact Evaluation (3ie).

McKernan, S.-M. (2002). The impact of microcredit programs on self-employment profits: Do noncredit program aspects matter? *Review of Economics and Statistics*, 84(1), 93–115.

MRA (2011). *NGO-MFIs in Bangladesh.* Dhaka, Bangladesh: Microcredit Regulatory Authority (MRA).

MRA (2014). NGO-MFIs in Bangladesh. Microcredit Regulatory Authority (MRA), Dhaka. Retrieved from http://www.mra.gov.bd/images/mra_files/Publications/finalvolx.pdf.

Mudahar, M. S. & Ahmed, R. (2010). *Government and Rural Transformation Role of Public Spending and Policies in Bangladesh.* Dhaka, Bangladesh: The University Press Limited.

Nussbaum, M. (1999). Women and equality: The capabilities approach. *International Labour Review*, 138(3), 227–245.

Osmani, S. (2011). Asset Accumulation and Poverty Dynamics in Rural Bangladesh: The Role of Microcredit. Dhaka, Bangladesh.

Osmani, S. R. (2014). Has Microcredit Helped the Rural Poor of Bangladesh? An Analytical Review of the Evidence So Far. Working paper No. 23. Institute of Microfinance, Dhaka.

Pitt, M. M. & Khandker, S. R. (1998). The impact of group-based credit programs on poor households in Bangladesh: Does the gender of participants matter? *Journal of Political Economy*, 106(5), 958.

PKSF (2014). Annual Report. Dhaka, Bangladesh.

Rahman, R. I. (1996). Impact of Grameen Krishi Foundation on the Socioeconomic Condition of Rural Households. Working Paper 17. Bangladesh Institute of Development Studies, Dhaka.

Rashid, F. (2011). Impact of Microfinance Programmes on Poverty in Bangladesh. Dhaka, Bangladesh.

Roodman, D. & Morduch, J. (2009). The Impact of Microcredit on the Poor in Bangladesh: Revisiting the Evidence. (No. 174).

Shah, M., Rao, R. & Shankar, P. S. V. (2007). Rural credit in 20th century India: Overview of history and perspectives. *Economic and Political Weekly*, 42(15), 1351–1364.

Spooner, L. (1846). *Poverty: Its Illegal Causes and Legal Cure*. Boston: Bela Marsh.

Wahid, A., Hasan, M. & Rabbani, A. (2015). The Outreach-Profitability Tradeoff: Evidence from an Ultra-Poor Program in Bangladesh. Dhaka, Bangladesh.

Zaman, H. (1998a). Assessing the Poverty and Vulnerability Impact of Micro-Credit in Bangladesh: A case study of BRAC. Dhaka, Bangladesh.

Zaman, H. (1998b). The Links between BRAC Inputs and "Empowerment Correlates" in Matlab, Dhaka. BRAC-ICDDR, B Working Paper Series No. 28.

Chapter 9

Conclusions

Christopher Gan*,§, Gilbert V. Nartea†,¶ and Judy Li Xia‡,‖

*Professor in Accounting and Finance,
Faculty of Agribusiness and Commerce,
Department of Financial and Business System,
PO Box 85084, Lincoln University, Christchurch, New Zealand

†Associate Professor, Chairperson, Department of Finance,
Waikato Management School, University of Waikato,
Private Bag 3105, Hamilton 3240, New Zealand

‡Lecturer, New Zealand College of Business,
149-151 Hereford Street, PO Box 6064,
Upper Riccarton, Chirstchurch

§Christopher.Gan@lincoln.ac.nz
¶narteag@waikato.ac.nz
‖Judy.Li@lincolnuni.ac.nz

Abstract

Credit is scarce and capital does not flow naturally from the rich to the poor. The poor have low access to bank credit because of the lack of collateral and because traditional financial institutions find it costly to deal with small credit transactions. Microfinance largely facilitates the poor's access to institutional credit and has both economic and non-economic impacts including poverty alleviation, women empowerment, and promotion of gender equality. However, microfinance is not a panacea for poverty alleviation and credit remains inaccessible to certain sectors of society especially the poorest of the poor. To benefit greater segments of society, microfinance should be part of a broader strategy that combines it with other social protection programs.

Keywords: Microfinance, credit, credit accessibility, poverty, empowerment.

Despite the importance of financial services in helping the poor to improve their living conditions, poor people are excluded from the formal financial system and such exclusion ranges from partial exclusion in developed countries to full or nearly full exclusion in less developed countries (LDCs) (Brau & Woller, 2004). Traditional financial institutions (FIs) are reluctant to serve the poor mainly because poor people fail to meet the selection criteria such as the requirement of physical collateral set by FIs. The perceived high risks and costs arising from processing and servicing unsecured small loans also make FIs shy away from financing the poor, mainly due to the concern of financial viability. Lacking access to formal credit, most poor and low-income people continue to rely on meagre self-finance or informal credit, which limit their ability to actively participate in and benefit from the development process (Li, 2010).

Credit is a scarce resource by its nature and the availability of credit differs among borrowers due to risk assessment by lenders. Stiglitz and Weiss (1981) introduce the credit rationing theory based on two main assumptions: (i) lenders cannot differentiate degrees of risk associated with safe and risky borrowers and (ii) loans are subject to the limited liability of borrowers to repay loans at the end of the investment period (i.e., if the project returns are less than the debt obligations, the borrower bears no responsibility to pay out of pocket). Because of the presence of asymmetric information, lenders judge borrowers' creditworthiness based on the available information before and after a loan is offered. The imperfect information creates at least two types of problems in microfinance — adverse selection and moral hazard. The adverse selection problem arises in the screening process where transaction costs involve differentiating between good and bad borrowers as reflected in the cost of borrowing, that is, interest rate. Increasing the interest rate to compensate for high transaction cost in small loans may drive out good borrowers from the pool of borrowers, hence, only bad borrowers with high-risk projects are able to borrow but not the target group. The moral hazard relates to the monitoring and enforcement mechanism where the borrowers may not make every effort to repay after receiving the loan since they know their lenders are sharing part of the risk (Pham & Lensink, 2007). In general, lenders decide whether credit is granted and how much is granted based on a set of information that they obtain, i.e., not all borrowers will receive the credit they apply for. This credit rationing leads to a problematic situation wherein households and small-scale enterprises face credit constraints regardless of their repayment capability (Aghion & Morduch, 2005).

Capital does not naturally flow from the rich to the poor in rural credit markets, particularly rural credit markets in developing countries because of market imperfection and asymmetric information (Aghion & Morduch, 2005; Stiglitz & Weiss, 1981). Risk assessment of borrowers defines credit accessibility which, in turn, is determined by adverse selection and moral hazard behaviours. Given their limited credit worthiness (for example as evidenced by lack of collateral), the poor can hardly borrow from formal credit institutions in the rural credit market. Some sectors advocate government intervention in terms of public policies that can correct market malfunctions, thereby expanding credit outreach; however, these policies if they stand alone cannot assure a better solution for the rural credit market. Pro-poor policies, starting with implementing microfinance programmes, face a trade-off between profit maximisation and government subsidy, and with third party's incentives in the lending practice (Adams & Vogel, 1986). Profit maximisation and third party's incentives help explain inaccessibility to microfinance programmes. The interlinked relationship of different parties in the rural credit market is embraced by different economic theories but a theory that is sufficiently robust to justify the existence of a rural credit market and for it to work efficiently towards the goal of poverty reduction and rural development needs to be evolved.

The poor face two main problems related to accessibility to bank credit (Beck & Demirgüç-Kunt, 2008). First, poor households have no collateral and they are not able to borrow against their future income.

Second, FIs find it costly to deal with small credit transactions, such as microloans. Without any external support, the rural poor can never gain access to microloans. Hence, they seek alternative sources of credit. The development of microfinance is perceived as a strategic tool to provide credit accessibility to the poor. Although government intervention in the rural credit market is controversial, this external support to the poor is widely accepted because it can overcome the rural credit market's failures (Phan, 2012). Aghion & Morduch (2005) provide a number of reasons for the government to intervene to expand credit access to rural households. However, most rural credit markets have been governed in one way or another towards delivering credit for the rural sector. Consequently, a large proportion of rural households have been excluded from the formal credit market. The collateral requirement imposed on farming households when they apply for loans to finance agricultural production raises concerns about their ability to access formal credit. When it comes to rural lending practices, Pham & Lensink (2007) indicate various strategies employed by different lenders to avoid adverse selection and moral hazard problems. For example, in the adverse selection problem, formal credit providers tend to associate the probability of default with contract-related items, such as interest rate and loan repayment, as a part of the client's previous credit history. In the moral hazard problem, informal lenders tend to link default risk to household related characteristics, particularly the presence of the lender–borrower relationship and social norms. As a result, there is always a proportion of rural households that are unable to obtain credit. To fulfil credit demand, rural households have to seek informal sources of credit at higher interest rates to support their production and consumption. This informal debt is believed to marginalise household income and likely leads the borrower into a cycle of debt and poverty. This market failure is eminent in many developing countries where the rural financial market is not functioning well (Phan, 2012; Musinguzi & Smith, 2000).

Hermes & Lensink (2011) argued that access to finance may contribute to a long-lasting increase in income by means of a rise in investments in income-generating activities and to a possible diversification of sources of income for low-income groups particularly rural households. Microfinance enables rural households to accumulate assets, smooth consumption in time of economic shocks, reduce the vulnerability due to illness, drought and crop failures, and better education, health and housing of the borrower's household. For rural households, improving microfinance accessibility can start from the household themselves by actively participating in a credit group. The poor, in this case, are physically poor due to capital constraints; they have insufficient land and working capital to generate a sufficient income level for a living. Given that pre-condition, microfinance shows its positive impact on the target household (Phan, 2012). However, it is difficult for the extremely poor to benefit from microfinance because they need pre-support (e.g., special aids, community support) to overcome internal rationing. Extremely poor people like people suffering from under and/or malnourishment, illnesses, lack of skills, etc., cannot be a target of microfinance that aims to provide small credit for income-generating activities. In this case, intervention in the form of microfinance will not be an efficient solution; instead a mixture of welfare and a microfinance programme is required for this target group. Microfinance should always be seen as the next step after they (the poor) are able to work (Gibbons *et al.*, 2000; Seibel, 1989).

The primary goal of a microfinance programme is to provide credit to the poor by extending small collateral free loans that purposely enable the borrowers to actively generate a range of improvements in their economic condition (World Bank, 2010). Islam (2007) hypothesised that microfinance can create a circle of growth for poor borrowers in that 'low income households need credit for investment to create more income and more credit and more income'. In other words, microfinance enhances income growth, which increases a household's consumption level, hence, contributes to an immediate welfare improvement. For example, an enhanced income from borrowing encourages the poor to increase investment in working capital as well as physical assets. Capital and physical asset accumulation attributed to microfinance reinforces the income-generating capabilities of borrowers (Aghion & Morduch, 2005; Hossain & Diaz, 1997). Hulme (2000) further illustrates that a conventional microfinance programme provides microcredit that lead to changes in household income, which leads to changes in economic security, education and work skills. Ultimately, these changes lead to a modification in household welfare and social political relations and structures. Thus, providing loans through microfinance programmes is a tool to create a desired impact on the target group of poor and low-income households. For example, households with higher annual income have higher probability of accessing microfinance because they tend to have more investment opportunities, leading to stronger potential need of credit support. Higher income households are more inclined to access credit because they are more capable to repay loans than low-income households (Li, 2010).

As a special form of financial service, characterised as small-scale lending, microfinance largely facilitates the poor's access to institutional credit by removing obstacles in traditional lending. Improved access to credit at reasonable cost enables the poor to smooth consumption (food and non-food), better cope with crises, develop self-employed businesses, enhance income earning capacity and build up assets gradually. The poor can use the generated income to pay for the instalment of loans while leaving their original capital intact. Consequently, their capital base usually increases in large amounts as they borrow continuously, which gives them opportunities to make medium and long-term investments. Therefore, microfinance borrowers are likely to sustain long-term development by participating in entrepreneurial activities and as a result, shake off poverty with economic growth.

Microfinance has impacted the poor in various aspects via improving their accessibility to credit, and such impacts can either be economic or non-economic, which are also referred to as social impacts (World Bank, 2006). By extending small collateral free loans to underprivileged people at affordable costs, microfinance enables its borrowers to actively take up job-creating activities which generate a range of improvements in their economic conditions. Islam (2007) notes that microfinance can positively impact the poor's welfare in terms of income, employment, assets/capital accumulation, and productivity. According to Islam (2007, p. 101), microfinance can create a 'virtuous circle' for poor borrowers: low income, credit, investment, more income, more credit, more investment and more income. The continued growth in income will then push up the total consumption levels of the households, which constitutes an immediate welfare result from borrowing from microfinance programmes. In addition, enhanced income from borrowing encourages the poor to increase investment in working capital (for example, raw materials, seeds and fertilisers) and assets (physical, such as machinery and financial such as cash savings).

As the microfinance loan is repaid in small instalments at relatively short intervals (usually one week), it is easy for a borrower to pay the instalment from their income, while leaving the original capital untouched (Aghion & Morduch, 2005; Hossain & Diaz, 1997). Capital/asset accumulation, which is a long-lived welfare effect brought about by microfinance, in turn reinforces the income-generating capabilities of borrowers (Islam, 2007).

Microfinance has been universally accepted as an efficient tool for fighting poverty due to its positive impact on the poor households' economic well-being such as increasing income/consumption levels and creating employment opportunities. In addition, microfinance has the potential to empower the poor, women in particular, which reflects the social impact of microfinance. Microfinance generally targets poor women who are the most marginalised group among the poor in many developing countries, being both economically and socially disadvantaged (Ang, 2004). The rationale for lending to women also relates to the fact that women are a better credit risk and have a greater tendency to use increased earnings to improve their family's well-being, compared to male borrowers (Ang, 2004; Mourji, 2000).

In addition to working as a powerful instrument in fighting against poverty, microfinance has the potential to promote gender equality by directly empowering poor women. Since microfinance programmes have generally targeted poor women as clients, access to microfinance can empower poor women by increasing their contribution to household income and asset building, which is a significant contributor toward their increased self-worth and improved family status. As a consequence of participating in microfinance programmes, women borrowers become more financially independent, more likely to participate in social networks and commercialisation processes, and able to better confront systemic gender inequities (Li, 2010). A regional study by the World Bank (2006) reveals that 90% of women borrowers from Self-Help Groups (SHGs) in India can freely visit local markets and make small and large purchases independently, while 68% of women borrowers in Nepal can make independent decisions on property, children's education and marriage.

Osmani (2007) described how poor women can be empowered through participation in microfinance programmes. First, microfinance enables poor women to earn an independent income and contribute financially to their families, which immediately raises their self-esteem as well as their esteem in the eyes of others. This is supposed to give women greater power within the household. Second, women will free themselves from the narrow confines of household precincts and move into a wider world in the process of taking out loans and using loans to initiate income-generating activities. The exposure to the outside world, together with the formation of networks with other women in the community, is expected to help women foster self-confidence and courage so as to exercise more power both within and outside households. Women's empowerment can be manifested in various dimensions, such as increased decision making, a more equitable status of women in the family and community, and being more active and mobile in participating in social networks.

Accessing microfinance also allows poor borrowers to enjoy some privileges such as accessing education and healthcare, which otherwise would be impossible for them if there is no microfinance. Due to the great potential of reducing poverty and empowering women, microfinance has been promoted as an effective development intervention programme by many countries and has become one of the key driving mechanisms towards meeting the Millennium Development Goals (MDGs) set by the United Nations (UN). The MDGs range from halving extreme poverty to halting the spread of HIV/AIDS and providing universal primary education by the target date of 2015 (UN Millennium Project, 2005). The importance of microfinance is further underscored by the designation of 2005 as the International Year of Microfinance by the UN, which called for global attention to build up a sustainable microfinance industry to serve the poor.

According to Basher (2007, p. 1), microfinance functions as a catalyst in transforming its participants' from a "passive credit recipient to a well responsive and active agent in economic and non-economic aspects of life". Because of the potential to reduce poverty and empower women, microfinance plays a major role in many countries' gender and development strategies.

While microfinance significantly contributes to alleviating poverty, it is not a panacea for poverty reduction. It may be less successful, or even counter-productive in helping the poorest of the poor raise their living standards because the worse-off borrowers use loans less effectively than the better-off borrowers due to the relatively weaker economic base of the former. Islam (2007) found that microfinance borrowers who are extremely poor experienced a further deterioration rather than improving their situation. Islam (2007) noted that those who experience further deterioration are either trapped in previous debts from informal lenders so that they could not use microfinance loans for productive purposes; or for any natural calamity or illness, or sudden incidents such as theft or death of livestock purchased with microfinance loans. Likewise, MacIsaac (1997) observes that microfinance is less effective, or even counter-productive, in helping the poorest of the poor to raise their living standards. This may be because the worse-off borrowers use the loans only for consumption or invest in less risky (and generally less remunerative) activities compared to the better-off borrowers who tend to invest in riskier and more productive ventures including technological improvements, which provide opportunities for generating a greater income to improve their living standards.

Mohamed (2003) also revealed that the cumbersome lending procedures and rigid conditions set by the rural FIs have restrained the rural households from accessing formal credit to a larger extent. This view is supported by Atieno (2001) who observed that lending terms and conditions reflected in collateral, application procedures and repayment schedules have considerably restrained the poor in Kenya from accessing formal credit and, in turn, forced the poor to find alternatives such as informal credit. Similarly, an empirical study by Umoh (2006) also revealed that inadequate collateral security, difficult loan-processing procedures and high interest rates are three major obstacles in obtaining formal credit by microentrepreneurs in Nigeria.

Microfinance cannot ultimately reduce poverty by itself, and it will be more effective when combined with other financial interventions such as savings and insurance (Islam, 2007; MacIsaac, 1997). For example, Islam (2007) emphasises that accessibility to reliable and monetised saving facilities can improve the economic security of the extremely poor and it is only when they acquire some economic security that accessibility to credit can help lift them out of poverty by increasing the productivity of their businesses or creating new sources of livelihood. Khandker (1998) suggests that the ultra-poor need initial help provided by public work programmes to get over the food, health or labour market thresholds before they can respond to the positive changes brought by any financial programmes.

Therefore, microfinance should be involved as a part of broader poverty eradication strategy combining with other intervention programmes such as social protection programmes (Chowdhury, 2004). In addition, microfinance remains inaccessible to the poorest of the poor because microfinance institutions intend to protect their self-sustainability at the expense of larger scale of poverty reduction (Druschel, 2002).

References

Adams, D. W. & Vogel, R. C. (1986). Rural financial markets in low-income countries: Recent controversies and lessons. *World Development*, 14(4), 477–487.

Aghion, B. A. & Morduch, J. (2005). *The Economics of Microfinance*. Cambridge, Mass: MIT Press.

Ang, M. H. (2004). Empowering the poor through microcredit. *Entrepreneurship and Innovation Management*, 4(5), 485–494.

Atieno, R. (2001). *Formal and Informal Institutions' Lending Policies and Access to Credit by Small-scale Enterprises in Kenya: An Empirical Assessment.* Nairobi, Kenya: The African Economic Research Consortium.

Basher, A. (2007). Empowerment of microcredit participants and its spillover effects: Evidence from the Grameen Bank of Bangladesh. *Journal of Developing Areas*, 40(2), 173–183.

Beck, T. & Demirgüç-Kunt, A. (2008). Access to finance: An unfinished agenda. *The World Bank Economic Review*, 22(3), 386–396.

Brau, J. C. & Woller, G. M. (2004). Microfinance: A comprehensive review of the existing literature. *Journal of Entrepreneurial Finance and Business Ventures*, 9, 1–26.

Chowdhury, A. K. (2004). Implementation of the first United Nations Decade for the Eradication of Poverty (1997–2006). Statement in the Second Committee of the 59th Session of the United Nations General Assembly. Retrieved from http://www.un.org/special-rep/ohrlls/ohrlls/UNGA59/HR's%20state-ment%2015%20Nov%2004-item89a-Eradication%20of%20Poverty.pdf.

Druschel, K. (2002). Microfinance in China: Building Sustainable Institutions and a Strong Industry. Master's thesis, School of International Service,

American University, 2002. Retrieved from www.american.edu/sis/idp/resources/Druschel%20SRP.pdf. Accessed on August 16, 2007.

Gibbons, D., Quiñones, B., Remenyi, J. & Seibel, H. D. (2000). *Microfinance for and by the Poor: Lessons from Experience. Microfinance and Poverty Alleviation: Case Studies from Asia and the Pacific.* London and New York: Pinter, pp. 253–269.

Hermes, N. & Lensink, R. (2011), Microfinance: Its impact, outreach, and sustainability. *World Development*, 39(6), 875–881. dx.doi.org/10.1016/j.worlddev.2009.10.021

Hossain, M. & Diaz, C. P. (1997). Reaching the Poor with Effective Micro Credit: Evaluation of a Grameen Bank Replication in the Philippines. *Journal of Philippine Development*, XXIV(2), 275–308.

Hulme, D. (2000). Impact assessment methodologies for microfinance: Theory, experience and better practice. *World Development*, 28(1), 79–98.

Islam, T. (2007). *Microcredit and Poverty Alleviation.* Aldershot, England; Burlington, U.S.A.: Ashgate Publishing.

Khandker, S. R. (1998). *Fighting Poverty with Microcredit: Experience in Bangladesh.* New York, U.S.: Oxford University Press.

Maclsaac, N. (1997). The Role of Microcredit in Poverty Reduction and Promoting Gender Equity. Discussion paper, Canadian International Development Agency, Quebec, Canada.

Mohamed, K. (2003). Access to Formal and Quasi-formal Credit by Smallholder Farmers and Artisanal Fishermen: A case of Zanzibar, Research Report No. 03.6. Dar es Salaam, Tanzania: Research on Poverty Alleviation (REPOA).

Mourji, F. (2000). Impact Study of the Zakoura Microcredit Program. Microfinance Gateway. Retrieved from http://www.microfinancegateway.org/p/site/m//template.rc/1.9.25435.

Musinguzi, P. & Smith, P. (2000). Saving and Borrowing in Rural Uganda. Southampton, UK, University of Southampton, Discussion Papers in Economics and Econometrics, 0016, p. 20.

Osmani, L. N. K. (2007). A breakthrough in women's bargaining power: the impact of microcredit. *Journal of International Development*, 19(5), 695–716, doi: 10.1002/jid.1356

Pham, T. T. T. & Lensink, R. (2007). Lending policies of informal, formal and semiformal lenders. *Economics of Transition*, 15(2), 181–209.

Phan, D. K. (2012). Microcredit: the Rural Credit Market in the Mekong River Delta, Vietnam. Unpublished PhD Thesis, Faculty of Commerce, Department of Accounting, Economic and Finance, Lincoln University, Christchurch, New Zealand, p. 230.

Seibel, H. D. (1989). *Finance with the Poor, by the Poor, for the Poor. Financial Technologies for the Informal Sector, with Case Studies from Indonesia. Social Strategies* 3/2. Basel: University.

Stiglitz, J. E. & Weiss, A. (1981). Credit rationing in markets with imperfect information. *The American Economic Review*, 71(3), 393–410.

Umoh, G. S. (2006). Empirical investigation of access to micro-credit in an emerging economy: Evidence from Nigeria. *Journal of African Business*, 7(1/2), 89–117.

UN Millennium Project (2005). *Investing in Development: A Practical Plan to Achieve the Millennium Development Goals: Overview*. Washington, D.C: Communications Development Inc.

World Bank (2006). *Microfinance in South Asia: Toward Financial Inclusion for the Poor*. Washington D.C., U.S.: Pangraphics.

World Bank (2010) Access to Finance for the Poor. CGAP Annual Report 2010.

Chapter 10

Accessibility and Impact of Rural Credit Cooperatives Microcredit Programmes to Rural Households: A Case Study from Hubei Province, China

Mohamad D. Revindo*,‡ and Christopher Gan†,§

*PhD Candidate, Faculty of Agribusiness and Commerce,
Department of Financial and Business System,
PO Box 85084, Lincoln University, Canterbury, New Zealand

†Professor in Accounting and Finance, Faculty of Agribusiness
and Commerce, Department of Financial and Business System,
PO Box 85084, Lincoln University, Christchurch, New Zealand

‡Mohamad.Revindo@lincolnuni.ac.nz
§Christopher.Gan@lincoln.ac.nz

Abstract

Microcredit programme was introduced in China in 1994 to ameliorate rural poverty in a financially sustainable way. Since the year 2000, microcredit programmes have been mostly carried out by Rural Credit Cooperatives (RCCs) that have successfully expanded the financial access to farmers and at the same time achieved high timely repayment

319

rate. This chapter draws the case of RCCs' microcredit in Hubei Province and looks at whether the implementation of RCCs' microcredit is an effective instrument to improve the rural households' welfare and whether it actually reaches the poorest population in rural areas. The evidence show that poor rural households are still constrained to access the microcredit due to some household-related factors as well as obstacles at RCCs' institutional level. The RCCs' microcredit marginally improve borrowers' welfare and the positive impact on welfare only takes effect as the cumulative amount of loan grows. RCCs' microcredit also enables women in rural China to have better social status which is manifested in several dimensions of women empowerment.

Keywords: Microcredit, accessibility, welfare impact, women empowerment, rural credit cooperatives, rural households, China.

10.1 Introduction

Rural farmers in China have been constrained from acquiring formal credit not only because of the risky nature of agriculture business and their small-scale farms, but also because China implements a village-based communal land-tenure system in which the farmers are not entitled to the land on which they farm and thereby they cannot collateralise the land in the formal financial institutions (Lin & Zhang, 1998). The limited access to formal credit has forced the rural households to resort to informal borrowings that charge higher interest rate (Linton, 2007) and hindered them from production expansion and improvement in their living standards, which in turn hampered economic growth and poverty alleviation in rural China (Cheng & Xu, 2004; Park, Ren & Wang, 2004).

To tackle this problem, the Chinese government initially introduced subsidised-loan programme in 1986 that aimed to ease the loan's interest rate burden borne by the poor. This programme successfully promoted overall regional economic development but failed to reach the poor and was not financially sustainable due to high default rates (Heilig *et al.*, 2006; Park & Ren, 2001). To bridge the gap in credit access for poor rural households, in the mid-1990s the Chinese government launched microcredit programme aimed to ameliorate rural poverty in a financially sustainable way (Park *et al.*, 2004). The microcredit programme was initially carried out by NGOs or quasi-official institutions (1994–1996), expanded by government agencies and policy banks (1996–2000) and by Rural Credit Cooperatives (RCCs) (year 2000 onwards) (Li, 2010). Characterised by flexible lending scheme, RCCs microcredit has expanded the financial access to farmers and at the same time achieved high timely repayment rate. In early 2010, there were 33,000 RCCs throughout China and the RCCs' microcredit had been accessed by 82.42 million rural households, equivalent to 33.5% of all rural households (Han, 2004; Lucock, 2014; Zhang & Loubere, 2015).

At the implementation level, however, questions remain on whether the microcredit programme has actually reached the poorest population and whether it is an effective instrument to improve the rural households' welfare. Few attempts have been made to test the welfare impact of microcredit in China, with the exception of Park & Ren (2001) & Li, Rozelle & Zhang (2004). Evidence show that large numbers of poor farmers still do not have access to microcredit because they are regarded as marginalised people in their villages due to their weak social connections and economic conditions. In addition, women in rural China are still disadvantaged in accessing any form of formal credit including microcredit and on some occasions they have to use their husbands' names to apply for microcredit loans (Dyar *et al.*, 2006; Han, 2004; Unger, 2002).

This chapter discusses a case of microcredit services provided by RCCs for rural households in Hubei, the largest agricultural province in China, based on the studies by Li (2010), Li, Gan & Hu (2011a, 2011b, 2011c). The first section discusses the accessibility of microcredit for the rural households. The next two sections discuss the microcredit impacts on the rural households' welfare and women empowerment, respectively.

10.2 Accessibility to RCCs' Microcredit Services

Li *et al.* (2011a) examined the microcredit accessibility from the demand side (households) by using observations on household borrowings as follow: households who have secured microloans and those who have never secured microloans from RCCs. They used a logit model to estimate how the probability of a household successfully secures microcredit is influenced by household-related factors. They identified 12 factors that significantly affect the accessibility of RCCs' microcredit (see Table 10.1).

Table 10.1: Factors Significantly Influencing Household Accessibility to Microcredit

Household factors	Expected sign	Estimated marginal effect
Household size	(+/−)	−0.0236
Household income	(+/−)	0.0012
Household head's engagement in self-run business	(+)	0.0547
Economic dependency ratio	(−)	0.0558
Value of household assets	(+/−)	−0.0064
Household savings with RCC	(+)	−0.1895
Household attitude towards debt	(−)	−0.1676
Alternatives/access to other sources of credit	(−)	−0.1002
Household member working in village or township committee	(+)	0.0724
Household's share in RCC	(+)	−0.1544
Dwelling place's distance to RCC office	(−)	−0.2495
Educational attainment of household head (secondary school)	(+)	0.1797

Source: Li *et al.* (2011a); Li (2010).

Four household-related factors positively affect microcredit accessibility including household income, household head's engagement in self-run business, the educational attainment of household head and household member working in village or township committee.

Households with higher annual income have higher probability of accessing RCC microcredit. One possible reason is that high income households tend to have more investment opportunities, leading to stronger potential need for credit support. High-income households may also be more confident in repaying loans that they borrow (Okurut, 2006). The probability of borrowing from RCC microcredit programmes would increase by 0.12% on average with every RMB1,000 increase in household income.

The probability of accessing microcredit increases when households become involved in self-employed businesses apart from agriculture production because investing in self-run enterprises requires additional capital. The probability of being a microcredit borrower would increase by 5.47% when the household is engaged in self-employment.

Households with members working as village or township officials may have greater need of credit for off-farm investment or may access microcredit easier due to their good relationship with local financial institutions such as RCCs. Having household members working as local officials increases the probability of accessing microcredit by 7.24%.

The estimated result for household heads' education, however, should be interpreted with caution. Li *et al.* (2011a) used three categorical variables to represent education: no education (as the base variable), secondary school and post-secondary school. Only the coefficient of secondary school is significant where the probability of microcredit accession of secondary school graduates' household heads are 17% higher than those with no education. However, the accession probability of household heads with post-secondary school is not different to those with no education. While non-educated household heads were less able to secure the credit than the educated ones (secondary school graduates), the most educated ones (post-secondary school graduates) may not need the microcredit services in the first place (Vaessen, 2001).

Li *et al.* (2011a) also found five household-related factors that negatively affect microcredit accessibility, including household size, value of household assets, household attitude towards debt, alternatives or access to other sources of credit and dwelling place's distance to local RCCs' office.

Larger households are less likely to borrow from RCCs. They may have lower repayment capacity resulting from the smaller future expected income per capita, which lowers the probability of borrowing (Okurut, 2006).

Households' accessibility to microcredit decreases as the total value of the household assets increases. Assets correspond to a household's initial capital thereby households with higher asset values may be less budget constrained and therefore less likely to access microcredit. An additional RMB1,000 increase in household assets is estimated to reduce the household's probability of accessing RCCs' microcredit by 0.64%.

An adverse attitude towards having debt decreases the likelihood of accessing any type of credit by the households, including microcredit. The probability of accessing microcredit would decrease by 16.76% when the household holds a negative attitude towards debt.

Households that have access to other sources of credit are also less likely to access microcredit than those with no alternatives. The availability of other credit sources (such as informal credit) tends to reduce the probability of borrowing from RCC microcredit programme. This finding is consistent with Vaessen (2001) who observed that many poor households are more willing to use informal credit owing to low transaction costs and flexible loan contracts.

Likewise, microcredit accessibility is negatively affected by the distance between household dwelling-place and RCCs' offices. Holding other factors constant, the households residing more than 20 *lis* away from RCC branches have 24.95% lower probability of accessing RCC microcredit compared to those who live within 10 *lis* of RCC branches.[1] This is mainly due to the perceived high borrowing costs arising from the travelling expenses and opportunity costs of time.

However, Li *et al.* (2011a) reported three other household-related factors which estimated signs contradict previous studies, including economic dependency ratio, household savings with RCC and household's share in RCC.

Economic dependency ratio measures the ratio of household members without income to household income earners (Husain, 1998). The households who are less economically active are found to have higher probability of being engaged in RCCs' microcredit programme. One possible explanation is that households with higher dependency ratios have fewer family members taking up income-generating activities and therefore are more inclined to rely on loans (including RCCs' microcredit) for household activities such as consumption and children's education.

The inverse relationship between household savings with RCCs and credit accessibility suggests that households who deposit money with RCCs have lower probability to access RCC's microcredit. This is possible since these households may prefer to use their savings in RCCs when

---

[1] One *li* equals to half-kilometre (500 metres or 1,640 feet).

they need financial support, which in turn weakens the likelihood of borrowing microloans from RCCs.[2]

Finally, the households who bought shares in a RCC are likely to have surplus money in their own control, which reduces their intentions to borrow. This might account for the negative relationship between household's share in RCCs and households' access to RCCs' microcredit.

Li *et al.* (2011a) also reported that other variables such as age and gender of the household head, geographic location of the village where households are dwelling (mountainous or low lying area) and farm size do not have significant effects on households' access to microcredit.

However, Li (2010) found that many rural households never attempted to borrow from RCCs because they had no knowledge about the microcredit programme operated by RCCs. The unawareness of the microcredit programme are mainly caused by the lack of understanding of 'microcredit' concept, inadequate promotion of the microcredit programme by RCCs and the unawareness of the RCC branches nearby.

Some rural households did not apply for microcredit simply because they had no need to borrow money during a certain period. Some other households decided not to apply for RCC microcredit when they need to borrow because: (1) their meagre income is not sufficient to repay the loans, (2) the interest rate charged by RCCs is too high, (3) prefer informal loans over RCC microcredit because the former can be easily obtained, (4) complicated application procedure adopted by RCCs in terms of documentation requirements and processing time, (5) the lack of proper collateral and (6) poor credit records (Li, 2010).

Li (2010) also reported that many rural households who signalled credit needs had actually applied for microcredit from RCCs but were not granted the loan. As a result, some households had resorted to either other formal lenders (e.g., Agricultural Bank of China) or informal lenders (e.g., friends, relatives). The perceived major reasons for microcredit applications rejection include: (1) the loan officers from RCC branches perceived the households as risky in repaying loans due to low household

---

[2]Savings in RCCs are not compulsory to collateralise the microloans issued. Instead, households can deposit money voluntarily and access savings freely.

income, (2) inadequate collateral or the inability to find loan guarantors, (3) creditworthiness, such as the poor credit history due to the previous loan defaults and (4) the difficulty in meeting the required documents by the RCC loan officers (Li, 2010).

In short, households' access to microcredit are attributed to both credit supply and demand factors. Microcredit access can be limited due to the low or zero credit needs of the households. Household income and availability of alternative credit sources (e.g., informal credit) significantly influence the households' borrowing decisions, and consequently, influence their access to microcredit. On the other hand, institutional-level factors such as interest rate, documentation requirements and loan-processing time can potentially harm the households' access to microcredit: leading to either loan rejection or reluctance to apply. This is consistent with Umoh (2006) and Atieno (2001) findings who note that the access problem is also created by the lending policies of financial institutions. In addition, there is an imperative for RCCs to enhance promotion of their microcredit programmes among the rural households and make the households fully aware of the features of microcredit (e.g., collateral free) to improve the access to microcredit by rural households.

10.3 Impacts of RCCs' Microcredit on Households' Welfare

Chinese microcredit programmes have been implemented on the assumption that microcredit is an effective tool to mitigate rural poverty similar to those in Bangladesh and Indonesia (Sun, 2003). However, Li *et al.* (2011c) studied whether RCCs' microcredit actually affects households' welfare by examining the change in borrowers' household annual income (HAI) or annual consumption (HAC) between 2002 (i.e., before RCCs' microcredit programme implementation) and 2008 (post-programme period).

Difference-in-difference method is used to observe the differences between borrowing and non-borrowing households. A set of household characteristics is controlled including age of household head, number of school-age children, household size and number of income earners in the household. The fixed effects method is adopted to control for the households' unobserved heterogeneities that affects both household's participation in the programme (or receipt of credit) and the welfare outcome investigated (i.e., selection bias).

The study found no significant impact of programme participation on the improvement of either welfare indicator (HAI or HAC). However, different results were obtained when the involvement in RCCs' microcredit programme was measured by the cumulative loan amounts borrowed by the households. The cumulative borrowing of microcredit provided by RCCs is found to have a positive and significant impact on the household welfare outcomes. On average an additional RMB1,000 in microcredit borrowing raises a HAI by 0.29% and HAC by 0.23%. Since the average total loan amount borrowed by the borrowing households in the sample is RMB44,012, the results imply that, on average, the borrowing households increase their annual income and consumption by approximately 12.76% and 10.12%, respectively, compared to the non-borrowing households. Thus, the households will benefit more as they become more involved in the programme (signified by the growing loan size). These findings are consistent with Cuong *et al.* (2007) and Pitt & Khandker (1998) who reported positive and significant relationships between the loan size and a set of household outcomes measured in income and consumption.

Although the impact of microcredit on welfare is pronounced from the statistical perspective, the magnitudes of the impact are not significant in economic sense (0.0029 in income and 0.0023 in consumption). The small values of welfare impact suggest marginal or economically insignificant effect of microcredit on the real levels of rural households' income and consumption (Niño-Zarazúa, 2007).

Moreover, it is difficult to examine whether RCC microcredit's positive impacts actually enable poor households in China to escape from poverty, mainly because the RCC microcredit programme does not primarily focus on the poor population alone. Li *et al.* (2011c) reported that a large proportion of the borrowing households were not categorically poor before they participated in the microcredit programme. Using the national low poverty line, the poor in the sample in 2002 accounted for only 0.3% of the borrowing households compared to 6.3% for the non-borrowing households.[3] Hence, the fact that no borrowing household in the sample were classified as poor anymore in 2008 (post-programme

---

[3]For the details of the construction of national poverty and income lines, see National Bureau of Statistics of China (2004).

period) compared to 2.1% of those in non-borrowing households did not give sufficient evidence of poverty alleviation impact.

Likewise, when classified by the national low-income line, in 2002 only 1.8% of the borrowing households in the sample were poor compared to 8.4% of the non-borrowing households.[4] Hence, although in the post-programme period (i.e., 2008) the poverty incidence across the sample showed no household in the borrowing group was classified as poor anymore compared to 5.2% poor households in non-borrowing group, no sufficient evidence of poverty alleviation impact can be detected.

There are at least two main reasons why the RCCs' microcredit programme does not explicitly target the poor population. First, the main goal of the RCCs' microcredit programme is to facilitate the credit accessibility for rural households as required by the People's Bank of China. There is no specific client target requirement for the RCCs and hence the microcredits can be granted to any household who is registered as rural residents who engaged in land farming or other agriculture-related business (The People's Bank of China, 2001). Unlike the microcredit programmes provided by NGOs or government agencies, which are specifically designed to reduce poverty by providing loans to the poor only, the RCCs' microcredit programmes have been carried out to increase the provision of credit services in rural areas and their participants are traditionally rural middle-income households (Druschel, 2002; Du, 2004, 2005; Sun, 2003).

Second, RCCs are formal financial institutions that assume sole responsibility for the profits and losses. To ensure the financial viability of the microcredit programme, RCCs emphasise loan repayment performance and are thereby likely to exclude poor households, who may neither be able to use credit effectively nor repay loans punctually, from participating in the microcredit programme (Cheng, 2007; Du, 2005). While previous microcredit programmes provided by NGOs and government agencies paid more attention to poverty alleviation and social development, the RCCs' microcredit programme instead focuses on business sustainability and risk management (Du, 2005).

---

[4]*Ibid.*

10.4 Impact of RCCs' Microcredit on Women Empowerment

The social status of Chinese women has improved greatly in the past two decades. However, gender inequality still exists in almost all social aspects including political power, education, health, employment and asset possession. The gender inequality problem is far more prevalent in rural, poverty-stricken areas where women usually lack sources of income (Dyar *et al.*, 2006). In addition, patriarchy still prevails in Chinese rural families where women continue to be relatively disadvantaged in matters of survival, health, nutrition, literacy and productivity (Jie & Kanji, 2003). Therefore, microcredit is expected to contribute to the empowerment of rural women in China by enabling them to be financially independent.

Li *et al.* (2011b) studied how microcredit affects five dimensions of women empowerment in rural China: control over financial assets, mobility, purchase making ability, involvement in decision making and freedom/legal awareness. They used logit model to examine how the state of empowerment (empowered and not empowered) is influenced by microcredit participation by controlling for households' socio-economic features, women's personal characteristics and village factors. In order to include the control group (non-borrower) and incorporate the cumulative effect of loan at the same time, they used categorical variable to denote four possible cumulative loan that the woman has borrowed from RCCs including no loan (non-borrowers), borrower for amount of RMB30,000 or less, RMB30,000–60,000, and RMB60,000 or more. They reported that microcredit has a positive and significant impact on various dimensions of women empowerment in rural China, which is consistent to the findings reported by Hashemi, Schuler & Riley (1996), Zaman (1999) and Pitt, Khandker & Cartwright (2003).

The use of microcredit enables women to have a greater control over their own financial resources and assets such as income and savings. In the literature women's control over financial assets is referred as one form of economic empowerment and the economic empowerment is the foundation for other dimensions of women empowerment (e.g., social and political empowerment) (Ansoglenang, 2006; Mayoux, 2002; Zaman, 1999).

Microcredit borrowing also strengthens women's family standing reflected by their greater role in the family decision-making process.

Six indicators of women's involvement in family decision making are positively and significantly influenced by the microcredit borrowing including involvement in deciding farmland lease, children's education, types of livestock and farming machineries to purchase, types of consumer durables to buy and joint decisions on opening saving accounts at banks. However, the RCCs' microcredit borrowing has no significant impact on women's involvement in the decision making regarding house repair/construction, types of crops to grow and decision to have a child.

The RCCs' microcredit also influences the mobility of women. The probability of going to the city alone is greater for the women borrowers than that of the non-borrowers. For example, women with cumulative loans between RMB30,000 and RMB60,000 and greater than RMB60,000 are 27% and 29% more likely to go to city alone than the non-borrowers, respectively. However, the chance of visiting parents' home without asking for husband's consent is not statistically different for the women who are borrowers and non-borrowers.

Participation in microcredit programmes also augments women's autonomy in making purchase for various households needs except for clothes. Borrowing women have increasing ability to independently make small purchases such as utensils and furniture as well as large purchases such as jewellery, livestock and farming machineries.

Li *et al.* (2011b) further reported that even after controlling for knowledge-related variables such as education level, being a microcredit borrower contributes greatly to enhancing women's freedom and legal awareness. Compared to the non-borrowers, women who have borrowed from RCCs are more likely to understand that women have the rights to protest against domestic abuse, being aware of the use of contraception, understand that parents should not arrange marriage for their children and aware of the minimum legal marriage age. The loan, however, does not significantly affect the probability of women to know the legal means of divorce. Care must be taken in assessing the impact of RCCs' microcredit programme on the 'freedom/legal awareness' because the employed indicators may reflect female perceptions of empowerment rather than their real behaviours. Whether any of the awareness would be actually put into practice is unknown but it can be argued that stronger legal or freedom knowledge plays important roles in increasing women's consciousness of fighting for their rights within the household domain or even at higher levels such as community and society (Zaman, 1999).

However, Li *et al.* (2011b) found that there is a threshold loan size beyond which microcredit can have significant effect on one or some dimensions of women empowerment. For most women in the sample, the loan threshold was RMB30,000 before it will significantly affect the empowerment with regards to control over financial assets, ability to make purchase and involvement in family decision making. In other words, significant impact of microcredit on these indicators emerges when women's borrowings reach RMB30,000 or above. In addition, the level of empowerment manifested in women's freedom/legal awareness begins to rise significantly only after the loan size reaches RMB60,000. These findings confirmed Zaman (1999) who argues that women's borrowing should at least reach a certain amount to allow for a significant effect of microcredit on the female empowerment.

Finally, microcredit not only has a positive and significant impacts on female empowerment, but such impacts also increase as the cumulative loan sizes grow larger (Li, 2010). This implies that the microcredit programme can further empower women who participate in it and the level of a woman's empowerment is likely to rise as she becomes more involved in the programme (reflected by the growing loan sizes) compared to her starting-level of empowerment. This finding helps to address the self-selection bias problem in the impact assessment where women who are already relatively more empowered, even in the absence of the microcredit programme, may have higher tendency to participate in the programme than others. In other words, a true impact can be reflected by this upward trend in women's empowerment along with their involvement in the microcredit programme (Hashemi *et al.*, 1996; Osmani, 2007).

10.5 Summary and Conclusion

This chapter presents the case study of RCCs microcredit in rural China, with reference to Hubei Province, the largest agricultural province in China. The case examines how the microcredit programmes provided by RCCs' may improve rural households' welfare and women empowerment in China. The case also discusses the factors that may affect microcredit accessibility by the rural households.

Some household-related factors influence the microcredit accessibility including household size, income, household heads' engagement in self-run business, economic dependency ratio, value of assets, households' savings with RCCs, attitude towards debt, alternatives/access to other sources of credit, household members working in village or township committee, households' share in RCCs, dwelling place's distance to RCCs' offices and educational attainment of household heads.

Some rural households opt not to apply for microcredit due to the low or zero needs for credit. However, some other households in need of funds are reluctant to apply for microcredit or having their application rejected due to several institutional-level obstacles such as interest rate, collateral and documentation requirements and loan-processing time. These lead to many rural households resorting to informal lenders where high interest rates are more than compensated by low transaction costs and flexible loan contracts.

The RCCs' microcredit increases rural households' welfare (measured by HAI and HAC) although its impact is marginal in magnitude. Furthermore, the microcredit only begins to take effect on the borrowers' welfare as the cumulative amount of loan grows. Moreover, from the poverty alleviation perspective it is difficult to examine the impact of RCCs' microcredit programme because it does not primarily focus on the poor population alone. The RCCs' microcredit programme are provided to rural residents in general who are engaged in land farming or other agriculture-related business. As a formal financial institution that assumes sole responsibility for the profits and losses, RCCs ensure the financial viability of the microcredit programme by emphasising on loan repayment performance and are therefore likely to exclude poor households who may not be able to use credit effectively and repay loans punctually.

RCC microcredit also improved the social status of rural women manifested in several dimensions of women empowerment. Microcredit enables rural women to have more mobility and freedom/legal awareness as well as to have more control over financial assets, purchase making ability and involvement in household decision making.

In conclusion, RCCs' microcredit improves borrowers' welfare and empowers women in rural China but poor households and households with weak social status and connections are still constrained to access RCCs' microcredit. RCCs' microcredit is not a substitute for informal credit which have flexible loan contracts and simple lending process. Hence, RCCs' microcredit may promote rural development in China in general but is not a programme specifically crafted to eradicate poverty in rural households. In order to carry out the task of rural poverty alleviation, a different micro-credit scheme that specifically targets rural poor population should be provided. Alternatively, RCCs microcredit should modify its microlending policies and its microloan products to allow for more flexible terms and conditions to better cater the diverse needs of the rural households.

References

Ansoglenang, G. (2006). *Rural Women and Micro-Credit Schemes. Cases from the Lawra District of Ghana*. Hansine Hansens: University of Tromsø.

Atieno, R. (2001). *Formal and Informal Institutions' Lending Policies and Access to Credit by Small-scale Enterprises in Kenya: An Empirical Assessment*, Vol. 111: African Economic Research Consortium Nairobi.

Cheng, E. (2007). The demand for microcredit as a determinant for microfinance outreach — Evidence from China. *Savings and Development*, 31(3), 307–334.

Cheng, E. & Xu, Z. (2004). Rates of interest, credit supply and China's rural development. *Savings and Development*, 28(2), 131–156.

Cuong, N. V., Pham, M. T., Minh, N. P., Thieu, V. & Toan, D. (2007). *Poverty Targeting and Impact of a Governmental Micro-Credit Program in Vietnam*. Quebec: PEP-PMMA.

Druschel, K. (2002). *Microfinance in China: Building Sustainable Institutions and a Strong Industry*. Massachusetts: American University.

Du, X. (2004). Attempts to Implement Micro Finance in Rural China. Paper presented at the Workshop on Rural Finance and Credit Infrastructure in China, Paris (pp. 271–284). Paris: OECD.

Du, X. (2005). *The Regulatory Environment for Microfinance in China*. Washington, DC: Microfinance Regulation and Supervision Resource Center.

Dyar, C., Harduar, P., Koenig, C. & Reyes, G. (2006). *Microfinance and Gender Inequality in China*. Michigan: International Economic Development Program, Ford School of Public Policy. University of Michigan.

Han, J. (2004). The creation of a favourable environment for investment in rural China: Current situation and future prospects. Organisation for Economic Co-operation and Development (OECD), Centre for Co-operation with Non-members, Rural finance and credit infrastructure in China, 23–33.

Hashemi, S. M., Schuler, S. R. & Riley, A. P. (1996). Rural credit programs and women's empowerment in Bangladesh. *World Development*, 24(4), 635–653.

Heilig, G. K., Zhang, M., Long, H., Li, X. & Wu, X. (2006). Poverty alleviation in China: A lesson for the developing world. *Geographische Rundschau*, 2(2), 4–13.

Husain, A. M. (1998). *Poverty Alleviation and Empowerment: The Second Impact Assessment Study of BRAC's Rural Development Programme: BRAC*. Dhaka: Research and Evaluation Division.

Jie, D. & Kanji, N. (2003). Gender Equality and Poverty Reduction in China: Issues for Development Policy and Practice: Department for International Development. Retrieved from http://webarchive.nationalarchives.gov.uk/+/http:/www.dfid.gov.uk/pubs/files/gender-equality-china.pdf.

Li, X. (2010). An Empirical Analysis of Microcredit on Rural China Household. Unpublished PhD Thesis, Faulty of Commerce, Department of Accounting, Economic and Finance, Lincoln University, Christchurch, New Zealand, 250 pp.

Li, X., Gan, C. & Hu, B. (2011a). Accessibility to microcredit by Chinese rural households. *Journal of Asian Economics*, 22(3), 235–246.

Li, X., Gan, C. & Hu, B. (2011b). The impact of microcredit on women's empowerment: Evidence from China. *Journal of Chinese Economic and Business Studies*, 9(3), 239–261.

Li, X., Gan, C. & Hu, B. (2011c). The welfare impact of microcredit on rural households in China. *The Journal of Socio-Economics*, 40(4), 404–411.

Li, H., Rozelle, S. & Zhang, L. (2004). Micro-credit programs and off-farm migration in China. *Pacific Economic Review*, 9(3), 209–223.

Lin, J. Y. & Zhang, F. (1998). The Effects of China's Rural Policies on the Sustainability of Agriculture in China Symposium Conducted at the Meeting of the 11th Biannual Workshop on Economy and Environment in Southeast Asia, Singapore.

Linton, K. (2007). Access to capital in China: Competitive conditions for foreign and domestic firms. SSRN Working Paper Series (1031223).

Lucock, D. (2014). *The People's Republic of China: Knowledge Work on Credit Growth in Microfinance and Rural Finance*. Manila: Asian Development Bank.

Mayoux, L. (2002). Microfinance and women's empowerment: Rethinking 'best practice'. *Development Bulletin*, 57(76–80).

National Bureau of Statistics of China (2004). China Statistical Yearbook. Retrieved from http://www.stats.gov.cn/english. Accessed on November 18, 2015.

Niño-Zarazúa, M. (2007). The impact of credit on income poverty in urban Mexico. An endogeneity-corrected estimation. An Endogeneity-Corrected Estimation (March 2007). Sheffield Economic Research Paper (SERP) No. 2007005.

Okurut, F. N. (2006). Access to credit by the poor in South Africa: Evidence from Household Survey Data 1995 and 2000. Department of Economics, University of Botswana Stellenbosch Economic Working Papers, 13(06).

Osmani, L. N. K. (2007). A Breakthrough in Women's Bargaining Power: The Impact of Microcredit. *Journal of International Development*, 19(5), 695–716.

Park, A. & Ren, C. (2001). Microfinance with Chinese characteristics. *World Development*, 29(1), 39–62.

Park, A., Ren, C. & Wang, S. (2004). Micro Finance, Poverty Alleviation, and Financial Reform in China. *Rural Finance and Credit Infrastructure in China*. Paris: OECD, p. 256.

Pitt, M. M. & Khandker, S. R. (1998). The impact of group-based credit programs on poor households in Bangladesh: Does the gender of participants matter? *Journal of Political Economy*, 106(5), 958–996.

Pitt, M. M., Khandker, S. R. & Cartwright, J. (2003). Does micro-credit empower women? Evidence from Bangladesh. Evidence from Bangladesh (March 2003). (World Bank Policy Research Working Paper No. 2998).

Sun, R. (2003). The Development of Microfinance in China Symposium Conducted at the Meeting of the International Workshop on Rural Financial Reforms in China, Beijing, China.

The People's Bank of China (2001). *Guidelines on Rural Household Micro-credit by Rural Credit Cooperatives*. Retrieved from http://www.microfinancegateway.org/. Accessed on February 22, 2017.

Umoh, G. S. (2006). Empirical investigation of access to micro-credit in an emerging economy: Evidence from Nigeria. *Journal of African Business*, 7(1–2), 89–117.

Unger, J. (2002). Poverty, credit and microcredit in rural China. *Development Bulletin*, 57, 23–26 (electronic version).

Vaessen, J. (2001). Accessibility of rural credit in Northern Nicaragua: The importance of networks of information and recommendation/Accessibilité du Crédit Rural Dans le Nord du Nicaragua: L'importance Des Réseaux D'information et de Recommandation. *Savings and Development*, 25(1), 5–32.

Zaman, H. (1999). Assessing the Poverty and Vulnerability Impact of Micro-Credit in Bangladesh: A Case Study of BRAC. World Bank Policy Research Working Paper no. 2145, Washington, DC: The World Bank.

Zhang, H. X. & Loubere, N. (2013). Rural Finance, Development and Livelihoods in China. Universität Duisburg-Essen Working Paper on East Asian Studies No. 94.

Chapter 11

Rural Microfinance Banking Viability and Outreach: A Case of Bank Rakyat Indonesia

Mohamad D. Revindo*,‡ and Christopher Gan†,§

*PhD Candidate, Faculty of Agribusiness and Commerce,
Department of Financial and Business System,
PO Box 85084, Lincoln University, Canterbury, New Zealand

†Professor in Accounting and Finance, Faculty of Agribusiness
and Commerce, Department of Financial and Business System,
PO Box 85084, Lincoln University, Christchurch, New Zealand

‡Mohamad.Revindo@lincolnuni.ac.nz
§Christopher.Gan@lincoln.ac.nz

Abstract

Bank Rakyat Indonesia (BRI) provides an example of large-scale rural microfinance banking services that are financially sustainable due to its commercial banking and capital self-sufficiency principles. BRI is also exceptional in the outreach of its microfinance services, with its 8.539 microoutlets in almost all sub-districts throughout Indonesia providing simple and flexible microfinance banking products that in 2015 served 43 million microsavers and 7.85 million microborrowers nationwide. This chapter gives a historical overview of BRI and its successful transformation from government-reliant towards commercial and capital self-sufficiency microfinance banking without overlooking its main mission in catering the rural poor population. The chapter shows how a well-managed microfinance banking system can weather economic crises and help the rural poor cope with economic shocks. The chapter also highlights some implications for the microfinance institutions, BRI in particular, as well as the government as the policy maker.

Keywords: BRI, microfinance banking, commercial banking, capital self-sufficiency, financial sustainability, outreach, Indonesia.

11.1 Introduction

Bank Rakyat Indonesia (BRI) (People's Bank of Indonesia), commonly referred to as Bank BRI, is the oldest and one of the largest banks in Indonesia, operating for more than 120 years. It is also the largest microfinance banking provider in the country and, arguably, one of the largest in the entire developing world (Das, 2015; Gerber, 2013). At the end of 2015, BRI microfinance banking business had a total of 43 million microsavers and served 7.85 million microborrowers catered by 8,539 microoutlets that spread in almost all sub-districts in rural areas throughout Indonesia (BRI, 2016).

BRI's microfinance banking services' scale and scope are enormous, but even more importantly it operates on *commercial and capital self-sufficiency principles*. However, it was not until 1984 that BRI reformed its microfinance banking business towards the adoption of fully commercial and self-sufficiency practices (Maurer, 1999; Seibel, 2000). The successful reforms have allowed BRI microfinance banking business as well as the entire BRI institution to weather the 1997/1998 Asian financial crisis and the 2008/2009 global economic crises and enabled BRI to keep expanding its services to most rural areas throughout the country (Seibel, Rachmadi & Kusumayakti, 2010). These reforms, therefore, may provide scholars and policy makers with some insights for the implementation and development of microfinance banking in other developing economies.

This case study aims to draw some lessons from BRI's microfinance banking reform and development. The case begins with a brief history of BRI and its microfinance banking services. It then discusses how BRI transformed its microfinance banking business towards commercial and capital self-reliance practices and how it helps the bank withstood economic crises. The case also highlights the future challenges for the government and BRI both at the corporate and microfinance banking business levels.

11.2 Brief History of BRI

The history of BRI dates back to more than 120 years ago and is summarised in Table 11.1. In 1895, Raden Bei Aria Wirjaatmadja, an aristocrat in Purwokerto in the (then) Dutch East Indies (now independent Indonesia), founded *Hulp en Spaarbank der Inlandsche Bestuurs Ambtenaren* (Help and Savings Bank of Indigenous Civil Servants).[1] His main aim was to

Table 11.1:   Historical Development of BRI

Year	Events
1894–1895	Founded in Poerwokerto, Central Java (in the (then) Dutch East Indies).
1942–1945	Became *Shomin Ginko* (People's Bank) under Japanese occupation.
1945–1946	Nationalised by Indonesia's newly formed government, following Indonesia's independence in 1945.
1968–1969	Became commercial bank and given task to finance the green revolution and integrated rural development.
1983–1984	Began the reform towards commercial microbanking.
1992	Became a limited liability company with 100% ownership by the Government of the Republic of Indonesia.
2003	Became a publicly-listed company by listing its shares on the Jakarta Stock Exchange (now Indonesia Stock Exchange).
After 2003	Expanding loan outreach to remote areas and wider segment of borrowers and enhancing the use of information and communication technology (ICT).

Source: BRI (2015), Seibel & Ozaki (2009), Apriyono (2015).

---

[1]Wirjaatmadja began money lending activities for the needy indigenous in 1894 through *De Poerwokertosche Hulp en Spaarbank der Inlandsche Hoofden* (Help and Savings Bank for Purwokerto's Aristocrats) initially using his own money and mosque fund. Purwokerto was a small regency in Java Island in the Dutch East Indies, a Dutch colony that later became modern Indonesia.

help indigenous farmers, workmen and civil servants escape indebtedness. He collected funds from donors and then disbursed loans through simple schemes and flexible repayment terms (Apriyono, 2015).

During the Dutch colonial period, the bank went through several changes before finally settled with *Algemene Volkscredietbank* (People's General Credit Bank, AVB) in 1934. AVB focused on helping indebted rural households and became the largest financial institution in the (then) Dutch colony (Seibel & Ozaki, 2009). During the Japanese occupation in the World War II (1942–1945) the bank became *Shomin Ginkou* (People's Bank or People's Treasury), which carried on AVB's previous mission with some additional tasks including credit provision for rice mills business and collection of people's savings. *Shomin Ginkou* also targeted indigenous middle class businessmen with a vision to replace departing Dutch businessmen (Apriyono, 2015; Seibel & Ozaki, 2009).

Following Indonesia's declaration of independence in 1945, the bank was officially nationalised by the new government and then renamed BRI in 1946. The new national bank was mandated to provide lending to the government, small enterprises in the informal sector and enterprises of the emerging middle class (Seibel & Ozaki, 2009). In more than two decades that followed, as a state bank BRI underwent several changes in its business orientation and strategy as a result of various political and economic turbulences in the new independent state. However, as Indonesia gradually moved towards political stability in the end of 1960s, BRI was re-established as a commercial bank in 1968 (BRI, 2015).

Despite its commercial status, BRI carried out the government's mission of integrated rural development and green revolution financing. As a result, BRI's services were overshadowed by subsidised rural credit programmes designed by the government and donor agencies (Seibel *et al.*, 2010). In 1969, BRI was appointed as the sole bank to disburse a government subsidised-credit programme for agricultural (mainly rice) intensification on a massive scale that enabled BRI to establish an extensive network of *Unit Desa* (village units) in most of sub-districts throughout Indonesia (BRI, 2015; Kuiper, 2004).[2]

---

[2]Despite its name, a village unit is established at a sub-district level to serve the villages within that sub-district. Village units operate as retail windows of the district/regency level branch offices.

However, the government discontinued the subsidised-credit programme following the drop in global oil price in 1982 that reduced the country's oil export revenue (Seibel *et al.*, 2010). Instead of closing the village units, which was unprofitable at that time, BRI management opted to reform them in 1984 with the encouragement from the Minister of Finance (Maurer, 2004). The decision became the most important milestone in BRI history for its success in turning the village units into commercial microfinance banking units.

In 1992, BRI underwent a legal status change and became a limited liability company as the base for future partial privatisation (Maurer, 1999). However, the state initially maintained 100% ownership before the bank eventually went public in 2003 with 30% of its shares listed on the Jakarta Stock Exchange (now Indonesia Stock Exchange/IDX). As of 2015, the government still held the majority of the shares (56.75%), followed by foreign investors (33.78%) and domestic investors (9.46%) (BRI, 2016).

In recent years, BRI expands its service outreach by: (i) extending the microfinance banking services to reach distant villages, isolated areas and small islands; (ii) targeting middle class population and medium-sized businesses that have flourished along with Indonesia's economic growth (BRI, 2015; Kikkawa & Xing, 2014). To support those tasks, BRI enhances its services by utilising the ICT, including the introduction of e-banking and self-service (hybrid) banking, as well as expanding its service outlets. As of 2015, BRI had 5,360 village units, 2,543 *Teras* (windows), 636 mobile *Teras* and 22,792 ATMs operating in 34 provinces across the archipelago (BRI, 2016).

11.3 Reform towards Commercial and Self-reliant Microfinance Banking

BRI has always been designated to cater small-scale customers since its birth 120 years ago. However, as a government bank its institutional design and status, its operation strategy as well as its main targeted segments and economy sectors often changed along with the changes in the mission and direction of the government regimes. This was evident during the Dutch colonial government, Japanese occupation and even after Indonesia's independence (Seibel & Ozaki, 2009). However, in 1984 BRI began a reform towards fully commercial microfinance banking practices and self-reliance sources of funding, both of which have been crucial in the sustainability of microfinance banking services and the expansion of the loans' outreach (Robinson, 2004).

Interestingly, the preceding event that led to BRI reform was the discontinuation and failure of the heavily subsidised government programme that had initially helped BRI to expand its network infrastructure (branches and units). In 1969, BRI was appointed as the sole bank to channel BIMAS (*Bimbingan Massal*, Massive Guidance/Counselling), a subsidised-credit programme for agricultural (mainly rice) intensification with liquidity support from the central bank. The scale and scope of the BIMAS programme allowed BRI to establish a network of village units, placed at the sub-district centres and designed to serve several surrounding villages.[3] The village unit numbers grew rapidly from just 18 in 1969 to 3,617 in 1982, practically covering almost all sub-districts in the country (Seibel *et al.*, 2010).

The subsidised-credit programmes gave BRI a leading role in rural finance in Indonesia but BRI's business orientation became increasingly overshadowed by government and donor agencies' propaganda (Seibel & Ozaki, 2009). Two years after the introduction of the BIMAS programme, BIMAS loans accounted for 15% of BRI outstanding loan value and 80% of loan accounts. The boom of the oil price in 1973 further increased the government provision of cheap credit, as well as local and rural development grants (Kuiper, 2004). In 1974, the village units were assigned to collect savings with interest rate offered was 3% higher than those charged on loans and the loss from the inverted interest rate structure was covered by the government (Seibel *et al.*, 2010).

However, as noted by Seibel *et al.* (2010), the subsidised credits posed some major problems for BRI. The benefits of the cheap credit to the borrowers were to a large extent offset by several stringent factors that crippled the credit accessibility including high transaction costs which burdened the borrowers, onerous procedures, limited loan purposes (for agricultural production), frequent delays beyond the agricultural input

---

[3]BRI has recently changed the "village unit" into "unit". However, we use the village unit terms throughout the chapter for consistency.

time and illegal extra charges by loan officers. In addition, many loans missed the target borrowers as they mostly were not granted to farmers but rather to village authorities and individuals who were not related to agricultural activities (see also Park & Ren, 2001).

Another problem that characterised the BIMAS loans was the slow repayment. The loan officers receiving illegal transaction fee were hesitant to enforce repayment, compounded by the fact that many beneficiaries perceived the credit as a grant. In the absence of incentives for small farmers to repay and for the staff at the village units to enforce repayment, in 1971 the village units' loss ratio reached 17.5% with one-third of the BIMAS clients in arrears. By 1982, the default rate had reached more than 50% and none of the 3,617 village units were profitable (Robinson, 2004).

Following the falling global oil price in 1982, and hence the shrinking government revenue from oil export, the Indonesian government could no longer financially support cheap credit policy. The government reversed its rural finance policy by eliminating interest rate cap and subsidy, removing credit ceilings, reducing central bank liquidity credit and terminating the subsidised-credit programme in BRI village units. The new policy severely affected BRI whose loan portfolio was dominated by subsidised BIMAS loan. With none of the village units profitable, BRI only had two strenuous options, close or reform them. A newly appointed BRI management decided to pursue the latter option — reform the units — with the support from the Minister of Finance (Kuiper, 2004).

In 1984, BRI began to implement the reform, with which the village units were transformed into commercial microfinance banking units, with technical assistance from the Harvard Institute for International Development (HIID) (Kuiper, 2004). The new design of the commercial microfinance banking village units differed from previous system in the terms of organisational setup, the market segment and the products.

At the organisational level, the village units had independent administrative structure that were separated from the branches (Robinson, 2004). The village units were designed to be self-sustaining profit centres with clear reward and punishment system for the managers and staffs. The village unit managers' lending authority and career prospects would be removed when arrears exceeded 5% but substantial profit-sharing incentives were offered in the case of profitable units. Unprofitable village units would be closed or downgraded to service/window posts. The task of channelling all government and donor-supported programmes were handed over from the village units to the branches. The staff size of the village unit was standardised to 4 personnel with possible expansion to 11, beyond which the additional village unit would be established (Seibel *et al.*, 2010).

The market segment was redefined and broadened. Rather than the previous commodity approach with the emphasis on farmers, agriculture crops and seasonal loans, the new credit product targeted any credit-worthy person and income-generating activity in the sub-district, including petty-trading, agricultural input trade, industry, services, agriculture, horticulture, small plantations, livestock and consumer credit (Kuiper, 2004). The units used more proactive approach to target potential customers who were able to save or repay loans. To support this new approach, village units were moved from rice planting areas to local business centres, mostly at the sub-district administrative centre or traditional market, to be more accessible to both the farming and non-farming population (Seibel *et al.*, 2010).

Finally, the products were also impacted by the reform. The loan product was modified to serve the new strategy and in addition a new saving product was introduced because the credit-emphasised approach was replaced by an equal importance on product innovations in savings and credit. As the village units should operate on a commercial basis, both microsaving and microcredit products were offered with commercial interest rates based on vigilant calculations of the transaction costs (Seibel *et al.*, 2010).

On the loan side, BRI launched *Kredit Umum Pedesaan* (general rural credit, KUPEDES), a non-targeted microcredit product provided for any purpose and to any creditworthy person. Its main features included simple procedures, short maturities, regular monthly instalments for borrowers with non-agricultural income, flexible collateral requirements (none for small loans up to $500), incentives for timely repayment, repeat loans contingent upon successful repayment of previous loans and market rates of interest (Kuiper, 2004). Loan sizes were granted from as low as $310 up to a maximum of $5,000. Loan interest rates were calculated on a monthly flat rate with constant monthly payments, which can be easily managed by both staffs and borrowers. Interest rates were set at 2% flat per month on working capital loans and 1.5% on investment loans, which were equivalent to gross effective rates of 44% and 33% per annum, respectively, minus 11% reward for the borrowers for timely repayment. Therefore, the net effective interest rates for the majority of borrowers were 33% and 22% per annum, respectively, sufficiently covering all BRI's costs and risks (Seibel *et al.*, 2010).

On the saving side, BRI introduced *Simpanan Pedesaan* (rural savings, SIMPEDES), a microsaving product with unlimited withdrawals and a lottery component with prizes in monthly public events, to complement the demand for time deposits and other savings products (Kuiper, 2004). The gross interest rate was set at 13%, of which the savers received 11.5% while another 1.5% was pooled into the prize fund. The savings thus offered the savers positive returns in real terms because the net interest rates were higher than the inflation rates that were always single digit except during the 1997/1998 Asian financial crisis. SIMPEDES immediately gained popularity and served as a BRI's effective instrument for resource mobilisation in rural areas (Seibel *et al.*, 2010).

At the initial stage of the village units' commercialisation, the savings deposits were not sufficient to fund the KUPEDES loan. Hence, two more sources of capital were made available to the BRI units: (i) an injection of RP210 billion ($196 million) of seed capital in 1984 by the Government as start-up liquidity; (ii) a World Bank loan of $97 million to be disbursed in 1989 (Seibel *et al.*, 2010).

The reform came to fruition in a relatively short period of time. As of 1986, most of village units already recorded profits and in 1988 they accounted for 30% of BRI's total net income. In 1989, the village units broke even in terms of the balance of mobilised savings and outstanding loans and thus began generating surplus liquidity. Therefore, the disbursement of the World Bank loan in 1989 was reallocated to the branch network (Seibel *et al.*, 2010). More importantly, despite the market interest rates charged on KUPEDES, the rural population, particularly the women, had better access to loans due to relaxed procedure and requirements (Yaron, 1994).

The villages units have continually been recording net profits and becoming capital self-reliant through the mobilisation of their own resources. Furthermore, the surplus liquidity within the village units' network continues to grow. Self-reliance in terms of fund mobilisation and profitability have provided the base for village units' autonomy and freedom from political interference which previously affected BRI negatively (Kuiper, 2004; Seibel & Ozaki, 2009). When the new government-backed credit programme, namely *Kredit Usaha Rakyat* (People's Business Credit, KUR), was incorporated into the village units in January 2008, BRI had already learned from reform experience and therefore separate it from BRI's KUPEDES loan product.[4]

11.4 Weathering Economic Crises

11.4.1 *The 1997/1998 Asian financial crisis*

When the financial crisis hit Asian countries in 1997/1998, the Indonesian Rupiahs (IDR) plunged against the US$ and the commercial banking sector collapsed due to both external regional factors and internal weaknesses. BRI was not an exception. In just 2 years (December 1996– December 1998), BRI's total assets fell from US$14.44 billion to US$4.25 billion (largely due to depreciated IDR), gross loans outstanding from US$11.23 billion to US$5.41 billion, deposits from US$8.10 billion to US$5.34 billion, total equity from US$0.76 billion to US$3.08 billion and income before tax from US$0.14 billion to US$3.31 billion (Seibel & Ozaki, 2009).

Interestingly, BRI's insolvency was to a large extent precipitated by the failure of its corporate portfolio rather than the village units (microfinance banking) operations (Patten & Johnston, 2001). In fact, the monetary crisis affected the village units in a positive way. The number of deposit accounts (guaranteed by government) held by the village units grew at higher rate than before, from 16.1 million in 1996 to 21.7 million

---

[4]KUR had 70% credit guarantee by the government and aimed to reach new feasible micro and small businesses that had previously been unbankable (failing to meet BRI's collateral requirements) (Seibel & Ozaki, 2009; Seibel *et al.*, 2010).

in 1998. During the initial 12-month crisis period from September 1997 to August 1998 the total savings deposits in the village units almost doubled from RP7.98 trillion to RP15.13 trillion. During the 3-month peak crisis period (June–August 1998), 1.3 million new deposit accounts were opened and an additional RP2.84 trillion (US$354 million) were deposited in the village units (Seibel *et al.*, 2010).

On the loan side, the rural population held back from applying for credit lines because of uncertainty over the future (Patten & Johnston, 2001). The number of borrowers with loans outstanding from the village units fell from 2.6 million in 1997 to 2.5 million in 1998, at the time when many donors were prepared to provide extra funds to strengthen the rural credit supply. The amount of loans outstanding remained almost constant in nominal IDR terms (despite substantial decline in US$ terms). As a consequence, deposits exceeded loans outstanding by even a wider margin in the village unit system (Seibel *et al.*, 2010).

Likewise, the economic crisis had only a moderate effect on loan repayment of the village units (Patten & Johnston, 2001). The non-performing loan ratio (overdue $\geq$ 1 day) increased from 3.7% in 1996 to 5.7% in 1998, indicating delays in repayment. Nevertheless, repayment delays at village units were much less dreadful than BRI entity as a whole where NPL ratio increased from 10.6% to 53.0% in the same period. The village units' 12-month loss ratio increased slightly from 1.6% in 1996 to 2.2% in 1997 but right after the peak of the crisis in August 1998 there was remarkably negative 1-month loss ratio (0.21%), which indicated that more than the due loans had been repaid. These facts could be explained by several combined factors including the effectiveness of timely repayment incentives, the resilience of the microborrowers and the borrowers' avoidance to payment delay because they might not be able to repay in the future given the severely distressed economy (Seibel *et al.*, 2010).

BRI's microfinance banking business remained profitable during the Asian financial crisis. Profits dwindled to half in 1997 in US$ terms due to the IDR depreciation but they remained stable in 1998 and doubled in 1999. Return on assets (ROA) declined from 5.7% in 1996 to 4.7% in 1997 but quickly recovered to 4.9% in 1998 when the crisis was still at its pinnacle (Seibel *et al.*, 2010).

Simply put, while BRI gained a worldwide reputation of banking excellence, it should be credited mainly to the combination of outreach and financial performance of the village units (or microfinance banking network). The village units' performance and reputation were perhaps the decisive factor that drove the Indonesian government to rescue the whole BRI entity through the crisis (Maurer, 1999).

11.4.2 *The 2008/09 global economic crisis*

The 2008/2009 global economic crisis had limited impact on BRI village units. From 2008 to 2009 the deposits account in the village units grew from 19.6 million to 21.2 million and the deposit balance rose from US$5.9 billion to US$8.0 billion (even with the depreciation of the IDR). The number of loan accounts grew from 4.5 million to 4.7 million and the amount of loans outstanding rose from US$3.9 billion to US$5.8 billion, both without any change in the direction of the trend since the year 2000. In the same period the net profit rose from US$563.8 million to US$786.7 million. Likewise, ROA increased from 9.8% to an all-time high of 10.2% in the same period (Seibel *et al.*, 2010).

The only adverse effect of the crisis on the village units was the arrears that slightly climbed from 1.0% in 2008 to 1.4% in 2009. However, further investigation revealed that this was not caused by the crisis but rather to a less performing KUR (new government-backed credit programme), incorporated into village units in January 2008 (Seibel & Ozaki, 2009; Seibel *et al.*, 2010). KUR's high arrears ratio of 6.0% affected the overall arrears ratio of the village units. During the crisis, KUR loans outstanding in the village units also decreased from US$408 million in 2008 to US$303 million in 2009 (Seibel *et al.*, 2010).

Removing KUR from the equation, there is no significant negative effect of the 2008/2009 global economic crisis on the village units. When the crisis hit in 2008 the village units already had 25 years of reform and the experience from previous 1997/1998 Asian financial crisis, both enabled the village units to withstand such external shocks. However, the underperforming KUR loan raised the question on the sustainability of donor or government-backed credit programmes once again.

11.5 Lessons Learned

Most of households, including the rural near-poor, have demand for savings service (Kikkawa & Xing, 2014). Hence, serving their need to save is just as important as their demand for credit. For the microsavers, the well-crafted saving products that suit rural households' needs would help them to manage their finance and to prepare for the uncertainty. For the bank, self-reliance in terms of fund mobilisation would safeguard its autonomy and freedom from political interference which have negatively affected the banking system (Maurer & Seibel, 2001). From a wider perspective, it would also further spur rural development because it helps mobilise funds from households with excess money to those with liquidity needs.

Most microborrowers are willing and able to repay the loan at the market interest rate. Therefore, addressing the credit accessibility issue including the simple procedure and easy collateral requirement is more crucial than providing cheap credit (Maurer & Seibel, 2001). From the bank's perspective the interest rates charge on loans should be sufficient to cover bank costs and risks so that the bank can be financially viable in the long term. Hence, the bank should be given freedom in approving credits based solely on the borrowers' willingness and ability to repay (Seibel & Ozaki, 2009).

Serving microsavers and microborrowers in rural areas may incur high operating cost to the banks (IFAD, 2001; Okurut, Schoombee & Berg, 2005). However, BRI experience shows at least two strategies to deal with such problem. First, credit should be made available to all creditworthy microcredit customers rather than specific purposes or economic activities. In this way, the overhead costs can be spread and minimised. Second, the organisation should be arranged such that there is a combination of simplicity and transparency, standardisation and delegation of authority and responsibility to the lowest operating units (Maurer & Seibel, 2001; Seibel & Ozaki, 2009).

It would, of course, be almost impossible to expect a government-owned bank to be fully free from government influence and intervention. However, in the case of BRI, the government interventions were limited to providing initial capital and setting up the ceiling for KUPEDES loans so that the village units can have managerial autonomy as well as survival responsibility (Maurer & Seibel, 2001). The government roles are more appropriate and required at the macropolicy level. As the case of BRI reform, the government of Indonesia deserves a compliment for their strong political will to reform the BRI village units in the time of crisis, for formulating a farsighted blueprint for a new village unit banking system and for appointing professional and able figures as BRI's board of directors (Maurer & Seibel, 2001).

11.6 Challenges Ahead

Despite the overall success of BRI in reforming its village units and weathering two economic crises over the past three decades, some challenges remain ahead or at least to be anticipated. The challenges exist at BRI entity level, BRI village units' microfinance banking as well as for the government of Indonesia as BRI's main shareholder.

At BRI entity level one of the challenges is to use the lessons from the microfinance banking business reform as an example to improve the overall BRI businesses. In 1997/1998 Asian financial crisis most of BRI units (i.e., the branch network) have been running losses for several years and 56% of the branches' loan portfolio, mostly large corporate loans, had to be written off (Maurer & Seibel, 2001). As result, in 1998 the consolidated BRI was technically insolvent and effectively bankrupt. It was the survival, outreach and the profitability of the village unit networks that convinced the government to salvage BRI by recapitalising and transferring non-performing loans to the Indonesian Bank Restructuring Agency (IBRA) (Maurer & Seibel, 2001; Seibel & Ozaki, 2009). Therefore, BRI may emulate the village units' reform to transform the overall BRI businesses to become fully commercial, financially viable and sustainable in the long run.

Another critical point at BRI level is how to optimally reinvest the profits from the village units to ensure microfinance banking sustainability. BRI should not use the village units' profits to cross-subsidise the non-profitable businesses of other divisions as previously practiced (Maurer & Seibel, 2001). Rather, the village units' profits should be reinvested in the village units' infrastructure in order to improve the services to their borrowers and savers.

At BRI microfinance banking business level, the successful village units also face the challenge of how to channel the excess funds from their operation back to the rural population. Since 1989, savings mobilisation from SIMPEDES has exceeded KUPEDES lending and the excess funds were mostly deposited in the BRI urban branches network (Maurer & Seibel, 2001). The economic crisis widened the gap further when 70% of the deposits were channelled off to the BRI branches in 1998 thereby mobilised funds from rural households to urban economy instead for rural development.

BRI may reconsider how to use the excess funds to expand its outreach in rural population. Despite BRI's extensive rural lending outreach, there is still a large unmet demand for loans in rural Indonesia (Johnston & Morduch, 2008; Robinson, 2004). The distribution of KUPEDES loans outstanding by economic sector showed a clear concentration of loans in small trade and for fixed salary employees while only small portion of the loans were channelled for agriculture and small industries. Hence, BRI has only reached the smaller part of the potential customers in all sectors of the economy. There is still large potential credit demand in agriculture and agriculture-related activities, housing and consumer finance in rural Indonesia (Maurer & Seibel, 2001). When rural areas become more developed and rural population's economic activities become increasingly diversified and heterogeneous, BRI may also consider to craft new loan products that can conform the new demand, thereby increase the outreach in particular sectors/areas and to spur rural development further.

However, expansion in lending requires adjustment in organisational setup, operation strategy and supporting infrastructure. There is a productivity ceiling for loan officers (i.e., the number of borrowers that could be handled by each officer) (Maurer & Seibel, 2001; Patten & Johnston, 2001). Hence, expansion of loan outreach requires additional staffs otherwise sacrificing the service and loan quality. Expansion in lending to more remote areas, smaller villages and small islands may also be considered but with careful costs consideration.

Finally, some challenges should also be addressed to the government. The main challenge is to restrain from intervening the successful BRI village units as an outlet for government programme. Government's deep involvement in BRI's microfinance banking reform in its early development including assistances in institutional set up, initial capital and human resources training are undoubtedly important for the success of the village units. However, government's banking deregulation that liberated the interest rate, discontinued the cheap credit liquidity and freed up the village units from government policy were at least as crucial in the village units' success (Maurer & Seibel, 2001). The underperforming of KUR programme incepted into the units in 2008 reconfirms the potential menace of deep intervention in the microbanking operations.

Another challenge for the government is to create healthy competition in the rural financial sector (Kikkawa & Xing, 2014). Despite the growing competition in some areas from small private rural banks (*Bank Perkreditan Rakyat*, BPR) operating at the sub-district level and village credit institutions (*Badan Kredit Desa*, BKD) at village level, BRI village units have retained its dominant position in the rural financial system in Indonesia. BPRs struggled to compete with BRI units because their deposits are not backed by government-guarantee and most of them are independent unit banks with no vertical risk diversification and with no access to a liquidity pool. Likewise, BKD struggles to compete with BRI units as their financial muscle is limited to small loans (Maurer & Seibel, 2001; Seibel & Parhusip, 1998).

The village units' dominant position in rural financing may be preferable from BRI's point of view as it allows a considerable profit margin. However, from policy makers and regulators' perspective, competition is important for at least two reasons. Competition is the driving force for innovations and adaptations that are crucial to cope with rapidly changing environment in Indonesia, in Asia and in the global economy (Maurer & Seibel, 2001; Robinson, 2004). Competition is also important for medium and long run development of microfinance as it would challenge the microfinance banking providers to maintain and continuously improve the quality of their financial services and the efficiency of their operations. Further, competition would ensure that profits are reinvested back to the rural customers instead of cross-subsidising poor performance and inefficiency in other parts of the organisation (Maurer & Seibel, 2001; Robinson, 2004).

11.7 Summary and Conclusion

BRI is the oldest bank and the largest microfinance banking provider in Indonesia and arguably in entire developing world. In 2015, BRI microfinance banking business served 43 million savers and 7.85 million borrowers, catered by 8.539 microoutlets spread in almost all sub-districts throughout Indonesia. More importantly, BRI microfinance banking business has been operating on commercial and capital self-reliance principles since its successful reforms in 1984.

Prior to the reform, BRI carried out various government rural finance policies, including the large-scale BIMAS subsidised-credit programme for rice intensification that initially helped BRI to expand its village unit networks throughout the country. The village units' operation were dominated by BIMAS subsidised-credit programme and hence none of the units was profitable. The discontinuation of the government subsidy and liquidity support in 1983 due to oil price shock forced BRI to reform its village units. The village units were transformed into autonomous microfinance banking units operated on commercial base.

The village unit reform includes the removal of government programme to the branch offices, clear incentive for performing managers and staffs and standardisation of management system. A new microloan product (KUPEDES) was introduced, with appealing features such as simple procedures, short maturities, regular monthly instalments, flexible collateral requirements, incentives for timely repayment, repeat loans contingent upon successful repayment of previous loans and market rates of interest. The microloan is offered to any creditworthy person and income-generating activity including petty-trading, agricultural input trade, industry, services, agriculture, horticulture, small plantations, livestock and consumer credit. In addition, BRI also introduced SIMPEDES, a microsaving product that allowed for unlimited withdrawals, offered interest rate above inflation rate and monthly prizes.

The village units' microfinance banking business enabled BRI to withstand the 1997/1998 Asian financial crisis and 2008/2009 global economic crisis. During the crisis, the number of borrowers and outstanding loans held by the village units slightly changed but the repayment rate remained high because many borrowers were motivated to repay the loans timely to maintain good record for future loan application. The economic crisis also increased the demand for microsavings because rural household need to keep some spare funds to cope with economic uncertainty.

BRI's successful village unit reforms offered some lessons for the microfinance banking discourse. Market interest rate does not constrain rural households from accessing the microloan but onerous procedure and inflexible loan terms do. Hence, for rural households easier access to credit is more important than the provision of cheap credit. Market interest rate also allows the banks to cover all the costs and therefore allows the microfinance banking services to sustain and develop. In addition to demand for credit, rural households also need a flexible microsaving product. From the bank's point of view, the saving deposits could be an important source for capital/liquidity.

Despite BRI's microfinance banking success, some challenges lie ahead. BRI should look to emulate the village unit reforms to the rest of the bank entity (i.e., corporate and retail businesses in branch offices). BRI should use the profit from microfinance banking business to further improve the microfinance banking services, such as improvement of village units' infrastructure (i.e., ICT system) and staffs capacity building, rather than cross-subsidise non-performing BRI businesses. BRI should also channel the excess liquidity in the village units back to the rural development rather than to fund the urban development projects.

Above all, government has to restrain from intervening the rural microfinance banking operation with their policy finance, apart from initial capital and managerial capability building assistances. The government should also ensure healthy competition in rural microfinance banking sector. A healthy competition will force the microfinance banking providers to improve their financial services as well as be adaptive to the change in the financial needs of the rural population and the ever-changing global economic environment.

References

Apriyono, P. (2015). *Dinamika Bank Rakyat Indonesia Tahun 1946–1965 (Kajian Sejarah Lembaga Perkreditan Rakyat Di Purwokerto)*. Central Java: Universitas Sebelas Maret.

BRI (2015). BRI's 2014 Annual Report: Continuous Innovations in Extending Services, Built Upon Integrity and Cutting Edge Technology. Jakarta: BRI.

BRI (2016). BRI 2015 Annual Report. Jakarta: BRI.

Das, A. (2015). Slum upgrading with community-managed microfinance: Towards progressive planning in Indonesia. *Habitat International*, 47, 256–266.

Gerber, J. F. (2013). The hidden consequences of credit: An illustration from rural Indonesia. *Development and Change*, 44(4), 839–860.

IFAD (2001). *People's Republic of China: Thematic Study on Rural Financial Services in China*. Rome: International Fund for Agricultural Development.

Johnston, D. & Morduch, J. (2008). The unbanked: Evidence from Indonesia. *The World Bank Economic Review*, 22(3), 517–537.

Kikkawa, K. & Xing, Y. (2014). Financial Inclusion in Indonesia: A Poverty Alleviation Strategy. *Financial Inclusion in Asia*, 45.

Kuiper, K. (2004). *Act or Accident? The Birth of the Village Units of Bank Rakyat Indonesia*. Eschborn: Deutsche Gesellschaft für Technische Zusammenarbeit (GTZ) GmbH.

Maurer, K. (1999). Bank Rakyat Indonesia (BRI), Indonesia (Case Study). Working Group on Savings Mobilization. Eschborn, Alemania: CGAP.

Maurer, K. (2004). Bank Rakyat Indonesia: Twenty Years of Large-Scale Microfinance. Consultative Group to Assist the Poor & World Bank Financial Sector Network, Scaling up Poverty Reduction: Case Studies in Microfinance.

Maurer, K. & Seibel, H. D. (2001). Agricultural Development Bank Reform: The Case of Unit Banking System of Bank Rakyat Indonesia (BRI): IFAD Rural Finance Working Paper No. B 5.

Okurut, F. N., Schoombee, A. & Berg, S. (2005). Credit demand and credit rationing in the informal financial sector in Uganda. *South African Journal of Economics*, 73(3), 482–497.

Park, A. & Ren, C. (2001). Microfinance with Chinese characteristics. *World Development*, 29(1), 39–62.

Patten, R. H. & Johnston, D. E. (2001). Microfinance success amidst macroeconomic failure: The experience of Bank Rakyat Indonesia during the East Asian crisis. *World Development*, 29(6), 1057–1069.

Robinson, M. (2004). Why the Bank Rakyat Indonesia Has the World's Largest Sustainable Microbanking System. *Symposium conducted at the meeting of the BRI International Seminar*, Bali, Indonesia.

Seibel, H. D. (2000). How an Agricultural Development Bank Revolutionized Rural Finance: The Case of Bank Rakyat Indonesia: Working Paper/University of Cologne, Development Research Center.

Seibel, H. D. & Ozaki, M. (2009). *Restructuring of State-owned Financial Institutions: Lessons from Bank Rakyat Indonesia*. Manila, Philippines: ADB.

Seibel, H. D. & Parhusip, U. (1998). Attaining Outreach with Sustainability: A Case Study of a Private Micro-Finance Institution in Indonesia. *IDS Bulletin*, 29(4), 81–90.

Seibel, H. D., Rachmadi, A. & Kusumayakti, D. (2010). Reform, growth and resilience of savings-led commercial microfinance institutions: The case of the microbanking units of Bank Rakyat Indonesia. *Savings and Development*, 277–303.

Yaron, J. (1994). What makes rural finance institutions successful? *The World Bank Research Observer*, 9(1), 49–70.

Index

A

AAOIFI, 256
ABC, 105, 136
access, 308
access the microcredit, 320
access to a liquidity pool, 352
access to credit, 27, 38, 43
access to formal credit, 122
access to microcredit, 326
access to rural credit, 44
accessibility, 319
accessing credit, 43
Aceh province, 242
ADBC, 106, 136
adverse selection, 308
adverse selection issues, 258
Agri–Agra Reform Credit Act of 2009, 182, 186–187
agricultural, 310
Agricultural Bank of China, 325
agricultural cooperatives, 162

agricultural credit, 123, 178, 183, 195, 211, 216
agricultural insurance, 137
agricultural lending, 115–116
agricultural loans, 105
agricultural production, 115
agricultural rural credit, 210
agricultural sector, 255
Agriculture and Fisheries Modernisation Act (AFMA), 184–186, 211
    AMCFP, 185
agriculture businesses, 84
agriculture commodities of China, 102
agriculture production, 101
agriculture productivity, 101
agriculture sector, 100–101
agriculture-related business, 332
agriculture-support policies, 113
Ahon sa Hirap Inc, 183

alternative credit sources, 326
  administration fees, 62
  Amanah Ikhtiar Malaysia (AIM),
    47, 49, 60, 81, 252
  background, 64
  charity-loans, 62
  established, 61
  general loan, 62–63
  group lending scheme, 64
  loan schemes, 62–63
  loans for fishermen, 62
  loans for social and recovery
    purposes, 62
  loans to single urban mothers, 62
  members, 62
  microlending, 61
  non-performing loan, 64
  political motives, 61
  Projek Ikhtiar, 61
  reforms, 62
  repayment rate, 64
  uncollectible loans, 62
  welfare and well-being fund, 64
annual member meeting, 241
Asian financial crisis, 50, 346, 350,
  353
asset-reducing strategies, 81
asymmetric information, 256, 308
asymmetric responsibility, 120
attitude towards debt, 323–324
AusAID, 125
authorities, 263
autonomy, 349

B

Bank for Agriculture and Agricultural
  Cooperatives (BAAC), 151
Bank Koperasi Tani Nelayan
  (BKTN), 231

Bank Muamalat Indonesia (BMI),
  246
Bank of Thailand (BOT), 151
Bank Perkreditan Rakyat (BPR), 85
Bank Rakyat Indonesia (BRI), 137,
  228
  access to loans, 345
  arrears, 348
  Asian financial crisis, 347
  autonomy, 346
  bankrupt, 350
  BIMAS, 353
  branches, 344
  capital self-reliance, 353
  capital self-reliant, 346
  capital self-sufficiency, 337
  collateral requirements, 344
  commercial, 353
  commercial banking, 337
  commercial microfinance
    banking, 342–343
  corporate portfolio, 346
  credit accessibility, 342
  default rate, 343
  deposit accounts, 346
  deposit balance, 348
  domestic investors, 341
  Dutch colonial period, 340
  effective interest rates, 345
  excess funds, 350
  foreign investors, 341
  general rural credit, KUPEDES,
    344
  government of Indonesia, 350
  historical development, 339
  instalments, 344
  interest rate, 342
  Japanese occupation, 340
  Kredit Umum Pedesaan, 344

Kredit Usaha Rakyat (People's
Business Credit, KUR), 346,
348, 352
KUPEDES, 345–346, 351, 353
loan product, 344
loans accounted, 342
loans outstanding, 346–348
loss ratio, 343, 347
market segment, 344
microborrowers, 337–338
microcredit, 344
microfinance banking, 338, 350,
353
microfinance banking business,
347
microoutlets, 337
microsavers, 337–338
microsaving, 344
microsaving product, 345
nationalised, 340
net profit, 348
non-performing, 347
outreach, 337, 341, 348,
350–351
outstanding loan, 342
payments, 345
privatisation, 341
profits, 347
reform, 338, 341, 343, 345, 348,
350, 353–354
reinvest the profits, 350
repayment, 343–344, 347
return on assets (ROA), 347
Rural Microfinance Banking,
337
saving product, 344
savings deposits, 347
self-reliance sources of funding,
342

self-sustaining profit centres, 343
service outlets, 341
Simpanan Pedesaan (rural
savings, SIMPEDES), 345
SIMPEDES, 345, 351
sources of capital, 345
subsidised rural credit
programmes, 340
sustainability, 342
target borrowers, 343
total assets, 346
village units, 340, 342–348, 350,
352–354
Bank Syariah Mandiri (BSM), 246
banking deregulation, 351
banks, 273–275, 277, 290, 292–293,
299, 302
Barangay Microbusiness Enterprise
Act (BMBE), 185
BBRI, 232
BIMAS (Bimbingan Massal, Massive
Guidance/Counselling), 230, 342
blacklisted, 84
BMBE Act of 2002, 185
BMT, 253
borrowers, 3, 308
borrowers' business decisions, 79
borrowing, 28
BRAC, 275, 278, 283–285, 287–289,
298
BRI microbanking division, 229
BRI units, 231
BRIAGRO, 234
BRIFAST, 235
BRIngin Remittance Co. Ltd (BRC),
234
BRISyariah, 234
BRItAma, 236
Bumiputera, 49, 54–55, 70

buoyant effect, 79, 81
business certificate, 250
business decisions, 80
business financial management, 84
business financing access, 70
business premises, 76
business projects, 84
business records, 84

C

capital demands, 113
capital investment returns, 121
CARD, 208–209
causal effect, 251
challenges, 262
cheap credit, 349, 352, 354
children's education, 78, 82
China Rural Credit Cooperatives
  (RCCs), 11
Chinese rural families, 329
collateral, 5, 110, 134, 136
collateral requirement, 349, 353
collateral free, 124
collective land-ownership system,
  103
commercial banking practices, 125
commercial banks, 218–219
commercial lending, 123
commercial loans, 136
commercial services, 106
commercial viability, 126
commitment savings account, 205
competition in rural microfinance,
  354
competition in the rural financial
  sector, 352
competitive advantage, 235
consumption loans, 114
consumption smoothening, 273

conventional deposit rates, 259
conventional lending, 5
cooperatives, 192, 218
coping with negative shocks, 79,
  81–82
covariant risks, 116
credit, 2, 308
credit access, 2, 31, 37, 42, 93, 95,
  124, 134
credit accessibility, 23–24, 31, 133,
  349
credit constraints, 309
credit delivery system, 178
credit demand, 33, 42, 114–115
credit demand and credit supply, 44
credit gap, 113, 122, 135
Credit Information Corporation
  (CIC), 182
credit information system, 219
Credit Information Systems Act
  (CISA), 185
credit markets, 6, 113
credit policy, 43, 137
credit pollution, 217
credit programme, 39
credit providers, 42
credit rationing, 122
credit shortage, 112
credit supply, 24–26, 32–33, 122,
  129
credit supply and demand, 33
credit support, 103
credit utilisation, 295
creditworthiness, 110, 117, 308

D

debt-like instruments, 257
debt-relief measures, 168
default, 118, 120–121

default rates, 320
default risks, 115
demand for credit, 34, 42, 113, 349, 354
demand for microcredit, 34
demand for microsavings, 353
demand for rural credit, 34
demand for savings, 349
demands for loans, 34
difference-in-difference (DD), 251, 326
DSN-MUI, 251
dual urban–rural economic structure, 134
dwelling place's distance, 323

E
economic dependency ratio, 324
economic development, 49
economic growth, 50
economic impact, 82
economic reform, 95, 99, 104
economic shocks, 9, 310
economics of microfinance, 272
education, 314
effective interest rate (EIR), 286, 291–292
employment provision, 100–101
empowerment, 14, 314
Engle-Granger error correction method, 259
entrepreneurs, 255
equity participation, 240
ethnic groups, 55
excess demand for rural credit, 122
excess liquidity, 354
explanatory research, 258
exploitive interest rates, 122
extreme poverty, 98

F
family decisions, 80
family food expenditure, 78
farm accounting knowledge, 169
financial assistance, 261
financial authorities, 229
financial crisis, 249, 263
financial inclusion, 179, 207, 228, 271–272, 274, 280, 297, 299, 302
financial institutions, 103
financial literacy, 169
    deposits and loans, 183
    deregulation of interest rates, 183
    financial market reforms, 183–184
    minimum capital requirements, 183
    rediscounting facility, 183
financial market reforms and liberalisation, 181
financial performance, 237
financial regulations, 170
financial report, 261
financial self-sufficiency, 125
financial services, 272, 276–277, 280, 288–289, 297, 299–300, 302
financial sustainability, 61, 125, 135
financial system, 29
financial viability, 121–122, 332
financially sustainable, 320
flexible lending scheme, 111, 135
flexible loan contracts, 324
foreign exchange, 236
formal, 2
formal and informal credit, 34
formal and informal credit sectors, 31, 33
formal credit, 25, 32–33, 42–43, 103, 114, 139, 150, 320, 321

formal credit financial institutions, 188
  commercial and development banks, 188
formal credit sector, 25
formal financial, 38, 308
formal financial institutions, 103, 107, 112, 122, 187, 189, 332, 328
  cooperatives, 191
  credit cooperatives, 191
  rural banks, 189
  thrift, rural and cooperative banks, 189
formal financial sector, 105
formal financial support, 134
formal financing, 110
formal lenders, 111, 325
formal loans, 33
formal microfinance institutions, 156
formal RFIs, 128, 136
formal sector, 25
formal, informal and semi-formal, 42
fraud, 262

G
GDP per capita, 96
gender equality, 13
gender inequality, 329
general and presidential election year, 238
Gini coefficient, 98
GINI index, 53
global economic crisis, 348, 353
global financial crisis, 50
government assistance, 263
government intervention, 35, 260, 349
government microcredit programmes, 128
government policies, 37, 43

Government Savings Bank (GSB), 156
grace period, 83, 285–286, 292
gradual disbursements, 82
Grameen Bank, 48, 60, 67, 81, 85, 124, 126, 137, 275, 297
Grameen Bank Approach, 183
grassroots citizens, 167
group lending methods, 137
group lending scheme, 61, 82–83
group members, 6
group-based approach, 272

H
haram, 253
hardcore poverty, 53, 55–56, 66
hardware requisites, 178
Harvard Institute for International Development (HIID), 343
healthcare, 314
high default rates, 95
high inflation rate, 237
household annual income (HAI), 326
household assets, 82, 323
household economic portfolios (HEP), 74
household income, 76, 78, 82
household savings, 324
household size, 323
household-related factors, 320–323, 332
households, 77
households' debt problem, 153
households' expenditure, 80
Hubei Province, 319–320, 331
human development index (HDI), 48
human development indicators, 51

I

imbalanced growth, 134
impact, 74–75, 251, 319
impact on individual borrower, 79
impact on the household, 76
impact on the individual, 78
incidence of poverty, 53
income disparity, 94
income disparity between the urban
  and rural population, 55
income equality, 48, 98
income-generating activities, 54, 252,
  324, 344
income inequality, 47, 52–54, 95, 99
independent financial accounting,
  128
index-based weather insurance (IWI),
  137
individual lending scheme, 82
Indonesia economic growth, 238
Indonesia stock exchange, 232
Indonesian Bank Restructuring
  Agency (IBRA), 350
Indonesian labour, 235
Indonesian Rupiahs (IDR), 346
Indonesian working force, 236
inequality, 97
informal, 2, 43
informal borrowings, 93–94, 103,
  320
informal credit, 25, 29–31, 43, 112,
  114, 150, 193–194, 272–273, 298,
  308, 324, 326, 333
    input–output traders, 193
informal finance, 110–113
informal financial sector, 139
informal lenders, 43, 110–112, 122,
  325, 332
informal loan, 25, 29, 33, 115

informal microfinance institution, 165
informal sector, 25, 31, 33, 138
information asymmetry, 210
innovations, 2
instalments, 353
Institute for Development Studies
  Sabah, 66
institutional-level factors, 326
institutional-level obstacles, 332
insurance, 315
insurance culture, 205
interest rate, 103, 111, 127, 273, 277,
  279, 285–286, 291, 294, 301, 309,
  320
interest rates cap, 135
international best practice standards,
  127
international donations, 124
international poverty line, 97
IPO, 232
iron law of interest rate restriction,
  119
Islamic finance concept, 257
Islamic investment rates, 259

J

joint liability, 6, 124
joint venture, 245

K

Kelompok Swadaya Masyarakat
  (KSM), 242
key policies, 36
kickbacks, 116
Kuala Lumpur, 57

L

lack of collateral problem, 169
lack of financial support, 99

land holdings, 76
land tenure security, 102, 136
land-tenure system, 99, 101–102
largest Muslim population in the
　world, 262
legal status, 135
lenders, 308
lending policies, 39, 43, 326
level of indebtedness, 155
licence revoked, 239
life expectancy, 50
linkages between the formal and
　informal sectors, 139
liquidity constraints, 115
loan appraisal, 116
loan outstanding, 28, 280–282, 284
loan repayment, 286, 292, 296,
　301–302, 310
loans, 6, 308
loans for agriculture activities, 83
loan-to-deposit ratio, 152
logit model, 321
low transaction costs, 324
low-income, 11

M
Majelis Ulama Indonesia, 247
Malaysia, 47, 81
Malaysian government, 85
maqasid al-shari'ah, 257
marginalised, 15
market failure, 189
　information asymmetry, 189
market interest rate, 349, 354
market-based credit policies, 215
market-based financial and credit
　policies, 184
market-based policies, 211
Mekong River Delta, 25, 39

MFIs, 58
micro enterprises, 182
micro entrepreneurs, 214
microbanking, 233
microborrowers, 349
microcredit, 5, 26–27, 37–40, 44, 214
microcredit accessibility, 321, 332
microcredit impact, 77
microcredit loans, 74, 76, 78, 80–82
microcredit participation, 81
microcredit policies, 43–44
microcredit program, 24, 27, 38–44,
　54, 84–85, 95, 123–124, 127, 135,
　326, 331–332
microdeposits, 208–209
microenterprise, 74–75, 112, 213
microenterprises land holdings, 76
microenterprises revenue, 75
microentrepreneurs, 218
microfinance, 2, 32, 35–37, 44, 106,
　179, 182, 184, 189, 191, 195–197,
　207, 209–210, 213, 215, 217–219,
　308
　　microfinance NGOs, 192–193,
　　218
microfinance banking, 354
microfinance banking providers, 352
microfinance industry, 213, 219
microfinance institutions (MFIs), 47,
　49
microfinance programmes, 31–32,
　154
microfinance regulatory agency, 171
microfinance services, 43
microinsurance, 3, 199, 205–206,
　289, 294, 301–302
　　commitment savings account,
　　204
　　housing microfinance, 201, 206

insurance penetration, 206
microdeposits, 203
microentrepreneurs, 201
microinsurance institution, 200
microsavings, 203, 209
microlending policies, 333
microlending rates, 137
microloan, 321, 353
microloan products, 333
microsavers, 349
microsaving product, 354
microsavings, 208
Middle East, 244
milestones history of BRI, 230
Millennium Development Goals
  (MDGs), 314
mission drift, 15
misuse of microcredit loans, 84
mixes commercial and social
  attributes, 243
MMU, 253
monetary stability, 239
moral hazard, 259–260, 308
mosque-based association, 230
MSME Law, 185
Muhammadiyah, 243
mutual aid, 136

N
nano-finance scheme, 167
National Development Policy (NDP),
  54
national low income line, 327–328
national poverty line, 53, 56–57
nazhir, 248
negligence, 245
New Economic Policy (NEP), 54
NGO microcredit programmes,
  125–126

non-financial institutions, 138
non-governmental organisation-
  microfinance institutions
  (NGO-MFIs), 273, 277, 279,
  281–282, 284, 286, 289, 291, 294
non-governmental organisation
  (NGO), 54
non-poor population, 118
non-targeting issue, 118
not-so-poor people, 82
NPLs, 82

O
objective of shari'ah, 257
off-farm self-employment activities,
  115
operating cost to the banks, 349
operational self-sufficiency (OSS),
  272
orgware essentials, 178
outreach, 84, 126, 139
outstanding loans, 28, 40
overlapping loans, 301

P
Palli Karma-Sahayak Foundation
  (PKSF), 280, 285–287, 289–290,
  292, 296
patriarchy, 329
pawnbrokers, 110
People Bank loan project, 160
People's Bank, 85
People's Bank of China (PBC), 103,
  129, 328
people's credit bank, 238
performance, 82
personal savings, 80, 82
perusahaan perseroan (persero),
  231

pilot study, 261
policy banking, 135
policy makers, 262
policy reforms, 136
policy-based banking business, 106
poor, 308
poor and low-income households, 42
poor families, 3
poor farmers, 116
poor households, 34, 40–42
poor targeting, 119
poorest of the poor, 16
poorest population, 321
postal savings, 123
poverty, 49, 52, 54, 59, 95, 97, 272,
    274, 276, 278, 280, 285, 287–288,
    293, 297, 299–300
poverty alleviation, 81, 94, 124, 133,
    178, 213, 332–333
poverty eradication, 48, 139
poverty gap, 53
poverty incidence, 55–56
poverty level, 51
poverty line, 53
poverty loan utilisation, 121
poverty measurement indicators, 253
poverty rate, 57
poverty reduction, 97, 128, 309
poverty-focused, 5
poverty-oriented institutions, 60
pre-agreed basis, 245
pre-determined return, 254
preferential tax policies, 137
private money lenders, 30
production cycle, 113
production loans, 114
profit and loss sharing (PLS), 243
provide credit, 27, 33
providing microcredit, 43

providing rural credit, 27
provision of credit, 34
Pusat Pengembangan Ekonomi
    Muhamamdiyah (PPEM), 250

R
RCC microcredit programmes, 322
RCCs' microcredit, 320, 324–329,
    332–333
    application procedure, 325
    collateral, 325–326
    credit accessibility, 328
    credit history, 326
    credit records, 325
    financial viability, 328
    flexible lending scheme, 321
    household heads' education, 323
    interest rate, 325
    microcredit accessibility, 322–324
    microcredit programme, 321
    microloans, 325
    off-farm investment, 323
    poverty alleviation, 328
    probability of being a microcredit
        borrower, 323
    programme participation, 327
    promotion, 325–326
    rejection, 325
    repayment, 321, 323, 328
    risk management, 328
    self-employment, 323
reform, 134, 138–139
regulatory authority, 279, 302
reinforces, 9
remittances, 10
remote areas, 233
rent-seeking activities, 119
repayment, 82–83, 110, 113, 120,
    125, 127, 134–135, 137, 319, 353

repayment capacity, 155
repayment structure, 111
reserve funds, 239
resource mobilisation, 139
resource mobilisation in rural areas, 345
revenue-generating businesses, 128
RFIs, 122–123
riba, 245
riba al-buyu, 254
riba al-qarud/qard, 254
Ridho Gusti cooperative, 249
risks, 4, 308
risk-sharing, 255
ROSCAs, 241
rural and poor households, 44
rural and urban, 4
rural areas, 100–101, 250
rural banks, 190–191, 214, 218
rural China, 331
rural communities, 256
rural credit, 28
rural credit cooperatives (*see also* RCCs), 105, 107–109, 115, 117, 122–123, 128–129, 133–134, 136, 138, 319, 331–333
    agricultural lending, 131
    ambiguous governance, 107–108
    collateral, 129
    compulsory savings, 130
    credit culture, 133
    credit supply, 132
    creditworthiness, 129
    deposit mobilisation, 133
    financial sustainability, 109, 130
    financial viability, 133
    formal financial institution, 130
    governance, 132
    governance ambiguity, 109
    group-liability, 129–130
    individual borrower accountability, 129
    institutional sustainability, 108
    interest rate ceilings, 132
    land farming, 129
    lending procedures, 138
    loan applications, 117
    membership fees, 117
    microcredit, 107
    microcredit programme(s), 129, 131, 133–134, 331
    mixed lending approach, 138
    net profit, 109
    NGOs, 131
    non-interest costs, 117
    non-performing loans, 109
    non-recoverable loans, 109
    outstanding loans, 109
    policy finance, 108
    profitability, 133
    programme replicability, 130
    promotion, 138
    repayment, 132–133
    repayment capacity, 138
    savings deposits, 107
    start-up capital, 107
    total assets, 109
    transaction costs, 132
rural credit market, 23–27, 29, 31, 33–35, 37–38, 42–44, 94
rural credit policies, 37
rural development, 309, 333, 349, 354
Rural Development Corporation (RDC), 66
rural development grants, 342

rural economy, 271, 274, 293, 296, 300
rural farmers, 134
rural finance, 36, 38, 43, 107
rural finance policy, 343
rural finance system, 28, 106, 113, 135, 139
rural financial institutions (RFIs), 93, 104
rural financial market, 2, 31, 37–38, 178, 187, 196
rural financing, 109, 136
rural formal financial system, 109
rural households, 33, 37, 349
rural households' welfare, 332
rural infrastructure, 105–106
rural land market, 103
rural poor, 28, 40, 42
rural population, 110, 351
rural poverty, 135, 319–320, 326
rural poverty in Thailand, 148
rural reforms, 104
rural women, 332
rural–urban income inequality, 99

S
Sabah State, 64
sadaqat, 248
Satelit BRI (BRIsat), 232
saving and credit cooperatives, 162
saving products, 349
savings, 3, 272, 277, 279–283, 285–286, 288–290, 292, 294, 296–298, 302, 315
savings and loan cooperatives, 228
savings deposits, 112
savings for production group, 163
scarce resource, 308
seasonal credit demand, 116

Selangor, 61
self-employed businesses, 322
self-esteem, 80, 82
self-help groups (SHG), 85, 241
self-reliance, 349
self-sufficiency, 84
self-sustainability, 16
semiformal and formal credit, 43
semi-formal credit, 24, 31–32, 43
Semi-formal microfinance institution, 161
shari'ah compliance, 235
shari'ah supervisory board, 251
shari'ah system, 240
sharia economic movement, 247
short-term projects, 260
Sidogiri, 253
simple procedures, 353
small lending, 116
small private rural banks, 352
smallholder farmers, 150
small-scale enterprises, 309
social collateral, 6
social connections, 321
social impacts, 312
social network and commercialisation process, 13
social networking activities, 164
social policy lending, 37
social-welfare commitment, 258
software needs, 178
Southeast Asia, 48
spiritual treatment, 261
state-owned bank, 152
structural transformation, 100
subsidised credit, 117
subsidised loan policy despite, 119
subsidised loans, 120
subsidised-credit policy, 121